CORPORATE GOVERNANCE AND LABOUR MANAGEMENT

Corporate Governance and Labour Management

An International Comparison

Edited by
HOWARD GOSPEL
and
ANDREW PENDLETON

OXFORD
UNIVERSITY PRESS

OXFORD
UNIVERSITY PRESS

Great Clarendon Street, Oxford OX2 6DP

Oxford University Press is a department of the University of Oxford.
It furthers the University's objective of excellence in research, scholarship,
and education by publishing worldwide in

Oxford New York

Auckland Cape Town Dar es Salaam Hong Kong Karachi Kuala Lumpur
Madrid Melbourne Mexico City Nairobi New Delhi Shanghai Taipei Toronto

With offices in

Argentina Austria Brazil Chile Czech Republic France Greece
Guatemala Hungary Italy Japan South Korea Poland Portugal
Singapore Switzerland Thailand Turkey Ukraine Vietnam

Oxford is a registered trade mark of Oxford University Press
in the UK and in certain other countries

Published in the United States
by Oxford University Press Inc., New York

British Library Cataloguing in Publication Data

Data available

Library of Congress Cataloging in Publication Data

Data available

ISBN 0-19-926367-1

3 5 7 9 10 8 6 4 2

Typeset by Newgen Imaging Systems (P) Ltd., Chennai, India
Printed in Great Britain
on acid-free paper by
Biddles Ltd., King's Lynn, Norfolk

Preface

Corporate governance has long been a subject of considerable interest and controversy, but debates on this topic have become much more prominent in advanced industrial economies over the last ten years. Primarily, these debates have concerned relationships between shareholders, corporate boards, and managers. For the most part and in most countries, the role of labour in corporate governance has been less of a focus of interest. However, at the present time, with pressures and changes in both corporate governance and in employment and labour relations systems, there is a growing need to bring the two together, both theoretically and empirically, and to understand their interaction in historical perspective. The Political Economy and Industrial Relations literatures are beginning to do this, and this book contributes to this important development.

One of the main factors in recent years driving changes in corporate governance and labour systems has been the opening up and liberalization of product, financial, and labour markets. These trends have accelerated recently, especially in continental Europe and Japan. As a result, national socio-economic systems have become more exposed to market pressures emanating from outside national boundaries. On top of these developments, privatization programmes and social welfare reforms are shifting the boundaries between markets, states, and business corporations. Together these trends have affected the ownership of firms and the relations between owners, managers, and employees.

These developments have put pressures on companies and sectors which in the past have acted as leaders in providing extensive social benefits. They have also raised serious questions about labour inclusiveness and participation in governance. A deeper issue still concerns the extent to which distinctive national patterns of economic and social organization can be sustained. For example, in a context of growing liberalization and marketization, can Germany sustain its system of 'Rhineland' capitalism? Can Japan maintain those aspects of its system that have long prized employment security and seniority within the enterprise community? Or will the so-called 'Anglo-Saxon' marketized systems of governance and employment, with their reduced voice for labour, prevail?

Answers to these questions are by no means straightforward. The national case studies in the book show that there are countervailing forces which make for complex outcomes. Thus, there are strong path dependencies and national inheritances which influence and nuance the way in which market pressures impact on social and economic institutions. Resistance to changes among social actors are strong, especially in the industrial relations area. In Germany, for example, there is the strongly instituationalized position of labour within the firm and in the national political economy. In Japan, prevailing social norms and political traditions mean that popular support for changes in the way that business corporations function is constrained. In Italy, France, and Spain, there are both political and social obstacles to change.

In addition, of course, economic and social systems are immensely creative. The form which corporate governance takes is subject to negotiation and accommodation among key actors, including owners, managers, labour, and governments. Outcomes cannot be simply predicted from observing the objectives and instruments of shareholders and global financiers. The most likely result is that greater exposure of national 'varieties of capitalism' to financial market pressures will generate complex and contradictory effects on labour management. This very complexity, however, will embody profound changes in the way that labour is organized and managed. Employment practices may become more varied within national economies. Employment protection, good social benefits, and voice in corporate affairs may come to be increasingly restricted to a core of workers in large firms who will constitute islands in a more liberalized sea. In turn, this will mean that it is more difficult for labour to mobilize on the basis of class or across firm and sectoral boundaries.

This book had its origins in a series of seminars, supported by the European Science Foundation, and held in Manchester and Cologne. It provides an overview of the debates about corporate governance and labour management in a number of countries and seeks to make linkages between the three main actors involved in these complex interactions. For those interested in the relations between corporate governance and labour management, it provides a useful and stimulating analysis.

Wolfgang Streeck
Max-Planck-Institut für Gesellschaftsforschung, Cologne
January 2004

Acknowledgements

This book has grown out of two workshops held in Manchester, UK, and Cologne, Germany, financed by the European Science Foundation (ESF). All of the authors are appreciative of the support given by the ESF. We would also like to thank Christine Czechowicz of Manchester Metropolitan University for organizing the Manchester workshop and Wolfgang Streeck and the staff of the Max Planck Institute for their hospitality in Cologne. We would like to record our thanks to Julie Froud and Richard Warren for their participation in the Manchester workshop, to Renate Mayntz for her involvement in the Cologne workshop, and to participants in the symposium we held at the Society for the Advancement of Socio-Economics annual conference in Aix-en-Provence in Summer 2003.

The authors of the chapters would like to thank their families and colleagues for their support and forbearance while the chapters were under preparation. We would also like to thank Matthew Derbyshire and David Musson of Oxford University Press for their support for the project. Finally, we record our gratitude to Christine Czechowicz for her sterling work in preparing the final manuscript.

Howard Gospel
Andrew Pendleton

Contents

List of figures

List of tables

Notes on contributors

RUTH V. AGUILERA is Assistant Professor in the Department of Business Administration and Institute of Labor and Industrial Relations at the University of Illinois at Urbana-Champaign. Her Ph.D. is from Harvard University and her research interests are in economic sociology and international management. Her current research in comparative corporate governance and cross-border mergers and acquisitions has been published widely in American and European journals. She is the co-editor of *Corporate Governance in a Changing Economic and Political Environment: Trajectories of Institutional Change* (Palgrave 2004).

TAKASHI ARAKI is a Professor of Law at the University of Tokyo, from where he received his bachelor's, master's, and doctoral degrees. He has been a visiting scholar at Harvard Law School, the Catholic University of Leuven, Columbia Law School, and Cambridge University. He is a Commissioner of the Labour Relations Commission of Tokyo Metropolitan Government and a Senior Research Fellow at the Japan Institute of Labour and Training. His most recent book is *Labour and Employment Law in Japan* (Japan Institute of Labour 2002).

GEERT BRAAM is Associate Professor of Accounting in the Nijmegen School of Management in the University of Nijmegen. He is qualified as a Register-Accountant and has previously worked as an auditor and business controller. His research focuses on corporate governance and performance management.

BERND FRICK is Professor of Personnel and Organizational Economics at the University of Witten-Herdecke. His Diploma, Doctorate, and Habilitation were received from the University of Trier. He has previously been a professor at the University of Greifswald. He has written extensively on corporate governance, industrial relations, personnel economics, and the economics of sport.

HOWARD GOSPEL is Professor of Management at King's College London, a Research Associate of the Centre for Economic Performance, London School of Economics, and a Fellow of the Said Business School, University of Oxford. He has published widely on labour management and industrial relations, in historical, contemporary, and comparative perspective.

MICHEL GOYER is a lecturer in the Industrial Relations and organizational, Behaviour unit, Warwick Business School. He has a Ph.D. in Political Science from MIT. He has held previous appointments at Boston University and the London School of Economics and has also been an associate at the Center for European Studies at Harvard University. His research interests focus on the political economy of West European nations, with a particular focus on corporate governance in France and Germany.

BOB HANCKÉ is Reader in European Political Economy at the London School of Economics. He has a degree in Sociology from the Free University of Brussels and a Ph.D. in Political Economy from MIT. He has been a Senior Research Fellow at the Wissenschaftszentrum, Berlin. He is the author of *Large Firms and Institutional Change: Industrial Renewal and Economic Restructuring in France* (Oxford University Press).

MARTIN HÖPNER is Research Scientist at the Max Planck Institute for the Study of Societies in Cologne. After completing his Ph.D. in Political Science at the Fern Universität Hagen, he was a Visiting Fellow at the Center for European Studies at Harvard University (2002–3). His research interests include comparative political economy, industrial relations, and corporate governance. He is the author of *Wer beherrscht die Unternehmen? Shareholder Value, Managerherrschaft und Mitbestimmung in Deutschland (Who Controls the Firm? Shareholder Value, Managerial Control and Codetermination in Germany)* (Campus Verlag 2003).

GREGORY JACKSON is Senior Lecturer in Strategy in the Management Centre at King's College, London. He has degrees from Wisconsin-Madison and Columbia Universities, and has held research posts at the Research Institute of Economy, Trade, and Industry (RIETI) in Tokyo and at the Max Planck Institute for the Study of Societies in Cologne. He has published widely on comparative and historical aspects of corporate governance, industrial relations, and institutional theory, especially in relation to Germany and Japan.

SANFORD M. JACOBY is Howard Noble Professor of Management, History, and Policy Studies at the Anderson School, University College of Los Angeles. He has degrees from the University of Pennsylvania and the University of California, Berkeley. He has written extensively on human resources, industrial relations, and labour markets, and is the author of *Modern Manors: Welfare Capitalism since the New Deal* (Princeton University Press 1997).

ANTJE KURDELBUSCH works as an expert on payment systems for the works council of DaimlerChrysler. She completed her Ph.D. in Sociology at the Ruhr-Universität Bochum and was a doctoral fellow at the Max Planck Institute in Cologne between 1999 and 2002.

ERIK LEHMANN is Assistant Professor in the Department of Business Administration and Economics at the University of Constance. He has a Diploma in Business Administration from the University of Nuremberg and a Ph.D. from the University of Rostock. His research interests are in corporate governance, personnel economics, and the economics of education and sport.

ANDREW PENDLETON is Professor of Human Resource Management at the University of York. He has degrees from Oxford and Bath and has held academic posts at the universities of Bath, Bradford, and Kent. He has written extensively on employee share ownership and stock option plans, and is the author of *Employee Ownership, Participation, and Governance* (Routledge 2002).

ERIK POUTSMA is Associate Professor in Labour Relations in the Nijmegen School of Management, Department Strategic Personnel Management. He manages the PARTNER Research Group and is Director of the Share Ownership Research Group at Nijmegen. He has published extensively on entrepreneurship, financial participation, and employee participation.

WOLFGANG STREECK is Professor of Sociology and Director of the Max Planck Institute for the Study of Societies. He has degrees from Frankfurt, Columbia, and Bielefeld, and has held appointments at Wisconsin-Madison and the Wissenschaftszentrum, Berlin. He has published in sociology, industrial relations, and comparative political economy. His recent books include *Germany, Beyond the Stable State* (with Herbert Kitschelt, Frank Cass 2004) and *The End of Diversity: Prospects for German and Japanese Capitalism* (with Kozo Yamamura, Cornell University Press 2003).

SANDRO TRENTO is Deputy-Director in the Economic Research Department of the Bank of Italy, where he is in charge of industrial and structural analysis. He studied Economics at the University of Rome, at Northwestern University, and at Stanford University. He has published on corporate governance, regulation, and technological change, and on competition policy.

1

Corporate Governance and Labour Management: An International Comparison

HOWARD GOSPEL AND ANDREW PENDLETON

1.1. Introduction

How firms are governed and how labour is managed are central issues for all industrial societies. Both have implications for economic wealth and for the broader welfare of nations. Yet, systems of corporate governance and labour management are often considered quite separately of one another. The aim of this book is to explore these two important issues, the governance of the firm and the management of labour, over time and in different national contexts. The further aim is then to go beyond this and to consider how corporate governance and labour management have interacted with one another and how this interaction has shaped distinctive national patterns of political economy.

The book relates to a number of topical debates. At the present time, there is a growing public concern about the nature of the corporation—whether it exists exclusively or even primarily to promote the interests of shareholders, whether the maximization of returns for shareholders leads to losses for other stakeholders, and whether recent trends have increasingly created unfair remuneration for senior executives. This has coincided with a number of major scandals and business failures which have given rise to concerns about managerial practices and the regulation of firms. In the popular Management literature, there have been a number of forceful critiques of shareholder value-orientated business and its possible negative effects (Hutton 1996; Porter 1997). As a result of all this, debates about corporate governance have taken place in business and political circles in many countries—such as the United States, the United Kingdom, France, Germany, Italy, the Netherlands, and Japan—over the last 10 years, and most have embarked on programmes to reform aspects of corporate governance. However, too often these debates and policies have focused on relatively narrow issues, such as the composition and responsibilities of company boards, with the result that broader questions about corporate objectives and practices have not been fully addressed. A further debate in both business and academic circles has considered the extent to which national corporate governance systems are converging towards a single model often seen as likely to partake of the Anglo-Saxon form (Kitschelt *et al.* 1999; Hansmann and Kraakmann 2000).

At the same time, there have also been debates about changes in employment and industrial relations systems. In some countries, such as the United States and the United Kingdom, comment has focused on the apparent increase in job insecurity, growing pay inequality, and the erosion of benefits such as final salary pensions. Some commentators have attributed these in part to the decline in employee voice at work and the assertion of managerial prerogatives (Hutton 1996; Kommission Mitbestimmung 1998; Cappelli 1999; Blair and Kochan 2000; Millward, Bryson, and Forth 2000; Dickens, Wadsworth, and Gregg 2001). In countries such as Germany and Japan, at the present time, there is considerable discussion as to the viability of their employment systems. Thus, in Germany, debate centres around whether a system of employee voice through works councils at the workplace and collective bargaining at the industry level can continue to exist in a context where financial pressures on firms have intensified and where some argue a need for major changes in corporate governance (Kommision Mitbestimmung 1998; Streeck 2001; Lane 2003). In Japan, the system of lifetime employment is said to be under threat, pay is being driven more by market forces, and effective employee voice mechanisms are weakening (Sako and Sato 1997; Inagami 2000). In this context, an appreciation is growing that these various phenomena, the financing and governance of the firm and the management of labour, may be interconnected.

This book seeks to bridge a gap between several different academic literatures. Various perspectives have recently started to consider the possibility that financial structure and corporate governance may influence the management of labour. The comparative Political Economy and 'business systems' literatures have examined relationships between national patterns of business organization, including finance and governance, and systems of employment (Lane 1995; Whitley 1999; Dore 2000*a*, *c*; Hall and Soskice 2001*a*, *b*). Recently, a strand of literature, based in part in Comparative Law, has considered the extent to which national governance systems of corporate governance are converging and whether this entails that labour management practices will also converge (Cioffi 2000; Hansmann and Kraakman 2000). Within Financial Economics, a recent strand of enquiry has focused on the impact of capital structures on employment, wages, and employee representation (Bronars and Deere 1991; Perotti and Spier 1993; Sharpe 1994; Hanka 1997). In turn, these literatures are beginning to influence Industrial Relations and Human Resource Management (HRM) analysis (Cappelli *et al.* 1997; Blair and Kochan 2000; Gospel and Pendleton 2003). Some others have argued that, though the power of labour may have been reduced in many countries, both its strength and its weakness are important for shaping and facilitating corporate governance arrangements (Roe 2003).

1.2. Governance, Finance, and Labour

Throughout the book, corporate governance and labour management are broadly defined. This is so that the breadth of interconnectedness between these different aspects of corporate behaviour can be fully identified.

Corporate governance is about the relationship between three sets of actors or stakeholders—capital, management, and labour. It is concerned with who owns and controls the firm, in whose interest the firm is governed, and the various ways (direct and indirect) whereby control is exercised. These three sets of actors may work with one another, form alliances, or oppose each other (See Chapter 11, this volume). Their relative roles and power vary considerably between countries and have important consequences for a whole set of management decisions. The justification for identifying these three actors is that all make investments (financial or human capital) in the firm. At the same time, however, it should be added that others argue that an even wider group of stakeholders have an interest in the governance of the firm, such as suppliers and local communities. Those interested in 'corporate social responsibility' especially emphasize a wide group of stakeholders.

Our perspective on governance can be contrasted with the focus in much of the business management and public policy debate about corporate governance which focuses on issues such as the composition of boards of directors and the pay of top managers. These are important matters, but must be set in a broader context. Our perspective, focusing on the broad set of relationships between key stakeholders, also goes beyond the conventional model in Financial Economics. Here, the approach has tended to view the firm as a 'nexus of contracts' and views governance as about how shareholders control managerial opportunism through the alignment of incentives (Shleifer and Vishny 1997: 740–8). We diverge from this so-called 'principal–agent' view on several grounds: it involves a reductionism which excludes one key actor (labour); it abstracts investor–management relationships from their institutional context; and it fails fully to engage with the diversity of interests among investors, managers, and employees (Blair 1995; Aguilera and Jackson 2003: 6).

The management of labour is defined broadly to cover a set of major decisions and resulting outcomes. These are taken to cover three main areas—work relations, employment relations, and industrial relations (Gospel 1992). Employment relations deal with the arrangements governing such aspects of employment as recruitment, training, job tenure, and reward systems. Work relations concern the way work is organized and the deployment of workers around technologies and production processes. Industrial relations is defined to cover the voice aspirations of employees and resulting institutional arrangements, such as joint consultation, works councils, and collective bargaining. Throughout the book, the emphasis will be on major strategic patterns in these three areas as they have developed, especially in large private sector firms, over a long period of time. Wherever possible, an attempt is made to deal with all these three aspects of labour management.

As already stated, corporate governance derives in part from, and is closely related to, finance. Here, there are a number of key features of finance which may be identified and which emerge in the various chapters: the sources and types of finance; the objectives of finance providers; and the intervention rights and practices associated with different forms of finance. These provide a set of constraints and opportunities which influence managerial choices, including in the labour area.

Sources of finance are essentially threefold—internally generated funds, debt, and share equity. Once established, most firms rely mainly on internally generated funds and these can give managers significant discretion over how resources are used. However, the exposure of firms to pressures from other financiers and claimants can have a powerful influence on the allocation and sought-for returns from these internal funds. From time to time, firms have to raise capital from outside. Debt can be a considerable constraint on firms and is viewed in the theoretical literature as underpinning strong governance (Stiglitz 1985; Hart 1995); but, where large and long-term, debt may draw lenders into a close relationship with management. Share equity can also be a considerable constraint. Where shareholders are many and small, investors may compensate for weaknesses in their relationship with managers by exerting pressure via market trading; where ownership is concentrated, equity owners may intervene more directly with management. An important dimension of finance refers to the means by which finance providers exert influence on managers. Here, it is possible to see a continuum from indirect involvement to direct intervention in governance. At one extreme, holders of tradable bonds or share equity may eschew any direct involvement and instead exert influence via market mechanisms (e.g. by the threat of selling or the actual sale of their investment). At the other extreme, those with financial claims may play a very direct role by occupying seats on the corporate board. Similarly, the objectives of those holding financial claims against the firm are important. Some may be speculative, others may have longer-term, more patient time horizons, and this in turn impacts on management and consequently has implications for labour (Manne 1965; Stiglitz 1985; Hart 1995).

The approach of the chapters in this book is based on a multi-stage perspective. First, the chapters consider the role of capital, the structure of corporate ownership, and patterns of business financing. Second, they examine the key role of top management and the strategic choices that they make, subject to constraints imposed on them by capital. Third, they then examine the influence which capital and management have on labour and the systems of labour management which are put into place. At the same time, however, the chapters point out that in certain circumstances labour itself can shape capital and management. Thus, there is a circularity in the perspective and the different chapters begin their analysis at different stages.

1.3. National Systems of Corporate Governance and Labour Management

As a further starting point, to guide the analysis, we suggest that there are a number of bodies of literature and broad typologies of national systems of corporate governance and labour management.

The authors of the following chapters draw on and develop these. However, simultaneously, the chapters seek to go beyond the traditional typologies and in addition cover countries which fit less easily into some of the literatures and typologies.

One approach is to view corporate governance in a historical perspective. Thus, there are a number of stages in the development of finance and governance. The first might be seen as the period of 'personal capitalism' during which period financing was often a personal or family or small group partnership matter and when ownership and control were closely interrelated. Later, from the early twentieth century onwards, 'managerial capitalism' emerged, at first in the United States and the United Kingdom. During this period, more active equity markets start to develop, share ownership becomes more dispersed, and control begins to be separated from ownership, with managers having considerable discretion to manage corporations in the interests of themselves and other insiders, including employees (Berle and Means 1932; Chandler 1962; Galbraith 1969). By contrast, in other countries, such as Germany and elsewhere in continental Europe, there was the development of a form of 'cooperative capitalism' in which outside finance comes significantly from large banks or from other firms or from the state and, as a result, where ownership and control are less dispersed (Chandler 1990: 587–92). This is the form, it is claimed, also taken in post-Second World War Japan. Later still, around the 1960s, there was in the United States and the United Kingdom a tendency towards 'conglomerate capitalism', under which managers used their autonomy and the ability to acquire other companies through the market in order to build up highly diverse enterprises. This then came under pressure in the 1980s, when it was felt that such companies were worth more in their parts than in their whole and when the beginnings of a re-concentration of equity ownership shifted power back to investors, including increasingly institutional investors, such as trust, insurance, and pension funds. This sees the growth of the 'shareholder value' concept, defined as the promotion of returns to shareholders, as the prime or exclusive objective of the firm (Lazonick and O'Sullivan 2000). According to some, the latest development is the spread of this 'shareholder capitalism' model to countries which have hitherto retained the more cooperative form of capitalism. This can be ascribed to the rise of foreign (mainly US) ownership, the growth of equity markets, and the development of more active markets for corporate control in many countries (Lazonick and O'Sullivan 1997*b*; Jürgens, Naumann, and Rupp 2000; Morin 2000; O'Sullivan 2000*b*).

Another typology for understanding finance and governance systems comes from the Financial Economics literature. Here, a useful distinction has been made between 'market/outsider' and 'relational/insider' systems (Mayer 1990; Franks and Mayer 1997*a*; Allen and Gale 2000). Market forms of financing are ones where emphasis is placed on finance via public equities and market-based debt. In these systems, equity markets are extensive and there is usually a high turnover of shares and corporate bonds. Investors have diversified portfolios and may easily sell their investments. Under such arrangements, there exists an outsider form of governance based on relatively strong legal rights for investors and on an active market in corporate control (mergers and acquisitions, especially hostile takeovers). This contrasts with relational forms of finance where more reliance is placed on bank and other loans, where securities markets are weak, and where investors are more likely to be long term. This is said to create a form of insider governance, where large owners have a more stable and direct relationship with the management of the firm, but where smaller investors and the market for corporate control exerts less discipline. The United States and the United Kingdom are said to have market/outsider systems, Germany and Japan to have relational/insider systems (Mayer 1990; Franks and Mayer 1997*a*).

This insider/outsider perspective offers useful insights and will inform some of the analysis in the following chapters. However, it may be criticized as too broad a bipolar typology which fails to capture both differences and similarities between systems. Thus, the United Kingdom now has growing concentration of ownership which allows for a few large investors to play a quasi-insider role and for these investors to reduce the emphasis on short-term returns (Armour, Deakin, and Konzelmann 2003; Chapter 3, this volume). Equally, in Japan, as well as powerful banks with influence within firms, there exists a highly developed and widely-held equity market (see Chapter 10, this volume). Furthermore, the insider/outsider distinction does not really incorporate the distinctive characteristics of Southern European regimes, where the state has traditionally played an important role, directly or indirectly, in corporate ownership and governance (see Chapters 7–9, this volume). For the most part, also, as utilized in the Financial Economics literature, this perspective assumes that labour has no role in corporate governance and it fails to say much about consequences for labour management.

In another approach, La Porta *et al.* (1997, 1998, 1999, 2000) have argued that national legal systems shape finance and governance.

Commercial legal systems have derived from four major legal 'families', respectively the English common law, French, German, and Scandinavian civil law traditions. These families have provided contrasting support for shareholders and credit-holders. In countries where such investors have more protection (the common law countries), there have developed larger and broader equity and debt markets and share ownership is more dispersed. This has not been the case in the civil law countries, though with the exception that German civil law countries afford strong protection to secured creditors. The legal systems approach has the advantage that it examines a large number of countries and provides us with measures for various aspects of governance, especially measures of shareholder and creditor protection. In essence, the approach turns on whether legal systems create relatively stronger financiers–investors or stronger entrepreneurs–managers and the consequences of this. This perspective may have implications for labour and *inter alia* it prompts the question as to whether investor protection is correlated with labour protection or whether, under investor protection, economic risks are shifted to labour. However, again, to date, this literature has had little to say about labour outcomes.

In the Political Economy tradition, the 'varieties of capitalism', and 'business systems' literatures have also placed considerable emphasis on forms of finance and corporate governance as key elements of national economic systems and important determinants of corporate behaviour (Lane 1995; Whitley 1999; Dore 2000*a*, *c*; Hall and Soskice 2001). Finance and governance arrangements are said to influence relationships between owners and managers, the nature of business strategies, and the extent of cooperation between firms. Again, some of these authors (Hall and Soskice 2001) discern two major varieties of capitalism: the 'liberal market' economies, typically the United States and the United Kingdom, and the 'coordinated market' economies, typically Germany and Japan. The 'varieties of capitalism' approach has the advantage that labour market institutions and outcomes are central to the thesis. Thus, in liberal market economies, dispersed ownership and financial constraints are said to exert strong pressure on employment systems and job tenure. By contrast, in coordinated market economies, different governance arrangements, including the involvement of labour, mean that financial pressures are more likely to be absorbed by shareholders and less likely to impact negatively on labour. Other institutional complementarities are also seen to follow in areas such as training, wage systems, and forms of employee representation.

The 'varieties of capitalism' approach has much to commend it and is drawn on by the authors below. However, it can be criticized in that much of the literature has again used a few national ideal types (typically the United States and the United Kingdom versus Germany and Japan). It is also based on the suggestive, but somewhat problematic, notion of complementarity, defined as the interaction of two institutions in a way which raises the returns from each. This implies that complementarity takes an almost evolutionary or Darwinian form, that is, 'deviant' institutions will eventually be forced out by the combined weight of complementary institutions. Thus, stable systems composed of mutually reinforcing elements will be created. Since the emphasis is on systemic cohesion, this approach tends not to consider which institutions have the most powerful effects. The chapters in this book try to deal with such issues and to go beyond the ideal types.

In the area of labour management, there are again some broad literatures and typologies which may be cited as signposts in later discussion. We outline these, suggesting some linkages with corporate governance.

The first body of literature to which we refer is again historically based and identifies a number of stages in the development of labour management. The argument here is that, by the beginning of the twentieth century and superseding earlier small-scale and craft-based production regimes, there had emerged a system in large firms which was based on mass production and bureaucratized employment relations. The latter eventually provided for internal labour markets, based on the possibility of long-term jobs, pay partially related to seniority, and welfare benefits such as pensions. In brief, this was the system which Jacoby refers to in the US chapter as 'welfare capitalism'. This system developed early in the United States, but gradually spread to Europe and Japan. In the post-Second World War years, it came to be supported by a system of collective bargaining between employers and unions that took wages out of competition in many cases and further embedded these arrangements. Some have referred to this as a 'Fordist' stage in labour management, typifying large-scale manufacturing enterprise. In general terms, it coincided with the era of managerial or cooperative capitalism in different countries, as outlined above (Jacoby 1985, 1997; Boyer 1990; Gospel 1992).

According to this historical perspective, more recently and gradually, over the last quarter century or so, this system has come under pressure and a new pattern has emerged. Mass production has given way to more flexible production arrangements (sometimes referred to as

Post-Fordist production systems). Along with this, internal labour market arrangements have begun to dissolve, with less secure jobs, more 'atypical' employment, new contingent pay systems, and the decline of company benefits. Subsequently, there have developed pressures on industrial relations: trade union density has declined, collective bargaining has become increasingly decentralized or has disappeared altogether, and it has been replaced by other voice arrangements based on direct participation or joint consultation. There has, thus, developed more firm-specific HRM, sometimes highly sophisticated and benign (the so-called 'high road'), sometimes harder and more malign (the 'low road'). Again, one variant of the history suggests that moves in this direction began in the United States and the United Kingdom, but pressures are now such that similar developments have taken place in countries where previously the practice of 'welfare capitalism' or 'stakeholder capitalism' had been predominant or persisted longer (Piore and Sabel 1984; Jacoby 1985, 1997; Boyer 1990; Gospel 1992; Hazama 1997). Various factors lie behind these transformations (technological change, increased product market competition, sectoral shifts from manufacturing to services, and more diversified labour markets). However, it is now also increasingly suggested that changes in finance and governance (e.g. shorter-term, shareholder value forces, and the market for corporate control) may also lie behind such developments (see Gospel and Pendleton 2003 for a review).

Other typologies of labour management are more contemporaneously focused and overlap with the notions of employment relations, work relations, and industrial relations as outlined above.

Some of these literatures revolve around notion of systems which are more or less market-orientated. Thus, some countries have labour management systems which are essentially based on market signals: firms adjust recruitment and lay-offs according to the state of the market; labour turnover is relatively high and average job tenures low; employers hope to acquire skills, in which individuals have invested, in the external labour market; and pay often has a high contingent element, based on individual or firm performance. Such systems are said to exist in Anglo-Saxon countries, such as the United States and the United Kingdom. Other systems are less subject to market pressures: labour turnover is lower and jobs are longer term; firms are more likely to invest in skills within the firm; and pay is based on seniority or job grade and less subject to external market forces. Such a system exists in Japan and to some extent in Germany and some other continental European countries. This notion of 'marketization' or 'commodification' clearly relates to liberal market versus coordinated market systems and has certain similarities with the 'varieties of capitalism' approach referred to above (Hall and Soskice 2001).

A variant on this approach typifies countries according to their production systems and work relations. Thus, some countries are said to have production systems which favour incremental improvements in processes and products. These are countries where the so-called numerical flexibility (the ability to hire and fire) is low and where functional flexibility (the ability to deploy labour with ease within the firm) is high. In such countries, labour tends to cooperate with management and restrictive labour practices are few. Again, at extremes, this would include Germany and Japan with their so-called 'flexible quality' and 'lean production' regimes (Streeck 1992*a*; Aoki 1994; Wada 1995). These countries then tend towards a 'productionist' orientation, emphasizing improvements in existing processes and products and the acquisition of market share. By contrast, in other countries, production systems have tended towards the mass production end of the spectrum, in part because there is less functional flexibility, less training in broad skills at the intermediate level, and less employee cooperation in production. In such countries, labour is less cooperative and, if able, may be more likely to engage in 'hold-up' activities. However, such countries may be better at non-incremental product innovation, because their more active labour and capital markets allow firms to move quickly into new areas. The United States is usually cited as a good example of this kind of work relations (Soskice 1999; Gospel and Pendleton 2003). Countries such as the United States and the United Kingdom tend towards a less 'productionist' orientation and are more driven by the 'marketization' or 'financialization' of their economies.

Somewhat similar notions underlie a broad typology of industrial relations systems. On the one hand, it might be argued that there are countries where employees have little or no formal voice in corporate governance. Voice in workplace matters may be via direct employee involvement (quality circles, team briefing), by voluntary joint consultation, or (as a last resort for employers) via trade union collective bargaining. Where unions are recognized, management prefers to deal with them on a decentralized firm by firm basis, negotiating terms and conditions to suit particular market and firm contexts, often in a distributive and adversarial manner. This has come to be the model in the United States and the United Kingdom. However, increasingly in those countries, managements have also preferred to move away from union-based voice systems to arrangements based on direct employee involvement or consultative committees and on profit-sharing or share-ownership schemes. By contrast, there are countries where the basis of national systems is that labour has some voice in corporate governance which in turn encourages a notion of 'social partnership'. This might be legally based as in Germany and some other countries in continental Europe or based on voluntary practices as in Japan. In such countries, also, management has tended to deal with trade unions in a coordinated manner through multi-employer bargaining at industry level. Such a system exists in Germany and some other continental European countries and to some extent in Japan via coordination by employers' organizations. In addition, in these countries, more elaborate consultation systems have existed within the workplace based either on law (Germany) or on custom and practice (Japan) (see Chapters 4 and 10, this volume).

One variant of this perspective allows that some countries fall in between the bipolar types—they may have statutory voice mechanisms in the workplace, but also trade unions and collective bargaining operating at a number of levels and in such a way that the system is less clearly either centralized or decentralized and is less articulated. They also lack well-embedded notions of social partnership and have more adversarial labour relations. These countries, such as France and Italy, tend not to get the best, but rather the worst of all worlds (Calmfors and Driffill 1988; Hall and Gingerich 2001). Hence, they have a big incentive, under growing financial and product market pressures, to move in one direction or the other (see Chapters 7–9 on France, Spain, and Italy below).

This prompts a final consideration concerning clusters of countries. Of course, we have already used the notion of an Anglo-Saxon cluster with distinctive corporate governance and labour management practices. There is then the obvious contrast with the so-called co-ordinated market economies of Germany and Japan, with certain purported common characteristics. However, this prompts the question as to where other countries are to be located. Thus, where does the Netherlands fit, with its interesting combination of both Anglo-Saxon and German characteristics? Or where does one locate the three 'Latin' countries, France, Italy, and Spain, which have some similarities with, but also differences from, both of the aforementioned models?

These latter three countries have traditionally had systems of governance based on state-led bank credit and strong cross-shareholdings (with, especially in Italy, pyramidal holding companies).

The state has played a key role in both ownership and control of a significant group of large firms. For its part, labour has not been directly involved in corporate governance and, moreover, trade union movements have often been opposed to any such involvement. In the case of these countries, there is certainly a challenge as to how to make the links between corporate governance and labour management. Briefly, in some countries, it would seem that there have been pressures, in part coming from financial markets and corporate governance, which have led to more marketized arrangements, an increase in contingent working, and variable pay systems. In the area of industrial relations, these factors may also be contributing to some shift away from multi-employer bargaining and indeed from collective bargaining altogether. However, for its part, labour has often been more likely to try to block developments than in either the Anglo-Saxon or coordinated market countries.

The authors of the following chapters draw on and develop these typologies. At the same time, however, it is hoped that the chapters go beyond the traditional typologies and offer the advantage that they cover countries which are less often considered in the literature. Furthermore, the detailed explorations of the characteristics of individual countries suggest that national systems are unique and more complex than simple typologies tend to allow. A strong theme which emerges in several of the chapters is the path-dependent nature of corporate governance and labour management regimes, and how these unique systems can never either be slotted simply into existing comparative classifications or be held to be converging neatly on one or other model.

1.4. Mechanisms Linking Corporate Governance and Labour Management

We turn now to the mechanisms whereby corporate governance and labour management may interact. This involves us taking one step back and asking the following questions. Why should corporate governance and labour management be related? How actually are links to be explained? How does one influence the other?

It should be recalled that the interaction is essentially between capital, management, and labour (Aguilera and Jackson 2003). In some cases, such as Germany, interaction is clearly visible at the level of employee involvement in the company through the mechanisms of board representation and the works council. Where labour has legal or customary rights of this type, it may impact directly on corporate governance: hence the presence of codetermination rights may in part be responsible for the comparatively small scale of the equity market and the absence of hostile takeovers in Germany. Notwithstanding this, the primary focus in the book is more on one particular set of relationships: the broader and more indirect impact of financiers' and owners' objectives and intervention rights on management decision-making in general and labour management in particular. Yet, straightaway it must be conceded that this reflects an Anglo-Saxon perspective on the question, and it is apparent from the discussion of other European countries in the book that labour in turn may influence corporate governance directly and indirectly by involvement in codetermination arrangements or by forming alliances with management or, more rarely, shareholders. In addition, of course, more broadly, labour movements influence the socio-economic and political context in which companies operate and corporate governance takes place (Roe 1999, 2003; Godard 2002).

Here, we focus on the way that finance and governance impact on management's approach to managing labour. For ease of exposition we use a two systems approach akin to the market/outsider versus relational/insider model to illustrate the argument, though we are mindful that this oversimplifies the array of governance regimes discussed later.

First, finance and governance create constraints on management and influence the balance of interests managers promote. Thus, in recent years, especially in market/outsider systems, equity owners have promulgated the notion that managers' primary responsibility is to them and that enhancement of shareholder value is the most important objective for firms. The threat of exit and consequent changes in control are powerful disciplinary devices to achieve these ends (Prowse 1995; Lazonick and O'Sullivan 2000). It has been argued that, in countries such as the United States and the United Kingdom, firms' attempts to enhance shareholder value have a negative effect on labour because the capacity of firms to achieve real increases in returns is limited. In other words, shareholder value shifts the distribution of claims against the firm but does not increase the surplus generated by firms. Hence, moves to enhance shareholder value will often be accompanied by measures to reduce workforces (though workers who remain may benefit from pay increases) (Froud *et al.* 2000). Similarly, Hall and Soskice (2001: 16) suggest that intensified pressure from investors has shifted the balance in managerial decision-making against labour because weaker statutory protection for labour in these economies allows this. By contrast, in Germany, direct representation of both financiers and labour in management provides a more even balance between the two interests; in Japan, prevailing norms require that managers are not seen to act against the interests of labour. In this way, the involvement of financiers in long-term governance relationships with firms in coordinated market economies may facilitate a greater awareness of labour's interests and the value of human capital among financiers. By contrast, the nature of finance and governance in Anglo-Saxon systems pressurises managers to place shareholder interests above those of labour.

The second way in which pressures on labour management are exerted revolves around time horizons. In more marketized systems, it is often argued the structure of governance and incentives encourage short-termism (Hutton 1996; Porter 1997). For instance, the managers of large funds, such as mutual or pension funds, are assessed on short-term performance, and this feeds through to pressure on managers, via market signals, to maximize short-term returns. The potential to exit and sell reinforces short-termism. By contrast, in relational-type economies, the closer integration of financiers into the firm, via equity ownership or long-term debt, facilitates a longer-term perspective by firms. These arrangements then feed through to managerial policies. In practice, the typical required pay-back periods for investment in outsider systems is much shorter than in insider systems. In turn, shorter pay-back periods imply a higher cost of capital. Together, shorter pay-back periods and higher capital costs mean that firms are less willing to invest in longer-term, intangible activities such as training and related forms of human resource development (Porter 1997: 7; Carr and Tomkins 1998: 221–3).

Third, as suggested above, it might be argued that variations in finance and governance affect business strategies, such as the pursuit of product market share as opposed to the pursuit of financial maximization. Thus, it might be argued, German manufacturing firms have sought to secure competitive advantage by producing relatively complex products involving complex production processes. Competitive advantage is maintained via incremental process innovation in production (Porter 1990: 356; Streeck 1992a; Soskice 1999: 113). Together these have allowed German firms to pursue market share in particular manufacturing sectors. By contrast, in outsider more marketized systems, the importance of financial returns (coupled with the cost of capital) tends to discourage investments in incremental product improvement and quality production. The pursuit of long-term market share is less emphasized. However, as suggested above, the more liquid equity markets and more active labour markets in the Anglo-Saxon economies may be conducive to radical product innovation by facilitating flotations and spin-offs of high-growth firms, as in the information technology and biomedical industries (Owen 1999: 403; Teece 2000: 57–9). In turn, then, these differences in product market strategies have implications for management decision-making in relation to employment patterns and workforce training.

Fourth, the market-based measures of performance and mechanisms of governance which are especially important in Anglo-Saxon economies tend to promote internal measures of firm performance which are primarily financial in nature. The emphasis on financial returns from equity markets percolates down through firms to influence many aspects of managerial behaviour (Carr and Tomkins 1998: 224). For instance, Porter (1997: 10–11) has argued that the decentralized strategic business unit model tends to be favoured by large firms in liberal market economies because it facilitates the use of financial measures in internal capital allocations. This has the twin effects of cascading financial imperatives down to lower levels of the firm, while at the same time divorcing top managers from the realities of organizing production and services. Thus, strategic decisions are made with little appreciation of their full consequences for lower reaches of the firm. A failure by managers to appreciate the importance of firm-specific human capital in production and service delivery may be a consequence. Related to this, managerial decision-making tends to discount the value of such intangible assets as human capital. In turn, this discourages investments in training and instead leads to a reliance on external labour markets for labour supply.

Fifth, in liberal outsider systems, the dominance of market-based transactions encourages the use of market-type devices to secure commitment and discourages employee institutions which may confuse such commitments and disturb the balance of interests mentioned earlier. In the absence of close relationships between owners and managers, there is a danger (stressed in principal–agent theories) that managers will pursue divergent interests from those of owners. Variable pay and stock options tend to be used in an attempt to deal with this agency or commitment problem (Pendleton *et al.* 2002).

Such payment systems seek to align managerial interests with shareholder value and shift downside risk to the recipients. Equally, at lower levels of the firm, managers may find it difficult to develop employee commitment via institutions of employee voice because they may restrict management's freedom to manoeuvre to meet imperatives emanating from shareholders. Once again, alternative market-based methods of securing employee commitment, such as variable pay and share ownership, may be sought. Simultaneously, these also shift risk from capital to labour. The converse arguments would apply to less marketized and more relational systems.

Finally, there is an argument that interlocking ownership in cooperative market economies, coupled with direct involvement in governance, may facilitate more coordination among firms (Soskice 1999: 116; Hall and Gingerich 2001). A good example of this is the vocational training system in Germany, where employers cooperate to develop general and occupational skills (Backes-Geller 1996). Similarly, ownership coordination also appears to be consistent with multi-employer collective bargaining, where firms are prepared to cooperate in the fixing of aspects of wages and conditions, while market-based systems seem consistent with company or plant bargaining, where firms try to relate wages and conditions to the performance of business units (Ulman 1974: 103–7).

In conclusion, there are various ways in which governance systems may influence management behaviour and decision-making. These contribute to several important labour management 'outcomes', including job tenure, training and skill formation, remuneration systems, work organization, and pay determination arrangements (Gospel and Pendleton 2003). For instance, internal labour markets have been especially well developed and quite persistent in countries like Japan (Aoki 1988: chapter 4; Koike 1988: 114–79), whereas they have been under pressure in countries such as the United States and the United Kingdom as shareholder value has taken root (Cappelli *et al.* 1997: 37–8; Lazonick and O'Sullivan 2000: 18–21). Similarly, countries in which shareholders have exerted influence via market means have tended to make greater use of contingent remuneration systems, especially for top managers, and these have more frequently taken a stock-based form. The use of company stock has provided an alternative instrument for securing commitment to the employee voice mechanisms (codetermination, legally mandated works councils, etc.) which are found in systems where governance takes a more relational form (Pendleton *et al.* 2002).

1.5. **Some Caveats and Further Considerations**

When work commenced on this volume, some of the authors (perhaps especially the editors) were attracted to the idea that finance and governance were major factors shaping labour management and employment outcomes. Indeed, this remains the key focus of the book. However, it soon became clear, especially outside of the Anglo-Saxon countries, that the causal link could run the other way. In other words, labour can shape governance and finance. This is clearly seen in Germany where, through board representation and works councils, labour is constitutionally a participant in corporate governance and can influence such decisions as the choice of finance, business unit disposals, and mergers and acquisitions. It is also seen in Japan where, though not legally based and less constitutionalized within the firm, labour has both direct and indirect voice which can influence decisions about finance and ownership. There is also a broader argument that organized labour can influence the general approach of governments to corporate regulation and wealth distribution, and that this can shape the business environment in which ownership and corporate governance have developed (Godard 2002; Roe 2003). This is most clearly seen in continental European countries, where labour and governments engaged in a social–democratic 'compromise' after the Second World War or where unions focused on political action (in some cases *in lieu* of activity within companies). These processes may be observed even in the Anglo-Saxon countries and it is arguable that at certain points in time, when labour has been strong, it has influenced the structure of ownership and governance via political action. Thus, Roe (1994, 2003) has argued that, in the United States, labour problems in the late nineteenth century were important factors leading to legislation which constrained big finance and favoured small shareholders. Arguably, at the present time in the Anglo-Saxon countries, a new influence of labour on governance takes the form of pension fund activism by trade unions (Ghilarducci, Hawley, and Williams 1997).

A second caveat which we would like to stress is that, though the aim of the volume is to explore the links between corporate governance and labour management, this is not to deny that other factors are important in shaping governance and labour. Thus, the state of product markets is also very important, with market extension and the intensification of competition ('globalization' in short) shaping corporate strategies and structures and also directly pressuring national employment and industrial relations systems. Changes in labour markets, not least the growing diversification of types and interests of labour market participants, are also reshaping traditional patterns of employment and industrial relations. Throughout the chapters it is abundantly clear that government intervention and non-intervention also have a profound effect on corporate governance and employment relations (this is particularly stressed in the French, Spanish, and Italian Chapters 7–9). Finally, as stated above, labour itself is not just some sort of dependent variable at the mercy of financial pressures and corporate governance: rather it can have an important autonomous effect on finance and governance.

As a final caveat, it must be pointed out that there is diversity within national systems. Though each of the chapters tries to give a broad overview of each country's system and linkages between their different components, they also show that there is variation within countries. Thus, not all Anglo-Saxon firms seem to act in a shareholder value orientated sort of way. So, for example, large pharmaceutical companies, such as Pfizer or GlaxoSmithKline, can take a long-term view of human capital development (Vitols *et al.* 1997); the same could be said for some high tech engineering companies such as Boeing and Rolls Royce (Lazonick and Prencipe 2002). Equally, some German firms, such as DaimlerChrysler and Hoechst, have moved towards a shareholder value orientation and (though at a slower rate) are adopting Anglo-American labour management practices, such as stock options (Jürgens, Naumaun, and Rupp 2000; Jürgens, Rupp, and Vitols 2000; Höpner 2001). These differences may in part reflect sector, technology, and size. However, they may also reflect the fact that shareholder portfolios are different. For example, the balance between small and large investors and between private investors and institutional investors of different kinds may provide more or less discretion and constitute more or fewer benign influences. It may also reflect the fact that managers have different relations with financiers, some developing long-term, more 'relational' type links which in turn facilitate certain kinds of labour practices (Deakin *et al.* 2002; Armour, Deakin, and Konzelmann 2003). Finally, of course, it must not be forgotten that it is managers, and not financiers, who manage labour and, albeit within constraints, the latter will let managers manage labour. This recognition of managerial choice allows within-system variation to be incorporated alongside between-system differences.

1.6. Outline of the Book

The main issues which the book addresses are the differences in finance and corporate governance between countries, how they affect labour management, and how in turn they are affected by labour. As Wolfgang Streeck suggests in the Preface this is to be seen in a context of growing liberalization of markets and growing privatization of state activities, including both physical assets and welfare systems. He therefore poses another major theme of the chapters, namely the extent to which national systems will converge, and suggests that this will always be constrained by path dependencies and national contingencies.

The chapters are presented in the following order. First, there are two Anglo-Saxon countries—the United States and the United Kingdom. These reveal certain well-known similarities, but also important differences, suggesting some questioning of the broad notion of an Anglo-Saxon variety. These are followed by two countries with Northern European-type systems, namely Germany and the Netherlands. The latter is notable for having some similiarities, but also important differences, with the Rhineland archetype. The next grouping provides examinations of France, Spain, and Italy. These countries provide interesting challenges for broad typologies of market-based versus relationship-based regimes. The final country chapter is Japan, with the author outlining both recent changes and the extent of continuity in that country. The book then concludes with a chapter which reverts to the broad literatures, typologies, and relationships considered in this introduction.

In Chapter 2, Sanford Jacoby examines the evolution of the US corporate governance system and its implications for labour over the last 50 years. He argues that, up until the 1970s, the prevailing model of large US business was 'managerial capitalism' with managers subscribing to a philosophy of 'welfare capitalism'. Thus, they perceived the corporation as a social institution with responsibilities to a variety of stakeholders. Managers saw their own role as balancing these multiple interests. In this system, managerial and shareholder interests were loosely aligned. The labour management implications of the model included long-term employment relationships, supplemented by an extensive package of employee wages and benefits, sometimes negotiated with trade unions. From the 1970s onwards, a shift in power has occurred inside the US corporation away from managers and employees and towards shareholders. This shift emanates from the growth of institutional investment, a growing assertiveness of investors, the development of new financial instruments (such as highly leveraged debt), and a lowering of the costs of entry and exit for personal shareholders. Together these developments have increased volatility and speculation in equity markets, heightened the power of investors *vis-à-vis* managers, and encouraged a short-termist orientation. Managers have found themselves exposed to greater risk and constrained to produce higher returns for shareholders; in turn, they have passed risks onto employees and sought to reduce the power of organized labour.

The result is that alongside the emergence of shareholder capitalism have come changes in the pattern of labour management. There has been a shift of pay and employment risk from the corporation and its shareholders to employees. Employment, especially for middle managers, has become more precarious. Although top managers have become increasingly subject to shareholder pressures, they have also been able to exploit the alignment devices—especially stock options—used by shareholders to guide managerial behaviour. As a result, pay differentials between top managers and ordinary workers have risen. In industrial relations, there has been a rise in unfair labour practices by employers and tougher anti-union activity, contributing to a long-term weakening of unions. Jacoby criticizes this set of developments on the grounds that employees are residual and undiversified claimants—they invest their human capital in the corporation and any stock holdings in the company typically constitute a significant part of their own wealth. Moreover, he claims, what is not recognized by managers is that, for both informational and incentive reasons, employees are also very well placed to monitor corporate practices and to contribute to performance.

It is true Jacoby sees some counter-trends. Some firms are adopting resource-based business policies, drawing on the strengths of their internal resources, including ordinary employees. Such approaches are associated with greater use of 'high performance work practices' and greater investments in workforce development. There has also been some modest growth in employee voice, especially in firms with employee share ownership. In addition, the chapter discusses recent legal and corporate governance reforms introduced in the wake of major business scandals. However, Jacoby argues, barriers to the further development of this model are many, especially the forces referred to above.

In Chapter 3, Andrew Pendleton and Howard Gospel then consider the United Kingdom, usually taken as the other main exemplar of the

Anglo-Saxon Model. The chapter begins by highlighting distinctive features of the UK system, such as the large number of listed firms and the dominance of institutional investors. The structure and nature of institutional investment reinforces tendencies towards market-based forms of monitoring and discipline. The evidence suggests that this leads to distinct patterns of management decision-making, including a greater emphasis on shareholder value than in other European systems and a shorter-term orientation towards investment. This appears to have distinct effects on labour management. At the same time as investor power has increased, the share of national and corporate income accruing to labour has fallen. Similarly, the market for corporate control has negative effects on employment security and has contributed to a growth in contingent employment. In addition, the UK ownership and governance system appears likely to contribute to a relatively wide pay gap between top managers and ordinary workers.

The chapter then proceeds to show how the UK finance and governance system is evolving. Significant developments are a growing concentration of ownership and reduced liquidity of investments. It is also noted that the disciplinary effects of takeovers may be less clear than was often assumed. Taken together, these developments are encouraging alternatives to market-based forms of monitoring and discipline. These include the emergence of relationship-based monitoring and of shareholder activism. Particular attention is given to the former, which takes the form of informal and private contacts between top managers and investors. 'Trust' is an aspect of this relationship. It is argued that these developments have contradictory effects on labour management. On the one hand, the development of relationships provides opportunities for managers to mould shareholder expectations. As a result, they may win investors over to resource-based strategies involving substantial investments in human capital. On the other hand, 'behind the scenes' activity facilitates powerful and speedy mobilization of influence by investors when companies hit hard times, with managers forced to make immediate and substantial changes to labour arrangements and employment relationships such as redundancies. Thus, finance and governance have an effect on labour management, especially during critical times. However, the impact is more complex than is suggested in some of the stakeholder capitalism and varieties of capitalism literatures.

The next two chapters consider various aspects of the German system of corporate governance and labour relations. Germany is given such prominence because of the unique role which labour has played in the system and its importance as a test case as to whether this role can continue under ever greater shareholder value pressures.

In Chapter 4, Gregory Jackson, Martin Höpner, and Antje Kurdelbusch provide a sociological and institutionalist analysis of corporate governance and labour management in Germany, teasing out complementarities, changing linkages, and growing tensions. They outline the main features of the German system of corporate governance and labour management as they have existed through most of the post-war years. Thus, the system of governance has been characterized by the importance of banks in external finance, high ownership concentration, patient long-term investment, and stable and dense corporate networks. This complemented a system of labour management, the main hallmarks of which have been relatively stable long-term employment, investment in worker training, flexible quality production, low variability and dispersion in pay, and strong employee voice allied with cooperative industrial relations. The authors argue that the corporate governance and labour management systems have been complementary, not in a mechanistic but in a complex manner related to economic circumstances, processes of negotiation, and shifting patterns of coalitions. These arrangements are now under pressure. Since the mid-1990s, there have been major changes in the corporate governance system—a decline in the role of banks, the unwinding of corporate networks, the rise of foreign and institutional investors, the emergence of a market for corporate control, and the growing financial orientation of top managers. Along with greater product market pressures and a growing political belief in the need to reform the welfare state and other institutions, these are putting considerable pressure on the labour management system. Drawing on recent research, the authors show that changes in corporate governance can be directly related to the shrinking of stable core employment and the growth of variable pay. However, the development of shareholder orientation has not undermined employee codetermination and collective bargaining, though it may have shifted the balance between what is done by the works council and the trade union. Both of these institutions are seen as more resilient to erosion and as playing a mediating role in the introduction of changes in employment relations. According to the authors, the key test for the future is whether German corporate governance and labour management will both move overwhelmingly in a more shareholder and market direction or whether they will develop and maintain a more 'hybrid' system. The authors predict the latter.

In Chapter 5, Bernd Frick and Erik Lehmann provide a meta-analysis of work on German corporate governance and labour management from a more Economics perspective. They set the context by demonstrating the importance of ownership concentration and the role of family, inter-firm, and bank ownership. However, their review of the literature suggests that the relationship between such governance characteristics and company performance is indeterminate and that any positive effects may be reducing over time as international competitive pressures increase. They then focus on those labour-related aspects of corporate governance unique to the German system and examine research on the legally mandated system of employee representation via board membership and works councils. Overall, they conclude board level codetermination seems to have had little effect on firm performance. However, works councils have a number of significant economic effects. This form of employee voice seems to reduce labour turnover, constrain the proportion of atypical employees, and increase the proportion of disabled employees (though not the recruitment of disabled newcomers). Firms with effective works councils tend to have higher wages and lower wage differentials. They also have greater functional flexibility in deploying labour and arranging working time, though they discourage the so-called 'high performance' work systems. The downside of all this is that a number of studies suggest a negative effect on profitability, though no effect on investment or innovation. Overall, the conclusion is that employee voice in German corporate governance has a positive effect on labour productivity and on economic performance. The authors conclude that recent changes in the legal framework will give even greater support for the works councils in medium and small companies.

In Chapter 6, Erik Poutsma and Geert Braam argue that the Netherlands combines elements of both Germanic and Anglo-Saxon governance and labour systems. The traditional mode of company finance and governance includes concentrated ownership and stable long-term relationships between shareholders and managers. Financial institutions provide a range of services to companies and this constitutes the basis for close, insider-style monitoring of corporate performance. However, there are signs that the system is moving in an Anglo-Saxon direction. Thus, foreign ownership has increased and the pattern of institutional investment is now similar to that found in Anglo-Saxon countries. Moreover, the Dutch stock market is dominated by a small number of major multinationals such as Shell, Unilever, and Philips. These are strongly exposed to influences from outside the Dutch system (especially Anglo-Saxon practices), though in some important respects they adhere to the Dutch model of governance. One of these is a German-style two-tier board system. Though there has been growing debate over the merits and demerits of this structure, on the whole government reforms appear to strengthen the role of labour, as well as capital, on boards.

The Netherlands has a system of works councils which have nomination rights to the upper board of the company. However, in most companies, the influence of such councils on governance appears to be limited. In terms of industrial relations, the chapter stresses the importance of centralized wage bargaining. Again, recently there has been debate about the need for decentralization, with works councils being given the right to sign company level agreements. However, in practice, there has been little change in the importance of sector level agreements, and many employers continue to value centralized arrangements. At the same time, there is some evidence of labour management evolving in ways which are typical of the Anglo-Saxon model: these developments include a trend towards rewarding top managers with share options, employee financial participation further down the organization, more use of performance-related pay, and an increase in flexible forms of employment. This has tended to occur in 'spaces' not strongly constrained by the centralized system. A continuing feature of the Dutch system, however, is employment protection: there are strong legal prohibitions on a 'hire and fire' regime. Thus, although there is a growing movement in favour of shareholder value approaches, these institutional features limit the opportunities available to firms to pursue labour strategies in line with these. The Netherlands is, therefore, an interesting hybrid with marketized capital but not too marketized labour.

There then follow three chapters on countries which may be seen as exemplifying a Latin or Southern European model, France, Spain, and Italy. All three have traditionally had concentrated ownership of large firms and state intervention, coupled with weak employee voice within the firm and a rather stronger role in centralized collective bargaining.

In Chapter 7, Michel Goyer and Bob Hancké consider 'Labour in French Corporate Governance: The Missing Link'. They argue that, despite attempts by governments to give labour a positive role in the firm, employees have traditionally been excluded from corporate governance, with trade unions playing at most a blocking role in the firm. The non-involvement of labour has allowed French firms to push through changes over the last 20 years which have made them approximate more to Anglo-Saxon companies in important respects. Thus, an older system of finance and governance, based on state-led, bank-based credit and on a close network of cross-shareholdings, has been greatly modified. The following major changes are stressed— major privatizations, the dismantling of conglomerate structures, the sale of cross-shareholdings, the rapid growth of foreign ownership, and the development of something more like a market for corporate control. In this context, senior managers have come to act more like their Anglo-Saxon counterparts, as seen not least in the introduction of stock options and other forms of variable pay for themselves and for others lower down the organization. Firms have chosen further to marginalize unions and to encourage weaker forms of employee voice. They have also, largely unilaterally, promoted flexible forms of working, based on management-sponsored teams and direct participation. To support this, they have fostered general rather than deep firm or occupation-specific skills, more in line with an external labour market orientation. Where they have had to bargain with trade unions, they have increasingly preferred to do so at company or plant level. In total, they have introduced policies and practices designed to promote the interests of shareholders, without having to take account of employee views or to negotiate these change.

In Chapter 8, Ruth V. Aguilera describes a system where there has been movement from what she suggests was a 'state-led' to a 'state-enhanced' corporate governance and labour relations system. She describes a system which was traditionally characterized by relatively high state ownership, strong state intervention, and an important role for banks, with labour excluded from corporate governance. From these origins, Spain has followed its own particular path to a new governance model shaped by its own traditions. It has moved towards a hybrid system, adopting practices from different countries, but in particular from the Anglo-Saxon model. As a result, there exists a tension between the new role of the state as a strong regulator, the uncommitted role of foreign capital, and the weak participation of labour within the firm alongside its stronger power in shaping macro-employment systems. The current Spanish corporate governance scene is characterized by a new role for the state as a relatively strong regulator, newly privatized firms in the hands of core investors (many of them foreign), a higher free float of capital on the stock market, but, still, a weak market for corporate control and the somewhat piecemeal introduction of Anglo-Saxon practices, such as increased transparency, accountability, and potentially more efficient boards. Anglo-Saxon-style codes of corporate governance practice and stock options have also appeared on the Spanish scene.

In terms of the labour management system in Spain, there is a tension between these changes and the power of labour in shaping broad national aspects of employment systems but in its weak participation in the firm. In Spain, there has developed a dual labour market system, where insiders enjoy employment protection and good benefits but alongside a significant precarious labour market of temporary labour. Recent legal changes have made it easier for managers to make employees redundant. Training arrangements are relatively underdeveloped. Firms, including the growing number of foreign multinationals, have tended to opt for labour-intensive production methods. Flexible forms of working are limited both by these production systems and by legal and institutional constraints. The strong bargaining power of unions at multi-employer level means they play an important role in shaping employment systems. Thus, as in the other Latin countries, major tensions exist between evolving corporate governance and labour management systems.

In Chapter 9, Sandro Trento argues that the Italian system cannot be classified as either market–outsider or relational–insider. Nevertheless, there are specific complementarities which arise from path-dependent patterns of historical evolution. On the one hand, the stock market has been underdeveloped, firms have relied on bank credit for investment, and ownership of large firms has been concentrated. Complex, pyramidal ownership structures, often involving family groups, have been a key feature of business organization. On the other hand, the bank–firm relationship does not exhibit the long-term character associated with relationship-based finance/governance systems. In support of the path-dependent development view, the chapter sketches the development of Italian capitalism over the course of the twentieth century. A key feature since the Second World War has been the extensive role of the state in economic activity. Although banks have been important suppliers of capital to industry, they have had little role in the ownership of industrial firms (unlike Germany) and do not actively monitor the firms to which they supply credit. Instead, the state has played an active monitoring role. As for the labour relations system, this differs from those found in both Anglo-Saxon and relational-based systems. Although there have been pressures towards greater labour flexibility in recent years, national/sector level bargaining continues to be very important. However, in contrast to relationship-based systems, there is a lack of employee voice within the firm. Historically, this derives in part from the particular organizing strategies and ideological perspectives adopted by the Communist trade union confederation.

By the early 1990s, it was increasingly felt that there were real weaknesses of the Italian model of governance: the stickiness of the family mode of control, collusion between top industrialists and government, and barriers to entry to new entrepreneurs. These were mirrored by a lack of flexibility in the industrial relations system. The last 10 years have seen some attempts to bring about change in corporate governance and labour management. Thus, there has been an extensive privatization programme, which in turn has contributed to the development of the stock market. However, the extent to which flexibility has been achieved in labour relations is limited. This is causing difficulties for firms which are coming under increasing pressures from globalization and investor pressures.

In the penultimate chapter, Takashi Araki describes the main aspects of the traditional Japanese corporate governance model in terms of strong cross-shareholdings, stable share ownership, and the absence of a market for corporate control. He also stresses control through directors mainly promoted from within the organisation and the existence of an insider monitoring system. These arrangements, he argues, support certain key aspects of Japanese employment practices and labour relations. They have underpinned long-term or so-called 'lifetime employment', wages and benefits which tend to rise with seniority and which result in low pay dispersion, a system of in-house training, and functional work flexibility. Though there is no legal basis supporting employee voice within the firm, Araki argues that enterprise unionism, management–labour joint consultation, and the relative proximity of top managers to ordinary workers means that employee voice is heard in corporate governance. However, at the present time, there are significant changes in the Japanese governance system. Long-term, stable share ownership is declining, there is a growth in foreign share ownership, and some leading firms are introducing Anglo-Saxon type boards with outside directors. Araki argues that in this context there is a greater emphasis on shareholder value type ideas. In turn, these may then be feeding into changes on the labour side. At the same time, other factors are also at work here, such as rising unemployment, greater workforce diversity, and declining union membership. The main changes in the employment system stressed by Araki are the growing number of atypical or non-regular workers and pressures on lifetime employment for many core employees. There is also some questioning of the traditional system of employee representation and, as a consequence, some commentators are coming to argue for statute-based voice arrangements on European lines so as to give labour a constitutional voice in corporate governance. However, though law has been important both in giving workers rights and in providing for new employer strategies, he argues that the Japanese system of corporate governance and labour management are practice-dependent rather than legally underwritten. This means that they can be more easily changed than, say, the German system. But, though he sees some of these changes continuing, on the whole he believes that there are sufficient counterpressures and continuities to maintain most of the key aspects of the Japanese governance and labour system.

In the final chapter, Gregory Jackson reverts to a more explicitly comparative analysis and draws out broader conclusions raised by the country case studies. He recommends the need to disaggregate the broad types found in the literature and understand links in a more configurational manner. However, he does see one fairly homogeneous clustering, namely the Anglo-Saxon group of countries, with their marketized governance and employment systems. On the other hand, the relational/insider or stakeholder/coordinated group of countries shows greater diversity, with rather more marketized elements than might often be thought and with considerable change at the present time.

The chapter identifies a number of major developments across countries. In terms of corporate governance, he suggests there is a shift towards stronger shareholder rights and more capital market orientation; firms are divesting from non-core and less profitable businesses; and differences in the area of financing, ownership patterns, corporate law and regulations, and executive compensation systems are narrowing. In terms of labour management, there is also a move towards more marketized systems. This is shown by the following: an increase in contingent pay of various kinds; the shrinking of employment security to a smaller core; the challenge to employee participation posed by new decision-making structures; and the decentralization of collective bargaining.

Jackson suggests some broad linkages between governance and labour management on the following lines. Though no one limited set of governance arrangements is a necessary or sufficient condition, some combinations are sufficient to produce labour outcomes.

In practice, very few counties have strong legal rights for both share-holders and employees; less marketized countries have more stable employment; few countries with predominantly market governance regimes have relational employment and industrial relations institutions. But, still, the linkages between governance and labour seem to be strongest at the extreme ends of the spectrum. Moreover, he cautions that it is difficult to differentiate between direct links between corporate governance and labour management and more indirect links which work through broader regulatory regimes and industrial relations institutions.

On the basis of this analysis, Jackson speculates that differences in both corporate governance and labour management will narrow, but not disappear. Patterns of change will continue to be complex, with different starting points, different degrees and mixes of market-ization, and often piecemeal adaptation. In future, differences may be more ones of degree than of kind.

1.7. Conclusions

Collectively, the chapters have important implications for debates about the future of corporate governance and labour management. Here, we conclude with a number of points which derive from the country chapters and which are returned to in the concluding chapter.

First, corporate governance and labour management are both defining sets of features in national political economies. The chapters also show that they are closely interlinked. In general, the more marketized is the position of capital, the more marketized is the system of labour management. However, the tightness of linkages varies. It varies between countries. So, for example, the link may be clearer at the two ends of the spectrum of countries: in other words, there are closer link-ages in the more liberal Anglo-Saxon economies and also in the more regulated cases of Germany and Japan. It varies also with the issues: so, for example, tighter links may be found between the marketization of capital and employment tenures and pay systems than with aspects of vocational training and industrial relations. Another way of putting this is that certain issues (such as employment and pay) are 'domestic' issues which are mainly internal to the firm (though obviously shaped by legal parameters). Here, finance and governance can more directly shape choices. Other issues are more external in that they involve more outside parties and legal norms. These include issues such as vocational training and employee representation, where government and legal factors mediate and moderate governance pressures on labour. However, in the area of industrial relations, there are new pressures on national collective bargaining systems, making for greater decentralization and more flexibility.

Second, there is the question of the direction of causal linkages. If there is a link which flows from corporate governance to labour and its management, there is also one which flows from labour to corporate governance. This again varies. It may vary over time, with labour being more significant in shaping systems under crisis, such as in the aftermath of two world wars. It also undoubtedly varies between countries. In Germany and Japan, albeit in very different ways, labour has shaped governance systems and is playing a continuing role in negotiating new accommodations. In France, Italy, and Spain, labour has been more of a bystander, playing at most a blocking role as far as it can. However, the political orientation of labour movements has had a significant influence on government regulation of the economy, and has thus indirectly shaped the context in which governance and labour management take place. In the Anglo-Saxon countries, labour has probably traditionally played and has certainly come to play the smallest role. In sum, this is another way of saying that the effect of labour on corporate governance varies with the strength of labour: where labour has real power resources and can mobilize these, it will have more influence on corporate governance and be less buffeted by financial and governance pressures.

Third, the chapters suggest that at the present time there may be an accelerated change in both corporate governance and labour management systems. Again, however, the chapters show that it is not possible to read off change in a 'one for one' sort of way. Moreover, the chapters show that there are also accelerating changes in other factors, for example, greater product market competition, growing workforce differentiation, and the changing priorities of governments as they look to maintain national competitiveness. Streeck in his Preface nicely brings these factors together in what he refers to as liberalization and privatization of many aspects of economic and social life.

Finally, there are trends making for some convergence between national systems. Thus, in countries such as France, Germany, and Japan, changes in corporate governance in a more Anglo-Saxon direction are occurring and may be contributing to some systemic changes in labour management systems. As the US and UK chapters show, there are also important changes in the Anglo-Saxon countries, for example, growing re-concentration of ownership and increasing large shareholder involvement in corporate governance. This opens the possibility for two-way convergence on some sort of hybrid model, perhaps of an 'enlightened shareholder value' kind. However, change is mediated by different national starting points and by different configurations of relations between the various actors, with the result that national diversities will be maintained both between countries and within countries (Katz and Darbishire 1999; Whitley 1999).

The governance of firms and the management of labour are central issues for all industrial societies. Both have implications for economic wealth and for the broader welfare of nations. It is becoming increasingly necessary to understand the interaction between the two.

2

Corporate Governance and Employees in the United States

SANFORD M. JACOBY

2.1. Introduction

Corporate governance comprises the rules, practices, and procedures by which managers are held accountable to those who have a legitimate stake in the enterprise. Major issues of corporate governance include the duties of directors, methods of financing the corporation, managerial compensation, acquisitions and divestments, and the monitoring of decision-making at the strategic and operating levels. These issues are of enormous importance, not only to corporations themselves, but to millions of people—shareholders, employees, customers, suppliers, and communities—who are affected by management decisions.

Although we live in an era of so-called globalization, systems of corporate governance remain stamped with distinctive national characteristics. This diversity is particularly evident when it comes to questions such as which groups have a legitimate stake in corporate governance, whether employees are one of those groups, and, if so, what should be the employees' role. Every nation has struggled with these questions and developed answers based on its legal and political traditions and its historical trajectory of labour relations. The Untied States, like every other country in this volume, has a distinctive pattern of corporate governance and a unique set of relationships between corporate governance and labour management.

Giving employees a voice in corporate governance is not coterminous with trade union collective bargaining. In countries with statutory provision for works councils or employee representation on company boards, representation typically occurs separately from collective bargaining procedures (though representatives are often linked to

This is a revised and updated version of an earlier paper (Jacoby 2001). The author is grateful to Marleen O'Connor for guiding his entry into this subject.

unions). On the other hand, unionized employees may eschew involvement with management decision-making because they prefer to keep labour and management roles separate. This has been the traditional practice in the United States.

Yet, as US union density has declined in recent years (now less than 9 per cent of the private-sector workforce), unions have become more involved in corporate affairs: through participation in corporate boards, through management of pension funds, and through employee involvement programmes that heighten employee influence at the operating (enterprise and workplace) levels. However, the right of employees to influence or monitor management inevitably comes up against the rights of other parties, especially shareholders. In the United States, there is a presumption that shareholders are the sole group with legitimate authority to monitor management decision-making. The link between shareholders and management occurs through corporate boards, which are legally required to represent shareholder interests, and through economic devices to align management decisions with those interests, such as stock options.

This suggests that efforts to expand employee 'voice' in the United States will have to contend not only with defects in labour law (addressed by the Dunlop Commission in the 1990s), but will also have to consider whether corporate law and regulation are barriers to greater employee voice in the enterprise (Weiler 1990; Jacoby 1995). The recent corporate scandals in the United States have focused attention as never before on issues of corporate governance. Reforms have been enacted by Congress, the Securities and Exchange Commission, and the private stock exchanges. Yet, few have considered the underlying assumptions of the US governance system or the perhaps heretical notion that some kind of employee representation at the corporate level might make a company less prone to malfeasance.

This chapter examines the evolution of US corporate governance and its implications for labour. It first analyses the development of the present US model of corporate governance over the last 40 years or so. Next, it analyses the costs and benefits of the US system. In recent years, in an effort to reduce costs, there has been substantial borrowing by US employers of practices from other countries, just as others have borrowed from the United States. To propel further changes in the US system, policy recommendations are advanced that would simultaneously reform corporate governance practices while creating a more favourable climate for employee representation.

2.2. **The US Corporate Governance Model**

The last 20 years have seen a shift of power inside the American corporation away from managers and other employees towards shareholders. One important development has been the capacity of shareholders and others to displace incumbent managers through hostile takeovers, often using new financial instruments such as junk bonds. The growth in institutional investment has been an important factor behind this. Institutional ownership of US corporate equities rose from 29 per cent in 1970 to 45 per cent in 1990 (Blair 1995: 45–46). The greater concentration of ownership associated with this made it easier for 'corporate raiders' to assemble majority coalitions to bring about changes in control (Donaldson 1994). Coupled with this has been a growing assertiveness of institutional investors—mutual funds and pension funds—arising partly from changes in securities law requiring them to disclose financial results, and thus to seek higher returns. Institutional investors, lacking inside information about the companies they invest in and having only a small capacity to influence management behaviour directly, base their buying and selling decisions on short-term movements in stock price. Either exempt from capital gains taxes (pension funds) or somewhat indifferent to them (mutual funds), these investors have high rates of portfolio turnover, and these increased from the 1980s onwards. In recent years, there also has been a move toward more speculative investments. In the 1980s, pension and mutual funds became major buyers of the junk bonds which financed takeovers.

Other factors leading managers to pay more attention to shareholders are the recent innovations which have induced individual investors to enter the market, to trade rapidly and cheaply, and to speculate on short-term price movements. These innovations include the rise of discount brokerages, the ability to trade on the Internet, and the spread of defined-contribution pension plans controlled by individuals (e.g. the so-called 401(k) plans which started in the early 1980s). Together, these changes have reduced the average amount of time a share is held and the turnover rate of individual portfolios. Again, the result is greater pressure on managements to produce short-term results and a quasi-speculative atmosphere in equity markets (Odean 1999; Shiller 2000: 39).[1]

A vast literature in Economics seeks to explain why principals and agents—owners and managers—have divergent interests and how they can be aligned. As compared to major investors, managers are relatively risk-averse. This is because investors have large, diversified portfolios, whereas managers' assets tend to be concentrated in firm-specific human capital and in their employer's stock. These concentrated investments incline managers to pursue long-term growth policies which minimize risk by providing them with career opportunities should one of the company's units encounter problems. As power shifted in the 1980s, managers found themselves exposed to greater risk and were forced to produce higher returns to satisfy investors and avoid takeovers (Coffee 1988; Useem 1996). In response, some senior managers took their firms private by mounting leveraged buyouts (LBOs); other, typically mid-level, managers have been major losers in terms of job security. Indeed, middle managers discovered that the elimination of their jobs was often the main goal of industrial restructuring. Much of the decline in aggregate job stability in the late 1980s and early 1990s was concentrated among long-tenure males in managerial occupations (Jacoby 1999).

The abrogation of implicit managerial contracts may be the reason why, according to one survey, some dissatisfied managers are wary of their employers and open to employee representation, although presumably of a non-union kind (Freeman and Rogers 1999: 59, 144). It may be that these managers see employee representation as a way of taking power back from shareholders and of moving away from corporate policies which expose them to undue risk. When managers pursue risk-minimizing policies such as diversification, earnings retention, and long-term growth, they and other workers benefit from higher returns on firm-specific training investments, greater career opportunities, stable employment, and higher wages. Thus, in many cases, workers and managers have common interests which do not always align with shareholder objectives.

Some recent empirical evidence indicates that those managers who are less exposed to shareholder pressure do not fight as strongly for shareholders as those who are monitored more closely. Evidence comes from the more than thirty states which adopted anti-takeover statutes in the early 1990s, in response to concerns that non-shareholder constituents needed protection from hostile takeovers and restructurings (Orts 1992; Roe 1993). The data show that annual wage growth is 1–2 per cent higher in those companies which are subject to anti-takeover laws (Bertrand and Mullainathan 1998).

However, even before the takeover wave of the 1980s and the rise of shareholder value ideas, American managers were never entirely left to their own devices. Then, as now, managerial decisions were coordinated with shareholder interests by use of instruments such as stock options, direct stock ownership, outside directors, and by a credo (reinforced by economists and lawyers) that the purpose of management is to maximize wealth for shareholders.

This credo—the Anglo-Saxon or neoclassical view—holds that the goal of the enterprise is to maximize shareholder value because shareholders have the greatest incentive to see that management runs the enterprise efficiently. Because shareholders are the residual claimants—although last to be paid, any surplus belongs to them—they have a direct interest in maximizing that surplus. But, in theory and in practice, one can question whether shareholders are, in fact, the only residual claimants. After all, employees have substantial firm-specific investments which put them at risk and give them an incentive to see that the enterprise is efficiently managed. Unlike shareholders, employees lack the protection of portfolio diversification and of limited liability. Hence, they may have an even greater incentive than shareholders to ensure that the enterprise is properly managed. Moreover, because they are 'close to the action', employees often know more about the firm than shareholders do. Thus, sharing governance with employees can be justified on efficiency grounds. It can also encourage employees to balance the long-term interest of the firm against their short-term self-interest. For example, employees may moderate wage claims to facilitate investment by companies. The benefits of these trade-offs are recognized in the governance systems of other nations, such as Germany and Japan, and arguably were also more fully recognized by American managers in the pre-1980 period.

During the decades up to the 1970s, the alignment of management and shareholder interests was looser—in both practice and ideology—than it has become today. As Berle and Means (1932) observed, the separation of ownership and control left American managers with substantial discretion. Fragmented and distant shareholders could not easily monitor managements, thus providing executives with autonomy to divide the corporate surplus between dividends, retained earnings, and wages. At the ideological level, at that time, American managers had a philosophy at variance with the current credo that maximizing shareholder value is the primary objective of the business corporation. Instead, managers were imbued with the ethos of what was called 'welfare capitalism' or 'managerial capitalism' (Jacoby 1997). They conceived of the corporation as a social institution—a corporate community whose members included employees, suppliers, and distributors—and managers saw themselves as stewards to balance the institution's multiple interests. For example, the medical company, Johnson & Johnson, even carved a set of principles in stone at its New Jersey headquarters stating that shareholders would get a fair return only after the company had ensured outstanding value to customer, employees, suppliers, and the communities where the company operated (Reichheld 1996: 293).[2]

A classic study in the 1950s, *The American Business Creed*, provides striking evidence of a managerial philosophy which would today be considered undesirable and heretical. As the authors of that study observed:

Corporation managers generally claim that they have four broad responsibilities: to consumers, to employees, to stockholders, and to the general public. . . . each group is on an equal footing; the function of management is to secure justice for all and unconditional maxima for none. Stockholders have no special priority; they are entitled to a fair return on their investment, but profits above a "fair" level are an economic sin. (Sutton *et al*. 1956: 64)

While Industrial Relations scholars usually think of management rights as a prerogative which managers defend against union encroachments, post-war managers actually had a broader conception of the term which included managerial autonomy from shareholder pressure. Management rights, then, meant 'a sphere of unhampered discretion and authority which is not merely derivative from the property rights of owners'. They included the authority to plough surplus cash back into the enterprise rather than pay it to shareholders, a practice that the National Association of Manufacturers defended as 'the way the American system works'. Apportioning profits between dividends and retained earnings (and other spending purposes) was seen in those days as 'one aspect of the general function of balancing competing economic interests which devolve on corporate management' (Chamberlain 1948; Harris 1982; Sutton *et al*. 1956: 85, 87).

This philosophy continued to hold sway in the 1960s and 1970s. As described by Donaldson (1994: 19), the typical mindset of senior management in those years was:

An introverted corporate view . . . focused on growth, diversification, and opportunity for the 'corporate family'. . . . It was a period when the social and legal climate encouraged management to adopt a pluralistic view of their responsibility to the various corporate constituencies. As career employees themselves, it was natural for management to identify with all constituents who were long-term investors in the enterprise and to view shareholders in the same light.

These decades were the highpoint of corporate social and community responsibility, as shown by the fact that by the 1970s forty-eight states had passed laws permitting corporations to give funds to charities without specific charter provisions. While courts conceded that these social activities might hurt shareholders in the short run, responding to the needs of various stakeholders was alleged to be 'good for the shareholders "in the long run" because the good health and well being of the communities in which companies operate was considered important for business' (Blair 1995: 215).

Did the looser coupling of management and shareholders which prevailed prior to the 1980s have consequences for labour–management relations? The post-war decades were far from being a golden age of industrial democracy. But it is hardly a coincidence that the era was one in which corporations willingly treated workers as stakeholders in the enterprise. While employees were not seen to be on a par with shareholders they were, nevertheless, seen as having status in the corporate family. Employment was construed as a quasi-permanent relationship which endured through bad times and good. Benefits and other emoluments served to underscore management's common interests with employees. As Donaldson (1994: 19) says of the 1960s, ' "Loyalty" was the key word—commitment to the success of the enterprise within which each constituent found economic and social fulfillment.'

As shareholders grew assertive in the 1970s, one change was in the industrial relations area where management hostility towards unions became more widespread. Examples include a rise in employer unfair labour practices, firings for union activity, the use of tougher dispute tactics, such as striker replacement, and sustaining operations during strikes (Perry, Kramer, and Schneider 1982; Freeman and Medoff 1984: 229–33). It is difficult to assess to what extent these changes were due to shifts in corporate governance because there were other concurrent events which contributed to a hardening of managerial attitudes (e.g. an intensification of domestic and global competition and a rise in the union wage premium). Even so, the increasing dominance of a credo which privileged shareholders over other stakeholders made it easier for companies to justify anti-union policies. Thus, changes in corporate governance promoted a growing resistance to union legitimacy.

Conversely, the weakening of unions contributed to the unravelling of 'managerialist' philosophies of governance, especially in large, paternalist non-union companies such as IBM and Kodak. With organized labour seen as less threatening, companies were freer to adopt market-oriented employment policies which transferred pay and employment risk from the corporation—including shareholders—to employees. More generally, the triumph of individualistic views in the 1980s contributed to the decline of those relatively egalitarian social norms that had been established during the New Deal and the Second World War. These norms had underpinned managerialist governance—the idea that everyone had a stake in the corporation's prosperity. It became easier to justify the redistribution of risk and of corporate rents once inequality and market values had become more socially acceptable. However, social norms were still strong enough that shareholders' distributional objectives were often cloaked under the guise of efficiency. Restructuring was claimed to be about becoming lean and mean though in practice it was often really only about becoming 'fat and mean', to use Gordon's (1996) phrase. Further accelerating the process of normative change was a set of thinkers—academics, journalists, politicians—claiming that 'managerialist' values were outmoded (Sunstein 1996). They claimed that a strong form of shareholder-oriented governance—buttressed with outsider Chief Executive Officers (CEOs) and heavy use of stock options—was necessary to reinvigorate American capitalism and return the country to the market-oriented individualism of the nineteenth century (Khurana 2002).

As has been suggested, not all business people were happy with the new emphasis on shareholders, share prices, and quarterly performance. Some of the opposition was motivated by pure self-interest. Middle managers were worried that strong shareholder governance would lead to downsizing, job insecurity, and stress. Hiring outside CEOs left fewer career opportunities for incumbent insiders. Other managers opposed shareholder governance because they questioned its effect on the corporation's long-term health. Instead they proposed a 'resource-based' view of the firm centred on the idea that competitive advantage emanates from internal resources which competitors do not possess and cannot easily imitate—everything from an idiosyncratic corporate culture to intellectual capital embedded in employees and their relationships to each other. According to this view, recognition of multiple stakeholders—including customers and employees—can better facilitate the accumulation of human capital, social capital, and other investments that enhance corporate performance and value over the long term. Advocates of this view are found among the corporate responsibility movement as well as among some executives and consultants (Jacobs 1991; Hamel and Prahalad 1994; Scott and Rothman 1994).[3]

Yet, as the 1990s progressed, less and less opposition to shareholder governance was heard from American management. With stock options diffusing throughout the management ranks—and with equity prices steadily rising—managerial compensation rose, leaving most managers feeling that the new business ethos was a good thing, both for themselves and for shareholders. The growth of options was phenomenal: fewer than a third of CEOs received options in 1980, whereas 20 years later nearly all CEOs had them (Murphy 1999). The share of CEO pay deriving from options rose steadily in these years until it overtook base salary as the largest single component of executive compensation. Other managers and even some non-managerial employees also had a growing share of their compensation tied to options (Bebchuk, Fried, and Walker 2002).

2.3. Benefits and Costs

Recent events in the United States, such as the Enron, Worldcom, and Tyco scandals show that the shareholder governance model carries a set of costs as well as benefits. The primary benefits claimed for it relate to economic performance, though it should be borne in mind that the shareholder model appears to perform less well in other Anglo-Saxon countries which embrace it, such as the United Kingdom and Canada. Hence, any attribution of America's economic performance in the 1990s to shareholder sovereignty (which also exists in the United Kingdom and Canada) is based more on faith than facts.

The US economic performance in the 1990s was mixed. On the one hand, the stock market boomed, job creation was higher, and unemployment was lower than in other advanced countries. On the other hand, pay growth was relatively slow and unevenly distributed. Output per hour (productivity) in the United States was about the same as levels observed in Western Europe. Neither productivity growth rates nor per capita growth rates were higher than in other advanced countries, including Japan and Germany. It is true that productivity improved in the United States in the late 1990s, and, if this turns out to be a cumulative phenomenon related to the so-called 'new economy', the United States might have something to boast about (Freeman 2000; Jacoby 2000). But currently it remains unclear how much of the productivity improvement is related to the new economy. Furthermore, the extent to which the new economy is driven by corporate governance-related factors (like venture capital and ease of lay-offs) or by potentially unsustainable first-mover advantages (as was the case with information-related technologies in the 1980s (Macher, Mowery, and Hodges 1998)) is not yet clear. Hence, caution is warranted. Productivity growth has been mixed in the early 2000s. This does not sound like a revolution. Indeed, economic history is filled with numerous examples of 'new eras' which forecast a brilliant future that never arrives!

Another shortcoming of the American governance model is the limited information possessed by dispersed shareholders, leading them to overfocus on stock price movements. Managers respond by emphasizing activities that bolster quarterly results, which, as noted, leads them to give short shrift to activities that are not easily quantified or whose payoff is long term in nature. While the US approach excels at funding new ventures and new industries, short-termism causes a failure to invest enough to secure competitive positions in existing industries. The consequences of short-term restructuring in the 1980s became apparent in the next decade as corporations with more 'patient' owners—either private firms with long-term owners or publicly held firms with concentrated ownership—outperformed companies with more dispersed and speculative owners (Shleifer and Vishny 1990; Grinyer, Russell, and Collison 1998).

The 'market for corporate control', via mergers and acquisitions, permitted the United States to move faster than other countries to shrink purportedly unprofitable industries, to reduce overcapacity, and to curb excessive corporate diversification by de-conglomeration. But restructurings also led to a host of internal problems. For example, LBOs are associated with cuts in plant expenditures—for training, maintenance, and the like—and with sharp reductions in R&D spending (Long and Ravenscraft 1993).[4] Furthermore, mergers and acquisitions have had substantial adverse affects. In 1995–2001, 61 per cent of US mergers resulted in a subsequent reduction of share-price value. Moreover, part of the value 'unleashed' by takeovers was merely a transfer of income to shareholders from retained earnings, from employees (whose implicit pay contracts were broken), and from present and future pensioners (whose pension plans were run down). Because the only stakeholders driving the process were shareholders, adjustment costs were disproportionately shouldered by employees and communities—the least diversified stakeholders (Shleifer and Summers 1988).[5]

While a chief virtue of American governance is the liquidity of equity markets, there is a downside risk. During the 1990s, consumption and business investment were buoyed by a surge of new investors into US equity markets. But with this came an increase in speculative trading behaviour, a jump in stock turnover rates, and greater market volatility, all of which ended with the dramatic fall of equity prices, especially on the NASDAQ market at the turn of the century. With the market not well anchored by 'fundamentals', it is difficult to accept the neoclassical claim that capital markets are the primary source of discipline on managerial behaviour (Shiller 2000: 135–168). Just as herd behaviour can lead to a sharp rise in equity prices, so a stampede for the exit can cause a market collapse. The stock market collapse has wreaked havoc on the real US economy, leaving states with large deficits and pension funds seriously under-resourced. The same forces which in the 1990s drove share prices up have shifted into the reverse, causing investment and consumption to decline, and venture capital to dry up.

Buoyant equity prices in the 1990s masked many of the problems with the shareholder governance model. The fall in equity prices, coupled with corporate scandals such as Enron, Worldcom, and Tyco, are now shedding light on the model's shortcomings. In the United States, a key presumption is that shareholders monitor management through corporate boards composed of 'independent directors'. Yet, independent directors usually hold only a modest portion of their wealth in the stock of the company they are overseeing, limiting the incentive to commit time and effort to scrutinizing management decisions. Alternatively, if they do hold significant levels of company stock, they become reluctant to bite the hand that is feeding them. Often these directors have little detailed knowledge of the company or broad business expertise (Sorkin 2002). In light of these shortcomings, some hope that institutional investors—who often hold large, illiquid stakes—will begin to function more like Japanese or German relational investors, that is, as representatives of banks, suppliers, and employees. However, this has turned out to be a false hope. Institutional investors—with a few exceptions—have turned out to have the same kind of short-term horizons as individual investors (Shiller 2000).

Because boards lack information and expertise, US executives were able to influence their own compensation. The belief that stock options were a 'magic' alignment device allowed CEOs to persuade boards to approve option mechanisms which richly rewarded top executives, regardless of how much—or how little—their own efforts contributed to the company's equity-price movements (Jacoby 2002). For example, in the United States there is almost complete absence of explicit indexing of stock options. As a result, the benefits of options to recipients can emanate from stock price movements or industry developments as much as from company performance. Also, executives can reload options so as to profit from share price volatility even when long-term share performance is flat.[6] It is not surprising that research finds that the highest paid CEOs are from companies with two characteristics: first, a large percentage of the directors have been picked by the CEO and second, shareholders hold stakes of less than 5 per cent (Bebchuk, Fried, and Walker 2002). Instead of incentivizing managers to act in the company's best long-term interests, options drove top managers to a single-minded focus on boosting share prices. Although shareholders benefited too, the main share of resources went to executives at the expense of employees and of long-term investment, and when stock prices fell, shareholders and employees were left to pick up the pieces.

To summarize, it would be an oversimplification to say that US economic success in the 1990s was due chiefly to its governance model, or that recent Japanese and European problems are due chiefly to *their* governance models, and to conclude that the solution for the latter is to emulate the former. Rather, each governance system comes with costs and benefits. The virtues of the coordinated market model come from concentrated ownership, which permits close monitoring of managers and attention to long-term growth factors, and also from a stakeholder approach which gives employees and others a voice in corporate affairs. However, the pace of change, both for restructuring and new ventures, is slow. The US advantage is the liquidity of its capital markets; capital is widely available to finance both restructuring and emerging industries. With management in charge, changes can occur fairly rapidly. On the other hand, the system is weakened by short-termism, weak monitoring, and the inequality that results from exclusion of legitimate stakeholders from corporate decisions (Franks and Mayer 1997a; Coffee 1999).

2.4. Two-Way Convergence

In the late 1980s, liberal commentators urged the United States to shed its institutions in favour of Japanese and German-type practices, while today conservatives are making the reverse argument. Both sides fail to realize that neither set of institutions is unambiguously superior to the other. Moreover, because governance institutions are complex, path-dependent, and embedded in complex social systems, haphazard borrowing does not guarantee an improvement in the borrower's economic performance. Still, there is piecemeal, pragmatic imitation of the US model taking place in Europe and Japan. What is less noted, but equally significant, is that borrowing is also taking place in the United States.[7]

An example can be found in the recent evolution of corporate strategies of large US companies. Traditional precepts of strategy are built around two elements: an external orientation associated with product market considerations of product differentiation and market power, and an internal orientation concerned with the financial aspects of administering a multi-divisional company (Chandler 1977; Porter 1980). To achieve competitive advantage, external strategies relied on clever marketing and product design, creating market power through scale economies, and entry-barrier pricing. As companies developed financial resources and management skill, they followed an internal financial strategy of diversifying into other (related or unrelated) industries with market opportunities. The diversified company functioned like an internal capital market, allocating funds to businesses with the most promising market returns. At one extreme, as in the case of a conglomerate, a company might be very broadly diversified, with little synergy holding its different units together.

Today, a number of US companies are shifting the emphasis from a financial approach to one based on competing on the basis of their internal strengths. This so-called 'resource-based' approach (Barney 1991; Foss 1997) is a familiar concept to Japanese and German companies, which tend to be less diversified and more focused than traditional US firms (Kono 1984; Itami 1987a, b). The strategy aims to develop inimitable or non-substitutable resources which other companies do not possess. These might include a firm's unique physical assets, its organizational structure (including a distinctive corporate culture or innovation organization), and its intellectual property or other human capital. While not a substitute for external strategies, this approach takes a less finance-driven approach to internal resources and focuses on strengthening organizational processes which make the company distinctive. It eschews unrelated diversification based purely on financial considerations in favour of diversification guided by core competency and potential synergies.[8]

Aside from the Japanese influence, a reason for the rise in the 1990s of a resource-based approach to business strategy was the tendency of corporate restructurings in the 1980s to split up diversified conglomerates into smaller, more concentrated units (Bhagat, Shleifer, and Vishny 1990). Another reason was the growing importance of intangible assets and the relative decline of financial capital as a source of competitive advantage. In the technology and service industries which increasingly dominate the economy, intellectual capital is typically a company's chief competitive advantage. Hence, 'it is no longer in product markets but in intangible assets where advantage is built and defended' (Teece 1998: 7).[9] With this has come greater attention to the internal corporate policies which facilitate employee morale, creativity, and retention. As the head of human resources at a software company put it, 'At 5 pm, ninety-five per cent of our assets walk out the door. We have to have an environment that makes them want to walk back in the door the next morning' (Groves 1998).

American managers realized that to compete on the basis of quality or innovativeness required attention across the company's internal resources (everything from its organization of work to its corporate culture). Hence, from the 1980s onwards, there was a vast effort to borrow from the Japanese their quality-oriented production techniques, keiretsu-style relations with a limited number of suppliers, team-based forms of organization, and employee involvement plans (Cole 1999). Efforts were also made to create or strengthen distinctive and inimitable corporate cultures. The Euro-Japanese ethos that human resources are a strategic asset began to develop inside some American companies (Pfeffer 1998). Today, there are US companies— like the software company mentioned earlier—that place as much emphasis on human resources as a large Japanese company (Jacoby and Saguchi 2002).

The transformation is striking, especially with respect to the so-called 'high-performance work practices'. Employer surveys show that of establishments with fifty or more employees, 32 per cent have self-directed work teams, 24 per cent utilize job rotation, 18 per cent have peer review of employee performance, and 46 per cent utilize total quality management techniques. These figures suggest that between one-fifth and two-fifths of mid-to-large-sized US establishments are utilizing at least one high performance practice (Gittleman, Horrigan, and Joyce 1998; Osterman 1999; Erickson and Jacoby 2003). Associated with these practices are larger investments in training. Also, there is greater linkage of individual compensation to organizational performance, as exemplified by employee stock ownership plans (ESOPs) and stock options. Currently around 13 per cent of US private-sector workers own stock in firms in which employee ownership is at least 4 per cent of the company's total market value.

ESOPs were especially popular in the 1980s as a way of inducing wage concessions or making a company more resistant to hostile takeovers. But some of their popularity was also due to a belief that they create more cooperative employee relations. Empirical research validates these suppositions: employee ownership has been shown to stabilize employment, while modestly improving performance (Blasi and Kruse 1991; Stabile 1998; Blair and Blasi 2000). Since the early 1990s, the big growth in employee ownership has come through stock options, which are now granted to an ever-larger proportion of a company's employees. This is the positive side of option proliferation.[10]

These changes in work organization are associated with modest increases in employee influence at strategic levels. A few US companies, particularly those with substantial employee stock ownership, have created mechanisms for bringing employee views to senior management and to the board, including formal representation systems and board seats for employee or union representatives. Combining ESOPs with strategic employee influence has been shown to improve corporate performance (Conte and Svejnar 1990). Another route for voice is to have senior human resource managers act as employee advocates—as found in Japan—although this 'advocacy' model of HR is struggling to sustain itself in the United States (Purcell 1995).[11] But, because of a presumption that employees are not stakeholders, the role of human resource executives on corporate boards remains extremely limited. Of the US Fortune 1000 companies, only six have their own HR manager on their corporate board, an astoundingly small proportion, whereas ninety-two include their Chief Financial Officer on the board.[12]

Efforts to increase employee voice in US companies confront a variety of other barriers. Labour law is a major obstacle since it is unlawful for employers to play a role in establishing representative bodies. Employee voice is also deterred by the legal presumption that boards represent the interests of shareholders. Despite the substantial investments which employees have made in firm-specific assets, they are not considered residual claimants with a justifiable basis for control. Furthermore, creating new forms of work organization is a protracted and expensive endeavour. The advantages are difficult to quantify and are not well captured by existing accounting techniques. As a result, investment analysts and shareholders—as well as financial officers within corporations—fail to appreciate the advantages of work reform and employee influence. Studies have shown investors to 'ignore information related to the degree to which firms value their employees [and] react negatively if firms use compensation to link pay to organizational performance' (Pfeffer 1998: 263).

These barriers deter many companies from adopting a high-performance approach, and help to explain why nearly 30 per cent of establishments employing fifty or more employees have not adopted a single high-performance practice (Erickson and Jacoby 2003). Even in companies which have gone down this route and combined it with employee participation, participation typically is limited to the work-group level and employee voice is much less common at the strategic level (Kochan, Katz, and McKersie 1986). Companies with significant employee ownership do not usually provide for employee representation on corporate boards and do not give employee owners influence in strategic decisions (O'Connor 1993; Blair and Kruse 1999).

2.5. Prospects and Prescriptions

The recent debacles at Enron and Worldcom, and other US companies may well be the kind of events which can trigger a shift in the balance of power inside US corporations. At the very least, these incidents have punctured share prices and investor confidence, and taken some of the air out of hyperbolic claims that US-style corporate governance is the best possible. There are important changes, especially after Enron. Thus, there is a growing scepticism that CEO-appointed boards, even small boards composed of apparent outsiders, are capable of monitoring managements effectively. There is also scepticism of the claim that huge CEO salaries and option grants constitute necessary and well-deserved incentives. Some commentators are now claiming that US-style corporate governance promotes 'rent extraction' rather than 'optimal contracting' (Bebchuk, Fried, and Walker 2002).

As a result of these events, it is no longer automatically presumed that a charismatic and outsider CEO can readily boost profitability and shareholder value by being incentivized with stock options.[13] In the future we can expect to see a greater number of CEO insiders, who have risen up the ranks within the company and are more in tune with, and loyal to, a corporation's stakeholders. The impact of a move back to insider CEOs will be felt further down the managerial ranks. There will be more attention paid to grooming internal talent and less reliance on headhunters, which means an enhanced role for HR staff. There will be less use made of financial incentives and greater reliance on implicit contracts, especially long-term understandings built up through internal executive development. HR executives will have more of an opportunity to influence the selection of CEOs, giving more weight to experience and loyalty.

It is also less likely that CEOs will come from finance backgrounds. The fall of share prices and the taint attached to stock options have called into question the centrality of finance to corporate decision-making. This diminution of the finance function creates opportunities for those with different perspectives on corporate-value creation. The old model, in which finance was first among equals, may give way to an approach in which HR, as well as areas like marketing and R&D, will have greater influence on strategic decision-making. Such a shift of power might be ratified by shareholders, who, at least for the moment, appear chastened by the collapse of the equity bubble. Relentless and unrealistic demands for share price gains have subsided, which opens the possibility for a longer-term approach to resource allocation decisions—an advantage for training, employee development, and other HR programmes. This could mean a return to more organization-oriented and less finance-driven types of corporate strategy.[14]

The diminished reputations of CEOs like Al Dunlap and Jack Welch—who were among the leading practitioners of the shareholder value approach to corporate restructuring—has called into question whether the job cuts of the 1990s were motivated by a single-minded search for efficiency (Madrick 2002). There is an emerging consensus, including among institutional investors, that at least some of those cuts were driven more by distributional desires than by efficiency concerns, that is, that money went into executive salaries which should have been reinvested or distributed to other stakeholders.

A further reaction to the recent corporate scandals has been a set of governance reforms introduced by the stock exchanges, Congress, and the Bush administration. The main legislative change is the Sarbanes–Oxley Company Accounting Reform and Investor Protection Act of 2002, which creates new requirements for CEOs (to certify the veracity of financial statements) and corporate boards (to forbid subsidized loans to executives). In addition, accounting firms are required to rotate the partners supervising audits and auditors are prohibited from immediately joining management at client companies. The law also creates the Public Company Accounting Oversight Board to replace self-regulation by the accounting profession, though it leaves unspecified an ethical standard for auditors.

Meanwhile, the Securities and Exchange Commission (SEC) is conducting investigations of major corporate scandals, such as the

WorldCom case. The SEC has proposed new rules to regulate the accounting profession, though some have claimed that they lack teeth. However, a recent SEC provision that mutual funds disclose their proxy votes has the potential of facilitating corporate campaigns and of permitting greater alignment of mutual fund votes with the desires of the individual investors whose shares are being voted (McNamee 2002).

The two major exchanges, the New York and NASDAQ markets, have adopted tougher rules to govern listed companies. Although both exchanges are private, their rules are more aggressive than those proposed by government, in part because the exchanges, which are desperate to see confidence in the markets restored, are less sensitive to corporate lobbyists than the SEC. The NYSE's rules include the requirement of shareholder approval for all stock option plans. As for boards, the NYSE requires companies to have a majority of independent directors, and only independent directors are permitted on the audit committee and on the committee that selects the CEO.

Taken as a whole, these changes reduce the power of CEOs and heighten corporate transparency. But they do little to shift corporate governance in the United States away from its present shareholder-sovereignty model towards a stakeholder model. The role of employees in corporate governance is never mentioned, except to the extent that employees invest their individual pension funds in a company's stock. The Sarbanes–Oxley Act, for instance, provides stronger protection for employee pension funds invested in the employer's stock (a particular problem at Enron).

The role of the union confederation, the AFL-CIO, in corporate governance reform is worthy of note. It has been vocal in support of the greater protection of employee pension funds provided by Sarbanes–Oxley. However, most of the AFL-CIO's efforts have been focused on seeking stronger regulations against management misdeeds rather than redirecting US corporate governance towards a stakeholder model. By and large, the labour movement has used its shareholder power in support of 'good governance' measures such as promoting more independent directors, eliminating poison pills, and separating the CEO position from the chairman of the board (O'Connor 2000). More recently, the AFL-CIO has been urging companies with former Enron directors on their boards to refuse their renomination, thus positioning the AFL-CIO as a player in the most recent round of governance reform debates (McNulty 2002). In its support for recent reforms, it functions as an ally of those institutional investors seeking to strengthen shareholder power *vis-à-vis* management, rather than just as a spokesperson for employees.

The AFL-CIO's role in the corporate governance movement predates the current corporate scandals by at least a decade. Because union pension funds hold significant amounts of stock, there is the potential for labour to influence corporate decision-making. But there are two problems here. First, no single union pension plan holds a great deal of stock in any one company. Second, even the combined holding of union pension funds are often only a tiny fraction of outstanding shares in large public companies. To rectify these problems, the AFL-CIO has tried to coordinate the voting practices of union pension funds and has worked with other members of the institutional investment community, seeking to form alliances wherever possible (Ghilarducci, Hawley, and Williams 1997).

Occasionally, labour has used its shareholder power in support of labour issues, such as union organizing and strike settlements at companies with which it has disputes (Schwab and Thomas 1998). The AFL-CIO has also been prominent in its efforts to criticize outrageous levels of CEO compensation, as with its popular 'Executive Paywatch' website. The AFL-CIO has recently joined institutional investors in pressing for governance reforms which would limit executive compensation levels by expensing stock options and tying options to a company outperforming its industry. Also, the AFL-CIO has joined with activist investors in an effort to give shareholders the right to place their own director choices on a proxy card. This would make it easier for investors to elect alternative directors. (This campaign is currently being contested by companies before the SEC.)

This is as close as US labour has come to challenging the corporate governance status quo, and it has done so under the name of 'shareholder democracy'. Yet the AFL-CIO has not taken the next step of advocating 'industrial democracy' and a stakeholder model of corporate governance by seeking a union (or employee) voice on company boards. The reasons for the AFL-CIO's reticence are not clear, although an important factor is likely to be that any expansion of employee board representation, formal or informal, would of necessity require loosening of the labour law's strictures on employer involvement in representation activities. The potential consequences of this are seen as a threat by much of the US labour movement.

There remains considerable room to improve on current voluntary, regulatory, and lobbying activities in support of governance reform. What follows are some proposals intended to nudge US companies in the direction of giving employees more influence in corporate governance. Some of these proposals are permissive: they make it easier for the parties to pursue institutional reform by changing incentives and enhancing information. Other proposals are more direct efforts to expand employees' influence, consistent with their status as residual claimants and as essential members of the corporate community.

2.5.1. *Information for stakeholders*

At present, few US employers provide information to employees relevant to their position as corporate stakeholders. Just as disclosure of information permits shareholders to monitor management, protect investments, and boost corporate efficiency, the same is true for employees. Employees should be regularly provided with data on financial performance, executive compensation, operating results, strategic plans, and business risks. Moreover, as the OECD (1999) recently recommended, employees should also receive information relevant to the employment relationship, such as disclosure of current and intended human resource policies. Such information would include training opportunities, details of compensation practices, and health and safety records. Probably the best way to accomplish this would be to place employee representatives on company boards, although this is unlikely to receive support from the AFL-CIO for the reasons noted earlier (Kochan 2002).

Equally, shareholders and potential investors should be apprised of a company's human resource investments and practices. Despite the growing importance to corporate performance of a company's intellectual capital, a recent study finds that 'little systematic high-quality information about the impact and value of firms' human capital investments exists' (Bassi *et al.* 2000: 335). Although a few companies are beginning to take steps more systematically to analyse and manage their human capital, the majority of companies continue to ignore their investments and returns in workforce development and other personnel management practices. Little or nothing in this regard is reported to shareholders, either on a continuing basis or during mergers and acquisitions (when such information is of particular importance) (Coff 1991; O'Connor 1998).

Creating systems for measuring human-capital investments and relating them to performance has multiple benefits. Measurement makes these investments more salient and impels managers to give greater attention to them. Another benefit of measuring human capital and returns is that it would encourage investors to evaluate factors contributing to corporate performance more accurately and thereby give greater credit to companies which are making investments in employees. However, it must be conceded that there is the possibility that positive returns to training are un-demonstrable in the short run or that investors will react negatively to companies making these investments.

2.5.2. *Linking ownership to governance*

Employee share ownership has grown in recent years through the creation of ESOPs and huge investments in employer stock by employee pension plans, including employee-controlled defined-contribution plans.[15] While a few ESOPs provide for employee representation on company boards, the vast majority of employee owners have no governance mechanisms available to express their unique interests as both owners and employees. Unlike other stakeholders, employee owners lack board representation. Moreover, trustees of defined-benefit pension plans which have substantial employee ownership in the employing company are required as fiduciaries to ignore any special interests of employee–owners and focus only on general shareholder concerns (Blair 1995: 316–18).[16] However, workers already elect representatives to pension funds in the US public sector and share in the governance of multi-employer plans such as those found in the construction industry. In principle, the same could be done in other areas of the private sector.

There are a number of ways to proceed. First, employee owners ought to be given board representation; this is consistent with their heavy investments—financial and human capital—in the employing company. Second, trustees of pension and ESOP plans should be legally permitted to give weight to the special concerns of employee owners. Third, policy-makers should encourage the adoption of other innovative mechanisms for bringing employee concerns to a company's strategic decision-makers. Examples can be found in American corporate history. In the 1940s and 1950s, for example, Sears Roebuck had an employee profit-sharing plan which owned over a quarter of the company's stock. The company created a Profit-sharing Advisory Council that comprised nineteen delegates elected on a regional basis by employees throughout the country. The Council met twice-yearly with the profit-sharing fund's trustees to convey non-binding suggestions. While the importance of the Council was perhaps more symbolic than substantive, it would not be difficult to design more effective structures for conveying the concerns of employee owners to pension trustees and corporate directors (Jacoby 1997: 110, 122). Finally, much could be done to expand employee ownership through the use of stock options. At the present time, the majority of options are paid to senior executives. If a greater proportion of options were passed to employees and if they could achieve a corresponding role in governance, the result would be a heightened concern for employee issues in the charting of corporate strategy (Blasi, Kruse, and Bernstein, 2002; Jacoby 2002).

2.5.3. *Corporate boards*

Following from the previous suggestion, corporate boards—like other fiduciaries—should be required to take into account the interests of major corporate stakeholders, including employees. There are two models for doing this: either public directors could act as mediators between conflicting stakeholder interests or they could function as optimizers who seek to maximize the joint welfare of all stakeholders contributing firm-specific resources to the corporation (Blair and Stout 1999: 298; OECD 1999: 22). These models are consistent with state anti-takeover laws which grant directors broad fiduciary discretion to consider stakeholder interests when assessing takeovers or other business decisions. The courts have been less sensitive than legislatures to stakeholder concerns, but there are some notable recent exceptions.[17]

An offshoot of this approach is the proposal to give employees and other stakeholders the right legally to challenge directorial decisions made on their behalf when those decisions breach implied fiduciary duties, as, for example, when lay-offs occur without the provision of adequate financial compensation (O'Connor 1991; Mitchell 1992). While the proposal may seem to have a utopian quality, it is worth bearing in mind that in recent years similar challenges have been mounted via shareholder resolutions on behalf of employees and other stakeholders. Although rarely approved, these resolutions nevertheless serve to place a board on notice that problems exist and that shareholders are concerned about them. For example, IBM recently converted to a cash-balance pension plan which cuts pension benefits for thousands of mid-career IBM employees. In response, employees mounted a national protest and developed a shareholder resolution opposing the change. Major institutional investors supported the proposal, including several multi-employer pension funds from the union sector as well as the giant California Public Employees'

Retirement System (CalPERS), which has more than a billion dollars (mostly from unionized public-sector employees) invested in IBM shares. The head of CalPERS said that it was 'bad business policy' for IBM to cut pensions because the productivity of IBM's workers was positively affected by having dependable and secure pensions. The proposal did not pass, but over 28 per cent of shares were voted in favour of it, thereby ensuring that it can be brought up again in the future.

2.6. Conclusions

The recent corporate scandals in the United States have started a movement away from the radical shareholder-sovereignty model which took hold in the United States in the 1980s and 1990s, a model which also had the perverse effect of creating incentives for managerial malfeasance. Nevertheless, despite some counter-tendencies referred to above, the United States is now far from the kind of modest stakeholder model which prevailed in large companies in the 1950s. Lay-offs continue to be a primary response to declining sales and falling share price. Corporate governance reforms face an uncertain future. Business strategy continues to be finance-driven and the human resources function continues to lack status.

It is unlikely that fundamental tenets of corporate governance will change unless and until there is an expansion of employee representation, either through traditional union-based structures or works councils and committees. At the same time, however, attention must be given to corporate governance. Governance reform opens up additional channels for employee voice in situations where representational structures are ineffective or unsuited to handling strategic, company-wide concerns.

The other important reason to transform US corporate governance practices is to change the current anti-employee attitudes of American managers. If the logjam in labour law reform is ever to be broken, it will happen only if managements shift from the priority they give to shareholders and give greater weight to other corporate stakeholders. Companies in other countries do this, it has been done in the United States before, and it can happen again in the United States. Unlike some 'third way' proponents of stakeholder capitalism, employee ownership and changes in corporate governance are not seen here as substitutes for more extensive employee representation. Instead, reform of corporate governance and employee representation are best viewed as complements in the context of the United States. Creating a presumption that workers have a legitimate voice in the enterprise opens up possibilities—in politics, the courts, and in labour markets—for giving workers what they want in the way of workplace representation. In the meantime, one should be sceptical of any American belief in the superiority of their corporate governance arrangements and recognize that there is no one best way in this respect.

NOTES

1. The turnover rate for NYSE stocks nearly doubled between 1982 and nearly tripled for NASDAQ stocks.
2. In the nineteenth century, there was a similar conception of the corporation as being endowed with societal responsibilities (Roy 1997).
3. The argument is sometimes made that share prices allegedly reflect all information presently available about a company and maximizing long-run value is equivalent to maximizing today's share price. This is the efficient markets hypothesis. In fact, the evidence for efficient markets is less compelling than one might think. After all, if prices were at their appropriate level yesterday, why did the NASDAQ market fall today? Moreover, institutional frameworks for trading equities affect managers' time horizons. High stock turnover rates create greater volatility and uncertainty in equity prices than exist under a system of more patient capital. If this is the case, and if uncertainty works against long-term projects, then it is possible that there exists a capital-market bias against long-term investments, a bias that would be heightened by the sensitivity of equity prices to near-term information. In fact, the evidence is ambiguous—much of it based on R&D figures that are not a reliable measure of 'long term'—and one can find empirical support on both sides of the issue (Lafferty 1996).
4. Partly to avoid the myopic constraints of public ownership, some LBOs in the 1980s were management buyouts which were associated with higher performance that was not due to lay-offs or to reductions in R&D expenditures (Kaplan 1989).
5. Bondholders also suffer during LBOs as a result of the increased risk associated with LBO debt financing (Smith 1990).
6. When an option is reloaded, the executive pays the exercise price by surrendering stock he already owns and for each share tendered he receives a new option with the same expiration date as the original options. In this way, the executive locks in a portion of the gain but loses none of the future upside potential. This enhances the ability to profit from temporary price rises in volatile situations. Reloading offers value to the executive but little obvious benefit to shareholders.

7. The Japanese have a long history of borrowing institutions and ideas from the West, although it is obviously easier to make incremental adaptations to existing institutions than it is to attempt major top-down change (Westney 1987).

8. There is evidence of a modest increase in median industrial concentration since 1980, which is consistent with de-conglomeration and relatively greater emphasis on internal strategies (Liebeskind, Opler, and Hatfield 1996).

9. Between 1978 and 1997, the book value of plant and equipment of publicly traded corporations, as a percentage of market value of claims on the firm, fell from over four-fifths to less than one-third of the market value of those claims (Blair and Stout 1999: 744).

10. Despite the proliferation of options, senior management still receives the lion's share. In 1998, the top managers of Fortune 500 companies received an average of 279 times the number of options given to each of the firm's other employees. Note that widespread use of options can have the effect of intensifying managerial myopia, because options create an incentive for managers to 'do everything they can to boost share prices . . . to undertake corporate initiatives whenever they think the market will respond to them, even if they themselves are doubtful of the value of these initiatives' (Shiller 2000: 23). Moreover, rather than aligning interests, options may drive a wedge between employee owners and shareholders, because companies often step in to protect employees when share prices fall, whereas nothing is done to cover shareholder losses (Financial Markets Center 2000).

11. Despite potential labour law violations, some 20 per cent of US companies with employee involvement plans also had a formal system of non-union employee representation (Kaufman 1999).

12. Data on corporate boards were kindly supplied by Caroline Nahas of KornFerry February 2002.

13. A recent study by the Federal Reserve Bank of New York reported that 'there is presently no theoretical or empirical consensus on how stock options affect firm performance' (Core, Guay, and Larcker 2003).

14. Heretical ideas about the importance of human capital are starting to appear in unlikely but influential places. *Business Week* has told its readers that,

    Corporate finance as it's taught in business schools takes for granted that shareholders are king. But theory doesn't match reality. At many companies, shareholders are no longer the owners in a conventional sense. That is because key employees are not simply hired help brought in to run the assets of the company . . . They are the company. (Coy 2002: 24)

15. Among the 1,000 largest US pension funds, the total share of investments in employer stock ranges between one-fifth and one-quarter of total plan assets (Stabile 1998).

16. One of the most famous ESOPs, United Airlines, has employee board representation. But the ESOP is currently being questioned and criticized by its employee–owners.

17. In Delaware, a bastion of traditional corporate law, the courts permitted Time to reject a hostile bid from Paramount and merge with Warner so as to preserve Time's culture of editorial integrity, even though a majority of shareholders preferred Paramount over Warner (Orts 1992). Bagley and Page (1999) call on boards to exercise corporate stewardship—a phrase reminiscent of traditional welfare capitalism—and propose that the SEC require companies to disclose in annual reports all board-level decisions which have a material impact on any stakeholder constituency, whether employees, management, customers, suppliers, creditors, the community, or the environment.

3

Markets and Relationships: Finance, Governance, and Labour in the United Kingdom

ANDREW PENDLETON AND HOWARD GOSPEL

3.1. Introduction

It has become widely argued, especially among those who desire a stakeholder model of the firm, that the UK finance and corporate governance system has adverse consequences for the performance of the firm and its employees. In a best-selling book, Hutton (1996) argues that the UK system prioritizes high returns to shareholders and subjugates the interests of firms and their workforces to the dictates of the City. The threat of takeover means that listed companies have to deliver high short-term returns to investors to secure their loyalty. As a result, 'technical innovation and building market share take second place to financial imperatives' (Hutton 1996: 134). Only those investment projects with high rates of return and low risk can be approved. The 'destructive relationship' between the City and industry means that investment, R&D, and workforces have to be sacrificed when firms face adverse economic circumstances.

This stakeholder line of argument has much in common with that found in the 'varieties of capitalism' literature and the corporate governance literature in Financial Economics. All emphasize the role of market forces in the UK capital and ownership system, with signals from stock trading activity as a key instrument causing firms to take particular courses of action. Hall and Soskice (2001*b*) view market-based forms of coordination between actors and institutions as the key characteristic of the US and UK economies ('liberal market economies'), contrasting this with relationship-based forms of coordination in the German and Japanese economies ('coordinated market economies'). 'Institutional complementarities' mean that large, active equity markets in Anglo-American countries are accompanied by a greater reliance by firms on external labour markets than elsewhere, along with relatively low levels of statutory labour regulation. As a result, firms typically respond to economic shocks by adjustments to labour management (for instance, lay-offs). By contrast, in coordinated market economies there is a greater likelihood that these shocks will be absorbed by capital.

This chapter assesses the impact of the ownership and governance system on labour management in large companies in the United Kingdom. We show how some labour management characteristics are associated with distinctive features of finance, ownership, and governance, in line with the stakeholder and varieties literatures. However, we also present evidence that is inconsistent with these critiques. The inference is that, while active equity markets are important in influencing managerial behaviour in listed firms, the relationship between ownership, governance, and labour management is less deterministic than the stakeholder critique suggests and less homogeneous than the varieties approach implies.

As part of a critique of these approaches, we focus on recent developments which are modifying the market model of governance in the United Kingdom. This evolution has several important features, including growing concentration of ownership and a reduction in liquidity. This 'locks in' major investors and leads them to find alternative means of corporate governance. Alongside public investor activism, a relationship-based system, characterized by a web of contacts between major institutional investors and top managers of firms, has come to be important. Influence is now often exerted privately via relationships as well as through market transactions. Thus, political and social models of governance are supplementing the market-based model (Pound 1993).

The emerging system has two opposing consequences for labour management. On the one hand, investor pressures when firms are in distress complement and reinforce market messages. Indeed, they may substitute for market transactions where investors are locked into their shareholdings. On the other hand, the nature of the relationships between major investors and managers provide managers with some degree of power and autonomy in determining their business and labour strategies for most of the time. In these relationships, the perspectives and social characteristics of the actors structure the content and outcome of interactions between the two, which take place in specific social and institutional contexts (Jackson 2000; Fligstein 2001; Aguilera and Jackson 2003).

In this chapter, we provide a brief outline of the main features of the UK ownership system and relate this to the market–outsider model typically used to characterize the UK system. We then identify the labour management consequences of this system, drawing on the extent of evidence to date. Then we consider the ways in which the system is currently evolving and draw out the implications of these developments for labour management.

3.2. A Profile of the UK System

Equity markets play a central role in the UK financial and industrial system. At the end of 2002, nearly 2,300 domestic and foreign firms had their shares listed on the London Stock Exchange, compared with just over 900 firms on the Deutsche Borse (World Federation of Exchanges 2002). Market capitalization of domestic firms listed on the London market is over double that on the German exchange and larger than those on Euronext (the combined Belgian, Dutch, and French exchange) (World Federation of Exchanges 2002). About 80 per cent of the largest 700 companies in the United Kingdom are quoted (Franks and Mayer 1997*a*, *b*).[1] London is the most important stock exchange, by number of firms listed and market capitalization, after the New York Stock Exchange, NASDAQ, and the Tokyo exchange.

Like the United States, ownership of listed firms is relatively dispersed, especially among firms with the largest market capitalization. Franks and Mayer found that only 16 per cent of the largest 170 quoted firms had a shareholder with 25 per cent or more of the equity, compared with 79 per cent in France and 85 per cent in Germany (1997: 283–4). A further notable feature of the UK equity market is that, despite ownership dispersion, it is dominated by institutional investors to a greater extent than the United States or Europe. At the end of 2001, the major groups of UK-based institutional investors—pension funds, insurance funds, unit trusts, investment trusts, and other non-bank financial institutions—together owned 50 per cent of UK equity (Table 3.1). Overseas investors, of whom a substantial proportion are financial institutions, own a further 32 per cent. Unlike many European countries, commercial banks have not invested in equities to any significant extent, though this has increased recently. Similarly, there is little cross-ownership of industrial firms by other industrial firms. Moreover, this fell throughout the 1990s to 1 per cent of total equity in 2001. Family ownership is also less significant than

Table 3.1. *Ownership of UK shares 1963–2001, percentage of total equity owned at year end by each investor type*

Investor type	1963 (%)	1975 (%)	1981 (%)	1990 (%)	1997 (%)	2001 (%)
Rest of the world	7	5.6	3.6	11.8	24.0	31.9
Insurance companies	10	15.9	20.5	20.4	23.5	20.0
Pension funds	6.4	16.8	26.7	31.7	22.1	16.1
Individuals	54	37.5	28.2	20.3	16.5	14.8
Unit trusts	1.3	4.1	3.6	6.1	6.7	1.8
Investment trusts[a]	n.a.	n.a.	n.a.	1.6	1.9	2.2
Other financial Institutions	11.3	10.5	6.8	0.7	2.0	9.9
Charities	2.1	2.3	2.2	1.9	1.9	1.0
Companies (non-financial)	5.1	3.0	5.1	2.8	1.2	1.0
Public sector	1.5	3.6	3.0	2.0	0.1	0.0
Banks	1.3	0.7	0.3	0.7	0.1	1.3

[a] Investment trusts were not recorded as a category until after 1981.

Note: n.a.: not applicable.

Source: Central Statistical Office (2002).

in countries such as France and Italy, though it was an important feature of corporate ownership even in very large firms up until the 1960s and continues to be significant among smaller listed companies (Chandler 1990).

The dispersion of share ownership in the Anglo-Saxon countries, and the resulting separation of ownership and control, has led to shareholder control of companies being achieved via market means. The primary form of discipline is said to be the market for corporate control: underperforming companies are subject to shareholder exit and consequent changes in ownership and control (Easterbrook and Fischel 1991). The fear among incumbent management of being replaced leads them to pursue shareholders' objectives. This type of regime is typically described in the Financial Economics literature as a market or 'outsider' system of corporate governance (Moerland 1995; Prowse 1995; Mayer 1997; Weimer and Pape 1999). It can be contrasted with continental European systems where a much greater concentration of ownership facilitates direct owner control. The German version, where bank and corporate cross-ownership are important, is often described as a relational or 'insider' system, whilst the Latin countries are notable for family and state ownership (Weimer and Pape 1999). The 'varieties of capitalism' approach distinguishes between 'liberal market economies' and 'coordinated market economies' on the basis of the relative importance of markets and relationships in other spheres of activity as well as ownership (though, arguably, it tends to ignore the Latin variant) (Hall and Soskice 2001*b*).

The nature of ownership adds to the intensity of market pressures associated with dispersed ownership. In general, the need for financial institutions to provide returns to customers and beneficiaries means that the motive for equity investment is primarily a financial one, rather than to secure 'private' benefits of control (such as social standing) (Thomson and Pederson 2000). The central role of pension funds (with over a third of the equity market by value) is also a 'peculiarity' of Anglo-Saxon regimes. It has a specific set of consequences. The substantial growth in private, occupational pension schemes post-Second World War, coupled with specific regulatory requirements in the United Kingdom (and US), meant that a sizeable proportion of pension assets were channelled into centralized pension funds rather than dispersed into insurance funds or invested in the employing firm, as occurred elsewhere (Clark 2000; Jackson and Vitols 2001). Whereas insurance funds tend to make substantial use of fixed interest assets such as bonds and of property (because of fairly predictable and stable outflows), pension funds in the United Kingdom were attracted to the high returns from equity from the 1950s onwards. Even among countries with well-developed pension funds, the UK pensions industry is notable for the proportion of assets invested in equities (HM Treasury 2001: 32). The massive flow of funds into the UK stock market from pension funds has had an important long-term dynamic influence on the size of the UK equity market (Froud *et al.* 2000*a*; Clark 2000). It has pushed up market capitalization leading to an emphasis on capital growth, as well as dividend payments, in UK equity investment.

The importance of the market for corporate control has been intensified by pressures towards short-termism and investor quiescence in governance, emanating from the structure of the institutional investment industry. Most large UK pension funds devolve asset management to specialist fund managers (the exceptions being public sector and ex-public sector funds such as Hermes) (HM Treasury 2001). Fund managers have weak incentives to participate in corporate governance because they bear the costs of intervention but do not take the gains (which accrue to the pension fund and its beneficiaries).

A preference for exit rather than intervention is reinforced by intense competition for business among fund managers on the basis of fund performance (Short and Keasey 1997). Although contracts are typically issued for 3–5 years, quarterly monitoring of performance by fund trustees is said to prioritize short-term financial performance. Furthermore, fund managers worry that activist corporate governance may alienate corporate clients. Moreover, the majority of pension fund trustees are company directors and they are disinclined to encourage institutional activism for obvious reasons (Plender 1998: 402). It is notable that self-managed pension funds, like insurance companies, have greater incentives to intervene actively in their investee firms because they reap the rewards of activism, and indeed these funds have been at the forefront of the emergent activist movement in corporate governance (Black and Coffee 1994; Faccio and Lasfer 2000).

The 'traditional' tendencies towards exit rather than voice are likely to have been added to by the dramatic growth in overseas investment in the UK equity market. While some of this growth is due to the trend among large listed firms to offer equity to US investors via the American Depository Receipts system (typically using a single nominee),[2] it also represents a significant increase in inward investment by foreign institutional investors and mirrors recent developments in other countries (see other chapters in this book). The costs of active governance can be high for overseas investors, and this favours active trading among these investors (especially as overseas stocks are often viewed as riskier components of investment portfolios).

3.2.1. *Influences on management decision-making*

One way of approaching corporate governance is to pose a simple set of questions: what do owners want, how do they get it, and to what extent do they succeed (Gospel and Pendleton 2003)? Following from these, how do investor objectives influence managerial actions, and what is the extent of any influence? The usual answer is that UK institutional investors want high, short-term returns (including capital growth) and that they achieve this mainly via the market for corporate control. The fear of takeover in systems with liquid markets and dispersed ownership forces managers to do what investors want and to prioritize the interests of investors above those of other stakeholders. Indeed, the success of one is achieved at the expense of the other.

In the stakeholder and varieties literatures, there are then several consequences. One emphasizes that the market system, coupled with weak employment protection, encourages managers to favour shareholders rather than labour in the distribution of returns from corporate activity. A second argument, associated with Porter (1997), argues that the influence of the market system is also felt indirectly. Market discipline and investor short-termism lead managers to pursue business strategies and practices which are less advantageous to labour than those encouraged by relational/insider systems (Gospel and Pendleton 2003). For instance, UK firms have a lower capacity to pursue strategies of 'diversified quality production' than German firms because of these constraints (Streeck 1992*b*). Pressures for high, short-term returns from equity markets discourage those long-term investments in sophisticated machinery and human capital needed for quality-based business strategies. At the same time, cost pressures force firms to 'sweat' existing physical and human assets. As a result, many UK industrial firms seek competitive advantage through long runs of relatively simple products, requiring modest human capital and accompanied by a strong emphasis on cost control. A third factor is an ideological one. The emergence of the credo of 'shareholder value' in recent years is seen to have intensified the pressures on managers to take actions which can have adverse effects on labour (Froud *et al.* 2000*b*).

An important issue, therefore, is whether UK managers have different priorities and patterns of behaviour than in relational systems. Preliminary evidence suggests that they do. Allen and Gale (2000: 52–53) report survey findings that 70 per cent of managers in the United Kingdom believe that shareholder interests should be given first priority, compared with 17 per cent in Germany and 22 per cent in France. The same survey finds that 89 per cent of UK managers believe that firms should maintain dividends even at the expense of employment reductions, compared with around 40 per cent in both Germany and France. These orientations towards shareholders are reflected in company practices. Carr and Tomkins (1998: 223) find an average pay-back period for investment projects of 3.3 years in the United Kingdom compared with 5.5 years in Japan, with the level of internal required return on investment projects being much higher than in Germany (23 versus 14 per cent) (p. 221). They also find that UK and US firms place three times as much emphasis on financial issues in key decisions as firms in Germany and Japan (Jürgens, Naumann, and Rupp 2000: 66). So, UK firms appear to make different 'strategic choices' (Child 1972) to those in relationship-based governance systems.

3.3. The Impact on Labour Management

Demonstrating causal relationships between these choices and labour outcomes is not easy because of the systemic nature of the posited relationships and the likelihood that many labour 'outcomes' have multiple causes. With this proviso, the remainder of this section identifies those aspects of labour management in the United Kingdom which seem likely to emanate from the governance system via managerial choices. We show that there is a body of evidence which is supportive of the relationships identified in the stakeholder and varieties literatures. However, there is also evidence which is inconsistent with their predictions.

The shares of national income accruing to labour and to capital provide a useful macro measure. Although the share of national income accruing to labour has historically been comparatively high in the United Kingdom, this fell from around 1980 while investment-related income started to rise (Ryan 1996). This coincides broadly with the rise of 'shareholder value' in the United Kingdom (and the election of an anti-labour Government). Focusing on the distribution of corporate income, the proportion of company profits paid out in dividends has risen from a low of 6.7 per cent in 1978 to 27.7 per cent in 1996. In addition, Mayer and Alexander find that a higher proportion of corporate earnings is paid out in dividends in the United Kingdom than in Germany (1990: 450). Overall, UK companies pay out more of their earnings to shareholders, and this appears to be at labour's expense.

This is confirmed by firm-level studies of income distribution. De Jong's (1995) study of the 100 largest European corporations (of which twenty-three were British) found that labour's share of net added value (sales minus the cost of sales and the wear and tear of assets) was considerably lower than elsewhere. Labour accounted for just 68 per cent of net added value compared with 88.6 per cent in Germany and 80.2 per cent in France.

A key element of the critique of market-based systems is that managers seek to maintain a high share price to deter takeovers, and an important way of driving up share prices is to control labour costs by job cuts or outsourcing. However, unlike the United States, there is very little systematic empirical evidence on market reactions to job cuts or lay-off announcements in the United Kingdom. Consistent with most US evidence, the only study so far finds that, contrary to the stakeholder critique, the market reacts negatively to lay-off announcements.[3] Positive market reactions can be observed in individual cases, but such price rises seem to occur when the market has already marked-down stock because of concerns about company prospects. In this context, job cuts signal that management is (belatedly) attempting to get to grips with poor performance. For instance, the share price of the steel maker Corus rose 10 per cent after the announcement of substantial job cuts in 2001, but this was in the context of earlier steep falls in share price due to sustained poor performance (Eironline 2001).

A further criticism of the UK system concerns both the threat and the actual effects of the relatively high incidence of takeovers on labour's interests. Such events may involve breaches of both implicit and explicit labour contracts, especially where labour regulation is weak, with adverse effects on wages and employment (Shleifer and Summers 1988). Takeovers, therefore, readjust claims against the firm and can shift wealth from labour to shareholders (in part to finance bid premiums). There are three reasons for expecting that restructurings in the United Kingdom will have pronounced adverse effects on labour. First, the relative weakness of statutory employment protection facilitates rewriting of contracts post-restructuring. Second, the importance of 'shareholder value' objectives for mounting restructuring transactions means that rationalization, with resulting job losses, is often a key rationale for restructuring. Third, the absence of labour from corporate governance institutions and the absence of works councils arrangements and associated information rights in most firms means that labour is ill placed to resist rationalisation and job cuts.[4]

The limited empirical evidence on this question provides some support for these predictions. The study by Conyon *et al.* (2000*b*) of mergers and takeovers over a 30-year period finds that mergers lead to net reductions in employment, especially where acquisitions are of related companies or are hostile. A further effect is that disappointing performance post-merger leads to further rationalization and job cuts. There are some dramatic instances of the adverse impact on labour of takeover activity in the United Kingdom. For instance, the hostile takeover of NatWest Bank by the Royal Bank of Scotland in the late 1990s was accompanied by a pledge to cut 18,000 jobs (to contribute to savings of £1 billion). This pledge arose from a competitive struggle with the Bank of Scotland to win the support of NatWest shareholders for the takeover by offering the largest bid premium (International Labour Office 2001).

However, the only other detailed UK study on this topic questions the extent of the negative impact of takeovers on labour. Beckmann and Forbes (2003) find that job losses after acquisitions are relatively modest and that shareholders and workers share 'joint misery'. Furthermore, workers who retain their jobs achieve wage increases relative to the past and to other workers in the sector.[5]

A distinguishing feature of the labour management system in the Anglo-American economies is pronounced income inequality between those managing corporations and the remainder of their workforces. This is most marked of all in the United States but is also substantial in the United Kingdom. A recent Towers Perrin survey of executive pay shows that the ratio between Chief Executive Officer (CEO) remuneration (including stock-based compensation) and the pay of manufacturing workers is 25 : 1 in the United Kingdom, compared with 16 : 1 in France, and 13 : 1 in Germany (www.towers.com). Furthermore, the gap between CEO and worker pay nearly doubled between the mid-1980s and mid-1990s, whereas it changed little in countries like Germany (Conyon and Schwalbach 2000: 516). Indeed, wage inequality grew more in the United Kingdom and the United States from the 1970s than in any other of the OECD countries (except Ireland) (Machin, 1999: 191).

These pay inequalities have two dimensions: higher remuneration for UK executives and lower average pay for manufacturing in the United Kingdom. The determination of these differences is complex and multifaceted but several aspects of the finance and governance system in the United Kingdom are important. First, high and rising levels of top executive pay are associated with active managerial labour markets, with the market for top managers driven to some extent by the emphasis on successful delivery of shareholder value. Furthermore, greater disclosure of executive pay in market-based systems 'ratchets up' total pay as CEOs exploit the comparability principle (Conyon et al. 2000a). The other side of the coin is that top executives are attempting to insure against job loss in their remuneration packages. Investor pressure for high returns has made the job of the CEO increasingly precarious, with the average job tenure of CEOs of FTSE 100 firms now down to 4 years (Steele 1999). Second, the extent of stock market participation by firms, the liquidity of stock markets, and the perceived need to provide incentives to top executives (in the absence of direct 'relational' control) has facilitated the use of stock-based remuneration. For some years, stock and stock option awards have accounted for a significant proportion of CEO pay, though a much lower proportion than in the United States (Pendleton et al.

2002). Currently, senior executives receive share options in 75 per cent of FTSE 350 companies (New Bridge Street Consultants 2002).

The other side of the pay inequality coin is the pay of shop-floor workers. A Towers Perrin survey indicates that the pay of manufacturing operatives is lower in the United Kingdom than in Belgium, France, Germany, Italy, Netherlands, and Sweden (see also Abowd and Bognanno 1995). The stakeholder critique suggests that worker remuneration in manufacturing in the United Kingdom is influenced by two features of the governance system. One is the orientation of managers towards shareholder interests, exemplified by the growth in dividend payments as discussed above. The other is 'low-road' business strategies, characterized by products which require simple production processes and modest human capital (Porter 1990; Soskice 1999: 113).

Further consequences of the finance and governance system might be discerned in the training area. The stakeholder critique argues that workforce training is a casualty of shareholder value. However, the evidence on training is complex and is not entirely supportive of the stakeholder critique. It is generally accepted that the United Kingdom has a weak system for initial vocational training (Estevez-Abe, Iversen, and Soskice 2001: 170) with the proportion of the relevant age cohort undergoing vocational training at secondary or post-secondary level about a third of that in Germany, Italy, and the Scandinavian countries (UNESCO 1999). Some of this difference might be attributed to the finance/governance system in so far as low levels of inter-firm ownership discourage employer cooperation in developing general skills at apprenticeship or similar level (Soskice 1999).[6] However, the provision of continuing vocational training by large UK firms compares favourably with the rest of Europe, with the amount of training time per employee exceeded only by countries such as France and the Netherlands. In terms of the employer spend on formal training (measured as training costs as a proportion of total labour costs), the United Kingdom comes top among European Union countries (OECD 1998b).[7] There is also evidence from individual companies that is at odds with the predictions of the stakeholder model. Lazonick and Prencipe (2002) provide a striking case study of how the aero-engine company Rolls Royce has been able to sustain innovation, based on a long-term commitment to developing human and organizational capital, despite vulnerability to stock market pressures.

The argument that outsider/market systems inhibit employer co-ordination can be extended to wage determination systems (see Soskice 1999; Hall and Soskice 2001a). The United Kingdom is notable in a European context for the exclusive use of single-employer collective bargaining at company or plant level rather than multi-employer bargaining. A further feature is that pay determination occurs via collective bargaining in only a minority of workplaces (31 per cent). Only 5 per cent of private sector employees are covered by multi-employer collective bargaining over pay while just 19 per cent are covered by single-employer bargaining at company or plant level (Cully *et al.* 1999: 108–109). It is difficult to demonstrate the causal role of finance and governance but 'institutional complementarities' are certainly plausible, especially as the shifts from multi-employer to single-employer bargaining and from collective bargaining to unilateral pay determination have coincided with the rise of 'shareholder value'.

A notable characteristic of employee remuneration in the United Kingdom is the extensive use of employee share ownership plans. In total, 25 per cent of private sector workplaces are covered by a share plan (Cully *et al.* 1999: 70), and a recent study shows that the United Kingdom has the highest incidence of all-employee share plans in Europe (Pendleton *et al.* 2001). Several features link share plans to the nature of the finance/governance system in the United Kingdom. First, an important determinant of share plan presence across Europe is stock market listing: the liquidity of stock-based rewards where stock is traded on open markets affects the attractiveness of this form of reward to employees (Pendleton 1997; Pendleton *et al.* 2001). Second, a primary reason for the use of these plans is the generation of employee commitment (Pendleton *et al.* 1998): it can be argued that share plans are used as a substitute for those mechanisms used to secure commitment in insider/relational economies such as incremental pay systems, promises of job security, and employee voice systems based on joint consultation. Third, share plans may assist in promoting legitimacy of 'shareholder value' among employees. They certainly help to generate interest in stock price movements (Proshare 1999). However, stock-based rewards very rarely substitute for 'core' wages in the United Kingdom context (Whadwani and Wall 1990; Pendleton 1997).

In contradiction to the above argument, it must be conceded that there is recent UK evidence which casts doubt on the extent to which a shareholder value orientation among UK firms has damaging effects on labour. Bacon and Berry (2003) distinguish firms with a shareholder value orientation from those with a stakeholder orientation. The differences between them in labour management practices are negligible in several respects. For instance, the incidence of union recognition is very similar, as is the communication of information to employees on finance and investment. The provision of training via the Investors in People initiative is equally likely in both types of company (around three-quarters of each). The likelihood of reducing employee numbers, measured by employment over a 5-year period, is similar between shareholder value and stakeholder companies (just over one-third of each).

Despite this counter-evidence, overall there is some evidence across a range of issues that is supportive of the argument that the market/outsider system of governance in the United Kingdom encourages a set of labour management practices which are relatively disadvantageous to labour. However, the support for some of the key links is limited and there is support which contradicts the simple determinism found in some stakeholder critiques. We need to look, therefore, for more complex explanations of the relationship between corporate governance and labour management. This is undertaken in the remaining sections.

3.4. The Evolution of the UK System of Ownership and Control

In this section we show that the UK governance system cannot be reduced to a simple market model and that the non-market aspects of the system are increasing in importance. This makes for a more complex relationship with labour management 'outcomes'. We highlight the importance of 'relationship' aspects of governance and show that the nature of investor–manager relationships gives managers more 'strategic choice' than a simple, market model implies. Thus, the effect of ownership and governance on labour management can be more open-ended than the literature predicts. Equally, these relationships can work together with market signals to intensify pressures emanating from the market or vice versa.

There are several important features of the UK ownership system which are modifying the market/outsider model. Most important, the dispersion of ownership (a key underpinning for the market model of governance) has declined significantly in recent years. Ownership is now more concentrated than is often implied in the literature. Mayer (2000) finds that the median shareholder holds 9.9 per cent of equity (nearly double that found in the United States) with the second and third blockholders holding 7.3 and 5.2 per cent, respectively. Even beyond the tenth largest block holding, the mean voting block is greater than 3 per cent. Not all of these investors are institutions: insiders such as family owners and individual directors are important holders of large blocks of shares (Franks and Mayer 2000). Even in the top 10 of the FTSE 100 (some of the world's largest firms by market capitalization), concentrated ownership can be found: in early 2003 three of these firms had a single shareholder with a stake larger than 10 per cent. For many firms, therefore, de facto control may rest with one or a small number of shareholders. Franks and Mayer, who otherwise emphasize the 'exceptionally dispersed ownership' in the United Kingdom, note that small coalitions of investors can now control 30 per cent of equity (the critical point for mounting takeovers in the City Takeover Code). Growing concentration of institutional ownership is the outcome of a number of developments, including an aversion to small company stocks among institutional investors, a 'herding' instinct among investment advisers, and mergers and acquisitions within the institutional investment sector (Golding 2001; HM Treasury 2001).

Concentration of ownership has several important consequences for the relationship between investors and firms. All these lead in the direction of greater use of alternatives to market discipline. First, concentration increases the benefits of monitoring and may thus encourage greater shareholder activism (Parkinson 1993: 163). Second, the smaller the number of major investors, the lower the costs of coordination among them. Third, concentration tends to 'lock in' major investors because of the difficulties in selling large block holdings.[8] In recent years, this decline in liquidity has been accentuated by share buy-backs (Golding 2001: 67). These developments combine together to inhibit active fund management and to encourage longer-term shareholdings. A further factor (which is both cause and effect) is the increasing use of indexing as a portfolio management instrument: around a quarter of the UK institutional investment market was indexed by the end of the 1990s (HM Treasury 2001). Finally, there are powerful counter-incentives to market activism among managed pension funds which mirror those said to militate against governance activism. Market activity generates immediate transaction costs for the fund managers, while the benefits of active trading

Table 3.2. *Turnover velocity of domestic shares 1995–2002*

Stock exchange	1995 (%)	2000 (%)	2001 (%)	2002 (%)
NYSE	55.5	87.7	86.9	94.8
NASDAQ	228.1	383.9	359.2	319.5
Deutsche Borse	106.3	128.6	118.3	125.1
Paris[a]	42.8	71.9	n.a.	n.a.
Euronext[b]	n.a.	n.a.	138.4	153.6
Tokyo	32.9	58.8	60.0	67.9
London	40.5	69.3	83.8	97.3

[a] The Paris Exchange became part of Euronext in 2001.
[b] Euronext is the combined exchange for Amsterdam, Brussels, and Paris.

Notes: n.a.: not applicable. Turnover velocity is the percentage of share trades by value against total market capitalization. The figures shown are the average monthly percentages over the year.

Source: World Federation of Exchanges (2003).

are uncertain. The poor performance of some active pension fund managers in the latter half of the 1990s has encouraged the steep rise in so-called 'tracker funds' and 'closet indexing'.[9]

As a corrective to the emphasis on market activity in stakeholder and other critiques, it is interesting to note the level of trading on the UK exchange. As Table 3.2 shows, turnover velocity of shares (the ratio of share trades to market capitalization) is *lower*, not higher, in the United Kingdom than in the main European exchanges. A significant proportion of UK trading activity by value is concentrated in the upper reaches of the FTSE 100 and in particular in the FTSE 100 top 10.[10] Thus, in January–March 2003, 86 per cent of share trades by value occurred in the FTSE 100, and nearly half of this in the ten largest firms. Many firms in the lower reaches of the FTSE experience little trading activity due to a combination of investor anxiety about liquidity and high transaction costs relative to the size of the trades.[11]

A further set of arguments concerns the efficacy of the market for corporate control as a means of influencing managerial behaviour. Franks and Mayer (1997a), for instance, question the disciplinary role of takeovers as the majority of hostile takeovers are not of poor performing firms. In fact, most takeovers in the United Kingdom are friendly rather than hostile: over 80 per cent of takeovers in 1991–5 were agreed rather than contested (Deakin and Slinger 1997: 418). The majority of takeovers are motivated by a concern to secure economies of scale or to expand product market share rather than to exert discipline (Froud *et al.* 2000*a*). The use of mergers and takeovers as a growth strategy by firms, rather than as a governance device by investors, fits into a long tradition in the United Kingdom of growth by merger and acquisition rather than organic growth (Chandler 1990).[12] Moreover, takeover activity is an episodic activity with long periods of quiescence in the market for control interspersed with occasional bursts of takeover activity. Thus, although the threat of takeover may be an ever-present one, it is not necessarily an especially salient one for most managers for most of the time.

The importance of other market-based forms of discipline should also be treated with caution. The market for new equity capital does not appear to be a strong influence on managerial behaviour because relatively little use is made of new equity as a source of finance by firms (Stiglitz 1985). UK firms make especially little use of equity markets for raising new capital, with retained earnings an even more important source of investment finance than in other countries. Corbett and Jenkinson (1996) found that 96 per cent of physical investment from 1970–89 was financed internally, compared with 91 per cent in the United States, 80 per cent in Germany, and 69 per cent in Japan. In the last few years (even pre-dating the stock market falls at the end of the 1990s), there has been a marked diminution in the use of equity issues for raising new capital. The number of rights issues has declined from a peak of 215 in 1987 to 23 in 2002. The number of new share issues (and fixed income securities) has fallen from a peak of 1,675 in 1996 to 741 in 2002. Major investors are generally wary of new issues because of the dilution effects and because new issues indicate, *pace* 'pecking order' theory (Myers 1984), that managers know something that investors do not (suggesting that company stock is overvalued).[13] For instance, British Telecommunications' (BT) share price fell by 10 per cent when it was announced that it had been holding discussions with some institutional investors about a rights issue (*Financial Times*, 9 February 2002).

Taken together, these developments suggest a departure from the 'pure' market model described in the stakeholder, varieties, and Financial Economics literatures. As a result, several forms of governance, besides the market for control, are important in the United Kingdom. Currently, there is a steep increase in the extent and significance of shareholder activism, encouraged by the recent regulatory requirement that company remuneration policies are voted each year at the annual general meeting (AGM) (though the vote is non-binding). The current approach to governance is well encapsulated in the statement of principles issued by the Institutional Shareholders' Committee in autumn 2002.[14] This requires institutions and their agents to develop clear, public policies on monitoring procedures, intervention strategies, and voting policies. The statement proposes that intervention should be considered by institutional shareholders and/or agents regardless of whether a passive or active investment policy is followed. It is accepted that monitoring may require information sharing and coordination with other investors. The issues which are seen as relevant for intervention include corporate strategy and performance, acquisitions/divestments, internal operational controls, top executive remuneration, corporate social responsibility, failure to comply with the Combined Code on corporate governance, and failure of independent directors to secure accountability of top management. Although this statement encapsulates an approach to governance which has been emerging for some time, it marks a clear break with the traditional view of investor passivity in corporate governance.

The most visible form of activist governance recently has been voting activity at AGMs. In the first half of 2003, substantial minorities of shareholders, including institutions, voted against remuneration packages at (in the FTSE top ten) Glaxo, Shell, and HSBC. However, though remuneration issues may be fought in the public domain, institutional investors do not view the AGM as a useful forum for monitoring companies. This is because they are able to secure higher quality information by alternative means, which we outline below (Barker 1998; Holland 1998).

Major investors and firms have built up relationships for the exchange of information and exercise of influence. Holland emphasizes the importance of these relationships, describing how 'close institution–company links revolve around co-operative stable relationships, with regular meetings and other channels for two-way flows of information, and feedback mechanisms after meetings. These relationships are comparable in many ways to close (commercial) bank–corporate relations' (1995: 19). He goes on to note that:

A close working relationship based on honesty, integrity, stable stakeholding, and regular contact was considered by the financial institutions to be one of the most effective means by which their influence could be exercised. These close relationships were active transaction channels for extensive reciprocal exchanges of capital, information and influence between companies and financial institutions. (1995: 21)

Contact between institutions and firms takes the form of one-to-one meetings, supplemented by site visits, group meetings, and other informal contacts. Major investors monitor up to around 300 companies a year in this way (Holland 1995; Hendry *et al.* 1997). This dialogue occurs mainly with companies in whom the investor has taken a 'core' stake.[15] For the company, active contacts are maintained with a fairly small group of major investors, involving between twenty and forty formal meetings each year (Barker 1998). Top executives in FTSE 250 companies now spend up to 25 per cent of their time developing relationships with City institutions (Pye 2001: 189).

From the company point of view, the objective is to manage 'investor relations' by generating trust in the capacity of the company and its management to continue to perform successfully. The rationale is that investor loyalty is more likely to be secured if investors understand and empathize with the company and its management. For investors, the importance of these relationships lies in their capacity to generate information to assist in interpreting current and projected financial figures. Investors seek to gain information in three main areas: financial projections, corporate strategy, and top management quality (Holland 1995, 1998; Hendry *et al.* 1997). Direct contact with firms supplements the 'narrow' financial information found in quarterly results and is seen to allow judgements to be made about more qualitative factors, such as the quality of management. It enables institutions to gain an understanding of company strategy and the capacity of managers to deliver it (Barker 1998: 14).

At the heart of these relationships is the generation of trust, and the biggest rifts between companies and investors in recent years have arisen out of perceived breaches of trust. Comments from interviewees (CEOs, Finance Directors, and HR Directors) make this very clear: 'it is important to build a high degree of confidence between the company and the investment community so that during difficult times investors retain their confidence in the company. To do that we need to ensure that both good and bad news is communicated. An open relationship helps to build trust and respect' (Holland 1995: 21). Again another interviewee states, 'It's all about developing a relationship. It means letting the investment community meet, see and have first-hand experience of the people leading and driving the company. Face-to-face exposure gives investors confidence that the company is in good hands' (Holland 1995: 36). In essence, companies build relationships with major investors to manage uncertainty and to establish trust. 'No surprises' is the institutions' mantra.

Relationship governance is not new, but it has become more important and has changed in form in the last 10 years or so. In the past, contact between firms and institutional investors was organized and controlled by intermediaries to a considerable extent (merchant banks and stockbrokers), but the reorganization of the City which took place after 'Big Bang' in the 1980s led to asset management firms developing direct contacts (Augar 2001). 'Sell-side' analysts working for investment banks still have a considerable role in collecting and disseminating information on companies and have developed a web of relationships with companies to do this. Nevertheless, they are treated warily by institutional investors because of various conflicts of interest (Barker 1998; Golding 2001).[16]

A key characteristic of the relationships between major investors and top managers is that they occur in private and 'behind the scenes'. Black and Coffee describe this as the 'hidden world of informal monitoring' (1994: 2002). A number of factors explain this secrecy: a culture of secrecy and politeness, the speed and efficiency of the process, the 'clubby' nature of the City, and a preference by all parties to avoid public disputes which could damage reputations of all concerned (Holland 1995: 26). Investors appear to be concerned not to cause irreparable damage to their relationship with the company given that they are to some extent 'locked in' to a long-term relationship with the firm (Parkinson 1993). Furthermore, 'behind the scenes' activity is less likely adversely to affect the share price of the company concerned.

Overall, this form of governance is well described by the Marketing Director of Schroder Investment Management Ltd:

We believe that direct and continuing communication between management and shareholders is the key to monitoring. . . . Therefore, regular, systematic contact . . . in order to exchange views is an important element in our investment process and we attempt . . . to meet senior executives of every UK company in which we invest at least once a year, and much more frequently with major companies. The value of such informal one-to-one discussion and monitoring should not be underestimated. It does not seem to be in the best interest of institutional investors to air shareholder grievances in public in the first instance. Many issues are very complex and can be better addressed in a less formal context. Matters of concern to shareholders should only be addressed at a public general meeting if direct dialogue with management has proved ineffective. (Wood 1996: 2–3)

The discussion so far highlights a basic characteristic of the relationship between major investors and top managers: the interaction between them is a social relationship not just a market transaction. A consequence is that the sanctions investors bring to bear on under-performing firms and their managers are social as much as economic. Given liquidity constraints and 'lock-in', investors take action by a variety of alternative means, though an important sanction for them is the threat to damage managerial reputation.[17] The strength of this sanction is such that compliance is usually achieved without overt conflict. Where top managers are proposing new strategic directions, they usually attempt to bring major investors 'on-side' before the strategy is formally accepted. On the few occasions where managers fail to take heed of investor opinion or where managerial competence is perceived to be a serious problem, investor actions include the 'planting' of stories in the press and 'whispering campaigns'. Where problems are felt to be serious, major investors typically coordinate their actions, with the ultimate sanction being the removal of the management (see Black and Coffee 1994 for an extensive discussion of these coalitions).

An excellent illustration of these processes is provided by Marconi in summer 2001 (then in the FTSE 100). Having assured an anxious City that order books were buoyant during spring (when other telecoms hardware companies were experiencing sales downturns), Marconi suspended share trading without notice on 5th July in conjunction with the issue of a profits warning.[18] The same day it was reported that five of the ten largest shareholders were planning to lobby Marconi's non-executive directors to press for a change of management. On the following morning the chief executive-designate was forced to resign after directors bowed to shareholder demands for a senior scalp. Even after this, the ten largest shareholders let it be known to the press that the chairman and replacement CEO needed to be replaced. Less than 2 months later both subsequently resigned. The competence of Marconi's management was severely criticized by institutional investors but the worst sin was seen to be breach of trust. In particular, Marconi management were perceived to have withheld relevant information from its shareholders and to have misled them about the company's prospects.

3.5. Consequences for Labour Management

What are the implications of this emerging system of corporate governance for labour management in the United Kingdom? We discern two influences on labour management. These work in somewhat contradictory ways. On the one hand, the nature of the relationships between managers and investors provides managers with some autonomy to devise labour strategies as they see fit. On the other, the network of relationships between firms and major investors provides a quick and effective means (supplementing or even substituting for market discipline) for investors to force changes on management when a firm is in difficulty. The first influence helps to explain varieties of labour management within the UK variety of capitalism. The second helps to explain how shareholders occasionally exert considerable influence on company managements, forcing them to make drastic adjustments at labour's expense.

To understand managerial autonomy, it is necessary to keep in mind that the relationship between core investors and corporate managers will be shaped by the social norms and interests of each party and will be embedded in specific institutional contexts (Aguilera and Jackson 2003). A powerful norm in the United Kingdom is that institutions should not 'micro-manage', that is, they should not involve themselves actively in operational management activity. Most areas of management, therefore, are seen as the preserve of company management, and investors do not normally seek to influence these. It is also generally accepted that there is little expertise in the City on human resource management. In particular, it is difficult to quantify labour management activities, and therefore investors find it difficult to assess company activities in this area. Two comments from fund managers illustrate these views: 'Anything about training is extremely difficult to quantify and the second problem is that no comparable figures are available from companies. There is therefore no basis for making comparisons between them.' 'There is no doubt that investment in training is a critical success factor, but from the fund manager's point of view it really is an internal issue for management' (Hendry *et al*. 1997: 70). Since managers have deeper knowledge and expertise in these areas, the expectation is that financiers should not attempt to 'second-guess' them.

These features of the company–investor relationship give managers more autonomy to devise their labour management strategies than the critiques of the UK system of governance generally imply. In so far as investors monitor labour management at all, their primary interest appears to be in the 'fit' between business and labour strategies rather than the content of labour strategies as such. As a result, major investors will support 'high-cost' labour management practices, including high levels of training, where management can demonstrate that this is appropriate for the delivery of future returns. For instance, Deakin *et al.* (2002) show how firms with a social partnership approach to labour management attempt to win over major investors to this strategy, and how some investors will support this. Furthermore, evidence from industries such as pharmaceuticals indicates that investors will back long-term, high human capital investment strategies where companies can demonstrate that these are supportive of competitive success (Vitols *et al.* 1997). There is some evidence suggesting 'matching' in equity markets: firms emphasising the importance of long-term employment relationships with skilled human capital attract institutional investors who are supportive of such long-term relationships (Deakin *et al.* 2002). Thus, in contrast to the stakeholder critique, which sees managers and firms as the passive victims of the finance and ownership system, firms may determine their labour strategies and seek to win investor support for them.

However, although relationship-based investing provides some autonomy for firms in their labour management, it also facilitates rapid and decisive action by investors when firms are in distress. This supplements or even substitutes for market-based signals. When firms are in distress, major institutional investors operate 'behind the scenes' to force changes to managerial policy and composition (especially the latter). The Marconi case mentioned above is good and illustrates how quickly major investors can force changes upon management. In other cases, action may take a more 'gentlemanly' form, such as a private dinner in the City. A good example is BT, which by summer 2001 had run up debts of £30 billion as a consequence of bidding for 3G mobile phone licences and a series of acquisitions and buy-ins in the mobile phone market. Investors dissatisfied with the 'civil service' characteristics of the top management planned to meet for dinner with the top management team and then request their resignation at the end of the dinner. Another good example is provided by the troubled steel maker Corus. Faced with a collapsing product market, Corus quickly announced significant reductions in capacity, with accompanying job cuts, to appease investors demanding swift remedial action. At the time of its profit warning in July 2001 Marconi announced 4,000 job cuts in an unsuccessful attempt to assuage institutional investors.[19]

Several observations may be made about this type of process. First, job cuts are sought by investors, or pre-emptively offered by managements, where there is strong evidence of product market difficulties. Thus, in the case of the Anglo-Dutch steel maker Corus, there was apparently heavy pressure on management to make dramatic reductions to the labour force. The weaker level of job protection in the United Kingdom also meant that job cuts had to be concentrated in the United Kingdom rather than in the Netherlands. Second, where management competence is seen to be at issue but product markets are healthy, job cuts are much less central to investor strategies. In the case of BT, where the problem was seen to be poor financial and strategic direction by an insufficiently entrepreneurial management, investor attention focused on changing the management, not downsizing the workforce. Third, a primary sanction in these kinds of intervention is the managerial labour market rather than the equity market and the market for corporate control. Investors' main sanction, both in 'behind the scenes' interventions and in voting at AGMs, is the damage that they can inflict on executive reputations and consequently on their employability.

3.6. Conclusions

In this chapter we have shown that the nature of the UK finance/governance system provides a clear set of parameters and constraints on management decision-making. To this extent, the UK case is consistent with the critiques and analysis found in the stakeholder capitalism and varieties of capitalism literatures. The extensive listed sector and the relative ease of mounting takeovers subject UK firms to equity market pressures to a greater extent than in other European countries. As shareholder value has come to be increasingly important, there appears to be a shift of returns from labour to shareholders. There are, however, two main caveats. The first is that there is some evidence which does not fit with this critique, such as that on company continuing training. The second is that the ownership/governance system is evolving in the direction of greater concentration of ownership with constraints on liquidity 'locking in' investors to some of their investments. The result is that activist and relationship governance is growing in importance relative to market-based forms. In these relationships management has certain advantages, emanating from informational asymmetries and superior competence in actual management. This gives firms a degree of autonomy in their labour management, at least for most of the time. Institutional investors appear to recognize that managers are better able to devise labour strategies than they are; and providing the approach is credible and consistent with business strategy and that management is credible, they appear to respect management's 'right to manage'. Investors do not know how to appraise human resource management activities, and therefore do not actively monitor company practices in any detailed way. However, the growing concentration of ownership also means that investor power to force changes on company management has grown in recent years. This power appears to be used sparingly, but it can be mobilized quickly and effectively when required. On occasions this can have dramatic effects on employment.

NOTES

1. In Germany, by contrast, only 51 of the largest 100 companies are traded on the Deutsche Borse (Höpner and Jackson 2001: 16).
2. In the case of BP, the UK's largest firm by market capitalization, 29% is held by J. P. Morgan Chase Bank, which acts as the depositary for BP's American Depositary Shares.
3. Smaller negative effects are found when job cuts are aimed at improving efficiency (Farber and Hallock 1999).
4. For some years there has been a legal requirement for firms to provide advance notification of job cuts to employee representatives, but the consultation rights have been limited. The implementation of the European Directive on Information and Consultation Rights is likely to strengthen consultation in this area.
5. A qualification to their assessment is that employment events in firms which are divested post-acquisition are not tracked.
6. Variations in state-sponsored educational and training provision will have a strong influence here.
7. To some extent, this may reflect a 'catching-up' process to compensate for the low level of initial vocational training (Green 1999: 133).
8. Partial but substantial divestments are likely to lower the value of the equity retained by major investors because of the signal divestment sends to the market, as well as necessitating discounts on the actual shares sold.
9. Closet indexing is where fund management is claimed to be active but where trading decisions are on informal indexes.
10. The top ten firms in the FTSE account for 40–50% of the total value of the All Share Index.
11. US evidence indicates that the growth of large institutional investors decreases demand for small company stocks, while the increased demand for large company stocks pushes up the price of these relative to small company stocks (Gompers and Metrick 2001).

12. Recent US evidence also contradicts the use of takeovers as managerial discipline. Mitchell and Mulherin (1996) find that takeover activity is concentrated in certain industries, and that external shocks generate restructuring activity.
13. Stock options, Long Term Incentive Plans (LTIPs), and bonus awards linked to earnings per share give top managers an incentive to avoid issuing new equity.
14. The ISC comprises the main trade associations in UK institutional investment: the Investment Management Association, the Association of British Insurers, the National Association of Pension Funds, and the Association of Investment Trust Companies.
15. Each major investor has a periphery of firms in which it has smaller stakes and where governance is either more passive or dominated by an 'exit' approach.
16. These include dependence on companies for information, reliance of investment banks on corporate finance business, and reliance on commission payments from share trades.
17. Routine monitoring of some issues is undertaken by the main trade associations. Both the Association of British Insurers and National Association of Pension Funds monitor top executive remuneration and attempt to secure compliance of firms with their remuneration principles. Where this fails, the trade association typically enlists the assistance of its member institutions who are major investors in the offending company.
18. Trading was suspended to complete a previously scheduled divestment while the profit warning went ahead.
19. The share price fell 54% on the day trading resumed, and more than 10% of the company's equity changed hands in a day.

4

Corporate Governance and Employees in Germany: Changing Linkages, Complementarities, and Tensions

GREGORY JACKSON, MARTIN HÖPNER,
AND ANTJE KURDELBUSCH

4.1. Introduction

In comparative debates, Germany is often viewed as a 'stakeholder' model of corporate governance. First, the ownership of German companies is highly concentrated. Banks provide substantial long-term external corporate finance, act as stable shareholders, and protect companies against hostile takeovers. These features support long-term capital investment and curtail managerial 'short-termism' in response to volatile capital markets. Second, Germany has the most far-reaching employee codetermination among OECD countries. Works councils enjoy extensive participation rights, and employees are also represented in the corporate boardroom. These institutions support long employment tenures and high skill patterns of work organization. Taken together, these two features contrast with the market or shareholder-oriented logic of Anglo-American corporate governance.

Existing literature presents two distinct views of the interactions between investors and employees within the German model. The 'varieties of capitalism' approach argues that patient capital and employee voice are mutually reinforcing, complementary institutions contributing to German industrial success (Soskice 1999; Hall and Soskice 2001b). Here, commitment by investors supports stable long-term employment,

This chapter was presented at the RIETI Conference 'Corporate Governance in International Comparison' in Tokyo (January 2003), the Conference of Europeanists, Chicago (March 2002) and a European Science Foundation workshop at the Max Planck Institute in Cologne (November 2001).

investment in worker training, and cooperative industrial relations. Management is able to build long-term organizational capacities by drawing upon both patient long-term investment and the high-trust work organization. These institutional complementarities are seen as key institutional preconditions for the dynamic (X-) efficiency in lower volume, high quality product markets that require high skills (Streeck 1992*a*; 1997*b*).

By contrast, the 'law and economics' literature has focused on how the role of employees impacts investors. Concentrated ownership and codetermination are again posited as complementary, but in the opposite sense. Codetermination is argued to hinder the emergence of dispersed ownership and shareholder-oriented corporate governance. Codetermination may reinforce poor managerial accountability by dividing the supervisory board into factional benches, diluting the board's overall powers and promoting collusion between management and employees (Pistor 1999). Roe (1999: 194) thus sees codetermination as increasing agency costs to shareholders, because 'diffuse owners may be unable to create a blockholding balance of power that stock-holders would prefer as a counterweight to the employee block'. Consequently, codetermination reinforces the weakness of capital markets and lowers the number of widely held corporations.

These diverse interpretations stem from different underlying causal assumptions and imagery. Ownership structure may be seen as facilitating or constraining patterns of human resource management (HRM). Conversely, labour institutions can be viewed as an independent variable that impacts investors. Understanding how capital and labour interact depends strongly on what models are used to specify these relations.

This chapter addresses these issues by examining German corporate governance within a sociological framework (Aguilera and Jackson 2003). Corporate governance involves various coalitions between capital, labour, and management (Cyert and March 1963; Aoki 1986). But these coalitions are shaped by their embeddedness within institutional settings which tend to be nationally distinct—including corporate law, accounting rules, financial regulation, pension finance, and industrial relations. Institutions shape the social and political processes by which actors' interests are defined ('socially constructed'), aggregated, and represented. While politics plays a central role in building institutions (Fligstein 1990; Roy 1997; Donnelly *et al.* 2001), institutional configurations exert joint effects that may have strengths and weaknesses for different types of economic behaviour.

Section 4.2 examines the basic features of post-war German corporate governance and HRM, as they existed through the late 1980s. Section 4.3 examines the institutional linkages between these features. Section 4.4 outlines the changes in corporate ownership and finance in Germany during the 1990s, in particular the declining role of banks and the emerging market for corporate control. These changes are related to observed changes in employment and industrial relations, particularly focusing on issues of remuneration and codetermination. The conclusion argues that linkages do exist between corporate governance and labour management, although the literature often overestimates the extent to which such linkages are tight and coherent. We interpret these results in terms of shifting patterns of coalitions among stakeholders.

4.2. German Corporate Governance in Comparative Context

The German 'model' defies easy categorization as an insider, employee-oriented, or stakeholder-oriented corporate governance.[1] Germany may be seen as a type of nonliberal corporate governance due to the limited role of markets as mediating mechanisms for both capital and labour (Jackson 2001). Both factors of production are institutionalized based on organizational commitment and voice within corporate governance. Here, Germany shares similarities with countries such as Japan, and is distinct from liberal market-oriented economies such as the United States or Britain. Yet, Germany has its unique features. For example, unlike Japan, German firms are subject to stringent legal regulation of its internal governance structures and external regulation through corporatist associations.

This institutional logic can be described as a 'constitutional' model of the firm where the voice of labour and capital is as a matter of public interest and supported through politics (Donnelly *et al.* 2001). Unlike a purely private association, corporations have features of a social institution which assigns non-contractual status rights and obligations to its members independent of their will and exchange value in the market. Governance involves both externalization of private interests onto corporatist associations, as well as internalization of societal interests within the firm. Outside the firm, governance is interwoven with industry-wide collective bargaining, membership in employers associations and chambers of commerce and industry, and obligations to train according to the public standards in the apprenticeship system. Within the firm, decision-making is densely regulated through a two-tier board

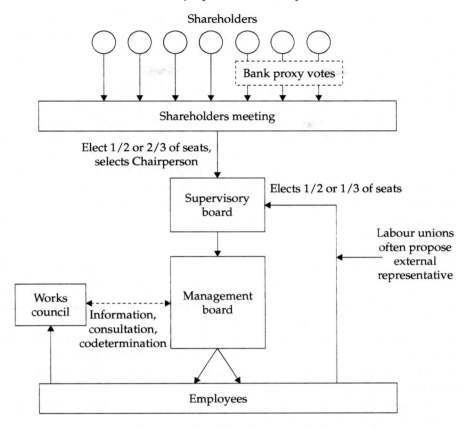

Figure 4.1. *The legal structure of corporate governance in Germany*

system that legally separates management and shareholder control, as well as opens the supervisory board to employee representatives (see Figure 4.1). Voice is shaped by strong legal institutionalization of public identities and class interests.

Next, we examine more specifically the role of investors, employees, and management in turn, focusing on the post-war era up through the 1980s. Our emphasis is on the relationship between institutional features and organizational commitment (limited role of markets) within German firms.

4.2.1. *Corporate ownership, finance, and monitoring*

Corporate ownership and finance in Germany has three well-known features: high ownership concentration, the predominance of strategic ownership ties among corporations ('coordinated capitalism'), and the importance of banks in external finance and monitoring. Open markets for corporate control are largely absent and banks play the central monitoring role among investors.

First, ownership concentration is high in Germany and minority shareholders play a limited role (Höpner and Jackson 2001). In 1998, the proportion of dispersed ownership averaged only 26 per cent among the 100 largest German companies. Families held 18 per cent, the state 14 per cent, foreign investors 17 per cent, and other companies and banks 14 per cent. This ownership structure has not changed much in the last 20 years. A high proportion of large firms remain unlisted private companies, while the number and market capitalization of listed corporations are low in international comparison.

Second, ownership is closely related to strategic interests of other organizations. Pyramidal conglomerate holding companies (*Konzern*) and dense bank–industry networks are both important (Beyer 1998). Sociologically, these ownership stakes involve high levels of commitment to particular enterprises, unlike the more diversified and liquid trading of US institutional investors (Jackson 2000). Whereas Anglo-American institutional investors are oriented to financial gains from share price appreciation and dividends, corporations and banks tend to pursue strategic organizational interests in promoting cooperation between firms and generating relationship-specific rents. Dense intercorporate networks suppress markets for corporate control and create incentives for voice rather than exit.

Third, German universal banks play a central monitoring role. Banks are closely linked to business through credit, large equity stakes, the exercise of proxy votes, and supervisory board representation (Edwards and Fischer 1994). Bank monitoring is an element of relational financing where debt and equity are commingled.[2] These multiplex relations alleviate agency conflicts between owners and creditors, as well as diminish information asymmetries. External corporate finance is dominated by bank loans and complements a strong capacity for internal finance in the absence of shareholder pressure (Borio 1990; Corbett and Jenkinson 1996). Given the different preferences of shareholders and creditors, strong banks may weaken the position of minority shareholders.

This pattern of ownership and control developed in close relation to several regulatory institutions. First, corporate law mandates two-tier boards that facilitate the representation of large shareholders. Second, voting rights deviated from the one share–one vote principle through multiple voting rights and voting caps. Banks also represent small shareholders by voting the shares held in their custodial deposits. Third, capital market regulations and accounting rules tend to weaken the position of minority shareholders and market mechanisms. For example, the German accounting rules are creditor-oriented and are considered to lack the same transparency as found in International Accounting Standards (IAS) or the US General Accepted Accounting Standards (GAAP).

4.2.2. *Employment relations, industrial relations, and work organization*

Employee voice is institutionalized through the legal institution of codetermination at the level of the supervisory board and works councils.[3] Works councils have extensive rights to information, consultation, and codetermination on matters relevant to employment. The works council is legally bound to represent the employees as a whole, maintain social peace, and promote the welfare of the enterprise and its employees. Employee representatives on the supervisory board provide a counterweight to shareholders in the appointment of management, as well as involving employees in monitoring of strategic business decisions. In certain companies, the appointment of a labour director to the management board by the employees reinforces the consensus nature of decision-making within the board.

Employment relations are characterized by a 'decommodification' of labour. Employment tenures are long and exhibit a low downward elasticity over the business cycle (see Tables 4.1 and 4.2). Unlike Japan, stable employment is not primarily generated through long-term incentives of internal promotion patterns and firm-specific skills. The returns to seniority in Germany are comparatively low.[4] While employees tend to be highly skilled, training takes place within a multi-employer and quasi-public system of occupational training.[5] These skills are portable and related to broad occupations rather than firm specific. These features reinforce each other, since strong occupational identities gravitate against generalist careers and elaborate internal promotion. The hierarchical span of control is flat and the occupational qualifications of supervisors tend to overlap with subordinates.

Stable employment relates to several other institutions. First, employees often lack incentives to change firms because wage differentials across firms, industries, and regions are relatively low due to

Gregory Jackson et al.

Table 4.1. *Employment tenure in various countries*

Tenure	Germany[a]		Japan[b]		UK		US	
	1990	1995	1990	1995	1990	1995	1990	1995
Under 1 year	12.8	16.1	9.8	7.6	18.6	19.6	28.8	26.0
1–5 years	28.2	31.4	27.6	28.9	36.3	30.2	32.9	28.5
5–20 years	42.3	35.6	43.3	42.2	35.4	40.8	29.5	36.6
Over 20 years	16.7	17.0	19.3	21.4	9.6	9.4	8.8	9.0
Average tenure (years)	10.4	9.7	10.9	11.3	7.9	7.8	6.7	7.4
Median tenure (years)	7.5	10.7	8.2	8.3	4.4	5.0	3.0	4.2

[a] Germany data (taken from the Socio-Economic Panel) refers to German-born citizens employed at the time of the survey.
[b] Japanese data refers to regular employees (persons employed indefinitely), temporary workers hired for more than one month, daily workers hired for over seventeen days, in private establishments with over nine employees.

Notes: Tenure figures are proportions of the employed workforce, except where shown.
Source: OECD (1993, 1997).

Table 4.2. *Stability of employment in various countries*

Tenure	Germany[a]		Japan[b]		UK		US	
	1980s	1990s	1980s	1990s	1980s	1990s	1980s	1990s
Lay-offs and quits as % of total employment[a]	1.6	4.3	1.9	2.4	4.4	4.4	5.1	4.0
Lay-offs as % of total employment	1.1	2.8	0.6	0.7	2.7	2.7	4.3	3.1
Separation rate as % of new hires[b]	25.0	27.2	n.a.	n.a.	40.5	42.9	60.5	65.9
Pace of employment amount adjustment 1974–93	0.14		0.04		0.21		0.45	

[a] Estimated separation rates for those currently unemployed or not in the labour force who left jobs within the past 6 months. The periods are Germany (1984, 1993–4), Japan (1987–8, 1996), United Kingdom (1983, 1993–4), and United States (1981–2, 1991–2).
[b] Estimated separation rates of employees with 1–2 years tenure (total population with tenure of up to 2 years minus those with tenure under 1 year) as a percentage of new hires (population with tenure under 3 months).

Notes: n.a.: not available.
Source: OECD (1997b).

industry-wide collective bargaining. Inter-industry wage differentials are significantly lower than Japan or the United States.[6] Likewise, earnings differentials by firm size in manufacturing are very low relative to Japan or the United States (Jackson 1996). Second, a central goal of works councils is to stabilize core employment. Legal protection against dismissals increases pressure for internal adjustment rather than external numerical adjustment. Works councils resist short-term lay-offs and mandate internal redeployment through training and transfers. Without their approval, dismissals are rendered null under German employment law. Employers are thereby forced to resort first to 'benevolent' methods of retrenchment such as natural attrition, early retirement, and transfers before involuntary dismissals. Works councils support such adjustment by negotiating 'employment pacts' involving measures to increase the productivity and flexibility of the workforce.

From the perspective of management, a key to stable employment is skills and training. Strong occupationally based skills contribute to functional flexibility in the workplace, which can to some extent substitute for recruitment on the external labour market. The German training system organizes occupations into categories of overlapping skills that create a wide 'substitution corridor' between occupations (Sengenberger 1987).[7] Polyvalancy creates a high capacity of internal adjustment to changes in technology and products.

Decommodification is also found in issues of payment schemes and wages. Payment systems are linked to both centralized collective bargaining and the firm-level works councils. Collective agreements set minimum rates with high thresholds, as well as outlining basic provisions and premium pay (e.g. overtime, shift work rates, and holidays) for each grade of employees. In manufacturing, most collective rates are time rates for each grade. Payment-by-results, such as piecework, are also common but do not result in much individual variation in wages. Collective agreements specify criteria for firms to categorize jobs into standardized grades by job evaluation methods, including detailed weightings for skill, knowledge, responsibility, and factors in the work environment (dust, gases, noise, vibration, etc.). Works councils play an important role in monitoring the implementation of industry-wide agreements at the company level.

Remuneration patterns have several notable features relevant to corporate governance. First, industry-wide bargaining considerably reduces the scope for firm-level variation of wages and working conditions. Though large and successful companies often pay a wage premium above the level of collective agreements, their scope remains limited (Bellman and Kohaut 1995*b*). Second, individual variability of pay is also reduced. Given union commitment to principles of equal pay for equal work, firm seniority plays little or no formal role in the determination of individual pay (hence, the flatter age–earnings profile). Employees are graded largely according to their qualifications. Works councils help assure that only workers with particular qualifications get access to certain jobs and prevent skilled workers from being classified into unskilled jobs—thus, the link between pay grades and qualification is not direct (e.g. everyone with this qualification must earn a standard salary) but is steered through the system of jobs. Third, income inequality is generally low given the flat wage structure and relatively high wages. Income differentials between top management and production employees are thus compressed relative to Anglo-Saxon countries.

Industrial relations are characterized by strong employee voice through codetermination within the firm, as well as multi-employer collective bargaining which regulates wages and conditions on an industry-wide basis. Employee influence thus has dual channels: employees represent their interests as producers in a particular enterprise through codetermination and their broader class-wide interests through collective bargaining. Works councils are closely involved in issues of work organization, working conditions, etc. Moreover, works councils also function as a long arm of the industrial unions by monitoring the implementation of collective agreements and occupational training.

Centralized, industry-level collective bargaining imposes comparatively uniform wages across firms and limits dispersion across industries. German unions pursue solidaristic wage policies that seek actively to narrow the earnings gap or promote uniform wage increases for all groups. Employers associations may discipline their members who pay too far above the premium. Standardized wage structures across firms eliminate or at least attenuate wage competition in the national market.

Work organization in industry is characterized by high functional flexibility and incremental patterns of innovation (Hall and Soskice 2001*b*; Boyer 2003). These features are closely linked to the characteristics of employment relations and industrial relations discussed above. German firms face high and uniform wages imposed by centralized collective bargaining, making wage differentials between low level unskilled workers and skilled workers small (Jackson 1996). Uniform wage increases mitigate the effects of supply and demand on the relative earnings at each skill level and create incentives for the substitution of skilled for unskilled labour. As Streeck (1992*a*: 32) argues, 'A high and even wage level also makes employers more willing to invest in training and retraining as a way of matching workers' productivity to the externally fixed, high costs of labour'. Firms accommodate high wages by migrating into 'high end' markets where competition is based on quality rather than price. This productivity whip is only functional as a constraint to the extent that high and flexible occupational skills are also present and contribute to the X-efficiency of work organization.

4.2.3. *Management*

German managers contend with strong voice from concentrated owners and banks, as well as employees and unions. Given this pluralistic set of interests, management faces dual pressures for both long-term profit maximization and employee utility (Aoki 1988). These pressures are somewhat attenuated by a highly consensus-oriented management culture. Interests must be negotiated in shifting coalitions which involve patterns of horse-trading, issue linking, and package deals between different groups of management. Several institutional features making up the social world of German management support this consensus orientation.

First, management careers tend to follow functional specializations, even within the management board. Educational backgrounds in science and engineering dominate the highest positions. Managers remain tied closely to their occupation (*Beruf*), and thus conspicuously lack a generalist orientation. The strong tendency for technical functions to be incorporated into the management hierarchy limits the relative importance of financial considerations (Lane 1993).

Second, managerial authority tends to be rooted in technical competence rather than supervisory or business-related skills. 'Management' is not so strongly set apart from other occupational groups in either educational background or forms of compensation. This productivist ethos of the business organization acts as an integrating mechanism, with strong focus on incremental technical innovation, quality standards, and build-up of long-term market share.

Third, the legal principle of collegiality in the management board works against strong dominance of the President and balances financial considerations with other management functions such as operations and personnel.

Fourth, moderately high rates of internal promotion and long management tenures help stabilize the long-term relations that top managers enjoy with their suppliers, customers, other corporations, banks, and works councils. The limited role of the external labour market also favours the orientation toward long-term profits instead of short-term success. Moreover, managerial compensation traditionally avoided high power incentives such as stock options.

4.3. **Institutional Linkages, Complementarities, and Tensions**

How do these institutional features of German corporate governance interact? What linkages exist between corporate ownership and control, on the one hand, and labour management, on the other? Institutions in different domains may be viewed as complementary when one institution becomes more viable in combination with other specific institutions (Aoki 2001). Complementarities do not imply economic efficiency in an absolute sense, but a process of mutual reinforcement. For example, the welfare effects of institution A may increase in combination with institution B, but not with institution C. Conversely, interdependence may create tensions because institutions imply conflicting principles of rationality (Lepsius 1990). For example, codetermination may be seen as diluting ownership rights, and thus hindering particular patterns of organization.

Important methodological issues arise in studying institutional linkages. First, complementarity does correspond to the self-similarity of organizational principles across domains. Contradictory organizing principles may provide beneficial countervailing checks and balances (e.g. state and market, unions, and managerial control) or be a source of requisite variety for organizations in supporting flexible and beneficial recombination of practices (Stark 2001). Second, specifying complementary relationships requires theoretical models linking economic functions across institutional domains. However, corporate governance influences multiple dimensions of economic activity, such as agency costs, transaction costs, and so on. We often cannot tell a priori which function will be most important for overall performance or social stability given changing external environments and strategic choices. The inherently selective focus of theoretical models may account for a tendency to overestimate the degree to which institutions are very tightly coupled and exert strong causal influence as complementary elements of a system.

Rather than presenting an economic model, we analyse these relationships as governance coalitions from a sociological standpoint.

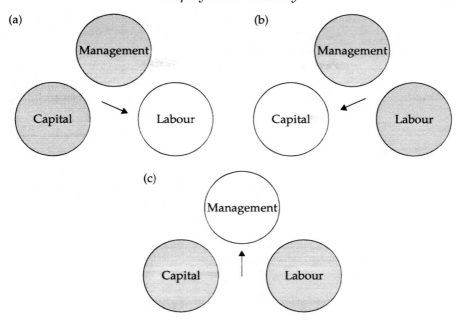

Figure 4.2. *Three types of partial coalition (a) class conflict, (b) insider–outsider conflict, and (c) accountability conflict*

Here, organizational goals may be the outcome of governance processes, rather than organizational goals determining the choice of governance institutions as in most economic models. Whether stakeholder interests exist in positive or negative-sum relation depends upon the issue area at hand, as well as the institutional definition and anchoring of control rights. By making interest constellations into a variable, three ideal-typical coalition patterns can be observed, as shown in Figure 4.2. Each of these coalitions embodies a particular axis of conflict: class conflicts, insider–outsider conflicts, and accountability conflicts.

1. *Class conflict* is manifested when shareholders and management have similar interests vis-à-vis employees, particularly regarding distributional issues such as wages or selected personnel and social issues.

2. *Insider–outsider conflict* may arise when employees and management have similar interests vis-à-vis shareholders. This is often assumed in agency theory, such as when insiders favour internal

diversification ('empire building') or may block efforts at restructuring. Likewise, corporate insiders may favour takeover defences at the expense of outside shareholders.

3. *Accountability conflicts* arise when shareholders and employees align their interests vis-à-vis management. Thus, both groups may favour measures to improve corporate transparency and disclosure. Good information on company performance may be used by both groups to control management, even when they oppose each other on how any surplus should distributed. Similar constellations may also appear around issues of risk management, in preventing perverse incentives in managerial compensation, and in some investment and restructuring decisions.

Whether these various potential coalitions and conflicts become manifest depends very much on the institutionalized relationships between each group of actors. Large shareholders may be more 'insiders' than smaller 'outside' shareholders, just as employees may be insiders or outside the core group. Thus, the discussion must be contextualized through a consideration of what interests dominant owners pursue and how these interests impinge upon the distributional outcomes for labour (and vice versa).

4.3.1. *Class conflict*

In Germany, several features of ownership were institutionally important in reducing class conflicts and facilitating mutually agreeable distributive outcomes. Inter-corporate and family ownership bind capital to the long-term fate of the firm, and stress long-term strategic interests of the firm over short-term pressure for financial results. Lower stock market capitalization stabilized a competitive rate of return to capital, while placing fewer constraints on the share of value-added going to labour. In addition, protections from hostile takeovers guard against 'breach of trust' (Shleifer and Summers 1988) that would otherwise endanger cooperative industrial relations, stable employment, and incremental innovation and learning in work organization.

Despite common views that shareholders are neglected, marginal returns to shareholders in Germany were quite favourable in comparative terms and gave investors little incentive to exit.[8] Comparisons of German and British corporations have shown that shareholder returns are quite similar at the margin when measured in price–earnings ratios or dividend yields (Höpner and Jackson 2001). Yet, top British corporations have higher market values. German shareholders could receive competitive rates of return as long as market capitalization remained low, for example, ownership remains concentrated among existing stable shareholders. As a consequence of higher market valuations, British corporations must produce higher operative rates of return to sustain similar returns to capital. Meanwhile, top German corporations may maintain greater commitment to employment and place greater priority on high sales growth, rather than profits.

Given the absence of strong distributive constraints from the capital market, German firms retain the option of pursuing business strategies other than maximizing return on equity (Ide 1998): firms can pursue higher market shares through strategies of forward-pricing; they can spend more on capital investments and/or R&D; they can absorb higher raw materials costs; they can concentrate on market segments offering lower returns but having large market size and relatively low risk; they can absorb higher labour costs, thus avoiding lay-offs more easily during cyclical downturns and thereby protecting employee morale and firm-specific human capital. These distributional options helped firms to accommodate employment rigidities, high wages, and strong employee voice as corporations specialized in strategies of 'diversified quality production' (Streeck 1992*b*).

It is worth noting that this distributive pattern is unlikely to be sustainable under an open market for corporate control. Here, the lower market to book values (price–book ratio) create high takeover premium and make firms vulnerable to predator firms with higher market valuation. Thus, De Jong (1996) argues that the absence of takeovers is a central pre-requisite for the high share of value-added going to employees in Germany.

4.3.2. *Insider/outsider conflicts*

Conflicts between insiders and outsiders were not predominant in Germany under conditions of rapid post-war economic growth. Resources generated by insiders were generally sufficient to be redistributed to outsiders without reallocation of control. For example, conflicts between inside and outside employees were limited by the ability to balance wage equality pursued by German unions and employment security pursued by works councils. Unions achieved a high wage floor that made German labour markets less 'dualistic' than in the United States or Japan. Labour peace was maintained within the firm by externalizing the costs of employment adjustment onto the German welfare state. But this balance changed as the core group of insiders has grown progressively smaller due to the decline of traditional industrial sectors. This tension presses unions and works councils to make strategic choices between their class-wide versus firm-specific interests. Union agendas of maintaining uniform wages face increased centrifugal pressures from firm-specific interests of works councils.

Likewise, insider–outsider conflicts among large blockholder investors and small shareholders were also relatively latent. As discussed above, small shareholders could benefit from relatively stable returns and low risk associated with the stable network of bank–industry relationships. However, slower growth and the rise of new individual and institutional investors sharpened conflicts with large investors who favour strategic interests or long-term relationships. Outside institutional investors often favour shifting resources from corporate insiders to be reinvested through arm's length market relationships. Moreover, the demands of institutional investors may create new patterns of cross-class coalitions with different employee groups. Outside investors and employee insiders may often share an interest in increased transparency, performance-oriented pay, and productivity orientation. But these coalitions may increase tensions with Germany's industrial unions who bundle interests outside specific firms.

4.3.3. *Accountability conflicts*

While post-war Germany had its share of corporate scandals and managerial excess, overall corporate accountability does not appear to have been deficient relative to other countries. The financial system remained quite stable, as have the fortunes of large industrial firms.

However, a first point of criticism is that accountability has relied largely on private information, rather than public transparency and information disclosure. For example, universal banks were thought to have extensive access to private information through their multiplex relationships as creditor, owner, and board member. Banks achieved economies of scope through comparable information from competitors and other firms throughout the sector. Likewise, supervisory board members sent from the works councils bring detailed knowledge about the actual operations in different divisions and often have extensive consultation with management within the economic committees of the works councils. Taken together, accumulation of private information may improve corporate accountability in the absence of more public information disclosure.

Similar debates surround monitoring within the board. Supervisory boards are often criticized for being too large, poorly informed, and hence too inactive in monitoring. Others question whether codetermination leads to factionalism within the board that induces ineffective monitoring. However, the virtues of the two-tier board system include the clear separation of management and monitoring functions now advocated worldwide. Boards also have a large number of outsiders who represent strategic stakeholders in the firm. Much debate remains as to whether more independence is required to prevent detrimental conflicts of interest or whether stakeholders also act to provide beneficial checks and balances. These debates cannot be discussed further here. However, no quantitative evidence exists to show that German firms are comparatively slow to remove poorly performing management (Kaplan 1994).

4.4. Changing Institutional Interactions since the 1990s

Germany proved to have a stable 'model' of corporate governance during much of the post-war period. Distributional compromises were able to reduce class conflict, while insider–outsider and accountability conflicts were held in check. But considerable pressures for change developed from the early 1990s onwards. Economic pressures of internationalization and political pressures for liberalization promoted a growing role of capital markets. New capital market actors, such as foreign and institutional investors, brought different investment strategies and an increased focus on financial returns. 'Shareholder value' became widely discussed as a new paradigm of management with greater focus on stock price, core competence, transparency, and investor relations activities. Debate ensued as to whether Germany would (or should) converge on a liberal US-style system of corporate governance which reflected international standards for investor protection.

How will trends toward shareholder or market-oriented corporate governance impact labour management and employee representation? As discussed above, the existing literature posits tight complementary relationships between capital market institutions and labour institutions, but offers divergent hypotheses about change. On the one hand, strong institutional complementarities may gravitate against change and allow only gradual 'path-dependent' evolution. For example, codetermination may prevent the emergence of dispersed ownership and active capital markets. On the other hand, institutional complementarities also imply that successful change in one set of institutions will lead to changes in the other linked sets of institutions. Change would ripple through the system like a house of cards and lead the German model to collapse. Thus, market-oriented capital would bring forth a 'fitting' set of market-oriented labour institutions, characterized by stronger external labour markets, numerical flexibility, variable pay, and fewer vested participation rights.

This section empirically examines how changes in capital market pressures are impacting German labour management and industrial relations by reviewing some selected empirical findings from our own research on the changes in corporate ownership and monitoring during the 1990s (Höpner 2001, 2003a; Höpner and Jackson 2001; Kurdelbusch 2002; Jackson 2003; Streeck and Höpner 2003).

4.4.1. *Changes in corporate ownership and management*

Since the mid-1990s, a number of important changes in corporate ownership and monitoring have become apparent. Several reforms of capital market regulations have liberalized markets and set up new regulatory agencies (Donnelly *et al.* 2001; Lütz 2002). New institutional and foreign investors have emerged as key capital market actors. The monitoring capacity of German banks has been substantially eroded by the change toward more market-oriented ownership patterns and new capital market regulation, leading many of the core private banks to move away from 'house bank' relationships and enter into the Anglo-American dominated field of investment banking. One result is a declining stability and density within the German corporate network. Given this 'marketization' of ownership ties among large firms, a market for corporate control has begun to emerge on a small scale. These trends are most pronounced among large internationally oriented corporations. A number of related points must be made.

First, data on the aggregate ownership of listed shares in Germany in the 1990s (see Table 4.3) show a rise among foreign investors, who are predominately Anglo-American institutional investors such as pension funds and mutual funds. Furthermore, domestic investment funds are growing. These groups are concentrated among large

Table 4.3. *Corporate ownership in Germany by sector*

Sector	1991 (%)	1999 (%)	Change in % 1991–9
Banks	12.7	13.5	+0.8
Insurance firms	5.5	9.0	+3.5
Non-financial corporations	39.4	29.3	−10.1
Government	2.6	1.0	−1.6
Pension funds	—	—	—
Foreign	12.7	16.0	+3.3
Investment firms and other	4.8	13.6	+8.8
Individuals	22.4	17.5	−4.9

Notes: Data is estimated from various sources using both market and book values.

Source: Bundesbank (2000).

corporations: for example, at Veba (E.on) 75 per cent, Bayer 68 per cent, SAP 55 per cent, BASF 73 per cent, Schering 74 per cent, Thyssen 78 per cent, and Bilfinger Berger 55 per cent of all shares were owned by institutional investors (Höpner 2001). In 1999, British and American funds alone held 40 per cent of Mannesmann shares, 31 per cent of DaimlerChrysler, and 27.5 per cent of Deutsche Telekom.[9]

These new investors have led to new types of pressures. Institutional investors pursue financial interests through their investments, thus favouring profitability over growth and shorter time horizons. Institutions also have a strong preference for liquidity ('exit' rather than 'voice') and generally refrain from active intervention in the fate of particular firms. Empirical studies show that institutional investors only rarely attempt directly to influence management (Steiger 2000). Their monitoring capacity lies in professionalizing information gathering and exit-oriented strategy. Therefore, stock prices are becoming more responsive to management decisions and more volatile. Investor activism targets the promotion of general practices of good governance, but rarely translates into strategic interest in corporate control.

Table 4.3 shows that the growing proportion of institutional investors coincides with declining shares among individuals. But declines were also seen for the government and other non-financial corporations. While growing 'institutionalization' increases concentration, a parallel trend exists toward de-concentration of ownership and unwinding of corporate networks. Privatization of government enterprises is one important factor. However, the density of corporate networks in Germany is declining substantially (Windolf 2002; Beyer 2003; Höpner and Krempel 2003). This trend will be likely to continue as large blocks are sold tax-free under new tax regulations introduced in 2000.

Second, the monitoring capacity of banks is substantially eroding. Bank credits to large corporations have declined, as these corporations have become largely self-financing (under conditions of slow economic growth) or have new alternative modes of finance (Jackson 2003). Several large private banks have undertaken a strategic reorientation toward Anglo-American style investment banking. The move from the *Hausbank* to investment bank paradigm contradicts their willingness to play a major role in the monitoring of industrial companies (Deeg 2001; Beyer 2003), because a close relationship to industrial companies would weaken their reputation among international customers of financial services. Banks' investment portfolios have also become more market-oriented and less focused on stable relationships. Thus, banks are reducing the size of their large ownership stakes and diversifying their investments. The withdrawal of banks is also evident in the declining number of supervisory board chairs held by bankers among large corporations (Höpner 2001). The Deutsche Bank has led this trend by reducing its supervisory board chairs by nearly half. Increasingly, supervisory boards are being chaired by former management board members from inside.

Third, barriers to hostile takeovers have significantly eroded and led to the emergence of a market for corporate control on a limited scale. The takeover of Mannesmann by the British Vodafone in 2000 was a watershed case illustrating the extent of change. Contrasting Mannesmann with other takeover attempts targeting German companies in the 1990s shows the erosion of barriers against hostile takeovers (Höpner and Jackson 2001). As large banks change from the *Hausbank* to the investment bank paradigm, banks are giving up their role as guardians against hostile takeovers. Krupp's takeover attempt for Thyssen in 1997 was the first case where the Deutsche Bank supported a takeover attempt. The corporate law reform (the *Gesetz zur Kontrolle und Transparenz im Unternehmensbereich (KonTraG)* (1998)) forbids voting rights restrictions. In the past, these restrictions were one of the most important of Continental's defensive actions against the takeover attempt of the Italian tyre company Pirelli. Legal reform (*Kapitalaufnahmeerleichterungsgesetz* (KapAEG)) in 1998 also made the economic worth of corporations more transparent. Moreover, codetermination seems no longer to act as a strong barrier to hostile takeovers.

A comparison of the cases of Thyssen (in 1997) and Mannesmann (in 1999/2000) shows that unions have changed their political attitude towards hostile takeovers from fundamental opposition against 'predator capitalism' in 1997 to a pragmatic acceptance of hostile takeovers as an inevitable instrument of economic behaviour in 2001.

Fourth, German management boards are also undergoing extensive change toward a greater finance orientation and away from the traditional science and engineering focus. This shift is symptomatic not only of shareholder demands, but also of the internationalization of managerial labour markets and the growing encounter of German junior management with Anglo-American management cultures. Information has been collected on the careers of all ninety top managers who were chief executives in the forty biggest listed industrial corporations in the 1990s (Höpner 2003a). A few findings on the development of the career and education of top managers in the 1990s can be summarized.

1. There is a strong trend towards further professionalization. The share of chief executives without higher educational training declined from just under 14 to 0 per cent in 1998 and 1999. The share of top managers who went through the German apprenticeship system is in decline (from 30 per cent in 1990 to 15 per cent in 1999).
2. The role of the external labour market is also clearly rising. In 1990, 17 per cent of the observed top managers were recruited from outside; in 1999, the percentage rose to more than 35 per cent. As a result, the role of in-house careers is declining.
3. The percentage of top executives who can be classified as financial experts with experience working in the financial division is rising. Thirty-nine per cent of chief executives have studied economics, 24 per cent have trained as lawyers, and 32 per cent have studied natural science or technical subjects.[10] Comparing these data with information on the 1970s (Poensgen 1982) suggests a strong decline in the role of natural science and technical subjects.
4. The average time in office among top managers is in dramatic decline, from more than 13 years in 1965 to less than 7 years in 1996.

These changes in the 'social world' of top managers help explain why shareholder-value strategies enjoy high reputation among managers. The changing social background and career incentives for management influences their perception of corporate goals. The emergence of a highly competitive labour market for managers requires the application of measurable performance criteria. At the same time, the willingness of supervisory boards to fire top managers is on the increase. In the 1990s, several chief executives were forced to retire from office because of bad performance and the resulting crises of confidence in the supervisory board, for example, Horst W. Urban (Continental), Anton Schneider (Deutz), Bernd Pischetsrieder (BMW), Heinz Schimmelbusch and Heinrich Binder (Metallgesellschaft), Bernhard Walter (Dresdner Bank), and Dieter Vogel (Thyssen Krupp). Beyond this, it can be argued that the increased importance of Financial Economics in education and career favours the willingness to utilize financial indicators.[11]

In sum, these changes can be expressed as a rise of a shareholder-value paradigm. In the early 1990s, the conglomerate VEBA was one of the first companies which sought to raise the importance of financial interests of shareholders within corporate policy. Numerous other companies such as Siemens, Hoechst, BASF, and Bayer followed suit (Vitols 2002). Shareholder-value strategies aim primarily at making the

Table 4.4. *Ranking of shareholder orientation of listed companies in the late 1990s*

Company	Score
Bayer	1.61
VEBA	1.48
SAP	1.33
Hoechst	1.20
BASF	1.14
Mannesmann	1.11
Henkel KgaA	1.09
Daimler-Benz	1.02
RWE	0.90
Siemens	0.86
Schering	0.74
Metallgesellschaft	0.72
Degussa	0.55
Viag	0.55
Preussag	0.45
MAN	0.36
Deutsche Lufthansa	0.28
Linde	0.22
Continental	0.21
Thyssen	0.17
Deutsche Telekom	0.16
Krupp	0.16
Buderus	0.04
Agiv	0.00

Source: Höpner (2001: 40).

market cost of capital the hurdle for corporate investment. In order to meet the minimum return to capital within each division or subsidiary, shareholder value aims to end cross-subsidization between the various segments within the firm. Alongside this strategy, key elements include transparency for outside investors and variable management remuneration linked to shareholder returns.

Table 4.4 shows a ranking of the shareholder-value orientation of the listed German non-financial corporations in the late 1990s (1996–9) (Höpner 2001). The ranking touches upon the three major dimensions of shareholder-value management.[12] The communication dimension involves greater transparency toward investors, via investor relations work, the adoption of international accounting principles, and reporting business results by business segment. The operative dimension aims at the implementation of value-oriented performance targets and monitoring systems. The management compensation dimension involves increasing percentages of pay contingent on the financial success of the corporation, particularly the performance of share prices. The degree of shareholder-value orientation varies substantially among German companies—which implies that the divergence in corporate governance inside the German economy is rising. This variation will be used in the following sections to examine the changes in other areas of labour management.

4.4.2. *Interactions with employment relations*

This section examines how shareholder value impacts key aspects of employment relations, namely stable employment and egalitarian wage dispersion. Increasing shareholder orientation is widely hypothesized to promote class conflict (as defined above) and a redistribution of wealth in favour of shareholders. As already discussed, the distribution of value-added between stakeholder groups varies strongly between corporate governance regimes (De Jong 1996). Germany is characterized by its high labour share and relatively small share to shareholders, supporting its high-wage economy. Furthermore, high rates of internal reinvestment and focus on growth rather than profits help stabilize employment of core employees. In this section, we show that growing shareholder orientation is associated with shrinking employment and the introduction of variable pay.

4.4.2.1. *Shrinking core employment*
Beyer and Hassel (2001) have analysed the changes in the distribution of value-added among large German corporations in the 1990s. Their

findings confirm that in shareholder oriented companies, the distributional position of shareholders improved modestly at the cost of employees. Shareholders benefited from high profits being distributed as higher corporate dividends. The redistribution effect is explained by the fact that shareholder orientation favours strategies of lower rates of growth and declining employment, while profits increase. Shareholder value thus introduces a form of redistribution that results not from declining wages, but from a declining portion of cash flow being reinvested at a lower rate of return. Collective bargaining can do little to stop this kind of redistribution, since bargainers normally cannot negotiate over the profitability targets set by management. Corporations remained committed to avoid involuntary lay-offs for core employees, but this core of stable employment is shrinking through the increased use of negotiated employment adjustment and benevolent methods such as natural fluctuation, early retirement, and part time work. For example, VEBA reduced its workforce by 29,000 people through early retirement with 90 per cent of previous salary.

As will be discussed below, shrinking core employment has not marginalized works councils. Works councils remain active in negotiating 'site pacts' to maintain jobs and keep high value-added production in Germany (Rehder 2003a, b). First, in order to assure investment in core plants, works councils grant cost-cutting concessions: lower social standards, the elimination of premium wages above collective bargaining rates, and cuts in bonuses for overtime and shift work (see also Nagel et al. 1996). Second, employment alliances involve concessions on wages or working hours in exchange for employment guarantees over a period of 2–4 years.[13] Work may be redistributed through reduced or flexible working time, or made cheaper by reducing company premiums above industry-wide rates. Often, these involve cross-class coalitions between local works councils and management, either against the centralized management seeking to impose new financial controls or with industrial unions seeking to impose uniform labour standards.

4.4.2.2. *Variable compensation as a consequence of shareholder value*

A sinking wage cost per employee is not the cause of the declining labour share described above. Although the overall share of net value-added which employees receive as wages is in decline, wages of the remaining core employees rise. This is possible because while less profitable business units are being closed or sold, core employees increasingly receive profit-oriented pay under new variable remuneration schemes.

Such compensation practices that link workers' pay more closely to individual and company performance have diffused rapidly among large German firms since the mid-1990s. These schemes exist both at the managerial level and for non-executive employees covered by collective agreements. A survey of the 100 largest German firms show that 70 per cent of firms had schemes with wage components based on individual performance evaluations or goal-setting targets (Kurdelbusch 2002). Fifty-one per cent of firms paid remuneration based on the profitability or performance of the enterprise as a whole and 57 per cent of firms had some form of employee stock ownership plans. This trend represents a departure from the historical stance of German unions in supporting a homogeneous wage structure, secure and stable incomes, and protection from ratcheting performance standards. From the point of view of 'traditionalists' inside unions, variable pay, therefore, introduces perverse effects which are likely to destroy solidarity and make works councils tolerate too much corporate restructurings.

While some firms introduced company-wide bonuses when profits were high, these 'on-top payments' are rare. Rather, variable pay is replacing fixed but company-specific wage components which in the past were paid above industry-wide wage agreements. Older forms of performance-related pay such as union negotiated piecework rates are being replaced by appraisal systems to monitor and reward individual performance. Such performance-related pay systems have been introduced to counter the egalitarian effects of collectively negotiated wages and introduce greater individual incentives. In addition, profit-related pay is being introduced that links the size of the performance-related budget to profits of the company or business unit.

These new variable pay systems are intended to enhance employee motivation and commitment in several ways. By giving employees a greater stake in overall corporate performance, variable pay is supposed to help focus employee effort on key job objectives and to clarify the links between such objectives and overarching business goals. Furthermore, variable pay is aimed at giving greater recognition to outstanding employees and thereby to increase motivation.[14] Thus, employees are encouraged to identify with the company. Entrepreneurial thinking is stimulated about how to generate revenue, reduce costs, and maximize profits. A special form of participating in the company's success—and a way of bringing shareholders' and

stakeholders' interests closer together—is employee stock ownership
plans or stock options. Here, the link between individual performance
and financial reward is less direct than with other performance-related
pay, profit sharing, or other annual bonuses, because the employee has
hardly any influence on the share price. But, for management, one
advantage is their long-term character which binds employees to their
company and enforces commitment.

Variable pay is also intended to increase the flexibility of business
costs over time. When profits are high, compensation will be higher
than without variable pay and lower when business is weak.
Employees have to accept risk to share in the rewards of improved
performance. Furthermore, managers expect a positive cost effect
because of increased productivity or at least a better form of cost control. Thus, flexible remuneration schemes are related not only to performance but also to financial management.

The details of variable pay programmes differ considerably across
companies, but all of them place an appreciable share of the pay of
employees at risk. To study its diffusion, an index was created looking at performance-oriented, profit-oriented, and share-oriented
components (see Table 4.5). The rise of variable pay in Germany can
partially be explained by increasing competition on product markets
and cost-cutting pressure. Nevertheless, a strong connection exists

Table 4.5. *Components of the remuneration index*

Pay system type	Score
Performance-related pay	
No performance-related pay	0
Performance-related pay implemented in parts of the company	1
Performance-related pay implemented throughout the whole company	2
Profit-related pay	
No profit-related pay	0
Bonus is set unilaterally by management	1
Works council and management negotiate	2
Bonus is set according to a fixed formula	3
Share-ownership	
No share ownership programme	0
Traditional share ownership programme	1
Extended share ownership programme	2
Total: Incentive-orientation of payment system	0–7

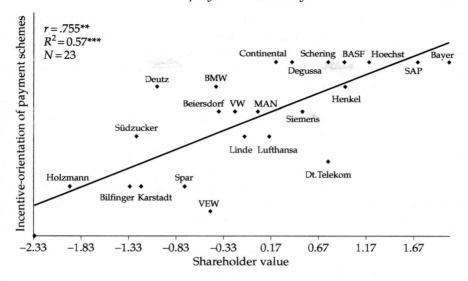

Figure 4.3. *Shareholder value orientation of companies and incentive orientation of their payment schemes for non-executive employees*

Source: Data bank of the 100 largest German companies, MPIfG.

between the use of variable pay and the adoption of shareholder-value strategies (see Figure 4.3). The rise of variable pay in Germany can thus partially be attributed to changes in the financial regime.

The spread of variable performance-related pay for managers—a key characteristic of shareholder value—is not surprising in the case of executives' compensation schemes. What is remarkable, however, is the rapid diffusion of performance-related pay among non-managerial employees. This phenomenon has several explanations. First, introducing performance-related pay for all employees is often simply an element of shareholder-value strategy. Investors see these pay systems as a signal for the congruence of employee goals and financial rewards. Works council members even argue that performance-related pay should be documented in the annual report in order to attract shareholders. Second, as bonuses for managers and dividends for shareholders rise, employees demand their piece of the cake as well. Bonuses for employees can reduce the conflict between shareholders and employees by giving a certain budget to the employees, instead of serving the shareholders first and letting employees divide the rest. Managers can also justify their own high income more easily as long as high bonuses are paid to the whole workforce. Third, companies with shareholder-value strategies can more easily introduce profit-related pay because relevant business indicators already exist. When target rates of return are set, reasonable rewards for meeting targets sound plausible. Finally, a block of employee ownership can also function as a protection against hostile takeover as investor pressures increase.

Once in place, how do variable pay schemes affect corporate governance? Profit-related pay may indeed reduce class conflict over the distribution of rewards between shareholders and employees. In Germany, it can be shown that in most companies where dividends increased, strongly profit-related pay was also implemented for lower level employees. The most direct way to align shareholders' and employees' interests is the introduction of employee stock ownership plans. However, the introduction of employee ownership is yet to have a impact on corporate governance. In some companies, employee shareholders have begun to exercise their voting rights as employee owners collectively, for example, to prevent hostile takeover bids. Nevertheless, the percentage of capital owned by employees rarely reaches the 2 per cent mark. Compared to employee ownership rates in the United States, this is a negligible proportion. The amount of shares held by single employees is also rather small, and far too small to place the interests of an employee shareholder as a shareholder above his interests as an employee.

4.4.2.3. *Variable pay and its impact on industrial relations*
Variable pay also has indirect effects on other linked institutions, particularly Germany's industry-wide collective bargaining. In principle, contingent compensation contradicts certain aims of German collective bargaining, namely a homogeneous wage structure, secure and steady incomes, and protection against high and continuously increasing performance standards. Yet, German variable pay programmes have been implemented in conformity with collective agreements. Up until now, company-specific pay systems coexisted within companies alongside collective wage agreements. Companies were always able to pay performance-related rewards above the collectively agreed basic pay. The high occurrence of variable pay in the banking and chemical industries, where wage drift is traditionally high, is evidence of this phenomenon.

Recently, new collective agreements incorporating new forms of profit-related pay have emerged, although exclusively at firm level. A new and highly recognized form of collective agreement was the one made at Debis (DaimlerChrysler Services AG) in 1999. It stipulates that up to 10 per cent of annual income depends on the individual performance and a further 10 per cent on the performance of the company. This collective agreement was made by metal industry union (IG Metall) and Debis. After Debis was purchased by Deutsche Telekom, a number of these innovations were copied in other parts of the company. Other collective agreements link part of the negotiated wage increases to the economic performance of the firm. Here, both parties agree in advance that, if a certain performance is reached, additional wage increases will be awarded (e.g. Schott AG).

With individual performance-related pay, an important trend is to replace formerly fixed payments or potential wage increases by a budget used for performance-related bonuses. During the recent round of collective wage bargaining, Deutsche Telekom AG agreed upon a model that increases wages by 1 per cent and uses a further 2.15 per cent for variable components. For the forthcoming year, an increase of 2.3 per cent was agreed upon. However, there will be no linear increase. The 2.3 per cent of wages will be distributed according to individual performance.

The regulation of variable pay via collective agreements has been discussed at the industry level. The main point of discussion is whether formerly fixed payments will be changed into a budget for flexible performance-related payments. But there are also discussions about the regulation of profit-related pay. The consensus seems to be that in the long run there will be an adjustment of collective regulations to remuneration practices at the company level, probably restricted to framework regulations which leave the actual scheme to be dealt with at company level in consultation with works councils. Thus, contingent pay does not only emerge 'in spite of' collective agreements but in some cases is also supported by the system of collective bargaining.

Incorporating variable components into collective agreements threatens the notion of industry-wide collectively agreed wages or at least lowers the portion of income regulated by collective bargaining. Thus one of the main functions of collective bargaining—to attain a homogeneous wage structure—would no longer be fulfilled. As collective agreements frame conditions for variable pay, they support the differentiation of wages over time as well as between firms and individual employees. In some companies, collective wage bargaining no longer provides steady and linear wage increases but leads to an increase in the volume of wages, depending on the performance of the company, which is distributed unevenly among individuals.

In sum, the emergence of company-specific remuneration systems (e.g. works agreement or company-level collective agreements) bring about two major changes in the process of determining individual wages. First, variable pay reinforces the decentralization of wage bargaining. Unions partially hand over their influence over earnings to works councils. These variable wage components do not substitute for base pay, but often replace collectively bargained elements (e.g. piece rates) or reduce their significance. The large rewards sometimes associated with variable pay may also be intended to weaken union penetration in new sectors such as IT.[15] Second, incomes are becoming more marketized. The determination of wages is to a greater extent based on individual performance and on market mechanisms in the form of business indicators, for example, cash flow or return on investment. Collective wage bargaining sets a smaller portion of the individual wage and a larger portion underlies entrepreneurial principles such as risk taking and competition.

4.4.3. *Interactions with industrial relations*

This section examines two questions. First, how do works councils and unions impact the implementation of shareholder-value management? Do they support, oppose, or remain indifferent and/or ineffective in this process? Second, how does the shareholder-value paradigm impact the existing institutions and practices within German industrial relations?

4.4.3.1. *The impact of industrial relations on shareholder value*
Organized labour has not blocked corporate restructuring but has played a subtle role shaping the implementation of corporate strategies aimed at improving share price performance (Höpner 2001; Höpner and Jackson 2001). This 'co-management' role has preserved a basic continuity in industrial relations institutions, but shifted its functions over time.

The role of the trade unions and works councils is most clear with respect to what above was described as the communicative dimension of shareholder value. Here, German trade unions have decided to side with shareholders. Unions recognize that international accounting standards, whether IAS or US GAAP, seem to be, at first sight, investor oriented. Yet, unions also see them as increasing transparency and accountability for employees as well. Company transparency is an old demand of trade unions, because the aim of codetermination is to control economic power and authentic information is a condition for control. Unions have supported the legislation on company finance (*Kapitalaufnahmeerleichterungsgesetz*) which facilitated the adoption of international accounting methods and have even called for an EU directive which requires German companies to use IAS. Works councils have strongly supported this demand due to their great interest in being able to compare the performance of subsidiaries in different countries, which is difficult where there are different accounting standards. In sum, German trade unionists argue that transparency is a tool for codetermination (Scheibe-Lange and Prangenberg 1997; Köstler 2000; Putzhammer and Köstler 2000).

Contrary to the rules of traditional German accounting (as laid down in the *Handelsgesetzbuch* (HGB)), international standards place constraints on accumulating hidden reserves in times of good performance. One could, however, argue that it might be in the interest of employees to hide finances in good times and have reserves in bad times. Trade union experts do not agree with this view. Hidden reserves, they believe, have a levelling effect on the balance sheets of companies. With regard to the distribution of dividends and earnings, the effect of German accounting rules is not anticyclical but procyclical. In bad times, companies using German accounting rules publish earnings that come from hidden reserves, while in fact there is no operating profit at all. Published earnings lead to distribution demands that may eat up substance of the firm, which is dangerous especially for employees. In contrast, in the context of high earnings, published profits are minimized despite the fact that the company would be able to distribute some of this to employees and shareholders.

Another dimension of shareholder orientation where the preferences of employee representatives and shareholder activists are similar is top management compensation (Engberding 2000). Unions share the view of capital market participants that top managers' salaries should be variable according to the level of company success. As with shareholder activists, unions criticize the trend towards escalating salaries.

The operative dimension of shareholder orientation is more complex. Works councils oppose profitability goals. In the late 1990s, an enormous wave of restructuring activity took place and was not stopped by codetermination. One reason was that in some cases, employees demand restructuring. Here, employees again share a broad interest with shareholders in promoting managerial accountability and in censuring poor performance. Another reason is that the negative impact of restructuring often has different impacts for core and peripheral employees within the corporation. Core employees may prefer a stronger core business, rather than continued support for ailing businesses which are less central economically. As we have seen, variable pay increases such incentives.

Case studies show that even the operative side of shareholder value sometimes appears as a conflict over managerial control. For example, during the conflict over the separation of subunits at Mannesmann (before the hostile takeover), both employee representatives and shareholders pressed management into restructuring. In 1999, Mannesmann was an extremely heterogeneous company, active in steel tubes, machine tools, automotive accessories, and the telecommunications sector. Telecommunications had become the focal segment within Mannesmann and attracted a growing proportion of funds for investment. One trade unionist at Mannesmann described the situation as follows: 'The development of telecommunications has slowly become dangerous for the other divisions. At the same time, as billions were being spent on the acquisition of Orange, in the classic businesses we had to fight for every hammer.' Organized labour supported the separation of these firms in order to allow these businesses to continue on an 'undisturbed' development. At the same time, trade unionists working in telecommunications preferred a break-up in order to remove the conglomerate discount which made acquisitions expensive and increased the danger of a hostile takeover.

Around the same time, a similar situation appeared at Thyssen Krupp, which was planning a (since revised) new company structure based on industrial services. The classic steel subunit was no longer a core business, but a peripheral activity. Therefore, Thyssen Krupp planned to spin-off Thyssen Krupp Steel and to list initially 30 per cent of the latter on the stock market. The works council chairman supported the planned stock listing demanded by shareholders: 'For two years now, we have observed that steel is no longer seen as a core competency. We do not attract high investments. . . . The scenario is either be sold or become stunted. Under these conditions, the stock listing might be a prospect. . . . Without stock listing, we would have no chance of becoming a core business' (Kroll 2000).

These cases show that spin-offs and return to corporate specialization can be undertaken with the consensus of organized labour. Here, capital market orientation and codetermination are hardly irreconcilable opposites. The mixture of core and marginal business is problematic for employees. Their representatives in the core businesses see the advantages of strategies to focus on core competencies, because these strategies strengthen the core companies and decrease stock price discounts. In the view of employees engaged in marginal activities, a change in the main shareholder may increase the chance to become a core business. In most cases, management and employees oppose shareholders' demands for radical restructuring. A good example of such an insider/outsider conflict is the demand of some major shareholders to break up the Bayer conglomerate into legally separate corporations.[16]

4.4.3.2. *The impact of shareholder value on industrial relations*
There is little evidence that companies adopting shareholder value attempt to discontinue codetermination. Shareholder orientation seems to strengthen trends that were already observable in the 1980s. Five trends in codetermination can be distinguished (Thelen 1991; Streeck 1996, 2001; Kotthoff 1998; Mitbestimmung 1998):

1. *System conformity*. Codetermination is no longer seen as an instrument for transforming the economic system into a mixture of capitalist and socialist elements (*Wirtschaftsdemokratie*). It is fully accepted that codetermination operates in firms whose natural goal is to generate cash flows and earnings.
2. *Efficiency orientation*. Democratic participation at the workplace is still one legitimizing force behind codetermination. However, increasingly codetermination has also to prove that it is not only the more democratic or social, but also the more efficient model for organizing the micro-relationship obtaining between employers and employees.
3. *Co-management and professionalism*. In practice, codetermination goes far beyond its legal foundations, interfering in and legitimizing company policy not only in social and personnel matters, but also in economic issues. The boundary between management functions and codetermination becomes increasingly harder to discern.
4. *Consensus orientation*. While confrontation between works councils and employers is becoming rare, codetermination seems to have committed itself as a cooperative process. Both sides see themselves as partners, not as opponents in class confrontation.
5. *Negotiation of rules*. Similar to the guideline on European Works Councils (EWC), evidence is growing that the role of legal foundations is decreasing, while the importance of negotiated codetermination rules is increasing. For example, several corporations have set up 'working teams of works councils' (*Arbeitsgemeinschaften der Betriebsräte*) which rely on negotiated rules instead of *Konzernbetriebsräte* that are based on legislation.

Codetermination practices are thus becoming more micro-focused and insider-oriented. This complicates the relationship between works councils and unions, since the latter see themselves as the macro-outsider force in the labour movement. The interests of employees as insiders in a particular company may contradict the interests of other employees who are outsiders. The unions' axiom that codetermination should go beyond the goals of existing company insiders has increasingly been undermined by practice. One example is the discrepancy of reactions to the hostile takeover attempt of Krupp in 1997. While IG Metall was fighting hostile takeovers as an illegitimate instrument of economic behaviour, Krupp employees were supporting the takeover attempt. When 30,000 members of IG Metall were demonstrating against hostile takeovers and the role of the Deutsche Bank in 1997, not even the works council members of Krupp participated. The heterogeneous and firm-specific employee interests were not overcome by common class-based interests. During a similar incident in summer 2003, works councils of large automobile companies protested against the Eastern German strike to demand a 35-hour week. Trade unions find it increasingly difficult to impose discipline and solidarity upon strong works councils who are involved with company-based cross-class coalitions. Because the interests of employees as producers in a particular firm are more heterogeneous than class interests (Streeck 1992a), the heterogeneity of interests inside unions increases.

Collective bargaining is also seeing a move towards controlled decentralization as discussed above in the section on variable pay. None of the large companies referred to here has opted out of central collective agreements (*Flächentarifverträge*). Shareholder-oriented companies even seem to avoid any sort of confrontation over pay policy. There are four reasons why large companies benefit more from centralized collective agreements than small companies. First, they enjoy greater productivity and would be confronted with higher wage demands if they opted out of central collective agreements. If unions base their wage claims on overall productivity development, highly productive firms tend to have decreasing unit labour costs, while less productive companies are faced with increasing unit labour costs. Second, union organization tends to be greater in large companies than in smaller ones, which increases the likelihood of strikes. Third, shareholder-oriented companies belong to the exposed sector, and are therefore more vulnerable than average in labour disputes. Shareholder-oriented companies are not indifferent to pay policy but have clear preferences: large corporations are particularly afraid of class conflict and are willing to place a premium on labour peace. Another reason why big firms do not opt out of central collective agreements is the existence of plant-level pacts, where managers and employees exchange job security against salaries above the centrally agreed scale (Rehder 2003*a*). There is no statistical correlation between shareholder-value orientation and the existence of plant-level pacts.

4.5. Conclusion

The post-war 'model' of German corporate governance was characterized a high degree of complementarity between patient bank-based capital and employee involvement. This complementarity was rooted in a specific class coalition where capital could receive favourable rates of return while allowing a distribution of value-added that favoured labour and internal reinvestment in the firm. 'Patient' capital thereby stabilized German employment relations and industrial relations. Meanwhile, corporate accountability was achieved by external contingent monitoring by banks, supplemented by internal accountability through consultation with works councils. Potential conflicts between corporate insiders and outsiders were held in check by high economic growth and the redistributive politics of the welfare state.

This chapter has shown that these institutional interactions have changed substantially due to changes in corporate ownership and finance and related diffusion of shareholder-value strategies. These resulting changes in employment and industrial relations remain a matter of degree and should not be interpreted as a convergence on the liberal corporate governance models of the United States or Britain. Market pressures continue to be mediated by the existing configuration of labour institutions. Here, we venture several conclusions.

First, a more marketized role of capital has led to changes toward more marketized employment relations in Germany. Stable employment is available to a shrinking number of employees, while the costs of 'benevolent' employment adjustment can no longer be effectively shouldered by the existing public welfare system. Variable pay is making wage setting more decentralized and contingent on the market position of the firm or business subunit. This trend suggests growing insider–outsider conflicts between core and peripheral employees, as well as between big firms and the larger society.

Second, the diffusion of shareholder value has not undermined the core institutions of German industrial relations, namely codetermination and collective bargaining. Particularly where labour is strong and supported by law, industrial relations institutions are relatively sticky even in the face of capital market pressures. These institutions continue to preserve labour peace within the firm. However, the economic functions of these institutions are evolving incrementally in light of new pressures and managerial strategies. Collective bargaining is struggling to maintain its past role in setting egalitarian and solidaristic wages. Unions are thus less able to exert a productivity whip on firms through high and uniform wages which were a 'beneficial constraint' on German work organization in the past. Now collective agreements are more defensive and steer the process of decentralization. Likewise, codetermination has an increasingly insider-focus on the interests of core employees. This shift is transforming codetermination from a politically guaranteed institution to a more private and contractual arrangement (Jackson 2003). While codetermination was the result of a historical effort to take labour and working conditions out of market competition in the interests of class solidarity, its function has changed more into the co-management of organizational change with the aim of making labour a competitive factor of production.

What can the German case tell us more generally about corporate governance and labour management? In returning to the two views of Germany discussed in the introduction, this chapter suggests that past literature has overestimated the degree to which capital and labour are tightly linked in a causal sense. Our chapter shows that since the mid-1990s, strong labour has not prevented the emergence of shareholder value in Germany, as implied by Roe (2000), nor has shareholder orientation undermined the distinctive institutions of German industrial relations. Roe stresses how employees may increase agency costs. However, we argue that this might be misleading because works councils may work in coalition to promote greater accountability and thereby actually decrease agency costs by monitoring managerial pay, fighting for transparency, opposing prestige investments, and also siding with shareholders in corporate restructuring. Likewise, committed bank finance does not appear necessary to support credible commitments by management toward labour. Capital market constraints are often more pliable, and labour can accommodate some new distributional constraints within the existing institutional framework of codetermination. However, we leave the long-term stability of these arrangements as an open question. In addition, while codetermination may coexist with capital market pressures, it also remains to be seen whether the distinctive German profile of comparative institutional advantage based on their past complementarities (Hall and Soskice 2001*b*) will be reproduced.

Change in the 1990s is consistent with a historical pattern of co-evolution, where these institutions revealed a largely unintended fit and their 'coherence' or 'systemness' as a national corporate governance model was attributed only in retrospect (Jackson 2001). Their stability often depended upon the fortune of ever-changing economic circumstances. Thus, institutional linkages are not established once and for all, but are in constant renegotiation—policy-by-policy and company-by-company. Institutions themselves are often ambiguous for actors, and the linkages between institutions indirect. Linkages are often made by the strategic choices on how to use institutions, as well as stakeholders entering into effective coalitions to promote and defend those strategies. A key example in this chapter was the finding that shareholder orientation is related to changes in the career characteristics of the German managerial elite. Shareholder-value management has spread rapidly because it is an important way for a new managerial generation to promote their careers. Here, strategic management plays an important intermediating role beyond a mechanistic relationship between inputs (functional pressures from product and capital markets) and outputs (shareholder oriented strategies).

Germany will remain an important test case as to whether labour can remain resilient in the process of adapting and inventing solutions to the new governance problems posed by market finance and shareholder-value management. The potential for a 'hybrid' model of corporate governance depends perhaps on the extent to which labour also impacts new shareholder-value practices. Will Germany adopt shareholder value in ways that differ from countries where institutionalized employee representation is weaker? This chapter documents several examples of the proactive role of labour in promoting an 'enlightened' form of shareholder value. Such a model would utilize employee voice alongside shareholders to promote greater accountability in issues of transparency and management pay, while continuing to avoid class conflicts and negative-sum solutions associated with the US or UK model. However, doing so will require Germany to confront the growing rift between corporate insiders and outsiders by developing new forms of interest intermediation and use of public power.

It remains to be seen whether an enlightened version of shareholder value in Germany can survive as a durable outcome, and one that is capable of generating a distinct profile of competitive advantage. Alternatively, we may be observing a slow transition process of what is, in fact, a convergence in labour management. While we think the prospects for a German 'hybrid' are strong, the scope for national diversity of employment relations is declining as financial systems are becoming more alike. The study of these linkages to finance and capital ownership is becoming ever more important for students of labour.

NOTES

1. For example, the characterization of Germany as an 'insider' model would overlook the importance of 'outside' interests such as industrial unions and employers associations which promote horizontal class interests. Moreover, the publicly guaranteed nature of codetermination rights do not fit well with the notion of an insider model.
2. On relational financing, see Aoki and Dinc (1997: 3). Empirical studies find that bank ownership reduces the sensitivity of investment to liquidity constraints, thus supporting the view of high financial commitment by banks (Elston and Albach 1995).
3. Works councils represent all workers at the level of the establishment and enterprise. Meanwhile, codetermination also extends to the supervisory board, where employees are represented with between one-third and half of the seats.
4. DiPrete and McManus (1995) find large differences between the United States and Germany in the returns to tenure while controlling for industry and occupation.
5. Germany has a distinctive system of vocational training in roughly 400 nationally certified occupations. Training is subject to corporatist administration by employers associations, labour unions, and state agencies (Hilbert, Südmersen, and Weber 1990). Apprenticeships combine elements of school-based and company-based instruction. In 1991, 72% of the West German labour force had completed apprenticeship training (Jackson 1996).
6. Inter-industry wage differentials are nearly twice as large in the United States even when controlling for differences human capital variables (Schettkat 1992: 36–37; Bellmann and Möller 1995: 152).
7. For example, apprenticeships in German metalworking occupations last 3.5 years. Six occupations share an identical basic training in the first year. In the second year, these occupations split into three 'groups' that share an additional half year of training. The next half year is spent in training in six broadly defined occupations. Finally, the last 1.5 years are spent within

one of seventeen specializations. Unions have pursued a strategy of lengthening and broadening occupational training, thereby drastically reducing the total number of occupations over the last decades.

8. The real rate of return on the national stock market index averaged 10.2% in Germany and 7.8% in the United States between 1950 and 1989 (Jackson 2001).
9. *Handelsblatt*, 8.11.1999.
10. These data were weighted for the duration of the time in office.
11. In interpreting these changes, the causality might be recursive. A given shareholder value orientation should also raise the demand for financially oriented managers. What is emphasized here is a distinct, non-recursive influence of 'management culture' variables on management behaviour. The professionalization and the marketization of management create a climate that favours some management ideologies more than others.
12. The indicator includes four items: the information quality of the corporate reports, the degree of investor relations efforts, the implementation of value-orientated performance targets, and the incentive compatibility of managerial compensation.
13. Pioneering examples are Mercedes Benz, Bayer, Continental, and Adam Opel.
14. However, the danger is that competition among employees for these rewards may reduce motivation for cooperation, passing along skills, and the sharing information.
15. Variable pay might make it more difficult for unions to organize low-level employees collectively, especially where works councils acknowledge principles of competition and risk taking as ways to raise the profitability of the company.
16. *Handelsblatt*, 21/22.07.2000, 24. Similar examples are Veba, Siemens, MAN, Degussa-Hüls, Deutsche Telekom. Most cases are a mixture: management tends to focus on core competencies, more (Veba) or less (Siemens) supported by works councils (Zugehör 2003), but shareholders' demands turn out to be more radical and are opposed by insiders.

5

Corporate Governance in Germany: Ownership, Codetermination, and Firm Performance in a Stakeholder Economy

BERND FRICK AND ERIK LEHMANN

5.1. Introduction

In most developed economies, the managers of (large) corporations are ultimately legally responsible to the shareholders. However, since Berle and Means (1932) published their seminal book, it has been argued that in practice managers tend to pursue their own interests rather than those of the shareholders. The separation of ownership and control, together with the fact that contracts are necessarily incomplete, creates a need to control managers and, in turn, this has led to the evolution of different systems of corporate governance (Hart 1995; Shleifer and Vishny 1997; Tirole 2001).[1] The main issue that has been considered in this context is how the interests of managers can be aligned with those of shareholders. Hence, corporate governance mechanisms assure investors that they will receive adequate returns on their investments. This is true for the owners of the firm who invested in physical capital as well as for the employees who usually invest in human capital. Both parties are highly vulnerable after the investment has taken place and may well become victims of a 'hold up'. Thus, corporate governance mechanisms tend to act as safeguards against opportunistic behaviour which, in turn, may increase the parties' readiness to engage in risky investments.

Compared to the Anglo-American model, found in the United States, the United Kingdom, and some other English-speaking countries (see Fabel and Lehmann 2001), the German model is idiosyncratic in at least two ways. First, due to 'codetermination', shareholders are not the only group to whom the managers of the corporation are responsible. Second, the far-reaching influence of big universal banks on corporate decision-making is also unparalleled in the Western world. More broadly, the main difference between German firms and those in the Anglo-Saxon countries is that their governance system is mostly shaped by factors that are internal to the firm. Hence, all of the 'stakeholders', managers, owners, banks, employees, and even the government, are more or less able to monitor and influence a company's performance and strategy.

Recently, the German system has attracted considerable interest because it is thought to address governance problems more effectively than the Anglo-American system. Among others, Pound (1995) has recently praised the 'governed' (German) corporation as the ideal governance model for restructuring not only corporate America but also other countries. In practice, however, the recent 'globalization' of input and output markets has already shifted the German system of corporate governance towards the Anglo-American system (Baums 1996; Fabel and Lehmann 2001). First, the foundation of the 'New Market' in 1997 (a special segment of the German stock market) increased the number of stock exchange listings from about 500 to more than 800 (about 350 small and medium-sized firms were listed in that segment in 2001). Second, legislation has recently reduced tax rates on capital gains. Hence, many banks and insurance firms plan to sell some of their shares in other firms. Third, the 1998 corporate law reform (the *Gesetz zur Kontrolle und Transparenz im Unternehmensbereich* (*KonTraG*)) strengthens the enforcement mechanisms for board member liability and abolishes limitations of voting rights in the case of interlocking shareholdings. This may well reduce ownership control.

Apart from the widespread appraisals found in the literature, the German system of corporate governance and its main characteristics (i.e. codetermination, bank control, ownership concentration, interlocking directorates, the virtual absence of a market for corporate takeovers, etc.) have recently also been blamed for a number of insolvencies that were apparently due to poor monitoring and a lack of pressure from the capital market (Wenger and Kaserer 1998).

In an attempt to evaluate the potential strengths and weaknesses of the German system of corporate governance, we discuss two characteristics about which there has been considerable debate in the literature: [2]

1. The German system of corporate governance may be a competitive advantage for German firms, but it may well be detrimental to

firm performance. In particular, the role of banks and the influence of workers' representatives on the supervisory boards need to be evaluated.

2. According to the Works Constitution Act, works councils have specific rights to information, consultation, and codetermination. They may either use their powers for the good of the company or they may exert a negative influence on the personnel policies (and, thereby, on the economic performance) of German firms.

While our primary intention is to present and review the available empirical evidence, we also try to relate the (sometimes contradictory and unconvincing) findings reported in the relevant literature to theoretical propositions derived from principal–agent theory, contract theory, and the new theory of the firm. To set the context, therefore, we briefly consider the broader context of corporate control and government in Germany on firm performance, before we turn to the influence of mandated codetermination and works councils on labour management strategies and the performance of German firms. We conclude with a short summary of our major findings and some speculation as to the likely future of the German system.

5.2. Corporate Governance and Firm Performance in Germany

5.2.1. *Ownership concentration and shareholder control*

5.2.1.1. *Descriptive statistics*

Corporate ownership is rather concentrated in Germany as compared to countries like the United States or the United Kingdom (Clarke and Bostock 1997; Boehmer 1998; Prigge 1998; Edwards and Nibler 2000).

From a control perspective, the ownership structure of domestic AGs (publicly traded firms) is a key figure. Table 5.1 reveals a long-term trend of increasing shareholdings of domestic institutional shareholders (see also Prigge 1998). Moreover, the data clearly show that share ownership of private households is traditionally of little significance, as are shareholdings by institutional investors. However, ownership by financial and non-financial companies is traditionally strong. It appears that shareholdings by investment funds and insurance companies have increased significantly while the percentage of shares owned by foreigners has decreased over the last 15 years.

Table 5.1. *Ownership structure of domestic shares, 1984–98 (percentages)*

Year	Banks	Insurance companies	Investment funds	Non-financial companies	Private households and organizations	Public sector	Foreign
1984	7.6	3.1	2.7	36.1	18.8	10.2	21.4
1988	8.1	2.7	3.4	39.3	19.4	7.1	20.0
1990	9.4	3.2	3.3	41.4	18.3	6.0	18.6
1992	9.7	4.8	4.2	42.4	16.8	5.5	16.6
1994	8.4	5.1	5.4	39.6	17.3	6.7	17.5
1996	9.5	5.6	5.5	37.5	15.7	10.9	15.3
1998	8.6	8.9	6.5	35.4	15.7	9.0	15.9

Source: Deutsche Bundesbank (2000: 32).

Table 5.2. *Voting rights controlled by the largest shareholder (percentages)*

Size of largest share directly held in % of total voting stock	Germany	Japan	US
0–9.99	3.2	61.1	66.0
10–24.99	6.9	21.3	17.4
25–49.99	16.7	12.9	13.0
50–74.99	31.9	4.9	2.1
75–100	41.3	—	1.5

Source: Dietl (1998: 124).

One decisive feature with regard to control is the size of the stake held by the different owners. If the intensity of control does indeed increase with the size of the stake, the ownership structure of German AGs would certainly be conducive to an effective control of management: ownership is often more or less concentrated in one hand with the remaining shares being more or less dispersed. As Dietl (1998: 124) shows, the largest individual shareholder owns more than 50 per cent of the total voting stock in nearly three out of four publicly traded companies in Germany (Frick 1999; Dilger and Frick 2000). As Table 5.2 indicates, the respective figure is less than 5 per cent in the United States as well as in Japan.

In a similar vein, Becht and Boehmer (1997) argue that the largest stake (with a median size of about 55 per cent) is by far the most important factor contributing to concentration. The second largest stake (and those further down) does not add very much to the degree of ownership concentration. However, stakes in Germany are by and large clustered at the legally important thresholds of 5 per cent (information disclosure), 25 per cent (blocking minority), 50 per cent (simple majority), and 76 per cent (super-majority). Franks and Mayer (1997*b*) document that out of 171 large corporations, 85 per cent have a shareholder owning more than 25 per cent, and 57 per cent have a shareholder owning more than 50 per cent of the equity. These findings have recently been confirmed by Edwards and Nibler (2000). They show that half of the firms in their database (156 large non-financial firms) and 47 out of 105 listed firms had a single owner holding more than 50 per cent of the equity. Only thirty of these firms had an owner holding less than 25 per cent (see also Prigge 1998; Boehmer 1999 for further details).

5.2.1.2. *The ambiguous consequences of ownership concentration*
According to Stiglitz (1985), one of the most important ways to ensure value maximization by managers is through concentrated ownership of the firm's shares. If, like in the United States, shares are held by a large number of investors, none of them has an incentive to control management, because of high monitoring costs associated with such activities. One large shareholder (or a limited number of them) may have an incentive actively to monitor the firm's management because he will be able to reap the benefits of such activities which, in turn, will induce management to maximize the market value of the firm (Shleifer and Vishny 1986).

Weigand (1999) shows that firms where ownership is concentrated do indeed experience significantly higher returns on assets (ROA) than otherwise identical firms with more dispersed ownership. On average and especially in the long run, bank and family-owned firms perform better than the reference group of manager-controlled firms. Moreover, Edwards (1999) finds evidence that the profitability of large German AGs and KGs is positively influenced by the extent of their ownership concentration, unless the large owners are public sector bodies.

Burkart, Gromb, and Panunzi (1997) examine the costs and benefits of concentrated ownership and show that, whilst close monitoring may indeed restrict the misuse of resources *ex post*, it may also be detrimental to managerial initiative *ex ante* which may then lead to under-investment in the long run. Their results point to a seemingly

Table 5.3. *Ownership concentration and firm performance in Germany: literature review*

Author	Sample	Method	Results
Thonet/Poensgen (1989)	300 large German firms (ownership structure for 90 firms)	OLS, Cross section	Concentration
Cable (1985)	48 stock corporations from Germany's 100 largest companies in 1974, 1968–72	Cross section	Positive impact of involvement on profitability
Schmidt (1996)	62 firms with bank ownership in 1990	OLS regression, analysis of variance	Positive of bank involvement on profitability
Chirinko/Elston (1996)	300 stock corporations ownership data for sub-sample, 1965–90	Long-run relationships, cross-section regressions voting rights and blockholding on ROA	Insignificant negative impact of both accumulated proxy
Franks/Mayer (1997*b*)	171 quoted companies, 1989–94	Fixed effects panel regression	No significant impact of ownership variables or turnover of blockholdings on firm performance
Edwards/ Weichenrieder (1999)	102 large listed companies, information about large shareholder from 1992	Cross section	Tighter control exercised by the largest shareholder lowers the market value of firms Increase in the control of rights of the second-largest shareholder increases the market value
Weigand (1999)	240 stock corporations, 1965–86	Balanced panel analysis	High bank and family ownership leads to higher ROA
Goergen (1998)	86 IPOs, 1981–8	Static and dynamic panel data regressions	Ownership concentration has no impact on profitability (cash flow/total assets)
Becht (1999)	DAX 100 companies from 1996–8		Significant negative impact of blockholding on liquidity (turnover/ market capitalization)
Lehmann/ Weigand (2000)	361 firms, balanced panel from 1991–6	3-step GLS panel estimations, 3-step GLS Instrumental value estimations	Significant negative ownership concentrations on ROA Ownership location matters, not concentration as such
Gorton/Schmid (2000*a*)	88 listed AGs in 1974, 57 listed AGs in 1985	Cross section	No impact of bank ownership on firm profitability for both samples

inevitable trade-off between control and initiative: while blockholding increases incentives to monitor, it very often also leads to a lack of liquidity (Bolton and von Thadden 1998*a*, *b*; Maug 1998).

Using a panel data set of 171 quoted firms for 1989–94 and employing a fixed effects panel regression approach, Franks and Mayer (1997*a*, *b*) cannot find a significant impact of ownership concentration on firm performance, which is consistent with findings reported by Kaplan (1994). Moreover, both studies show that the relationship between board turnover and firm profitability does not depend on ownership concentration. This latter finding can be interpreted in two different ways. First, if firms' shares are highly concentrated, the managers of all firms may be subject to a similarly high degree of monitoring, which is reflected in a turnover–profitability relationship that does not depend on whether ownership is concentrated or not. Second, it may also be the case that managers are simply not very closely monitored by large shareholders.

Another trade-off between costs and benefits occurs if the interests of large shareholders are different from the ones of minority shareholders. In this case, the former can pursue their interests at the expense of the latter which, in turn, would not only be detrimental to firm performance but would also lead to an expropriation-like redistribution of wealth. In other words, blockholders and controlling owners can obtain private benefits of control at the expense of minority owners.

Edwards and Weichenrieder (1999) analyse a small sample of 102 large listed German corporations of which 72 had a major shareholder with more than 25 per cent of the voting equity. They show that, other things being equal, the larger the control rights of the largest shareholder, the lower the market value of firms' equity performance. If, however, ownership of the second-largest shareholder increases, the share value of the companies increases too. Thus, they argue, the ability of the largest shareholder to obtain private benefits of control may be limited by extending the control rights of the second-largest shareholder.[3] Gedaljovic and Shapiro (1998) study the block holding-performance relationship of the largest firms from five major industrialized countries. For the ninety-nine publicly traded German stock corporations in their sample, they find a significantly negative and non-linear impact of ownership concentration on ROA over the period 1986–91. Thus, profitability first decreases in ownership concentration and then, at higher levels of concentration, rises again. This, however, contradicts the findings of Edwards (1999) who provides evidence that the relationship between profitability and ownership concentration for large German firms is not non-linear. Finally, Becht (1999) finds a significantly negative effect of ownership concentration on liquidity, measured by the ratio of turnover to market capitalization. These seemingly incompatible findings may be due to differences in the data sets used (the samples are small and not representative) and the ownership measures that have been employed. In a more comprehensive study, Lehmann and Weigand use a balanced panel of 361 firms for 1991–6. They find a significantly negative impact of ownership concentration on profitability, as measured by ROA. Furthermore, they show that the representation of the largest shareholder on the board of executive directors does not have any influence on profitability. This latter finding is certainly at odds with the assumption that large shareholders seek private benefits of control.

According to Demsetz (1983), ownership concentration may be the endogenous and efficient outcome of a firm's response to its competitive environment. Viewed from this perspective, governance does not affect firm performance, but is simultaneously determined together with firm performance by the forces of competitive markets. Januszewski, Köke, and Winter (1999) find only weak evidence that competition has a positive effect on productivity growth for firms with concentrated ownership. In addition, they show that concentrated ownership itself has a negative impact on productivity growth. They conclude that product competition can indeed compensate for the negative influence of dominant owners to a certain extent. Goergen (1998) supports these findings by studying eighty-six initial public offerings (IPOs) that occurred in Germany over the period 1981–8. Estimating both static and dynamic panel regressions, he finds that ownership concentration does not have any impact on profitability, measured by cash flow over total assets. He interprets his results as supporting the Demsetz hypothesis that ownership structure is chosen to maximize firm value.

Thus, is the seemingly high concentration of ownership beneficial or detrimental to the performance of German firms? Apart from rather technical explanations (emphasizing differences in sample sizes, cross-section versus longitudinal data, different time periods, balanced versus unbalanced panels), the type of firms included (listed versus not listed, different legal forms, etc.), the econometric tools employed (OLS-regressions, fixed or random-effects estimates, panel estimations), the seemingly incompatible results obtained for Germany may simply indicate that the relationship between governance and profitability has changed over the years (see Lehmann and Weigand 2000). While a significant positive relationship between ownership concentration and profitability seems to have existed for owner-controlled firms during the 1970s and the 1980s (Weigand 1999), this relationship seems to have vanished or even became negative in the 1990s (see Franks and Mayer 1997a, b; Becht 1999; Goergen 1998; Lehmann and Weigand 2000). This may be due to the fact that the globalization of product markets and increased international competition may have altered the profitability–ownership concentration relation since the late 1980s.

5.2.1.3. *The location of ownership and the performance of firms*

It has been argued by Cubbin and Leech (1983) that the location of control rights may be a more important determinant of the degree of control exercised by owners than the degree of ownership concentration. In this vein, Lehmann and Weigand (2000) show that the negative impact of ownership concentration found in the full sample of firms can be traced back to the different groups that own and (possibly) govern the firm.

Individuals or *families* may be better monitors than other corporate shareholders as long as they can avoid internal agency conflicts. If, however, the size of the group of individuals or family members (like the Siemens, Thyssen, and Krupp clans) exceeds a certain threshold value, the cost of coordination as well as the agency costs increase. Lehmann and Weigand (2000) show that firms that are governed by families or have a mixed ownership structure, experience a significantly lower profitability.

Foreign owners are another type of shareholder to be distinguished. According to the corporate governance literature institutional investors from the United States and the United Kingdom are likely to be very active shareholders (Roe 1994; Short 1994; Shleifer and Vishny 1997). As shown in Table 5.1, about 15 per cent of the shares of German firms are held by foreigners. If foreigners are indeed better monitors, then firms owned by them should outperform firms that are otherwise observationally similar. However, as Lehmann and Weigand (2000) show, the coefficient of the respective interaction term (dummy for foreign ownership multiplied by a measure for the concentration of shares) has a negative sign and an insignificant effect on ROA.

Moreover, other *industrial* firms may be a relevant group of shareholders. As Prigge (1998) points out, personal and capital links play a dominant role in German corporate governance (see also Adams 1999).

The German *Konzern* (large holding company of a conglomerate nature and with a pyramidal structure) is a major issue when looking at the links within the corporate sector. However, they do not show up in official statistics. Prigge (1998: 970) shows that about 73.6 per cent (by number) and 96.4 per cent (by statutory capital) of all AGs are part of a *Konzern*. Hence, ownership structures in Germany are characterized by an outstanding incidence of hierarchical linkages within the corporate sector. Lehmann and Weigand (2000) show that ownership concentration in those firms is exogenous (for 1991–6). Thus, there may be other reasons for linkages and cross-holding than economic performance. One major reason is to avoid unfriendly takeovers especially by foreigners (Franks and Mayer 1997*a*; Emmons and Schmid 1998). Franks and Mayer (1997*a*) illustrate the practice of pyramiding in Germany by analysing the case of the former Mercedes Holding AG (now DaimlerChrysler AG). It was established in 1975 with the explicit encouragement of government officials as an anti-takeover device. Another example is Volkswagen AG.[4] Hence, it would come as a surprise if firms owned by another industrial firm were particularly successful in economic terms (see Lehmann and Weigand 2000).

One main difference with other countries is the long-term relationship between German banks and their client firms: Germany banks hold both debt and equity and they actively intervene where the client runs into financial distress (Edwards and Fischer 1994; Lehmann and Neuberger 2001). The importance of equity ownership by financial institutions in Germany and the absence of a market for corporate control have led to the suggestion that the agency problem is solved by financial institutions acting as an outside monitor of the management of large corporations (Neuberger and Neumann 1991; Neuberger 1997).

Several studies have confirmed this hypothesis. Using a small sample of forty-eight stock corporations from Germany's largest firms in 1970, Cable (1985) estimates cross-section regressions for 1968–72 and obtains a positive and statistically significant impact of bank involvement on profitability (for similar results, see also Schmid 1996). In a further study, Gorton and Schmid (2000*a*, *b*) use a sample of eighty-two listed AGs in 1975 and a further sample of fifty-six listed AGs in 1986. They find that bank equity positions and shareholder concentration measures are positively and statistically significant related to firm performance. In contrast to Cable (1985), they do not consider the possible influence of bank supervisory board representation or bank lending on profitability. In this vein, Edwards (1999) argues that there is no evidence of German banks having an economically significant impact in corporate governance beyond that of being, along with many non-banks, owners of large equity stakes in some firms.[5] The findings presented by Agarwal and Elston (2001) point to a clear-cut negative influence. Using an unbalanced panel of 100 large German firms from 1970 to 1986 ($n = 1,660$), they conclude that bank-influenced firms do indeed benefit from increased access to capital, but that the interest payments to debt ratio is significantly higher for bank-influenced firms, suggesting that German universal banks engage in rent-seeking activities. This finding is evidence of conflicting interests between creditors and shareholders.

The panel study by Lehmann and Weigand (2000) provides evidence that ownership concentration does make a difference for firms that are governed by financial institutions. They conclude that the significantly positive influence of banks is in line with the standard reasoning that banks are the best monitors and are therefore most likely to enhance firm performance. However, it may very well be the case that banks are better at 'picking winners' rather than better at governance. Summarizing, it appears that although the statistical significance of the influence of bank ownership on firm profitability is not very strong, most of the estimates (with the exception of Perlitz and Seger 1994) are positive and significantly different from zero.

So far, one major problem has not been considered, namely that banks are themselves subject to the same agency problems as firms (see Lindner-Lehmann 2001). Therefore, past and recent institutional change is most likely to affect the future role of the banking sector in corporate governance. Following the enactment of the KonTraG, banks must inform customers whose shares they manage about their strategies to be pursued, so that customers may choose to have their voting rights exercised by the bank or by a shareholder association. Furthermore, a bank must inform its customers when it holds 5 per cent or more of the voting rights in cases where the company is listed or if the bank is a member of the company's most recent underwriting syndicate. Finally, a bank must also advise its customers if one of its managers or employees is a member of the management or supervisory board of the respective stock corporation. In the future, banks must also submit proposals on how to exercise the voting rights of customers and they must take organizational measures to ensure that their own interests will not influence such proposals.

5.2.2. *Codetermination, works councils, and firm performance*

5.2.2.1. *Codetermination and firm performance*

To date, a limited number of studies have investigated the influence of the different codetermination laws on the economic performance of German firms (FitzRoy and Kraft 1993, 2000; Benelli, Loderer, and Lys 1987; Gurdon and Rai 1990; Schmid and Seger 1998; Edwards and Nibler 2000; Gorton and Schmid 2000*a*, *b*). The overall conclusion one can draw from these studies, though they use rather different data and test designs, would be that the legislation of 1951 and 1976 had a rather modest—if any—influence on the sectors and firms affected. Until recently, the comparative analysis of codetermination has produced no clear conclusions. It is rather difficult to say that there is an effect, much less specify its direction or magnitude. There are several reasons why empirical studies have been rather inconclusive. First, the samples examined have been rather small. Second, the studies have usually been concentrated on single events (such as the introduction of the Codetermination Act 1976) and have not considered whether this legislation might have been anticipated by firms (and potential investors) since the late 1960s and early 1970s. Third, most of the studies had great difficulty in adjusting for all the appropriate factors, since in most cases no detailed data are available to indicate all relevant differences between firms (i.e. to control for unobserved heterogeneity).

One example is an event study that has been conducted by Baums and Frick (1998, 1999). In order to study the influence of labour representation on corporate boards, they use daily stock returns data from twenty-eight different firms that were subject to court decisions concerning the application of the Codetermination Acts of 1951 and 1976 during the period from January 1974 to December 1995. This permits measurement of the impact of codetermination on the stock price of the respective firm. In a second step they ask whether the introduction of the Codetermination Act, and the ruling of the Federal Constitutional Court that declared that Act as being compatible with the Basic Law of the Federal Republic of Germany, had any influence on the performance of those sectors most heavily affected by the decision. Combining longitudinal and cross-sectional analyses, they find that the average abnormal rate of return on the event date, that is, the date the respective court announced its decision, was slightly positive—although in half of all cases the decision was clearly in favour of the unions' or the employees' position. Thus, neither does a company's success in the respective lawsuit lead to a significant increase in the abnormal rate of return on either the event date or one of the following days, nor does a company loss have the opposite effect on the development of the relative capital market performance of the company affected. Moreover, neither the enactment of the Codetermination Act, nor the fact that it was later declared constitutional by the Federal Constitutional Court, result in a significant change in the average abnormal rates of return in any of the six sectors under consideration.

5.2.2.2. Works councils and firm performance

Until recently, the number of studies analysing the influence of works councils on firm performance was rather low and their quality poor. With the recent availability of several firm-level panel data sets, the situation has changed quite dramatically. The number of studies is increasing rapidly and these more recent studies suffer less from methodological problems than the ones that were published before the mid-1990s.[6]

The studies that have been published since then have used a variety of measures, including productivity levels and growth, financial performance and profitability, investment in human and physical capital, as well as in research and development and job generation. Contrary to the performance effects of worker representation on corporate boards, the existence of works councils seems to have clear-cut consequences for firm performance: the presence of a works council has—other things being equal—a significantly positive influence on labour productivity and a significantly negative influence on profitability. Moreover, works councils do not have an influence on investment behaviour and/or on innovations (neither product nor process innovations).

However, most of the empirical studies are unable to control for the capital stock of the companies and are thus unable to rule out the possibility that it is capital intensity rather than the presence of a works council that fosters better economic performance. Assuming that financial resources that have recently been invested to replace used capital goods are highly correlated with the capital stock, Frick and Möller (2002) estimate different types of production functions (Cobb-Douglas, Translog, and CES) with value-added as the dependent variable. Apart from information on capital and workers employed, the production function estimates include a wide range of variables identified as (potential) determinants of firm performance. The study uses information from the sixth and the eighth wave of the IAB-panel for firms located in West Germany and from the third and the fifth wave in East Germany (the data are for 1998 and 2000, with the number of firms being around 2,000 in both years in each part of the country).

The most important findings of that study can be summarized as follows. The Translog specification is the most appropriate functional form, suggesting that it is not only the amount of labour and capital used that matters, but that their interaction is also of paramount importance for the performance of firms. Moreover, controlling for a number of firm characteristics, the presence of a works council has a positive and statistically significant influence on economic perform-ance. The respective coefficients indicate that these effects are rather large and that they differ significantly between industry and service sectors. Together with the findings reported by Jirjahn and Klodt (1998, 1999) and by Bellmann and Kohaut (1995a, b, 1997, 1999), the estimates suggest that the presence of a generally accepted 'voice-institution' may foster the generation as well as the distribution of rents that would otherwise not occur.

5.3. Corporate Governance and Labour Management in a Codetermined Economy

5.3.1. *The potential benefits of mandated works councils*

Although the view of the firm as a 'nexus of contracts' (Jensen and Meckling 1976) was a significant step towards a better understanding of the terms of the relationships between its various participants, it is certainly not enough to look only at the relationship between shareholders and managers and to treat employment relationships as a separate topic. The influence of investments in firm-specific human capital on the performance of the firm implies that the nature of the employment relationship is central to the institutional arrange-ments which, in turn, constitute the governance system of the firm (Zingales 1998).

Two broad arguments have been directed against laws that mandate worker participation. The first argument—based on political economy considerations—has been advanced by Furubotn (1988: 178):

Efforts by governments to . . . reshape the firm have not led to particularly desirable results. The approach taken has emphasized the 'political' aspect of the firm and the importance of corporate governance while failing to give much attention to broader economic issues and to the relation between the firm's total property-rights structure and its performance. By granting workers major control rights without regard to their actual investment position in the firm, state programmes have violated an important rule for ensuring rational allocation, viz. the rule that those making decisions should bear the full costs of the decisions they make. This defect, together with the costly system used to apportion the firm's quasi-rents between workers and stockholders, means that the orthodox co-determined firm does not possess a truly efficient organizational structure.

The second argument—a market-oriented case against legally mandated codetermination—was given by Jensen and Meckling (1979: 474):

If codetermination is beneficial to both stockholders and labour, why do we need laws which force firms to engage in it? Surely, they would do so voluntarily. The fact that stockholders must be forced by law to accept codetermination is the best evidence we have that they are adversely affected by it.

In contrast, there are plausible arguments that even though codetermination may be able to provide gains to both workers and firms, it could still be under-provided by the market.

First, as Freeman and Lazear (1995) have shown, neither employers nor workers have incentives to voluntarily create councils with the power to maximize 'social value'. However, once created and vested with the optimal amount of rights, councils can reduce economic inefficiencies by moderating worker demands in tough times and by assuring that firms use worker-provided information to benefit labour as well as the firm. Moreover, councils can produce new solutions to the problems facing the firm. This is more likely when both workers and management have information that is unavailable to the other side.[7] If, however, works councils increase the joint surplus of the firm–worker relationship, why do they have to be mandated? The answer given by Freeman and Lazear (1995: 29) is simple:

Institutions which give workers power in enterprises affect the distribution as well as the amount of the joint surplus. The greater the power of works councils, the greater will be workers' share of the economic rent. If councils increase the rent going to the workers more than they increase total rent, firms will oppose them. It is better to have a quarter slice of a 12-inch pie than an eighth of a 16-inch pie.

Second, if workers invest in firm-specific skills, the firm's profits may well rise and thus help boost wages. However, in a world of informational asymmetries, the firm may be unable to check on the extent to which employees are making firm-specific investments.[8]

Moreover, workers may be reluctant to make such investments, because it makes them vulnerable. After all, such an investment will pay off only if workers can be assured of being with the same firm for some time into the future; otherwise they would suffer serious economic losses (i.e. in the case of a dismissal). Thus, if workers are protected by institutional or contractual safeguards, then they become willing to invest in the acquisition of firm-specific skills, and both parties can benefit (Alchian 1984; Furubotn 1985, 1988).[9] Therefore, codetermination is a type of governance structure that is capable of dealing with maximizing agents having conflicting interests.[10]

Given these seemingly incompatible positions, theory offers no definitive guidance as to the likely effects of mandated works councils. The beneficial as well as the detrimental effects of codetermination must therefore be demonstrated empirically.[11]

5.3.2. *The influence of works councils in various policy areas*[12]

5.3.2.1. *Labour turnover*

Using a representative sample of about 2,400 private sector firms in Germany, Frick (1996, 1997*a*) finds that during the 2-year period 1985–7, firms on average had a turnover rate of 35 per cent. In firms with a works council the respective share was only 26 per cent while in those without a works council it was 38 per cent. The number of dismissals per 100 employees was 7.8 in firms with a works council and 14.6 in firms without a council. The average number of voluntary quits was 10.4 in the former and 15.7 in the latter. Since dismissals and quits are influenced by the economic situation of the enterprise or by structural characteristics of the sector to which a firm belongs, as well as the presence of a works council, other possible determinants of dismissals and quits have to be analysed simultaneously. Controlling for a large number of potential determinants of firms' dismissal behaviour, it appears that firms with a works council have a dismissal rate which is 2.9 percentage points lower than in firms without a plant-level interest representation. Union density, on the other hand, has no association with the dismissal rate. Of equal importance is the finding that firms with a works council on average have a quit rate which is 2.4 percentage points lower than that in firms without plant-level interest representation. Once again, union density is not statistically significant (for similar findings, see Addison, Schnabel, and Wagner 1998, 1999; Addison *et al.* 2000; Dilger 2002). The respective estimates show that works councils neither oppose dismissals in shrinking firms nor inhibit hirings in growing firms. Under certain conditions, works councils can, in firms with at least twenty employees, explicitly oppose the recruitment of new employees. However, in practice, not even this fact seems to have any influence on firms' hiring behaviour.

As has been pointed out by several critics, if the works council unilaterally favours the interests of the incumbent workforce, the following events should occur. In shrinking firms with a works council, the percentage of younger and/or qualified workers should be disproportionately high among the leavers, if the works councils actually favour those with long tenure and reduced opportunities on the external labour market. This, in turn, would be detrimental to the firm's economic performance, because in the long run it might be left with its less productive workers, putting it at a competitive disadvantage compared to otherwise identical firms without a works council. In shrinking firms without a works council, the percentage of older and/or less qualified workers should be disproportionately high among the leavers, because of the firm's interest in retaining its most productive employees. The respective estimates show that the presence or absence of a works council does not have any influence on the qualification structure of those who leave or stay in the case of inevitable workforce reductions.

5.3.2.2. *Wages, fringe benefits, and pay systems*

In a series of papers, Bellmann and Kohaut (1995a, b, 1997, 1999) not only isolate the factors influencing per capita wages, but also answer the question as to why a sizeable minority of all German firms pay wages in excess of those stipulated by collective agreements. In 1992, about 72 per cent of all firms in West Germany had to obey collective agreements. Of these, 57 per cent paid higher wages than necessary. The wage gap (i.e. the difference between collectively agreed and effective wages) in that year was 7.6 per cent (based on all firms) or 13.4 per cent (based only on firms paying more than the going rate). In 1997, the percentage of firms that had to obey collective agreements had dropped to 59 per cent (West Germany) and was even lower in East Germany (41 per cent).[13] The wage gap had dropped to 5.5 per cent (all firms) and 11.4 per cent (firms paying more than the going rate) in West Germany. The respective figures for East German firms are 1.9 and 11.4 per cent (Meyer and Swieter 1997; Bellmann, Kohaut, and Schnabel 1998). Controlling for firm size, sector, the percentage of vacancies, the percentage of female workers, and the percentage of part-time employees, the presence of a works council has, other things being equal, a negative impact on the wage gap.[14]

With regard to the average wage (total wage bill divided by number of employees), the findings are rather different, although the authors use nearly the same control variables. Here, they find that the presence of a works council has a significantly positive influence (separate estimates for private sector firms in East and West Germany reveal quite similar coefficients).[15] These results are confirmed by Addison, Schnabel, and Wagner (1998) and by Jirjahn and Klodt (1998, 1999). They use one or more waves of the Hanover firm panel to isolate the determinants of per-capita wages in manufacturing firms located in Lower Saxony. Based on an unbalanced panel of 861 firms ($n = 1,888$, 1993–5) and estimating random effects models, the latter authors find that firms with a works council pay significantly higher wages.[16]

Using data from the fourth wave of the Hanover panel,[17] Hübler and Meyer (2000) analyse the determinants of wage differentials between skilled and unskilled blue-collar workers. To measure wage differentials within firms, the respondents were asked the following question: 'Can you tell us the approximate difference between the highest effective hourly wage rate of a skilled blue-collar worker and the lowest effective hourly wage rate of an unskilled blue-collar worker in your establishment? Temporary workers should not be taken into consideration'. Among the 617 firms (87 per cent) that answered the question, the average wage differential is 38 per cent. Controlling for a number of potential determinants of wage differentials, they report that union density has no influence on the internal wage structure. Given the institutional setting (especially the 'division of labour' between unions and works councils) this may be reasonable, because union representation at the establishment level is rather weak. Furthermore, the presence of a works council leads to a lower wage differential. Finally, the study shows that coverage by collective bargaining leads to a widening of the wage structure between skilled and unskilled workers. This finding is the most surprising one and certainly defies the demand for a more decentralized bargaining system.[18]

5.3.2.3. Working time arrangements and 'atypical' employment relationships

Dilger (2002) uses the sixth wave of the 'NIFA-Panel', a representative longitudinal survey of over 1,300 engineering firms, to analyse the influence of works councils on working time arrangements. He reports that the presence of a works council contributes significantly to the firm's flexibility in deploying its workforce. The data used in this study is novel insofar as it allows a distinction between firms that do have a works council and those that do not, as well as a closer characterization of the works council as viewed by the respective firm's management. Dilger finds that only two out of five 'types' of works councils are beneficial to the firm with regard to the introduction of flexible working time arrangements. While works councils that are considered to be a 'tough' or a 'cooperative' partner seem to foster such arrangements, this is not the case when they are 'antagonistic', 'disinterested', or when they are not involved by management in the decision-making process. Thus, although works councils may be seen as an institution that reduces the firm's 'external' flexibility (though the empirical findings quoted above do not seem to support that assumption), they apparently increase 'internal' flexibility by promoting among their constituents the introduction of working time arrangements that deviate from 'standard' working hours.

Düll and Ellguth (1999) distinguish between two different forms of 'atypical' employment relationships: fixed-term contracts and 'marginal' jobs. The holders of these latter jobs earn less than the minimum amount that creates the legal obligation to pay contributions to social security. Using a pooled data set with information from more than 4,000 firms in East and West Germany covering the period 1996–8, they find that in West Germany only 10 per cent of all firms have fixed-term employees (these people make up 3 per cent of the firms' workforces) while in East Germany 14 per cent of all firms have fixed-term employees. Controlling for a number of other possible determinants, the authors find that the presence of a works council has a significantly positive influence on the percentage of fixed-term employees in East and West German firms. The estimates suggest that works councils try to protect insiders by accepting new employees only if these recently hired people cannot be used by management to threaten the incumbent workforce in the sense that the latter must fear expropriation of their quasi-rents, that is, in the case of a dismissal.

Looking at the prevalence of 'marginal' jobs, a different picture emerges: among the West German firms with a works council, 45 per cent have marginal employees while in firms without a works council the respective share is 65 per cent (in the former firms, 5 per cent of all employees are in marginal jobs, while in the latter it is 22 per cent). In East German firms the differences are less pronounced, but still significant: 30 per cent of the firms with a works council and 35 per cent of those without such plant-level interest representation have marginal employees; the respective shares are 2 per cent in the former and 7 per cent in the latter firms. Even after controlling for other factors, it appears that the presence of a works council has a negative and statistically significant influence on the percentage of marginal employees (for similar findings, see Boockmann and Hagen 2001).

5.3.2.4. *High performance work systems*
Empirical evidence on high performance work systems in Germany is still very rare. One study that analyses the relationship between works councils and high performance work practices on the one hand and their both separate and joint influence on firm performance on the other hand is Frick (2002). This study finds that it is not the presence of a works council per se that influences the adoption of high performance work practices[19] but its 'level of activities' (measured by the number of firm-level agreements concluded during the last 3 years) and the 'type' of the works council as viewed by the management of the firm. Frick reports that, in firms with an 'antagonistic' works council, the number of high performance work practices is higher than in otherwise similar firms that have either a 'disinterested' or even an 'excluded' works council. Surprisingly, firms that do not have a works council adopted a larger number of high performance work practices than those with such representation.

Looking at the performance effects of such practices, it becomes apparent why works councils are often rather sceptical as to their consequences for employees: other things being equal, the adoption of the above-mentioned practices increases expected, as well as actually realized, firm performance (measured by changes in product demand, in sales, and in profitability), but at the same time it reduces the demand for labour. This means that firms do indeed benefit from such practices—but at the expense of workers.

5.3.2.5. *'Disadvantaged' employees*
According to the now amended German Handicapped Act of 1974, public and private employers with more than twenty jobs must have 5 per cent of severely disabled people among their staff. Otherwise they have to pay a monthly compensation of about 200 DM for each quota position they have failed to fill with a severely disabled person. One task of the works councils is to observe whether their employer fulfils his legal duties. According to both the Handicapped Act and

the Works Constitution Act, the workers' representatives are obliged to foster the integration of older and/or disabled employees. On the one hand, they have far-reaching consultation rights in the case of dismissals. According to Sections 15–22 of the Handicapped Act, public and private employees not only have to apply to a special Government office for permission to dismiss a severely disabled person, but they also have to consult the works council prior to the application. On the other hand, works councils should closely cooperate with the employer and the local labour office to foster the recruitment of disabled people. If the employer, nevertheless, decides to dismiss a disabled employee, the works council is obliged to participate in the respective public hearing.

There is broad empirical evidence that firms with a works council have a significantly higher percentage of disabled employees than firms where no such worker representation exists (Sadowski and Frick 1990, 1992; Frick 1992, 1994; Frick and Sadowski 1995). Given the above-mentioned legal restraints, it is surprising that the risk of dismissal for a severely disabled person is not very much less than that for a non-disabled employee. Approximately 80 per cent of employment relationships are terminated and only 20 per cent are continued when the procedures stipulated by the Handicapped Act are followed. Moreover, nullification contracts based on the mutual consent of the parties often serve as functional equivalents to dismissals. An employer's application is usually followed by a formal procedure, in which the employer, the employee, a representative of the local labour office, a member of the works council, and a spokesperson for the disabled person present their respective points of view. Following the oral presentation and after an appreciation of the parties' written statements, the public authority decides whether a continuation of the specific employment relationship is possible. The attitude of the works council can be interpreted as an 'early signal' to the employer of how the employees view the dismissal decision. No reaction at all or explicit approval may indicate that the employees do not view the dismissal decision as an offence against their 'reciprocity expectations'. The expression of misgivings or even a formal contradiction, however, may mean that the employees interpret the dismissal decision as a 'violation of legitimate norms'.

Overall, the works councils are usually supportive of the employer's point of view. In more than 70 per cent of all applications the works council either explicitly approves the employer's decision or keeps silent. In only 13 per cent the works councils express their misgivings (i.e. they consider the dismissal as socially unacceptable or criticize that no social compensation plan has yet been designed), and in 16 per cent they lodge a formal contradiction (arguing that the employer's arguments are not valid, that other employment opportunities within the firm exist, etc.).[20] The seemingly high degree of consensus between employers and works councils is at least to some degree a statistical artefact, because in more than 55 per cent of all cases the employees themselves have no objections against the dismissal either. If these cases are excluded, the percentage of applications for dismissal in which the works councils lodged objections increases from 29 per cent to more than 41 per cent. If the application is based on operational reasons—such as plant closing, lack of demand, technical reorganization—the percentage of objections is 49 per cent. In the case of personal misconduct of the employee (such as unsatisfactory performance, unjustified absence from work, violation of safety regulations), the respective share is 39 per cent only.

As reported in Frick and Sadowski (1995) the attitude of the works council is one of the most important factors influencing the outcome of the procedure. In cases where the works council supports the employer's point of view, either by explicit approval or by silence, the percentage of continued employment relationships is significantly lower (15 and 37 per cent) than in those cases where the works council either expresses its misgivings or formally contradicts the employer's arguments (27 and 48 per cent, respectively). The main reason for the considerable difference between operational and personal reasons (22 as opposed to 41 per cent) is that in the former case the discretion of the Government office is usually severely restricted.[21]

Thus, works councils do make an unambiguous difference in favour of the employment of disabled people. Although usually supportive of the employer's position, works councils above all tend to support those people who became disabled while working for their current employer. The works council's position significantly increases a disabled person's chance of reinstatement. Moreover, works councils considerably reduce the recruitment of disabled outsiders, particularly in large firms.[22] Here, works councils fall strikingly short of their legal and public policy task to foster the employment of disadvantaged groups of workers. Apparently, the associated costs of 'norm-violation' are rather low compared to the importance of 'solidarity' with health-impaired insiders.

5.4. **Summary and Future Prospects**

Our analysis suggests that the German system of corporate governance not only differs from the ones that prevail in the Anglo-Saxon
world by its predominance of banks and insurance companies as
large shareholders, but also due to the existence of legally mandated
works councils and worker representation on company boards. While
the enactment of the KonTraG reduces the power of banks and insurance companies, they remain dominant and powerful shareholders.
Moreover, the enactment of the amended Works Constitution Act will
certainly increase the powers of works councils in small and medium
enterprises. These recent changes in the institutional environment
clearly affect the distribution of property rights and will therefore
change the relationships between the stakeholders. Since these
changes affect a number of institutions, which are embedded in a
highly complex framework, it is far from clear who is going to benefit at the expense of whom.

International capital markets exert increasing pressures on German
corporate law. Recently, a commission established by the Federal
Government, and chaired by Theodor Baums, published its assessment of the German corporate governance system.[23] The final report
contains around 150 different proposals aimed at maintaining a
framework that is attractive for companies and investors alike. Many
of the proposals have the goal of improving the performance of
supervisory boards and of establishing transparency standards which
will not only increase management responsibilities but also provide
additional information for stockholders.

These recommendations will not be enshrined in law. The only
requirement publicly traded companies will have to fulfil is either to
state in their annual reports that they are observing the code or to
explain why they do not follow the recommendations. The underlying
assumption is that the capital market will value both types of behaviour.
Whether this is 'wishful thinking' or not remains to be seen. Finally, the
code does not contain any recommendations regarding the market for
corporate control—the most effective instrument to discipline managers. This problem, however, is not a 'typical' German one and thus is
not independent from what other countries in the European Union are
doing. As in the prisoner's dilemma, no country in continental Europe
has an incentive to be the first to reduce the barriers to (hostile)
takeovers by foreign companies or investors, given the predictable
consequences for the behaviour of utility-maximizing managers.

NOTES

1. Referring specifically to profit-oriented firms in the legal form of corporations, Schmidt (1997: 4) defines the term 'corporate governance' as 'the totality of institutional and organizational mechanisms, and the corresponding decision-making, intervention, and control rights, which serve to resolve conflicts of interest between the various groups which have a stake in a firm and which, either in isolation or in their interaction, determine how important decisions are taken in a firm, and ultimately also determine which decisions are taken'. The most important factors and mechanisms to be looked at are the law, the structure of the financial sector, the situation on input and output markets, and the distribution of information, abilities, and other resources or power bases.
2. For a general overview, see Beyer (1996), Sabel (1996), Jürgens, Naumann, and Rupp (2000), and Windolf (1994); for a selective survey of the literature see Grieger (2001).
3. See also Thonet and Poensgen (1989) who find significantly lower returns on equity for owner-controlled than for manager-controlled quoted stock corporations. However, since information on ownership structures was available only for about 90 of the 300 firms in their sample, their estimates are questionable.
4. The European Union has forced the German government to withdraw its voting restrictions from Volkswagen which are still based on the Volkswagen Privatization Act of 1960. There is an upper limit to the fraction of total voting stock a bank can represent at the annual meeting, including proxy votes from small shareholders. To avoid an unfriendly takeover, Ferdinand Piech, the CEO of Volkswagen, has recently tried to build an alliance with other firms through cross-holding activities.
5. Some other studies use samples of listed AGs where the firms are first classified as either being influenced by banks or not. Perlitz and Seger (1994) find that the profitability of firms subject to bank influence was lower than the profitability of the firms in their comparison group. However, their results have been criticized for a number of reasons (see Lindner-Lehmann and Neuberger 1995). A similar approach has been taken by Chirinko and Elston (1996). Using dichotomous variables indicating the extent of blockholding, they analyse data on 300 stock corporations over the period 1965–90. Due to incomplete information on ownership structures, they cannot take full advantage of the panel characteristics of their data. Moreover, like Perlitz and Seger (1994), they also cannot distinguish between the different channels of bank influence (like equity ownership, proxy votes, supervisory board membership, and loans).
6. For an overview of recent studies see Addison, Schnabel, and Wagner (1999, 2001). Studies published prior to 1997 are summarized by Frick (1997*a, b*).

7. For a further elaboration of this and similar arguments pertaining to the production and sharing of information, see Dilger (2002).
8. This 'network of specific investments which cannot be replicated by the market' (Zingales 1998: 498) constitutes the economic core of a firm. This is certainly different from a 'nexus of contracts' as described by Jensen and Meckling (1976). Sadowski, Junkes, and Lindenthal (2001) therefore argue that, in distributional conflicts about contractually unprotected rents, it is naive to expect an efficient voluntary agreement about the firm's constitution. Quoting Shleifer and Vishny (1997), they go on to argue that economic theory usually admits that a certain legal protection is necessary for outside investors while no such protection is granted to inside investors (see also Hart 1995).
9. For a detailed evaluation of the arguments presented in the discussion, see Dilger, Frick, and Speckbacher (1999) and Frick, Speckbacher, and Wentges (1999).
10. For further arguments in favour of mandating codetermination, see Levine (1989, 1991, 1992, 1993, 1995) and Levine and Tyson (1990).
11. Concentrating on firm performance in the sense of output, profits, value added, etc. leads to a rather conservative estimate of the influence of works councils, because investments in intangible assets, such as 'organizational capital', are not taken into account.
12. For an empirical analysis of the influence of works councils on initial training see Sadowski, Backes-Gellner, and Frick (1995) and Backes-Gellner, Frick, and Sadowski (1997). For a similar analysis of further training, see Gerlach and Jirjahn (2001).
13. Using the IAB firm panel and the Hanover panel respectively, Kohaut and Bellmann (1997), Schnabel and Wagner (1996), and Bellmann, Kohaut, and Schnabel (1999) try to identify the determinants of firms' membership in an employer association. This membership, in turn, obliges the firm to apply the conditions stipulated by the collective agreements concluded by their association. Moreover, Gerlach, Lehmann, and Meyer (1998) study the reasons why firms give up membership in an employers' association. In this case, the terms of all collective agreements concluded after the firm has departed have to be applied for two further years and only thereafter is the firm free to set pay scales as it—and its employees—wish. Meyer (1995a) shows that firms belonging to an employers' association do not pay higher wages than those which had recently left or had never been a member.
14. The data for these results is the first wave of the IAB firm panel in 1993. The number of firms is 4,300. Using a rather small and non-representative sample of 168 manufacturing firms, Meyer (1995b) reports similar findings.
15. Comparing the estimates for public and private sector firms, it appears that firm characteristics, such as size, personnel structure, technical

equipment, are rather weak predictors of per-capita wages in the private sector (Bellmann and Kohaut 1997, 1999).

16. In a second estimate based on a smaller sample of firms ($n = 604$ instead of $n = 861$) Jirjahn and Klodt (1998, 1999) also show that product market competition tends to reduce wages while membership in an employers' association (with the resulting obligation to pay wage rates that employers and union have agreed upon) does not influence per-capita wages.

17. This took place in 1997 with 711 participating firms.

18. A number of studies look at the (possible) determinants of pay systems (Carstensen, Gerlach, and Hübler 1995*a, b*; Heywood, Hübler, and Jirjahn 1998; Jirjahn 1998). Although pay systems are likely to influence pay levels (Lazear 2000), these studies will not be discussed here. Moreover, Schnabel and Wagner (1999) as well as Bellmann and Frick (1999) and Frick (2000) not only isolate the determinants of the existence of a firm-operated pension plan, but also look at the factors influencing the adoption of a 'cafeteria system' (a 'bundle' of benefits out of which utility-maximizing employees can choose up to a certain cash equivalent).

19. High performance work systems are defined as the reduction in hierarchy levels, the delegation of decision-making, the introduction of team work, the introduction of profit-centres, and the adoption of flexible working time arrangements.

20. In the case of all employees the latter two percentage shares are 6 and 8 per cent, respectively. This shows that works councils are more in opposition to the dismissal of severely disabled employees (Höland 1985: 98).

21. In cases where no works council exists, the percentage shares of continued employment relationships are very similar to the ones that occur if the interest representation supports the employer's decision (Sadowski and Frick 1992: 127–135).

22. The empirical evidence is documented in detail in Frick and Sadowski (1995: 62–65).

23. The report is available at www.otto-schmidt.de/corporate-governance.htm.

6

Corporate Governance and Labour Management in the Netherlands: Getting the Best of Both Worlds?

ERIK POUTSMA AND GEERT BRAAM

6.1. Introduction

The Dutch system of corporate governance is an interesting combination of the Anglo-Saxon market–outsider system and the German relational–insider system. On the one hand, there is emphasis on the importance of shareholder value. The firm has to act in the interest of the shareholders, and this implies a focus on short-term financial performance, flexible work, and performance-related labour management. On the other hand, low labour mobility and long job tenure, a well-established system of collective agreements, and strong protections against dismissal indicate that the firm also has to take account of the interests of other parties such as labour. Various phenomena, however, suggest that the degree and locus of power and decision-making is changing within this hybrid Dutch system. For instance, the works council in the major steel producer in the Netherlands has recently experienced a decline in influence on labour matters due to the change in corporate control arising from a merger with an English steel producer. Traditional systems of governance are being destabilized and new arrangements are emerging (Van Kersbergen and Van Waarden 2001: 10). The 'shifts in governance' suggest that a 'western wind' is blowing, that is, that an 'Anglo-Saxonization' of corporate governance and labour management is taking place. In this chapter we attempt to assess the extent and importance of these changes in the Netherlands.

Section 6.2 describes the framework of the research and the historical background and business structure of the Netherlands. Section 6.3 outlines the changes in financial structure and corporate governance that are taking place in the Netherlands and shows how labour management changes are linked to these shifts. In Section 6.4 we assess the proposition that 'Anglo-Saxonization' of corporate governance is affecting labour management in the Netherlands. Section 6.5 concludes.

6.2. The Dutch Context

6.2.1. *'Varieties of capitalism'*

Firms seek to coordinate aspects of their internal and external environments, and successful coordination of these appears to be a prerequisite of business success. Following Hall and Soskice (2001*b*), we believe that different varieties of capitalism solve these coordination problems in different ways. To compare national political economies, Hall and Soskice specified five spheres of coordination. These are corporate governance, inter-firm relations, industrial relations, vocational training and education, and employee relations. Corporate governance concerns the relationships with shareholders, banks, and other financial institutions. Within this context we define corporate governance models as institutional arrangements that are designed to control the relationships between stakeholders and which affect the actions of the different stakeholders (see Gelauff and den Broeder 1996; Goodijk 2001). Inter-firm relations refer to the relationships with other firms, suppliers, and clients to secure stable demand, supply, and access to technology. Industrial relations is where firms face the problem of bargaining over wages and related costs with representative bodies, possibly in coordination with other employers. Vocational training is about how firms secure a workforce with suitable skills. Employee relations is about ensuring that employees have the requisite competencies and ensuring that employees cooperate with management and each other so as to advance the objectives of the firm.

Based on the ways in which firms resolve these coordination issues, Hall and Soskice (2001*b*: 8) drew a core distinction between two types of political economies: liberal market economies (LME) and coordinated market economies (CME). Drawing on this perspective, three main questions for this contribution can be formulated. One, to what extent can the Netherlands be described as either a CME or an LME, or does it occupy a position between the two? Two, have there been any recent changes in these five spheres of coordination that would shift the position of the Netherlands in relation to this distinction? Three, are changes in the sphere of corporate governance clearly linked to changes in industrial relations, vocational training and education, and employee relations? Prior to addressing these questions, we first describe the historical background and business structure of the Netherlands.

6.2.2. *Historical background: the corporatist tradition*

The Netherlands is often seen as good example of a corporatist economy, with the extent of corporatist institutions only slightly less developed than in the Scandinavian countries and Austria. The Dutch economy is still regarded as one of the most coordinated economies in the western world (Soskice 1999; Slomp 2001). The Dutch system emphasizes concertation, cooperation, and consent in the interactions between economic and political actors. Based on the dominant view since the Second World War that labour and capital should develop harmonious relationships at sector level, a variety of issues have been delegated to institutions and business, such as stock market regulation, regulation of wages and working conditions, pensions and social security, and collective dismissals. Self-regulation mechanisms provided sufficient flexibility to facilitate adjustments in response to new challenges. For decades this set of institutional arrangements made for good economic performance and became known as the 'Polder Model' or the 'Dutch Miracle' (Visser and Hemerijck 1997; Delsen 2002).

The consequence of this 'path-dependent' history is that there are institutional complementarities between finance and corporate governance, industrial relations, vocational training, and employee relations of the typical type associated with CMEs. In the CME of the Netherlands, access to finance is not entirely dependent on publicly available financial data or current returns. Dense networks, cross-shareholdings, and securities regulation have been developed to ensure that access is provided and that relationships are stable over the long term. In this 'relational–insider' model, we expect to find company financial structures where there is more emphasis on internal funding and debt financing than in outsider economies. Equity funding is less developed. The focus on the longer-term and the relative lack of emphasis on equity finance suggest that labour management will be more loosely coupled to shareholder interests than in market–outsider countries.

The principle of concertation has influenced industrial relations and their outcomes. Collective labour agreements are still the main vehicle establishing the terms of employment. Despite an expressed intention to deregulate and decentralize, the government still supports this centralized instrument by maintaining the extension principle, that is, that collective labour agreements cover an entire sector or category of personnel, whether they are union members or not. At sector level various institutions that are jointly controlled by trade unions and employers' federations have been established. Examples include pension funds, training institutes, and institutes to promote health care and good working conditions. Labour management by firms is therefore constrained by institutionalized employee influence. The institutional cooperation between management and labour facilitates employment security and human capital development. Managements pursue business strategies that depend on workers with firm/industry-specific skills and high levels of commitment. These are secured by offering workers long-term employment, industry-based wages, and protective works councils. Vocational training schemes, supported by an industrial relations system that discourages poaching, provide high levels of industry-specific skills. Later in the chapter we will discuss recent changes to this pattern of institutional complementarities. Before doing so, we highlight important features of business structure in the Netherlands.

6.2.3. *Business structure in the Netherlands*

Compared with other countries in Europe, the Netherlands belongs to the smaller coordinated market economies. It has a pronounced dualist business structure, with a very small number of large companies accounting for about 44 per cent of employment in private business, and a large number of small and medium-sized businesses that on average are a bit larger in size than in the other small economies like Denmark and Austria.

Although the Netherlands has a long history of companies with publicly traded shares, the number of companies listed on the stock exchange is fairly small (see Table 6.1). However, several major multinationals such as Shell, Unilever, and Philips are listed on it, and they dominate the listed sector in the Netherlands. The largest company quoted on the Euronext Amsterdam (Shell) accounts for 22 per cent of total market capitalization. The combined market capitalization of the five biggest companies together is 55 per cent of the total market.

Table 6.1. *Companies listed on Euronext, Amsterdam, by sector, 2001*

Sector	Number	% of market (by capitalization)
Finance	12	28.26
Oil	2	22.73
Trade	23	7.63
Electronics (for industry)	58	15.97
Electronics (hardware)	15	9.36
Information, telecommunications, and media	42	12.91
Services and transport	20	3.14
Total	172	100.00

Source: Euronext Amsterdam (2001).

The value of the twenty-five largest companies is more than 90 per cent of total market capitalization. A second characteristic of the Dutch stock exchange is the important position of financial institutions. Together they account for nearly 30 per cent of the stock market by value.

The structure of the Dutch economy has two important implications for our analysis and interpretation of the linkages between finance providers, governance, and labour. First, the vast majority of companies are small private family companies where the debate on corporate governance and the role of labour is not anything like as relevant as in publicly held, listed companies. Labour management in these small and medium-sized companies is largely dependent on sector institutional arrangements, such as collective agreements and vocational training systems. This limits the opportunities for firms to pursue labour strategies and practices that are typically associated with shareholder value.

Second, the dominance of multinational enterprises on the stock exchange has a substantial impact on corporate governance and labour management. These Anglo-Saxon-oriented multinationals shift the locus of decision-making to higher levels than that of national company level. Parent company policies in substantive areas such as pay, employee involvement, and training are transmitted to subsidiaries through explicit, formal, routinized systems that also permit highly standardized dissemination (Veersma 1995; Ferner 2000). As a consequence, labour management tends to develop towards an LME type of management. This may diminish the importance of local coalitions between management and labour and may conflict with other institutions. Starting with this context, we now link shifts in finance, ownership structure, and corporate governance with changes in labour management.

6.3. Ownership Structure, Corporate Governance, and Labour Management

6.3.1. *Ownership structure*

Corporate governance analysis typically distinguishes between 'equity' and 'credit' countries. In the 'equity' countries, ownership is seen to be the primary source of control rights, and shareholders are considered to be the owners of the firm. Consequently, the firm has to act primarily in the interest of the shareholders. The emphasis on 'shareholder value' in these economies embodies a narrow financial conception of the firm. In the 'credit' countries, by contrast, a social institutional conception is dominant. The firm is seen as an independent legal entity with a social presence and purpose. According to this conception of the firm, companies have to take account of all interested parties, including labour and other financial institutions besides shareholders.

The differences between the two approaches are important for the system of corporate governance. For instance, in the 'equity' countries equity ownership is dispersed. The shareholders have limited access to internal information. Usually, no single investor has majority or effective control of a firm. This is said to give rise to a governance problem in that owners face high costs in preventing management opportunism and self-enrichment, while the benefits of intervention are public goods. To counter this, in market–outsider systems there will be pressure for full information disclosure and protection of minority investors. In the 'credit' countries financial institutions and institutional investors hold larger blocks of shares. These large shareholders are better organized than private shareholders. We expect, therefore, that they will exert pressure privately to gain control and to obtain more detailed information than is generally available to the public or minority shareholders. As a consequence, the differences in ownership structure have important consequences for the different interpretations given to corporate governance. Furthermore, the legal system appears to be strongly associated with ownership structure and practices. 'Equity' countries like the United Kingdom have a legal system that relies upon a limited amount of

Table 6.2. *International comparison of equity markets and governance systems*

	UK	The Netherlands	Germany	France
Equity market (size indicators)				
Listed domestic firms	2,399	214	741	784
Market capitalization of listed domestic firms (euros)	897	227	414	370
Domestic listed firms/ million people (1999)	45.2	14.7	9.0	13.4
Ratio of debt to debt plus equity (1994)	0.20	0.26	0.34	0.30
Voting power concentration				
Largest voting block (median)	9.9	18.2	52.1	20.0
Largest voting block (mean)	14.4	26.9	49.1	29.4

Source: Alexander and Nobes (2001); Gugler (2001).

statute law. In such a 'common law' system, the court interprets the law and builds up an extensive system of case law to supplement the statutes. Countries like Germany and France have a system of law that is based on Roman law.

Where should the Netherlands be located in relation to this two-system model? Some characteristics shown in Table 6.2 suggest that it is reasonable to place the country with the United Kingdom in the 'shareholder' group. However, the Dutch legal system conforms more to the codified system of law. With respect to the concentration of voting power, the Netherlands occupies a middle position, so the country can be characterized as an interesting mix between the liberal capital market system (the Anglo-Saxon model) and the coordinated or statist systems (the German and French models). Other characteristics that place the Netherlands in a middle position between liberal and coordinated market economies are the important role of large financial institutions in corporate ownership, the widespread use of takeover defences, limits on shareholder influence, and the increasing use of employee financial participation. It is clear, then, that the Dutch system incorporates elements of both the Germanic and Anglo-Saxon systems.

6.3.2. *Large shareholders (financial institutions) and takeover defences*

In the Netherlands, financial institutions are the dominant group of shareholders. They can have various relationships with companies. On the one hand, they provide loan capital to firms. This has a direct disciplinary effect on managers given that managers seek to avoid postponement of debt servicing payment or liquidation. These disciplinary effects are thought to have a positive effect on the firm's performance (McConnell and Servaes 1995). On the other hand, they can also conspire with a firm's management to realize their specific interests given that, as large shareholders, they have considerable voting power. In the Netherlands, financial institutions such as insurance companies, mutual funds, and pension funds, typically have fairly dispersed ownership of companies (between 5 and 20 per cent). They may participate in the board of directors and the supervisory board. Moreover, financial institutions also provide other financial and advisory services to companies. Because of this diversity of relationships, financial institutions have the motivation and opportunity to control and discipline companies. Recent research into the influence of financial institutions on corporate performance has found a negative relationship between the two, suggesting that financial institutions 'conspire' with management (De Jong *et al.* 2001*b*). The current system of governance favours financial institutions over other shareholders.

Takeover defences are aimed at preventing hostile purchases. Table 6.3 suggests that Dutch companies make a great deal of use of takeover

Table 6.3. *Use of takeover defences by non-financial companies on Euronext Amsterdam*

Takeover defence	Explanation	% of companies using it
Priority shares	Holders have specific rights such as to make binding nominations to the supervisory board	45
Preference shares	Holders have preferential rights over ordinary shareholders in takeovers or liquidation	56
Share certifications	A company-associated foundation owns the shares and issues certificates Holders of certificates receive dividends but the foundation holds the voting rights	34
Two-tier board	Supervisory board has to approve important resolutions of the management board	65

Source: Commissie Corporate Governance (1997).

defences such as priority shares, preference shares, and share certifications (Voogd 1989; Van der Hoeven 1995; Van Kampen and Van de Kraats 1995; Kabir, Cantrijn, and Jeunink 1997; De Jong 2001b). Research shows that in the Netherlands the negative use of takeover defences is correlated with a firm's performance (Kabir, Cantrijn, and Jeunink 1997; Van der Goot and Roosenboom 2001). The combination of large shareholders and the use of takeover defences is negatively correlated with an increase in shareholder value, suggesting that limiting the control exercised by minority shareholders has a negative influence on company performance (De Jong *et al.* 2001).

6.3.3. *The supervisory board: the current debate over the management of large corporations*

In 1972, the *Structuurwet* (Two-Tier Act) made a two-tier board structure compulsory for large companies in the Netherlands. Under this regime, which reflects corporatist influences on the development of institutions and regulation, the institutions of governance in large companies are fixed by statute. These institutions comprise a board of directors (executives only), a board of supervisory directors, the shareholders' meeting, and the works council. Large companies are defined as legal entities that have issued capital plus reserves of at least €27 million, a works council by virtue of other statutory obligations, and at least 100 employees in the Netherlands. The thinking behind this legislation was that dispersed shareholders cannot fully supervise large companies via the shareholders' meeting.

The supervisory boards were accorded important powers by the Two-Tier Act. One, they have to approve major resolutions of the board of directors, such as those concerning large investments or divestments, important strategic decisions, dismissal of a substantial number of employees, or far-reaching changes in their working conditions. Two, the board of supervisory directors is charged with the appointment and dismissal of the board of directors. Three, the board of supervisory directors has to accept the annual accounts and approve the dividend to be paid to the shareholders. In taking these decisions, the board of supervisory directors is required to act independently of the executive board of directors. In line with the consensual and corporatist tradition of the Netherlands, the supervisory board is required to consider the interests of all stakeholders, including shareholders, management, and employees. To date, there has not been a strong set of sanctions to enforce this approach. Recently, however, the appointment of a Commission for Corporate Governance (Commissie Corporate Governance (or *Commissie Tabaksblad*)) puts the requirements of the Act on a stronger footing.

It is clear that shareholders are kept at a distance from management decision-making in this two-tier system. Once a year, at the general meeting of shareholders, the shareholders have the power to approve the annual accounts, but the board of supervisory directors adopts this important document in advance. Shareholders are permitted only to approve or reject resolutions: they cannot file amendments to them. Furthermore, they cannot directly determine the appointment of the members of the executive board of directors.

Listing on the Amsterdam Stock Exchange does not automatically mean that companies are subject to the two-tier regime. It is estimated that about two-thirds of listed companies apply two-tier arrangements. Companies listed on the Amsterdam Stock Exchange will usually meet most of the conditions for the two-tier regime. However, if *more than half of the total employees* of a company work abroad, though the corporation is based in the Netherlands, the two-tier scheme does not apply. For example, Philips, a company that has approximately 80 per cent of its employees working abroad and whose 'holding' is based in Amsterdam, is not subject to the two-tier regime. The same applies to large multinational corporations that were originally Dutch, such as Heineken and Akzo Nobel. In these multinationals only the operating companies carrying out activities in the Netherlands fall under the two-tier regime. Yet, in these circumstances the applicable regime is a weakened version. Remarkably, a number of companies that meet the criterion of 'foreign-ness' still apply the two-tier regime voluntarily. The reasons for voluntary use include a concern to maintain Dutch characteristics, employee objections to abolition of two-tier arrangements, and protection against hostile takeovers. It is estimated that about 15 per cent of companies with a two-tier board do so voluntarily (Van het Kaar 1995).

The board of supervisory directors appoints its members itself, by means of co-option. However, the general meeting of shareholders and the works council both have the right to nominate candidates for appointment, and these two bodies also have the right to object to proposed appointments. A supervisory director is appointed for 4 years and can be reappointed up to his or her 72nd birthday. Members of the supervisory boards of large corporations appear to be members of an 'old boys' network', and this system is subject to increasing criticism.

In June 1997, the Peters Committee (the Corporate Governance Committee), established by the Amsterdam Stock Exchange authorities, made some forty recommendations to improve corporate governance in large companies. With respect to the two-tier system, the Peters Committee noted a number of shortcomings such as a lack of transparency with regard to the functioning and the composition of the board of supervisory directors. The Peters Committee was a 'private' committee that aimed to bring about voluntary changes in corporate governance. However, De Jong *et al.* (2001*a*) noted no significant changes in the regimes of large corporations since the publication of the report.

It is against this background that the Dutch government asked the Social and Economic Council (SER) in March 2000 for advice on this issue. Should the current two-tier system be maintained, reformed, or completely abolished? The Social and Economic Council's view was that the two-tier system serves a useful purpose and should in essence be maintained. However, several reforms were necessary, especially relating to the transparency of management, and the accountability and integrity of members of the board of supervisory directors. Most criticism was focused on the co-option system of appointment. In the new arrangements proposed by the SER, the final say on appointments to the board of supervisory directors should be in the hands of the general meeting of shareholders. However, the SER did not simply shift the power of appointment from the board to the general meeting of shareholders. The intention is that the board of supervisory directors makes a binding nomination to the general meeting of shareholders for the appointment or reappointment of its members. The nomination will be binding to the extent that only a two-thirds majority of the votes of the shareholders present (representing at least one-third of the total shareholders' capital) can overturn nominations to the board of supervisory directors. Furthermore, no more than one-third of the number of seats on the board of supervisory directors can be held by persons nominated by the works council. These two changes form the core of the new appointments procedure. In this way, both capital and labour appear to influence the composition of the supervisory board.

However, it is a moot question as to whether shareholders have got, or will be getting, sufficient influence as a result of the Social and Economic Council's proposal. Although formally given the right of appointment, some believe that the requirement to achieve two-thirds of the votes to overturn a nomination gives the shareholders less influence than is desirable. Moreover, it is also questionable whether those works councils that currently do not make much use of their right of nomination would be able to submit sufficiently substantial and suitable candidates for appointment to the board of supervisory directors in the new system. Although the government decided in 2001 that the changes proposed by the SER have to be incorporated into law, at the time of writing no law has yet been passed.

To improve the effectiveness of corporate governance, a new Corporate Governance Committee, known as Commissie Tabaksblad, was established in March 2003. Although the Netherlands had acquired a code of practice on corporate governance as a result of the Peters Committee, it had become clear that certain aspects of the code were no longer strictly observed, mainly because compliance had never been consistently or systematically enforced. Commissie Tabaksblad revised the corporate governance code of conduct in July 2003 drawing on the Peters recommendations and perceived best practice. The new code focuses on the bodies responsible for decision-making and supervision as well as procedures for information disclosure and corporate reporting. For instance, the code requires that the management board declare in the annual report that internal risk management and control systems are adequate and effective. An internal audit committee has to supervise risk management and disclosure of information. An independent supervisory board is required to supervise the management board and the general affairs and activities of the company. Management board decisions that are so far-reaching that they affect the core identity of the company now require the approval of the general meeting of shareholders.

The new code will be placed on a legal footing in January 2004 based on the now common 'comply or explain' principle. Companies will be required to report on their corporate governance policy in a chapter of the annual report. Non-compliance has to be explained in a clear and comprehensible fashion. The shareholders' meeting is required to approve corporate governance policy. In doing so it is assisted by the Netherlands Authority for Financial Markets, which verifies that a corporate governance chapter and a compliance statement have been produced and that they are consistent with each other.

6.3.4. *The influence of works councils*

Information and consultation procedures are well established in the Netherlands, mainly as a result of the Works Council Act of 1950

(Wet op de Ondernemingsraden (WOR)). This affords works councils a strong position compared with that in most other European countries. It is mandatory for companies with fifty or more employees to establish a works council. The works council has the right to information on most labour management issues. It has the right to give advice on strategic matters (like mergers) and has the right of approval for most decisions that concern personnel matters (for instance, reorganizations and social plans). Works councils have the right to nominate members of the supervisory board.

Some important amendments were made to the Works Councils Act in 1998. The most important was that works council and employers can develop company agreements, thereby enabling negotiations on the terms of employment at company level. Since then there is some evidence of specific company agreements, mainly focusing on working time arrangements. However, in only about 10 per cent of companies is there a collective labour agreement negotiated by the works council alone (Van het Kaar and Looise 1999: 174). The Supreme Court has restricted the scope of the Works Council Act (as amended) somewhat by stating that the primary terms of employment are not covered by the Works Council Act. This means that primary terms of employment are mainly covered by collective agreements with trade unions (and of course legislative constraints).

6.3.4.1. *The role of works councils in the supervisory board*
Works council nominations generally occur in companies where there is an agreement between the board of supervisory directors and the works council to nominate one or two seats on the board of supervisory directors. These directors are called 'confidential directors', 'social directors' or 'employee directors'. Van het Kaar's survey of works councils in two-tier companies found that there are one or two employee directors in 64 per cent of cases (Van het Kaar 1995). In practice, neither the general meeting of shareholders nor the works council makes much use of the right to make nominations. With regard to the shareholders, this hardly ever occurs, while only one-third of eligible works councils actually nominate candidates for seats on the board of supervisory directors (Van den Tillaart 1999). In most cases the supervisory board itself proposes candidates for the role of social or employee director, even in cases where the works council does not formally or actually request one.

The reasons why works councils make relatively little use of their rights of nomination and objection include insufficient knowledge of the membership of the board of supervisory directors, insufficient knowledge of the profile that is expected of a candidate, and inadequate familiarity with the activities of the boards of supervisory directors.

The right to make nominations does not guarantee the influence of works councils. This is because it is an obligation that the nominated person does *not* at any time hold a seat on the board of supervisory directors *on behalf of* the works council. A member of the board of supervisory directors has to be independent and must supervise the policy of the board of directors and the well-being of the company in its entirety, taking into account *all* interests not just those of employees. There are seldom any 'deals' or guidelines agreed between supervisory directors and works councils because this would violate the independence of the board member. Van het Kaar's survey (1995) indicates that agreements between works councils and employee directors are significantly related to conflict situations at the time of nomination. They arise where the works council had objections to the nomination and, as a result, guidelines were issued to govern contact between the board member and the works council.

Works councils are also not well informed about issues in the supervisory board. Van het Kaar (1995) found that in 73 per cent of cases works councils are never informed about issues by the supervisory board. Even where there are confidential directors on the supervisory board this percentage is only slightly lower. Disclosure of information to the works council comes mainly from the board of directors. Van het Kaar (1995) found that about half of works councils meet the director mainly at formal meetings with the board of directors, held under the auspices of obligations under the Works Council Act.

In general, the assessment by works councils of the role and functioning of the confidential director is slightly more positive than negative. Those works councils that consider themselves as influential, those where the membership is more unionized, and those where the council consists of higher-level staff members, are the most positive about the role of the confidential director (Van het Kaar 1995).

6.3.4.2. *Company policy and labour management*
A survey among more than 600 works councils in 1999 (Van den Tillaart 1999) suggested that the influence of the works council on company policies is limited. The survey found that 12 per cent of the works councils assessed their influence as practically none, 62 per cent judged that they had some minor influence, 25 per cent assessed their

influence as great, and only 1 per cent stated that they had very great influence. There do not seem to be clear determinants of these assessments: only company size was related to the influence of the works councils in this study. In companies with more than one thousand employees the proportion of works councils that reported that they had great or very great influence increased to 43 per cent.

The study indicates that works councils in large companies appear to be more able to exert some influence on management and supervisory boards. More influence is exerted with management staff than with the supervisory board. Table 6.4 shows that works councils have more regular meetings with management and staff in the largest companies. It also shows that in larger companies works councils influence the nomination of board members more often than in smaller companies. They also have more opportunities to discuss problems in meetings with management and supervisory board together.

Table 6.4. *Indicators of the influence of works councils*

Percentage of works council	Size of company (employees)					
	1–99	100–199	200–499	500–999	1000+	All
Supervisory board						
Receives management decisions submitted to supervisory board	13	10	10	8	18	12
Receives minutes of supervisory board	17	11	10	11	10	12
Influences nominations to supervisory board	14	14	24	38	40	23
Informal contacts with the supervisory board	15	11	18	25	24	17
Regular meetings with supervisory board and management on specific problems	13	16	23	33	30	21
Management staff						
Regular meetings with personnel department	41	45	71	76	85	60
Regular meetings with other management staff	38	33	43	58	68	44
Regular working conferences with management	30	26	37	47	59	36

Notes: Data obtained from works council secretaries.

Source: Adapted from Van den Tillaart (1999).

Looise and Drucker (2000) assess the influence of works councils on company policies based on surveys of management and works councils conducted in 1985 and in 1998. Both management and the works councils reported that the works council had a great deal of influence on organization and personnel policies. However, according to both parties the works council had practically no influence on commercial, financial–economic, and technology policies. For instance, only 20 per cent of management and 17 per cent of works councils stated that they had some influence on the financial–economic policy of the company. Looise also reported that there was practically no change in this position between 1985 and 1998.

It seems likely that works councils have more direct opportunities to influence the board of directors than small shareholders, especially on labour management issues. This means that the executive board of directors may position itself in coalition with labour, especially when the two-tier regime is in operation. However, the direct influence of works councils in strategic and corporate governance matters is clearly limited. It is possible that the SER recommendations and subsequent changes in legislation may have a positive impact here. In the recommendation works councils are given a more profound role in the election of board members. From a corporate governance perspective the works council may be a much more important institution than a small shareholder (Goodijk 2001) since they have better access to relevant information, underpinned by stipulations in the Works Council Act that require management to disclose information.

In the Netherlands, the position of the board of directors and its policy on labour management is not only constrained and influenced by the works councils. Important constraints are also found in industrial relations factors, more specifically the regulation of terms of employment and working conditions by collective bargaining. It is, therefore, to a discussion of trades union and collective bargaining that we now turn.

6.3.5. *Trade unions: collective bargaining*

After the Second World War corporatist views had a powerful influence upon collective bargaining. Collective labour agreements were tightly controlled by a central tripartite institution, in which successive governments played a major role by establishing the parameters of negotiations. This came to an end in 1982 with the signing of an agreement between the social partners to moderate wage increases for the sake of the national economy (*Wassenaar Agreement*). From then onwards the government decentralized the determination of terms of employment to the social partners. However, since 1982 there has not been as much differentiation in bargaining outcomes as might be expected from this relative freedom of the contracting parties. Coordination between the social partners persists as it appears to work. Indeed, this coordination is considered to be an essential part of the *Dutch Miracle* (Visser and Hemerijck 1997).

In the Netherlands, deregulation and decentralization in industrial relations are now widely discussed. However, it appears that policies to promote decentralization and deregulation may have led instead to further centralization and regulation. Despite discussions about the desirability of micro-flexibility, emanating especially from employers, most employers still embrace centralized collective labour agreements. There are some pressures to decentralize sector collective agreements, but so far only some larger companies have developed their own collective agreements with the trade unions. This development might be described as controlled and coordinated devolution of functions (Ferner and Hyman 1998), resulting in the creation of new institutions. Tros (2001), in his study of decentralization in Dutch industrial relations in the period 1980–2000, confirms that such a process has been taking place and that regulations were decentralized from national level to sector level. However, within sectors, some specific aspects of labour management became more centrally regulated than before. Overall, there has been no significant change in the relative importance of sector and company agreements. In 1996, sector-wide agreements covered 87 per cent of employees: by 2000 this figure had dropped only slightly to 86 per cent. Furthermore, the government has retained the traditional extension rule associated with centralized bargaining that makes sector agreements generally binding on all employees in the sector (despite trade union density being only 27 per cent).

The entrenched position of trade unions and employer federations in determining terms of employment is still being debated. There have been regular discussions about decentralizing the system and making it more voluntary. However, most of the proposals for change have come to nothing. Despite the rhetoric, both sides of industry acknowledge that the current system is well established, and that the institutions of labour management regulation operate largely successfully.

Due to the importance of collective labour agreements, works councils, and institutional regulations at sector level, management does not have much room for manoeuvre in labour management.

Because of these constraints, in corporate governance labour is at least as important as other stakeholders. From a corporate governance perspective the works council is a much more important institution than a small shareholder. The possibility exists, therefore, that management may join in coalitions with labour to stifle activity by shareholders. For instance, hostile takeovers may be inhibited by alliances between management and labour. The potential for such alliances is aided by the emergence of employee shareholders. We discuss this in the next section.

6.3.6. *Employee share ownership*

In the current debate on corporate governance and the role of shareholders in the Netherlands, growing attention is being paid to employee financial participation. Employee share options and share ownership plans are portrayed as mechanisms for overcoming the agency costs of the separation of ownership and control as they align rewards with capital growth. In August 2001, the chair of the biggest Dutch trade union argued in favour of including share option schemes on the negotiation agenda for new collective labour agreements. According to this trade union leader, option schemes had become the property of management and executive staff in companies, and now it was time for such schemes to be made available to all employees. Table 6.5 shows that share option plans are now open to manual and clerical personnel in around 20 per cent of business organizations with 200 or more staff (though management participate in such plans in double this number of organizations) (Pendleton *et al.* 2001). Other studies indicate that one-third of share plans are open to all employees (Poutsma and Van den Tillaart 1996).

The trade union leader cited above was primarily concerned with the financial advantages to employees of share and share option plans. However, employee share ownership also raises important

Table 6.5. *The growth of employee share option plans*
for various groups of staff

Year	Management	Professionals	Clerical	Manual
1992	19	12	10	10
1995	20	14	13	12
1999	43	27	21	20

Source: Pendleton *et al.* (2001).

governance issues. In quite a number of cases, employees receive shares with limited voting rights that negate the control implications. It is estimated that of the 10 per cent of listed companies that have all-employee share plans, approximately one-third offer their employees share certificates (i.e. without voting rights). If employees acquire an interest of 5 per cent or more in the company through collective share ownership, share participation is deemed to have the characteristics of co-ownership. In this situation the management of the company has to involve this group of employee–shareholders as a discussion partner. In practice, in a number of Dutch companies the employees have joined together to pool their shares in an association, foundation, or trust in order to secure and enhance their governance rights. In practice, the management of this legal persona consists of a board with an employee representative. The trustee receives the dividends and can distribute them among the participating employees. However, Poutsma and Nagelkerke (2003) show that the impact on changes in ownership structures and hence the possible impact on corporate governance is still limited. In general, ownership is much lower than 5 per cent and in only a few cases does ownership take a collective form.

6.4. Labour Management and Corporate Governance: A Change of Fit?

In the previous section we described recent changes in corporate governance, alongside a review of the character of labour's relationship to the governance system. In this section we assess the proposition that 'Anglo-Saxonization' of corporate governance is taking place in the Netherlands and that this is leading to changes in labour management. 'Anglo-Saxonization' implies increasing emphasis on contingent rewards (such as performance-related pay and share option schemes), flexible working practices, and fewer stable long-term relationships. It also suggests less focus on binding collective agreements, a weakening of hitherto influential works councils, less employment protection, less use of internal labour markets, and decreasing emphasis on long-term investments in human capital. Against this background, we attempt to discern whether such changes are taking place, and to assess their impact on labour. We will consider the development of share option schemes, performance-related pay (PRP), flexible working practices, protection against dismissal, and employee training and development.

6.4.1. *Share and share option schemes*

The literature shows that employee option and share schemes are far more common in market–outsider countries than in countries with relational–insider systems (Pendleton *et al.* 2001). As already mentioned, the Netherlands is assumed to be moving in the Anglo-Saxon direction. Dutch empirical evidence shows that financial participation schemes, which are mostly share or share option plans, are also a fast-growing phenomenon (see Table 6.6). The number of firms listed on Euronext Amsterdam offering opportunities for financial participation increased substantially in the late 1990s. Nearly 90 per cent of firms in 2000 had some form of financial participation compared with just under 70 per cent 5 years earlier (see Table 6.6). Eighty-two per cent of firms were operating employee share option plans, and 39 per cent stock ownership plans by 2000.

Employee option and share ownership plans may reduce the distinction between employee and shareholder interests and can be seen as elements of the shifts in labour management practices towards greater involvement of employees, more employee responsibility and stimulation of employees to position themselves as co-entrepreneurs. Table 6.7 shows which kind of firms quoted on the Euronext Amsterdam are using employee financial participation schemes. Large multinationals, young firms, knowledge-based companies, and service sector firms are most likely to have financial participation (Mol, Meihuizen, and Poutsma 1997). Perhaps unsurprisingly, all-employee share option plans are most common in young and knowledge intensive companies. Share ownership and share option plans occur less in smaller and unlisted companies (Table 6.8).

It is clear that, as in Anglo-Saxon countries, the role of stock options in executive remuneration has grown substantially in recent years.

Table 6.6. *The incidence of financial participation in listed companies*

Type of plan	1995		2000	
	No.	%	No.	%
Employee share options	94	65	136	82
Employee stock ownership plans	14	10	64	39
Profit sharing	—	—	8	5
Convertible debenture	—	—	4	2
Stock appreciation rights	—	—	8	5
Companies with any scheme	99	69	146	88

Source: Meihuizen (2000).

Table 6.7. *Proportions of types of listed firms with financial participation plans*

Company type	Number of Companies	Any plan	Stock options for managers	Stock options for employees	Allocated share plan
All companies	144	69	51	10	10
Large companies	72	76	60	13	11
Young companies	18	89	44	39	17
Knowledge-based	20	76	35	35	10
Service companies	71	76	54	14	7
Labour intensive	72	69	49	17	6

Source: Mol, Meihuizen, and Poutsma (1997).

Table 6.8. *Proportion of companies with share plans, 1996–7*

Company type	Number	Any share plan	Narrow-based share plan	Broad-based share plan
All firms with over ten employees	401	51	3	1
Listed firms	144	69	55	10

Source: Poutsma and Van den Tillaart (1996); Mol, Meihuizen, and Poutsma (1997).

Cools and Van Praag (2000) found that the contribution of options to executive pay packages ranged from 15 to 25 per cent in 2000, compared with 10 per cent in 1997. The use of executive remuneration in the Netherlands has involved a conscious imitation of Anglo-US practices. However, there are also other reasons why Dutch firms introduce share and share option schemes, such as stimulation of employee involvement and creation of flexible pay and bonus systems. The use of PRP and flexible working practices are also as much bound up with a concern to stimulate employee involvement as pressures to adopt 'shareholder value'-type practices.

6.4.2. *Performance-related pay*

'Anglo-Saxonization' suggests that Dutch labour management is increasingly oriented towards PRP. We have already pointed to the strong increase in the use of share options for higher staff and management indicating the possible effect of greater orientation to shareholder value. However, although competence-based job evaluation still appears to be the main basis for rewarding employees, the *Jaarboek Personeelsmanagement* (Year Book of Personnel Management of the

Dutch Association of Personnel Management) notes a shift towards performance-based pay (Vinke and Larsen 2001). Currently 38 per cent of male and 19.8 per cent of female employees are subject to forms of PRP. Performance-related pay is mostly found in workplaces not covered by collective agreements and is received by more highly educated employees in the 35–44 age group who are not members of a union (Verboon 2001: 67, 76). It appears that Dutch companies are adopting Anglo-Saxon elements of labour management in certain niches of employment that are not directly covered by the corporatist institutional arrangements of the industrial relations system.

6.4.3. *Flexible working practices*

'Anglo-Saxonization' suggests an increase in flexible working practices and less stable employment relationships. In the Netherlands, the number of part-time jobs increased by 66 per cent between 1987 and 1993, and then by 49 per cent from 1994 to 1999. The number of flexible jobs (including temping and on-call work) increased in the same periods by 18 per cent and 37 per cent, respectively. Full-time jobs increased by 16 per cent and 14 per cent in the same periods (Hoogendoorn 1999; Delsen 2002). In the Netherlands, part-time labour and temporary labour are more prevalent than the average in the European Union (Delsen 2002: 88). These developments can be explained by several factors. One, growth in the number of flexible contracts emanates from employer uncertainty as to whether increases in product demand are permanent (Delsen 2002: 89). Two, flexible workers can be dismissed more easily than full-time workers protected by collective labour agreements. In other words, employers seek to circumvent collective agreements. However, the extensive growth of part-time work and the spread of variations in working time has had a profound effect on the content of collective agreements. Part-time jobs now receive almost the same protection as full-time jobs in collective agreements (Slomp 2004). Three, there are strong indications that the Dutch labour market has become a dual labour market with a primary segment of core full-time employees and a secondary segment of flexible workers (Kleinknecht, Oostendorp, and Pradhan 1997). This is partly caused by outsourcing strategies of larger companies focused on enhancing short-term shareholder value. This strategy appears to be especially prevalent in multinationals with UK or US links, such as Shell, Unilever, and Philips (Van Witteloostuijn 1999).

6.4.4. *Preventive system of dismissal*

'Anglo-Saxonization' is assumed to increase dynamics in hiring and firing practices due to a short-term focus on labour costs. The more openly competitive practices associated with Anglo-Saxon labour market regimes support rent-seeking behaviour by both parties: while firms outsource some functions to freelance professionals to enhance the return on these functions, these workers attempt to extract high fees from firms through job-hopping. Are these practices being increasingly found in the Netherlands? We have already pointed to the lower mobility and longer tenure in the Netherlands. However, there is also a unique feature in Dutch employment relationships that hinders easy termination of labour contracts: the preventive system of dismissal. In this system, redundancies, individual and collective dismissal, and partial unemployment (including short-time working and temporary lay-offs) are subject to administrative rules in the form of prior administrative authorization by the Minister of Social Affairs and Employment. As a result, it takes longer to dismiss an individual in the Netherlands than in many other countries, and for an employee it takes longer to quit. This procedure is increasingly being avoided, however, by using a costly civil law procedure. Courts usually decide to give compensation based on months or years of salary to the employee who is dismissed. Although these 'golden parachutes' are much lower than in the United States, in many cases the amount outweighs the extra salary payment that would arise from adherence to the longer dismissal period associated with the authorization regime of the public employment service. This 'hire and fire' route appears to be especially likely to be taken in instances involving reorganizations and mergers of successful firms since it is believed that authorization via the public employment services will be less easy in these circumstances.

In the 1990s, there were attempts to get rid of the authorization system and change it into a repressive system where the dismissal can be judged in court after the event. However, the system has survived these attacks up to now. This is probably because of its potential benefits. The longer dismissal period has positive short-term effects on employment. It also supports a more cautious approach by managers towards seeking changes in the size of the labour force. It also has a positive effect on the attitudes of employees because they have employment security. In other words, it tends to support cooperation. Limiting or removing this protection could lead to higher transaction costs and unwelcome higher labour turnover.

6.4.5. *Employee development*

It is sometimes suggested that the short-term cost and performance focus found in Anglo-Saxon corporate governance regimes depresses long-term investments in employee training. However, at first sight there are no indications that Dutch companies have reduced their investment in training due to 'Anglo-Saxonization'. Eurostat data show that the proportion of both younger and older Dutch employees receiving employer-provided training is above the European average (Delsen 2000: 104). Only in Scandinavian countries are the proportions slightly higher. This indicates that lifelong learning is well developed in the Netherlands. In the United Kingdom the proportion is also higher than the European average though it may be that this compensates for inadequate initial training in the United Kingdom (Mancini and Visser 1995).

In the Netherlands, the higher proportion of employees receiving training is directly linked to the industrial relations system and cooperation between social partners at sector level. In almost all collective agreements, arrangements are made for the promotion of job and task-related training. However, Groot and Maassen van den Brink (1998) showed increasing under-investment in training in some sectors, and thus a more uneven use of training overall. Moreover, employers are increasingly applying to decentralize collective agreements that may erode this collective training system and may lead to under-investment in human capital (Delsen 2000: 105). Although the proportion of Dutch employees that receives training is above the European average, therefore, the trends suggest that Dutch companies may be reducing their investment in training.

6.5. Conclusions

The Netherlands has a corporatist tradition and is still one of the most coordinated market economies. Its business structure comprises a small number of large companies and a large number of small and medium-sized businesses. The large, multinational companies listed on the stock exchange, in particular, are having a substantial impact on the Dutch debate about possible shifts in corporate governance and labour management. Their labour management tends to adopt features that are typical of the LME. As a consequence, the Netherlands can be characterized as midway between the Anglo-Saxon liberal–outsider system and German coordinated insider system. On the one hand, it shows an increasing acceptance of the concept of shareholder value in debates about corporate governance and more focus on flexible working practices, PRP, and share options. On the other hand, concentrated shareholding (although mainly financial institutions), low labour mobility, lengthy job tenure, high investment in human capital, the high coverage of collective agreements, and preventive systems of dismissal, are interpreted as characteristics of the relational–insider system. As a consequence, the set of legal protections for labour, based in part on a corporatist system of industrial relations, limits the opportunities for firms to pursue labour strategies and practices that are typically associated with shareholder value. Empirical evidence, however, shows that firms can pursue shareholder value-type labour strategies in the 'spaces' not covered by the corporatist labour system. The Director of Human Resources at Unilever has suggested that this has provided significant opportunities for firms. In the 1990s, corporate HRM strategies increasingly determined labour management practices instead of the over arching industrial relations system. This opened the possibility for the development of greater alignment between employees' interests and 'shareholder value' interests of management and owners (Haveman 2003: 77).

Nevertheless, the centrally-controlled decentralization of industrial relations is considered a competitive advantage of Dutch business because it prevents labour conflicts and large shocks in the domain of labour management (Nagelkerke and De Nijs 2003: 187). The institutions of labour management appear to be only loosely coupled to corporate governance. In conclusion, the shifting institutional complementarities between corporate governance and labour management in the Netherlands appear to be an attempt to get the best of both worlds: the commitment of insiders and shareholder value.

7

Labour in French Corporate Governance: The Missing Link

MICHEL GOYER AND BOB HANCKÉ

7.1. Introduction

By the end of the 1990s, the character of French corporate governance suggested that large companies in France had gone far in adopting Anglo-Saxon practices (Parrat 1999; Goyer 2001; Morin 2002). The most notable changes are the following: several large firms have dismantled their conglomerate structures to focus instead on a limited number of business activities; cross-shareholdings among blue-chip companies have been sold; and stock options and other forms of variable pay are now extensively and substantially used to provide incentives to top management. This picture of substantial transformation of corporate governance contrasts sharply with conventional images of the French corporate system as one that permanently generates blockages to change (Hoffmann 1963; Crozier 1964).

In this chapter we explain the apparent contradiction between this image of France and the major shifts in corporate governance that have apparently taken place. Our argument is that the weakness of labour in French corporate governance explains to a large extent why and how corporate restructuring over the last two decades led to a pronounced turn towards Anglo-Saxon governance patterns. In contrast to many other European economies, labour is not represented in corporate decision-making structures: there are no specific legal provisions for independent directors to represent the workforce, and elected works councils have very few effective information and monitoring rights (Howell 1992; Desseigne 1995). These institutional arrangements have allowed management considerable unilateral control over business strategy and corporate reorganization. In particular,

We would like to thank Suzanne Berger, Pepper Culpepper, Howard Gospel, Peter Hall, Andrew Pendleton, and David Soskice for comments and discussion of the chapter.

employees have been unable to prevent the unilateral implementation of shareholder value practices by management.

However, the transition toward a greater 'financialization' of the economy in France has led to a rather peculiar model of Anglo-Saxon corporate governance (Williams 2000). Contrary to some expectations, the absence of institutional constraints on management by employees did not unequivocally lead to a wholesale adoption of US or UK-style shareholder value practices. Most important, the transformation of French corporate governance has been limited mainly to a small number of former state-owned companies. Furthermore, the adoption of shareholder value practices has focused mainly on corporate strategy and executive remuneration rather than on the full range of management decision-making. Our findings provide a mirror image of those for Germany in this volume (see Chapter 4). In the latter country, the strong legally embedded position of employees has not prevented the introduction of some shareholder value practices (Höpner 2001). In a similar vein, the weak position of French employees, resulting from the institutional framework in which they are embedded, did not translate into the wholesale adoption of shareholder value practices (Goyer 2003: 194–198). Within this implicitly comparative framework, our findings suggest that some aspects of shareholder value-oriented corporate governance might be easier to implement in contexts where labour shares responsibility with management for the economic performance of the firm.

The chapter starts with an analysis of the weakness of labour in the French political economy, both historically and structurally. We then go on, in Section 7.2, to demonstrate that the particular relationship between management and labour resulting from the strategic choices made by labour unions in the 1970s fed into the corporate readjustment path of the late 1980s, by forcing management to marginalize labour in their search for renewed profitability. The particular patterns of mutual ownership among the restructured companies in the first half of the 1990s served to protect management from undesired pressures emanating from the state, organized labour, and short-term-oriented capital markets. In the second half of the 1990s, the unravelling of these ownership networks and the subsequent restructuring of French capital took place without labour and allowed for a degree of managerial unilateralism unparalleled in any of the other continental European economies. Sections 7.3 and 7.4, the empirical core of the chapter, discuss the specific sources of pressure faced by privatized companies in France that led them to be at the forefront of the transformation of corporate governance. Section 7.5 then links the transformation of the system of corporate governance in France with the stability of its industrial relations.

7.2. Labour in Corporate Governance: Political Calculations and Missed Chances

Compared to most other continental corporate governance systems, France stands out because of the very low involvement of labour in corporate decision-making. Labour is neither involved directly through works council type arrangements, such as the ones found in Germany and the Netherlands, nor indirectly through seats on supervisory boards reserved for organized labour. What explains this French exception? Most analyses emphasize the historical exclusion of labour from economic decision-making and discuss how labour is confined to participation in state-led social policy arrangements and to sector-level negotiation (Ross 1982; Rosanvallon 1988). In this argument, the absence of labour in corporate decision-making is a consequence of the policies of the post-war French state to keep labour at bay. In fact, the few attempts in the mid-1960s to reform industrial relations are best understood as ways to keep organized labour, monopolized by the Communist Confederation Generale du Travail (CGT), out of company-level decision-making (Howell 1992).

Government proposals to reorganize French corporate structures on a basis that would include labour were only developed in the early 1970s, in response to the events of May 1968 (Howell 1992). Yet, these plans did not propose substantial power-sharing between management and labour. However, they foreshadowed the Auroux plans introduced some ten years later by the first Left government. Instead of being centrally organized around the labour unions as the workers' representatives, the 1970s plans take the workplace and the company as the central place for interaction between capital and labour and emphasize the non-union basis of the new arrangements. In short, since the state has traditionally been very sceptical of the involvement of organized labour in corporate structures, labour is virtually absent from corporate decision-making.[1]

The typical perspective on French industrial relations outlined above neglects two factors. The first is that the state was not just hostile towards labour, but also shaped the choices that trade unions made. By stepping in where unions might have had a direct impact, such as in company-level labour policies and wage-setting, the state substituted itself for any form of emerging 'social-democratic'-style labour unionism. The state played a direct role in wage-setting through its manipulation of the minimum wage, which then became the reference wage for all collective bargaining. In many of the state-owned companies, the state showed that capitalist success could be combined with a progressive social policy on such matters as wages, holidays, and working time. Moreover, the state took over the role performed by works councils or local unions in many other West European countries by making lay-offs subject to administrative authorization by labour inspectors.

The second neglected issue concerns the interaction between the labour unions themselves and the state. While the post-war French state certainly was not very hospitable to organized labour, the unions made important strategic choices during the post-war period (especially in the 1970s) based on political calculations. Their positions varied between extreme reluctance and positive hostility toward participating in corporate governance arrangements.

From May 1968 onwards, the French Left, including the unions, believed that a Left government that would use the centralized state to overthrow capitalism was imminent (Capdevielle 1981; Ross 1982). This prospect suggested that it would simply be a matter of time for the unions to be able to transform their role in French society. As a result, they saw no reason for them to get involved in the complicated restructuring of failing capitalist enterprises.

This approach had tactical and organizational implications. Company-level unions remained weak, even after their formal recognition in the 1969 Grenelle agreements, in large part because the central union confederations did not trust their own local unions. The leaders of the central union were concerned that the locals would cooperate with company-level management, and thus undermine the political struggle in which the leadership was engaged. As a result, they refused to hand over substantive decision-making authority or resources to local union organizations (Eyraud and Tchobanian 1985).

The result was that when proposals that could have given organized labour a direct influence in corporate strategy were floated in the mid-1970s, the unions refused to support or participate in them. They were convinced that more was to be gained from supporting the Left coalition. A possible French version of codetermination thus never developed. In fact, when these plans were resuscitated under the Mitterand government in 1981, in the form of the Auroux laws, they had the opposite effect (Howell 1992). Instead of a means for labour to influence corporate governance, the organizational weakness of unions within companies meant that managerial unilateralism became the norm for corporate decision-making.

7.3. **Large Firm Restructuring and Labour Relations in the 1980s**

The exclusion of labour from corporate decision-making influenced the corporate adjustment path of French firms in the 1980s. In 1980–5, large French firms faced a crisis. All of the former national champions experienced big financial losses. It was clear that the basic political–economic configuration which had served the French so well in the post-war period had become counterproductive and a radical reorganization was necessary.

In response to this crisis, large firms managed to disengage themselves from the state while becoming the central actors in the restructuring of the French political economy (Hancké 2002). Exploiting the weakness of labour and the possibilities offered by the new Auroux labour institutions, large firms reorganized by circumventing the unions. Since employees were unable to rely on any institutions for representation and negotiation, the adjustment path of large firms resulted in a situation where unions were largely irrelevant in the corporate restructuring process of the 1980s. The unions were therefore unable to organize more than symbolic resistance. They were defeated in the few instances where they constituted a real problem, most prominently at Renault in 1986–7. The long-term outcome has been that unions have played no significant role in French corporate governance.

The crisis of the French production regime was to a large extent resolved by the state, which owned or controlled many large exporting companies after the wave of nationalizations in 1981. Between 1984 and 1987, the French state injected much-needed capital into those companies it controlled and freed up resources for the others. According to some estimates, the state invested several times more in these companies than their private owners had done in the previous 20 years (see Schmidt 1996: 123–126). However, in a departure from the old French system, whereby state subsidies helped firms out of a crisis, on this occasion state grants and loans were linked to business plans which imposed profitability criteria on the firms.

The central issue for these large firms was that their profitability crisis had its roots in a combination of weak productivity and high relative wages. Resolving the profitability slump therefore required initiatives in two different but related areas. The first was how to reconfigure work organization and skills so as to raise productivity.

Within the West-European context, French firms were models of Taylorism. Organizational structures were not only inefficient but also incorporated a wide array of obstacles to change. The second issue had to do with union politics. In the 1980s, French unions were radical, unwilling, and organizationally incapable of supporting reform proposals, even if they were made by progressive management. However, since unions de facto had the capacity to block organizational changes, even though they otherwise lacked a voice in company decisions, workplace restructuring necessarily imposed a strategy that would marginalize them.

In essence, large firms restructured by using their new skill requirements as the basis for a new labour relations regime and relied on several supply-side government initiatives to restructure workplaces. They used the early retirement programmes to lay off older workers and relied on educational policies to increase the general skill levels of workers. The remaining, more productive workers were then offered improved further training programmes, clear career tracks, and tangible rewards, which allowed large companies to improve labour productivity and marginalize the labour unions at the same time.

The reorganization of the internal labour market of large firms came very soon after the turnaround of the companies. Since the early 1980s, the official goal of government policy had been to assure that by the mid-1990s, four out of five young people had a certificate of secondary studies (the 'Baccalaureat'). By 1995, around 75 per cent of the 1977 birth cohort had passed this exam, up from some 40 per cent in 1984 (Courtois 1995). Furthermore, with an eye on the well-performing German economy, French authorities also reorganized the contents of the vocational and technical training programmes. As was to be expected, these attempts to emulate the German training system fell considerably short of stated ambitions, since many of the institutional preconditions which made the German training system work, such as strong unions and employers associations, did not exist in France (Möbus and Verdier 1997; Culpepper 2001). However, during implementation the curriculum reforms often echoed the actual operational needs of large firms, and some firms even managed to create new technical diplomas, subsequently sanctioned by the state (Verdier 1997).

While it was an important step, the revision of the vocational and technical training programmes did not resolve the workplace reorganization problem. Most large firms still employed many older workers who were relatively ill-equipped for the new forms of work organization. In response, the existing workforce reduction pro-grammes were accelerated in an attempt to adjust the workforce to the new production processes and product market strategies which the large firms were adopting. The French government funded these soft lay-offs by including many of the older workers in early retire-ment programmes. Thus, they maintained their income but disap-peared from the factories without showing up in the unemployment statistics (Guillemard 1991). Most important, these measures allowed the large firms to replace relatively old, underskilled workers with younger, better-trained workers (Béret 1992; Midler and Charue 1993).

As a result of these government initiatives, the core human resources policies of these large firms changed fundamentally. The shifts in the educational system raised and customized the skill basis of young workers. However, note that these skills were not of the 'deep' tech-nological kind that the German system produces (Streeck 1991; Soskice 1997). Instead the reforms concentrated on general skills such as mathematics, IT knowledge, languages and their application in commercial activities, and on a set of 'social' skills, which facilitated the exchange of information between workers, units inside the com-pany, and the company and its suppliers. In other words, the reforms enhanced a wide variety of skills that were peripheral to most production processes, but which were, nevertheless, essential to large firms because they facilitated high-productivity-oriented work reorganization. In turn, the early retirement packages ensured that older workers could be replaced by younger ones. Relying on the institutional resources provided by the government measures, large firms were thus able to integrate a series of tasks into workers' jobs and thereby allow them to pursue novel and more sophisticated product market strategies than was found in classical mass production (Salais 1988, 1992).

Despite these changes, French workplaces remained essentially Taylorist in character (Linhart 1991; Duval 1996). In a way, that was exactly the point of the new education programmes and the way they were articulated with the new workplaces: they left the core contents of the job largely untouched, but provided employers with skills nec-essary for the administrative tasks *surrounding* the actual work. Since historically these had been the types of jobs—in control, administra-tion, maintenance, and supervision—of which French companies had disproportionately more than companies in other countries, reorgan-izing those tasks offered the possibility of significant productivity increases (Maurice, Sellier, and Silvestre 1986; Lane 1989).

Because of the trade unions' capacity to block organizational change, workplace reorganization was intimately tied up with the labour relations system. Restructuring workplaces, therefore, not only required changes along the lines discussed above, but also new forms of workplace communication that circumvented the unions.

In 1981–2, the government passed a series of labour laws, the so-called Auroux reforms. These introduced new methods of direct workers' participation on the shop floor such as direct 'expression' groups. While traditionally the unions regarded such government initiatives with a mixture of defiance and suspicion, on this occasion the two main unions, the Communist CGT and the Left-socialist Confederation Francaise Democratique du Travail (CFDT), dropped their radical rhetoric and attempted to make the reforms work. However, local trade unionists, who were meant to implement the reforms, were incapable of playing this novel role. Since unions had been highly centralized prior to the reforms, the local union sections had little or no experience with the type of 'social-democratic' workplace union activities which the Auroux laws had envisaged for them (Eyraud and Tchobanian 1985). Thus, the fundamental discrepancy between the new requirements and local union capacities seriously strained union organization.

Employers initially were very suspicious of the Auroux reforms (Weber 1990). Gradually, however, they began to see the advantages of the new institutions for shop floor workers' participation that the laws provided (Morville 1985). This was related to the structure of the Auroux reform project itself, which encapsulated two very different reform projects. One aspect of the Auroux project was a blend of German-style social-democracy and of self-management ideas carried over from the 1960s; a second, by contrast, was a form of workers' integration which borrowed heavily from Japanese teamwork and quality circles (Howell 1992). Since local unions were too weak to substantially influence the implementation of the reforms within companies, the second scenario, with its links to concepts of the flexible workplace, developed to a greater extent than the first. As soon as the initial boom of legally induced 'expression groups' subsided, there was a dramatic growth in management-led quality programmes and shop floor teams. These increased from approximately 500 in 1981, the year of the Auroux reform, to over 10,000 in summer 1984 (Weber 1990: 446). What was initially a worker-oriented reform package, became a management tool to defuse the conflict-ridden formal industrial relations system, and facilitated the development of a management model that integrated workers' skills into the production system without integrating unions (or workers) into the corporate decision-making structure.

What were the consequences of this pattern of industrial adjustment for the French system of corporate governance? As described, this pattern of restructuring led to the concentration of power in the hands of French CEOs and top managers as well as to the exclusion of employees from decision-making processes about business strategy. However, this adjustment process also resulted in a highly particularistic corporate governance structure. By the late 1980s and early 1990s, French corporate governance was organized around stable cross-shareholding networks, which encompassed banks, insurance companies, utility companies, and a number of industrial enterprises (Morin 1995; Schmidt 1996: 369–81). Companies held shares in each other and thus safeguarded management autonomy from predatory investors; they also helped keep the state and trade unions at bay. Cross-shareholdings were thus a means of excluding from corporate decision-making processes those interests that might obstruct reform. At the same time, however, the exclusion of employees from the decision-making process did not result in a stronger position for minority shareholders. Up to the mid-1990s, the pursuit of shareholder value practices was almost non-existent in France (OECD 1998*a*, *b*). Instead, the ownership structure of the French corporate sector allowed members of corporate networks to participate in long-term relationships based on a broad definition of their mutual interests (Morin 1996).

While the foregoing argument helps us understand the nature of labour exclusion in France, it sheds little light on the particular ownership structures which dominate French private sector firms today. Given the autonomy that cross-shareholdings gave large firms, it might be expected that they would be a durable feature of French corporate governance. However, from late 1996 onwards, the system of cross-shareholding networks began to collapse and the stage was set for a substantial transformation of the French system of corporate governance. We now turn to a discussion of these changes, and the reasons for them.

7.4. Corporate Governance Reform

By the mid-1990s, as the process of industrial restructuring began to bear fruit, pressures for corporate governance reforms were mounting.

While large firms had achieved strong positions in world markets (Amable and Hancké 2001; Hancké 2001), a series of financial indicators (such as return-on-investment, the level of stock market capitalization, and share price of equity capital) painted a less rosy picture, especially in comparative perspective. The cumulative rate of return on equity of French firms between 1993 and 1995 was 8.5 per cent, against 10.5 and 18.5 per cent for Germany and the United Kingdom (*Le Monde*, 14 February 1997). The stock market capitalization of large French companies remained extremely low *vis-à-vis* their foreign rivals: there were no French firms among the world top 100 by stock market capitalization in 1996, and only five in the top 200. While stock markets in Germany and the United Kingdom registered moderate increases between 1993 and 1995, the overall level of capitalization of the Paris bourse decreased by 7.6 per cent (*Expansion*, 21 March 1996: 71).

Poor financial results, which were concentrated among the recently privatized firms, increased the vulnerability and sensitivity of French companies to the demands of Anglo-Saxon institutional investors (see Table 7.1). In addition, the cross-shareholdings, which had been instrumental in the restructuring of companies in the decade before 1995, came under pressure because it turned out to be a very expensive system of control when companies were competing in rapidly-moving product markets. In combination, these two factors paved the way for the entry of large foreign institutional investors into the French corporate sector.

To a large extent, the low share price of large companies was a reflection of the way the government had initiated and organized their privatization.[2] In order to increase their operational flexibility at a time of tight budgets, public sector corporations in France were to issue up to 50 per cent of their capital in the form of investment certificates (i.e. shares without voting rights). However, firms issuing such non-voting shares are subject to a significant discount by investors (Helias 1997: 56). In addition, in an attempt to make the privatization process a political success by enlisting small shareholders, public sector corporations were sold at heavily discounted prices—usually between 15 and 20 per cent of their traded market value (*Expansion*, 14 February 1997). At the same time, the system of cross-shareholdings among friendly firms reinforced the pattern of under-capitalization because core shareholder groups in the newly privatized firms were public sector corporations and other privatized companies. Thus, a small group of relatively cash-poor firms held shares in each other. Moreover, the issue of free shares to individual

Table 7.1. *The control and performance of large French companies*

	Control (dominant position) in the executive body of the company	Market capitalization end May 1996 (FF million)	Return on own capital average 1991–5 (%)
LVMH	Family	115,328	19.1
L'Oreal	Family	105,007	17.8
Elf Aquitaine (privatized)	Cross-participation	104,082	5.7
Carrefour	Family	103,538	22.2
Total (privatized)	No dominant shareholder	82,524	8.6
Alcatel Alsthom (privatized)	Cross-participation	73,166	2.4
Générale des Eaux	Cross-participation	66,515	9.5
Air Liquide	No dominant shareholder	62,236	13.7
Axa	Midi participations	57,900	7.2
Groupe Danone	No dominant shareholder	55,682	12.5
Société générale (privatized)	Cross-participation	52,457	9.7
Saint-Gobain (privatized)	Cross-participation	51,712	8.9
BNP (privatized)	Cross-participation	41,629	4.3
Paribas (privatized)	Cross-participation	39,954	0.1
Rhône-Poulenc (privatized)	No dominant shareholder	39,695	6.9
Renault	State	37,453	11.0
Peugeot	Family	36,169	5.0
Pinault-Printempts-Redoute	Family	35,122	13.0
UAP (privatized)	Cross-participation	34,464	3.7
Suez (privatized)	Cross-participation	34,140	−2.0
Roussel-Uclaf	Hoechst	33,045	16.7
Schneider	No dominant shareholder	32,020	4.2
Lafarge	No dominant shareholder	30,535	10.8
Lyonnaise des Eaux	Cross-participations	30,125	6.7
Michelin	Family	29,319	2.4
Canal Plus	Hava, Générale des eaux	27,895	25.7
Havas (privatized)	No dominant shareholder	27,501	11.0
Promodés	Family	26,094	18.9
Eridania Beghin-Say	Montedison SPA	21,867	11.2
Legrand	Family	21,513	16.9
Accor	No dominant shareholder	20,761	8.2
Usinor-Sacilor (privatized)	No dominant shareholder	19,445	−3.6
AGF (privatized)	Cross-participation	19,209	6.2
Pernod Ricard	Family	19,013	14.9
Péchiney (privatized)	No dominant shareholder	18,614	2.0
Thomson-CSF	State	16,057	2.4
Bic	Family	15,759	14.2
Castorama	Family	15,455	20.3
Sodexho	Family	14,431	20.9
Docks de France	Family	12,571	19.6

Source: OECD (1997*a*: 127).

and employee equity holders who held their stocks for more than 18–24 months, so as to stabilize the ownership structure of privatized firms, reduced earnings per share, and thus further depressed their share price. Finally, French firms were allowed to issue dividends in the form of new shares. By the late 1980s, almost 100 companies resorted to this practice, among them all the newly privatized firms (*Journal des Finances*, 1 July 1989: 8). This strategy reflected the financial weakness of privatized companies, for whom a large amount of cash was immobilized in cross-shareholding schemes. This further contributed to their low earnings per share.

The low share price and market capitalization of large companies set the stage for strong pressures towards corporate governance reforms, as they made the companies easy targets for cash-rich foreign predators.[3] However, by taking controlling stakes in each other, the firms had been able to fend off this possibility of takeovers. Like the rest of continental Europe, the ownership structure of the French corporate sector is fairly concentrated (Becht and Roell 1999). A large segment of the French corporate sector is organized in a holding company structure, which allows for a maximum of firms to be controlled with a minimum of capital (Windolf 1999). In this respect, until the mid-1990s, France has been described as an insider model of corporate governance with ownership concentration as one of its main features (OECD 1998a, b).

However, this overall picture of concentration and tight control concealed several more dramatic underlying weaknesses. Up until the mid to late-1990s, the members of the corporate networks in France were engaged in long-term relationships based on a broad definition of mutual interests—often at the expense of shareholder value (Morin 1996). By the late 1990s, however, the ownership structure of large French companies had been substantially reshaped: ownership had become considerably dispersed and Anglo-Saxon institutional investors had entered the French market *en masse*. In 2001, twenty-one of the top CAC 40 firms had a highly dispersed ownership structure (Goyer 2001: 144–6).[4] Privatized companies represented the bulk of firms with a dispersed ownership structure.[5] The pattern of stability-inducing cross-shareholdings designed by the government in the mid-1980s and in the early 1990s had collapsed. The percentage of shares held by fellow domestic companies in the top fifty French firms fell to 3.5 per cent in 2001 from 15 per cent in 1997 (Morin 2002: 168). The decline in cross-shareholdings was particularly severe for privatized firms.[6] At the same time, foreign ownership rose rapidly in

France, reaching 41.29 per cent of the equity capital of CAC 40 firms in 2001 (*Le Monde*, 15 June 2001: 22).

The strategy of French policy-makers to develop an insider type of ownership structure had, under the conditions under which it was implemented, become a very costly project. In January 1996, more than FF 100 billion were immobilized in cross-shareholdings, a figure that is three times the amount raised by all French firms on stocks markets in 1995 (*Nouvel Economiste*, 28 June 1996: 51). Moreover, since cross-shareholdings took place in a context of low market capitalization, scarce capital was immobilized in the hard core shareholder group rather than invested in their core activities.[7] For these reasons, French firms sold their cross-shareholdings in a very short period between early 1996 and mid-1998. By late 1998, the cross-shareholding structure which had typified French capitalism had dissolved and Anglo-Saxon investors had taken large stakes in French companies (Morin 2002).

7.5. Labour and the Transformation of Corporate Governance

The pressures faced by large privatized French firms led to a substantial transformation of their system of corporate governance in line with some of the most important preferences of Anglo-Saxon institutional investors. The key changes included the following: the appointment of a growing number of independent directors to French boards of directors (Parrat 1999; Goyer 2001); the emergence of variable pay as an important component of management remuneration (Towers Perrin, various years); a focus by blue-chip companies on a limited number of core business activities (Goyer 2002, 2003); and the sale of cross-shareholdings by large companies (Morin 2002). Nonetheless, the transition of the French system of corporate governance to an Anglo-Saxon system is far from total. Most important, French companies have not adopted international accounting standards and still rely on deviations from the one share–one vote principle in order to protect themselves from unwanted takeover bids (Goyer 2003: 194–8).

The institutional arrangements of labour organization in France account to a large extent for the particular form the changes in the system of corporate governance took. The lack of institutionalized labour influence within the firm provided management with ample room to introduce shareholder value practices inside French firms. Moreover, at the same time, it complemented the organizational frameworks of large corporations. The concentration of power at the top of the firm, the ability to rapidly develop new strategic initiatives, the innovative design of products based on scientific research, and the virtual exclusion of labour from the corporate decision-making process characterize the business strategy of large French firms (Schmidt 1996; Ziegler 1997; Hancké 2001).

Yet, labour weakness at firm level has not necessarily meant the wholesale adoption of shareholder value practices. As research on the German case demonstrates (see Chapter 4, this volume; Höpner 2001), the introduction of shareholder value is perfectly compatible with strong employee participation at firm level. The unwillingness and inability of an important segment of the French labour movement to assume responsibility for workplace relationships and for the economic performance of the firm enabled them to block changes on specific issues when the firm need cooperation. This explains why the business strategies developed by top management in the 1980s and 1990s to deal with various crises was also designed to marginalize labour. The inability of French unions to serve as a strategic partner at the firm level— combined with their willingness to block institutional change—sowed the seeds for a nationally specific pattern of transformation. Thus, labour matters in two ways: weak employees are unable to block many managerial initiatives, yet are unwilling to participate in those reorganization schemes that require their cooperation.

While French companies have reformed their corporate strategy by focusing on core business activities, they have failed to enhance financial transparency. The specific organization of labour contributed significantly to this outcome. The process of de-conglomeration and refocusing on core competencies was likely to externalize costs onto employees. Simultaneously, employee representatives had very few means at their disposal to block these changes. In turn, financial transparency was eschewed by management because greater disclosure of information could have facilitated claims by employees for a larger share of company profits in the form of wages.

7.5.1. *The focus on core competencies*

During the entire post-war era, the conglomerate form of organization and the involvement in many (often unrelated) business activities had been an essential element of large companies in France (Whittington and Mayer 2000: 128–34). The diversification of business activities allowed firms to reduce risk by pooling the fortunes of unrelated businesses and furthered economies of scope as managers could exploit synergies between business units. However, the recent increase in foreign ownership of large French companies has led to a reconsideration of this strategy. Anglo-Saxon investors have expressed strong views against the maintenance of the conglomerate form (Markides 1995: 11–35). Conglomerates are perceived as an inefficient organizational form by investors since they frequently use cross-subsidies from profitable divisions to shore up loss-making ones regardless of their long-term growth prospects. Investors have therefore preferred to see portfolio companies focus on a limited number of business activities. As a result, they suffer from a 'conglomerate discount': their stock market value is lower than the potential sum of their individual divisions (Berger and Ofek 1995; Comment and Jarrell 1995).

Focusing on core competencies is likely to lead to a convergence of interests between top management and investors in France, since de-conglomeration tends to raise share prices, and thus enable higher investment. However, this strategy will almost certainly encounter opposition by labour.[8] In contrast to investors, employees benefit from the internal organization of conglomerates, whereby the central office can reallocate funds from fast growing units to poorer performing counterparts, because they facilitate extensive internal labour markets. De-conglomeration implies a dismantling of internal labour markets. Moreover, focusing on core competencies necessarily implies reductions in the workforce in most cases. For example, the process of conglomerate dismantling in the United States in the 1980s resulted in the reorganization of the portfolio of activities through a concentration on core business units, rapid turnover of peripheral segments, and the shedding of a substantial part of the labour force. The redistribution of wealth from employees to shareholders accounted for a significant percentage of the financial gains realized during the takeover wave of the 1980s in the United States (Shleifer and Summers 1988).

Table 7.2 suggests the French corporate sector underwent an important reorganization between 1994 and 2002 with respect to corporate strategy.[9] Many large French companies substantially reduced their degree of diversification and have done so more aggressively and faster than their German counterparts (Goyer 2002, 2003). How could we account for this shift in firm strategy? What is the role of labour in this transformation process?

The gains associated with the reversal of the strategy of diversification and the elimination of the conglomerate discount are contingent

Table 7.2. *Corporate strategy of French firms*

Company	1986	1990	1994	1998	2002
Accor	DIV	DIV	DIV	DIV	DOM
Air Liquide	DIV	DIV	DIV	DOM	DOM
Alcatel	DIV	DIV	DIV	DIV	DIV
Aventis[a]	—	—	—	—	DOM
Bic	DIV	DIV	DIV	DIV	DIV
Bouygues	DIV	DIV	DIV	DIV	DIV
Bull	SIN	SIN	SIN	SIN	SIN
Carrefour	DIV	DIV	DIV	DIV	DIV
Danone	DIV	DIV	DIV	DOM	DOM
Elf[b]	DIV	DIV	DIV	DIV	—
Lafarge	DIV	DIV	DIV	DIV	DIV
Lagardere	DIV	DIV	DIV	DIV	DIV
LVHM	DIV	DIV	DIV	DIV	DIV
Lyonnaise des Eaux[c]	DIV	DIV	DIV	—	—
Michelin	SIN	SIN	SIN	SIN	DOM
L'Oreal	DIV	DIV	DIV	DOM	SIN
Pechiney	DIV	DIV	DIV	DOM	DIV
Pernod Ricard	DIV	DIV	DIV	DIV	DOM
Peugeot	DIV	DIV	SIN	SIN	SIN
PPR	DIV	DIV	DIV	DIV	DIV
Renault	SIN	SIN	SIN	SIN	SIN
Rhône-Poulenc[a]	DIV	DIV	DIV	DOM	—
St-Gobain	DIV	DIV	DIV	DIV	DIV
Sanofi[d]	—	DOM	DOM	SIN	—
Sanofi-Synthalabo[d]	—	—	—	—	SIN
Schneider	DIV	DIV	DIV	DIV	DOM
Sodexho	DIV	DIV	DIV	DIV	DIV
Suez[c]	DIV	DIV	DIV	—	—
Suez-Lyonnaise[c]	—	—	—	DOM	SIN
Synthalabo[d]	—	DOM	DOM	SIN	—
Thale-Thomson	DIV	DIV	DIV	DOM	DOM
Total[b]	DOM	DOM	DOM	DOM	—
TotalElfFina	—	—	—	—	DOM
Usinor-Sacilor	SIN	SIN	SIN	DOM	SIN
Valeo	DIV	DIV	DIV	DIV	DIV
Vivendi	DIV	DIV	DIV	DIV	DIV

[a] Rhône-Poulenc changed its name to Aventis. Data is recorded for Rhône-Poulenc until 1998. For 2002, data is shown for Aventis.
[b] Data is recorded for Elf-Aquitaine and Total as separate companies until 1998. Data for 2002 is recorded for TotalElfFina.
[c] Data is recorded for Lyonnaise des Eaux and Suez as separate companies for 1986, 1990, and 1994. Data for 1998 and 2002 is recorded for Suez-Lyonnaise des Eaux.
[d] Data is recorded for Sanofi and Synthalabo as separate companies for 1990, 1994, and 1998. Data for 2002 is recorded for Sanofi-Synthalabo.

Notes: SIN: Single Business; DOM: Dominant Business; DIV: Diversified.

on commensurate changes in the structure of the decision-making process. Focusing on a limited number of business activities implies that inter-relationships among fewer but related units are exploited (Markides 1995: 135–41). Such a reduction in diversification invariably entails some increase in portfolio risk as more eggs are put in fewer baskets. Refocused firms must therefore exercise tighter control over their units (Hill 1988), and the head office is forced to acquire substantial knowledge of operational affairs in order to establish linkages between divisions. Moreover, top managers must be able to shift resources quickly to allow for a proper focus on the market niches seen as crucial for the profitability of the firm.

Substantial managerial autonomy (with respect to labour) over the organization of business unit activity works in favour of radical workplace reorganizations. Most important, the underdeveloped legal instruments available to French employees reduce their ability to substantially restrain managerial authority (Goyer 2002: 18–19). While French workers and their representatives have strong information rights they have no formal veto rights. As a result, French employees cannot punish firms which rely excessively on dismissals in the implementation of a refocusing strategy (Desseigne 1995).

In addition, the organization of work and skill formation in France facilitated a dismantling of the conglomerate structure and a concurrent focus on core competencies. In contrast to many other continental economies, especially Germany, the French economy is not based predicated on the presence of a majority of employees with certifiable skills. French employers in fact possess substantial autonomy in three areas in which their German counterparts are facing substantial constraints. First, skills are not a prerequisite for job promotion, but are often acquired *after* the promotion, often on highly idiosyncratic grounds (Maurice, Sellier, and Silvestre 1986: 77). Second, management does not face compulsory requirements to provide training (Marsden 1999: 98): state-led initiatives to impose training in the 1990s met with strong, and ultimately successful, opposition from employers. Third, the hiring of new employees with the requisite skills is not subject to the approval of the works council, but is often the exclusive prerogative of management and a few outside experts (Hancké 2001: 323–7; Goyer 2002: 26). The content of training and the resulting role of employees in the production process represent areas of pure managerial prerogative. Overall, the process of skill formation in France allows managers to bring about radical changes in corporate strategy.

The organization of the workplace in France is also characterized by the presence of extensive rules regulating the tasks to be accomplished, rather than the functions to be performed (Maurice, Sellier, and Silvestre 1986: 60–65; Marsden 1999: 103–104). Highly qualified engineers stipulate the development of products with employees following detailed instructions (Linhart 1994). Thus, the reliance on codified rules and procedures, and the bureaucratic controls associated with a rigid division of labour, significantly reduce the dependence of management on employee skills (Goyer 2003: 199–202). Since employees have limited knowledge of the full range of company operations, the development of performance standards in France is decided centrally by the CEO and top management (Linhart 1994; Casper and Hancké 1999).

7.5.2. *International accounting standards*

Institutional investors have a strong preference for continental European companies in their portfolios to adopt international accounting standards. International accounting standards enable transparent comparisons between their domestic and international portfolios (Zanglein 1998).[10] At the same time, financial disclosure based on international accounting standards provides a strong monitoring mechanism for shareholders and reduces risks associated with takeovers (Fox 1998). When continental European companies try to acquire a competitor through a stock-for-stock method of payment, Anglo-Saxon institutional investors insist they adopt international accounting standards and report on a quarterly basis (Coffee 1999: 649).

Despite the growing presence of institutional investors, the number of companies using an international accounting standard among France's largest 100 companies has increased only a little, from thirty-five in 1997 to thirty-eight in 2000 (Goyer 2003: 194). Again, we relate the reluctance of French companies to adopt greater degrees of financial transparency to the particular position of organized labour in the company. Traditionally, the institutional framework of corporate governance systems in continental Europe relied on relatively opaque financial reporting. While more transparent financial reporting allows shareholders to monitor management better, it might also lead to an increase in the influence of labour, since employees may improve their understanding of how well the firm is doing and can thereby demand higher salaries (Roe 2000: 568). However, extraction of a greater proportion of value-added by workers constitutes only one scenario.

In some countries, such as Germany, employees have long had access to privileged information, yet they have typically presented moderate wage demands. This suggests that the willingness of European companies to adopt greater financial transparency will be influenced to some degree by the extent to which employees internalize the interests and objectives of the firm.

The exclusion of French employees from firm-level decision-making processes, combined with their ideological anti-capitalist posture, significantly reduced the incentives for management to adopt greater financial transparency. Even if management introduced transparent accounting standards in France, it is unlikely to produce the outcome we find in other countries such as Germany, because the typical organization of workplaces in France does not provide employees with strong incentives to assume responsibility for the economic performance of the firm. The managerial strategy of removing skills from the shop floor in France in the 1980s was a direct response to the ability of key workers to prevent the introduction of new production processes (Hancké 2002). Within such a context of low-trust adversarialism, the danger is that the release of additional information will lead to higher wage demands without the quid pro quo of a constructive engagement in the restructuring processes.

7.6. Corporate Governance and Labour Relations

The major shifts in French corporate governance over the last decade confirmed the novel patterns of labour relations that had already emerged in the period prior to the collapse of cross-shareholdings in 1996. By and large, given the adjustment process of the previous period, large French companies faced very few problems addressing the needs of their new foreign owners in the 1990s. The adjustment period after the crisis of the mid-1980s reflected the need for large exporting companies to raise profitability, often by raising hourly labour productivity, and this involved lay-offs as well as a general increase in the skill levels of the remaining workers. Furthermore, the internal arrangements easily met the expectations of Anglo-Saxon investors since the adjustment was critically built on the idea that management had a relatively free hand in internal structures.

In terms of work relations, the core human capital strategy of the large firms, constructed around a high level of general skills (instead of deep industry-specific skills), did not change. If anything, the need for a combination of high profitability and internal management autonomy, which followed the shifts in ownership and corporate governance, reinforced this skills regime, since it minimized potential hold-up problems for management. It assured that the influence of workers in internal decision-making was limited to what was legally required and what was instrumental to management's productivity drive. Similarly, the organizational decentralization of the 1980s and 1990s, involving the establishment of semi-independent business units (including worker teams and quality circles), was expanded. By the late 1990s, an international survey reported that French companies led many of their continental counterparts in the adoption of teams and direct participation channels (Benders *et al.* 2000).

Even the few government initiatives which directly addressed work organization inside companies, such as the 1998 Aubry law on the reduction of working time, were easily adopted by large firms as a means of modernizing their work practices. Since the law simultaneously imposed a reduction in average annual working time and a plant-level negotiated reallocation of working time, it ultimately led to more flexible working time schemes. These allowed weekly working time to fluctuate in accordance with production schedules based around just-in-time production and delivery schedules (Trumbull 2002).

As a result, large firms began to develop more idiosyncratic forms of personnel management. Most French companies today have systems in place which offer workers long-term career tracks on the basis of their skills, often acquired in further training programmes, and on the basis of their willingness to move between jobs. Reflecting the capacity of employers to externalize adjustment costs onto individual workers, the basic idea is that 'employability' is ultimately the worker's own responsibility, and the contribution by employers is limited to evaluating company-wide skills needs and offering training programmes where necessary. While wages *de jure* still follow centrally negotiated wage scales, the 'pay-for-knowledge' component of wages has become an increasingly important part of the 'extra' negotiated at the plant or firm level.

This basic configuration of skills, in which workers are significantly more dependent on employers than the other way around, implies that labour shedding remains the crucial strategy when things turn sour for large firms. When large companies, such as Michelin, Danone, and Renault, faced problems in 2001, their immediate response was to lay off a large part of their workforce. This strategy led to calls for a change in the law to block highly profitable companies from adopting such crude workforce reduction strategies.

Within companies, therefore, the direct influence of labour on corporate strategy, including human resources plans, remains very small. Unions had been eliminated as countervailing forces in the early 1990s, and the new skill profiles disproportionately favour management's independence from their workforce. Not surprisingly, this has led to patterns of industrial relations which reflect the needs of companies and their owners.

Most important, France has become a haven of social peace. Despite periodic well-publicized major strikes, labour conflicts in France today are, in fact, very rare. In terms of 'working days lost' French strike figures are roughly on a par with Germany. Those strikes which do take place are disproportionately concentrated in the public sector, where lifetime employment guarantees still exist and unions are able to exert a significant influence due to above-average unionization rates and a law that grants them 'representative' status in wage negotiations.

While labour unions may have been weakened over the last two decades, employers' associations have not grown in strength either. Reflecting the increasing autonomy of large exporting firms from the broader institutional framework of economic and social policies, the national employers' association, the Confédération Nationale du Patronat Français changed its name to Mouvement des Entreprises de France to signal that it had become an organization which represented the interests of small firms. While it is still active in the preparation of wage negotiations, its main function is as a lobbying organization with privileged access to the right-wing government elected in 2002.

Wage bargaining systems have been quick to reflect changes in the French political economy. Even without the mandatory plant-level agreements which the 1997 law on working time reduction imposed, more plant-level wage agreements are concluded today than ever before. Their numbers increased by 10–15 per cent annually since the early 1990s and, as a result of the law on working time reduction, that pace accelerated (EIRO 2002). Despite having the lowest union density rate in Europe, France has the highest proportion of workers covered by collective bargaining. To a large extent this follows from the still important role of the state in wage-setting: wage agreements concluded in large firms become the formal signposts for wages in their industrial branch as a whole, and the wage settlement is then extended by administrative fiat to all the companies in the sector.

In turn, private sector wage growth becomes the informal wage norm for public sector negotiations, with the effect that over 95 per cent of French workers are covered by wage agreements. However, the large exporting firms are more important in this process than the state. Safeguarding profitability means that wages in the French establishments of these companies are set as a function of relative labour productivity vis-à-vis production units in other countries. Since large firms set wages as a function of labour productivity, and other companies adopt this wage rate, aggregate nominal wage growth in France never surpasses labour productivity growth. Thus, while monetary policy may have been transferred to the European Central Bank in Frankfurt, the large exporting firms continue to contribute to low inflation inside France as a result of their leading role in wagesetting.

The advent of foreign institutional investors and the adoption of corporate governance practices that reflect their interests and preferences thus confirmed the existing practices in French labour relations, which disproportionately favoured the interests of employers, especially in large exporting companies. International investors have at best an indirect influence on work, employment, and industrial relations. Paradoxically, they are a force of inertia, in the sense that most of the changes in labour relations often associated with the rise of foreign ownership and subsequent changes in corporate governance patterns, were already in place by the time French ownership patterns went through their revolution in 1997. Yet, as we argued earlier in this chapter, the causality is probably the inverse from what we see in other countries. Instead of imposing constraints on companies that force management to change their labour policies, the French case suggests that a prior, mostly endogenous, shift in labour policies has been rewarded by a rapid growth in foreign ownership. Once accomplished, the system then seems to find itself in a relatively stable equilibrium.

7.7. Conclusions

By the end of the 1990s, the French system of corporate governance had very little in common with the systems which preceded it— the state-led, bank-based credit system that France knew until the late 1980s and the dense networks of cross-shareholdings which characterized French capitalism between the late 1980s and the mid-1990s.

Instead, foreign investors had entered the French capital market in high numbers. In response to this presence of foreign investors, a large number of French companies have implemented policies designed to better represent the interests of their new shareholders.

The weak position of French employees in the firm is crucial for an understanding of this transformation of the national system of corporate governance. The institutional weakness of labour allowed management to introduce polices and practices designed to promote the interests of shareholders. The relative weak position of French employees also made them unattractive partners in the implementation of any reforms inside the firm. The lack of workers' influence over firm strategy reduced their incentives to cooperate and provided management with incentives to pursue corporate adjustment schemes which marginalized labour.

What are the broader insights to be gained from this analysis of the transformation of corporate governance in France? First, the weakness of French labour within the firm contrasts sharply with most other countries, especially in northern Europe. Second, in France the process of transformation was one of managerial unilateralism without compensation for employees. Comparing this outcome with the analysis of German corporate governance in this volume, where employees have been able to shape the terms of the introduction of policies and practices designed to promote the interests of their shareholders, makes clear how different systems of employee representation continue to lead to different outcomes.

Capitalism at the turn of the century thus retains different organizational forms, with different effects, even if the overall pressures are very similar. But they do not necessarily do so solely because of the social matrix offered by the organization of capital (Hall and Soskice 2001*a*). The extent and ways in which labour has historically been integrated in the political economy lays down equally important tracks for reform and change. The organizational weakness of French labour inside the firm, and the political calculations of French trade unions in the 1970s were at the basis for the marginalization strategy adopted by French firms in the 1980s and 1990s. These factors also continued to play an important role in how firms negotiated their relations with foreign investors in the latter part of the 1990s. 'Bringing labour back in' instead of solely focusing on the effects of how capital reorganises, makes the differences in coping strategies of the different systems intelligible, both in a historical context and in terms of the incentive structures which actors face.

NOTES

1. There are a few exceptions, primarily found in the public services, such as EDF and the SNCF (Chorin 1990). One could argue that de facto corporate governance in some state-owned companies such as Renault was built around a careful balance between the CGT and management. However, without underestimating the impact that these arrangements may have on corporate strategy, they are not institutionalized arrangements to proactively include labour in decision-making, but the expression of a particular balance of forces in the history of these companies. Overall, company organization has been the monopoly of top management (Linhart 1991).

2. For a full analysis of the impact of state policies on the financial development of public sector corporations, see Goyer (1998).

3. The bidding period in France at that time was only 25 days. This makes it difficult to find a 'white knight' and to organize a defensive counter-bid.

4. A dispersed ownership structure is defined as having a hard-core shareholder group (or single large blockholder) owning less than 20% of equity capital.

5. By contrast, the remaining members of the CAC 40 index were either family-owned firms or subsidiaries of another corporation. Both groups have a concentrated ownership structure (Goyer 2001: 145).

6. *Les Echos* (8 December 1998: III) lists them as follows: Accor (14.5%), Air Liquide (7.8%), Danone (12.9%), Elf (8.2%), Paribas (12%), Rhône-Poulenc (6.5%), Saint-Gobain (16.9%), and Vivendi (14.4%).

7. For example, Saint-Gobain had invested FF7 billion in friendly groups while its stock market capitalization was barely more than FF18 billion in 1996. The similar figures for Paribas were FF18 billion and FF39 billion, respectively (*Nouvel Economiste*, 28 June 1996: 51).

8. The opposition of employees to the dismantling of conglomerates is not necessarily a universal proposition, as Germany suggests (Höpner 2001: 44).

9. Table 7.2 extends to 2001 the results of previous studies on diversification carried out by the Harvard students of Chandler and their successors (see Whittington and Mayer (2000) for an overview).

10. The most striking example of this lack of uniformity is that of Daimler-Benz which reported a DM1 billion profit under German law and a DM2 billion loss by applying the GAAP standard in 1993.

8

Corporate Governance and Employment Relations: Spain in the Context of Western Europe

RUTH V. AGUILERA

8.1. Introduction

Corporate governance studies have traditionally focused on the relationship between managers and owners and have usually neglected the role of employees. Recently, there have been various attempts to understand how employees might be involved in the governance of the firm and how they interact with other stakeholders (Aguilera and Jackson 2003). Blair and Roe (1999), for instance, emphasize the relevance of the institutional context in which employees are embedded as a critical explanatory factor in understanding their influence in corporate decision-making. This type of approach is reinforced by arguments presented by O'Sullivan (2000a, b): she provides an 'innovative capabilities' account of labour in the corporate governance equation, underscoring that corporate governance is wider than just the monitoring of managers by investors. Finally, Gospel and Pendleton (2003) dissect the specific mechanisms by which governance and financial systems influence the role of labour–management relations in different corporate settings by contrasting liberal market economies and coordinated market economies. Their comparative research also points to the corporate governance idiosyncrasies of each individual country, and therefore implicitly rejects the arguments that corporate governance is converging on the pattern of investor–management relationships held to be typical of the Anglo-Saxon countries.

In the light of this research in comparative corporate governance, the purpose of this chapter is to illustrate the characteristics of corporate governance and labour management relations in Spain. It does so with reference to other industrialized countries considered in this book. The chapter therefore identifies the 'exceptional' traits of the Spanish economic organization model, its main transformations over time, and the complementarities and tensions between corporate governance and employment systems. The implication of the approach is that the dichotomy between liberal market economies and coordinated economies found in the 'varieties of capitalism' literature is simplistic. The Spanish case, along with Italy and to some extent France, can be characterized as conforming to a third type, the so-called 'Latin' model. Countries in this category are typically categorized by concentrated ownership of firms, strong state intervention, and weak labour participation at company level (Rhodes and Van Apeldorn 1997; Aguilera 1999). However, this Latin model of corporate governance is far from static and, just as Schmidt (2003) demonstrates for the French case, certain market-oriented reforms are moving Spanish capitalism from state-led to 'state-enhanced' capitalism.

The chapter argues that Spain has followed its own idiosyncratic path to a new model of corporate governance. This route has been distinct and unique, and determined by Spanish institutional legacies, constraints, and opportunities. The Spanish system is evolving towards a hybrid model that adopts practices from different systems, especially the Anglo-Saxon one. There is a strong tension between the state's new role as a strong regulator, the weakness of labour at company level but its strength in shaping national employment systems, and the central but uncommitted role of foreign multinationals. This tension is framed in a context of increasing internationalization of financial markets and the closer integration of the European Union (EU). In sum, key features of the current Spanish corporate governance scene comprise newly privatized firms owned by core investors (some of them foreign), a weak market for corporate control, a dual labour market system, an emphasis on passive labour market policies, and a sporadic use of Anglo-Saxon practices. The latter includes reforms aimed at increased transparency and accountability of firms, more efficient boards of directors, the development of professional managers, and innovations in workplace practices.

8.2. Institutional Background

Spain experienced massive political transformations in the last century, with the Franco dictatorship and the closed economic regime initially adopted by it being the most remarkable. The legacy of this era has conditioned the country's economic and social organization in unique, path-dependent ways. In terms of economic development, Spain was a latecomer to industrialization. It shifted from policies of autarchy during the first 20 years of the Franco regime (1939–59) to rapid industrialization and growth, triggered by liberal economic reforms and then a market-oriented approach to the international economy. The 'economic miracle' of the 1960s was based on tourism, the export of surplus labour to other European countries, and large foreign direct investment. The latter was promoted by the complete removal of barriers of trade coupled with government incentives to attract multinational companies in capital-intensive industries (Campa and Guillén 1996). With industrialization, economic development, and the lowering of trade barriers, the sectoral structure changed dramatically in a short space of time. For example, the sectoral composition of employment shifted from approximately 30 per cent in agriculture, 34 per cent in industry, and 37 per cent in services in 1967, to approximately 7 per cent in agriculture, 20 per cent in industry, 11 per cent in construction, and 62 per cent in services by 2000 (OECD 2001*a*).

One set of legacies of 40 years of dictatorship under Franco is the persistence of a protected banking system, extensive public ownership of industry, and paternalistic labour policies. This legacy shapes the character of corporate governance, labour management, and the interactions between them. These characteristics have diluted slowly, and their persistence (particularly in the labour market) presents serious obstacles to the country's economic development. Under the years of dictatorship, there was a particular complementarity between capital and labour, underpinned by a strong, interventionist state. The state and a privileged banking system were the main providers of capital to firms, resulting in little competition in capital and product markets, and few pressures to innovate. In turn this meant that there was limited demand for higher skilled labour. In addition, the state aimed for full employment by maintaining rigid rules to govern labour market entry and exit. This closed system intensified the tendency towards very limited investment in human capital. As will be discussed below, this labour–capital relationship has changed because of deregulation, privatization, and the development of financial markets.

In the democracy years (post-1978), and especially in the last decade, the following four developments have influenced both corporate governance and labour–management relations: (1) an extensive programme of economic restructuring to meet the requirements necessary to enter the European Community (EC) in 1986 and then to meet EU harmonization policies; (2) the privatization of state-owned companies; (3) an unemployment problem which rose to over 20 per cent in the mid-1980s and then to nearly 30 per cent in the mid-1990s; and (4) the presence of foreign capital in the form of subsidiaries of multinational corporations and foreign institutional investors. All of these factors are considered in the discussion of Spanish corporate governance and labour–management relations.

8.3. The Corporate Governance System

Corporate governance here is defined broadly to include both the institutional environment in which firm decisions are embedded (e.g. the legal system, the financial system, the market for corporate control, and the stock market), and mainstream governance character-istics such as ownership type and concentration. This section discusses some of the main institutional transformations which have influenced developments in corporate governance, prior to discussing current governance arrangements in Spanish firms.

8.3.1. *The privatization process*

Privatization has been an important phenomenon in Spain because of its contribution to the development of 'shareholder capitalism' and the weakening of labour protection. State-owned enterprises devel-oped under the early Franco regime as a strategic tool for the import-substitution model of economic growth and played a key role thereafter in Spanish industrialization. They were notably concen-trated within the state industrial holding company *Instituto Nacional de Industria* (INI), which emulated the Italian state-owned holdings developed under Mussolini (see Chapter 9 on Italy). Since the demo-cratization of Spain in 1978, these firms have been subject to rational-ization and restructuring, with successive waves of privatization as various governments sought to improve their efficiency. The privat-ization process was further motivated by government efforts to cut the public sector deficit so that Spain could enter the EC in 1986. State-owned enterprises, particularly in sectors experiencing heavy losses such as iron and steel, were subject to programmes of 'industrial reconversion' to increase their competitiveness. These programmes involved tens of thousands of job losses.

The main argument against extensive privatization in Spain rested on its potential to increase unemployment, particularly in the state-owned sector. Proof of this argument was demonstrated by the fall in employment in public sector industries, such as naval construction (58 per cent fall), mining (49 per cent), and defence (41 per cent) (Gámir 1999: 73). Often unions tried to stop privatizations or to intervene to minimize job losses. For instance, the partial privatization of Telefónica (the telecommunications monopoly) during 1991–7, coupled with a rationalization plan involving a 62 per cent reduction in the workforce of 180,000 provoked widespread protests from the unions. The bulk of Spanish privatizations took place after the enactment of the 'Spanish Privatization Plan' of 1996, with proceeds from privatization reaching their peak in 1997 and 1998. Only France and Italy secured larger sums from the divestment of publicly owned companies, though it should be borne in mind that their economies are also larger (OECD 2002: 46).

Although early privatizations took the form of trade sales to strategic buyers (as in France), in the 1990s initial public offerings (IPO) became the predominant method of sale. IPOs require sophisticated financial markets and a well-developed legal infrastructure. In practice, at first, they tended to place equity in the hands of institutional investors, some of them foreign. More recently, IPOs have included incentives to encourage the involvement of minority shareholders. For example, the privatization of the bank Argentaria in 1993 was the first one to provide minority shareholders with pre-IPO discounts and post-IPO protection (Gámir 1999). The subscription of minority shareholders has almost doubled since the implementation of the 'Spanish Privatization Plan' in 1996. Thus, privatization encouraged shareholder capitalism by increasing the number of traded firms and boosting the capitalization of the Spanish stock exchange. Both individuals and institutional investors became shareholders, with the state slowly bowing out of its hitherto dominant role in the management of these companies. Finally, some privatization initiatives also offered special share issues for employees, who then also become owners.

8.3.2. *The legal regulation of corporate governance*

In Spain, commercial law has historically protected large shareholders and left little room for minority shareholder voice. Like other Latin countries, Spain is a typical case of a country with weak anti-director rights, weak protection of minority investors, and concentrated owner-ship (La Porta *et al.* 1998). These features were accompanied by poor accountability and a lack of transparency. A major reform within the Spanish financial system has been the enactment of two new laws to improve shareholder rights. This legislation is a consequence of the increasing importance being attached to 'shareholder value', a key trait in liberal market economies. First, the Law on Measures to Reform the Financial System was passed in November 2002 to increase the effi-ciency and competitiveness of Spanish financial markets and strengthen investor protection. This law was also designed to incor-porate several EU Directives into Spanish law so as to prepare Spain for EU financial integration (Comisión Nacional del Mercado de Valores, CNMV 2002). Second, a Transparency Law was enacted in July 2003 to improve the transparency of ownership and corporate control. It main effect is in the area of takeover announcements. These laws bring innovative regulation in the following areas: they foster efficiency in the securities, credit, and insurance markets; they stimu-late competitiveness in the financial sector; they bring about greater transparency in corporate control; they protect the clients of financial services companies; they improve the financing of small and medium-sized enterprises; and they facilitate electronic trading (CNMV 2003). For example, the legislation has created the new post of Commissioner for the Defense of Investors to deal with abuses of financial institutions. None of this new legislation was aimed expli-citly at bringing about a 'shareholder value' model of Spanish capital-ism but, in its emphasis on greater efficiency, accountability, and transparency, it has helped to create an institutional environment that is conducive to this form of capitalism.

In addition, in 1998, the Spanish stock market approved the Olivencia Code of Good Governance to improve the governance of Spanish listed firms and in particular to reform the operation of boards of directors. In Spain, boards have traditionally been large, one-tier boards. But, like German boards, they establish dense net-works of directorship interlocks (Aguilera 1998). The Olivencia Code of Good Governance was designed and benchmarked against the British Cadbury Report of 1992. Hence, once more we find another trend towards Anglo-Saxon capitalism—if only for legitimation rea-sons (Aguilera and Cuervo-Cazurra 2004). The code is voluntary to the extent that listed companies are not compelled to comply with the code, but they are required to disclose in their annual reports the degree of compliance and to explain any reasons for non-compliance ('conform or explain'). The CNMV surveys all listed companies in order to assess their degree of adoption of the Code of Good Governance's recommendations. The conclusions of these annual surveys (1999–2002) are as follows: (1) the average firm fully adheres to approximately 75 per cent of the twenty-three recommendations listed in the code (although there is no indication that listed firms are increasingly adopting the Code recommendations); (2) firms with large free-float tend to comply more; (3) the least used recommendations are those related to transparency of remuneration, age limits for directors, and the establishment of control commissions composed solely of external directors; (4) there seems to be a significant increase in the presence of independent directors, and this is directly related to the presence of floating capital (CNMV 2002, 2003).

As a result of the new EU Directive on Market Abuse, partly incorporated in the 2002 Finance law, an updated Code of Good Governance, the *Informe Aldama*, was issued in January 2003. This code comprises a set of recommendations to govern the behaviour of listed firms. As before, the emphasis is on self-regulation and the Code does not have the force of law. The Code illustrates the active efforts taken by the Spanish governance community to promote further efficiencies in the governance system, though it is too early to assess its consequences.

Finally, one of the important effects of EU measures aimed at harmonization is the approval in 2002 of an EU decree that will require all firms trading in European stock markets to comply with the accounting norms formulated by the International Accounting Standard Board (IASB) by 2005. In reaction to this decree, the supervisory board of the Spanish stock market conducted a study (Libro Blanco) on the 'Characteristics of the Current Spanish Accounting Systems and Main Issues that need to be Reformed'. Transparency comes up again as an important concern in Spanish corporate governance. Moreover, the new financial law of 2002 includes significant measures towards accounting harmonization, particularly regarding the compulsory rotation of external auditors and the audit committee of the board of directors. Also, the US Sarbanes-Oxley Law of 2002 (enacted in response to US corporate scandals) will shape corporate governance practices worldwide and in particular those firms which are listed on any of the US stock markets.

8.3.3. *The financial system*

In the past, the Spanish financial system bore some similarities with that in Germany. Industrial banks were the main sources of financial capital, with strong cross-shareholdings and director-interlocks between banks and industry (Aguilera 1999). Recently, the Spanish financial system has experienced several major changes, and these are likely to encourage greater activism among investors. To illustrate this, it is necessary to discuss several institutions in the Spanish financial system: the banking system, institutional investment, the stock market, venture capital, and the nature of corporate control.

The Spanish banking system, particularly in the form of the industrial banks, was characterized by a privileged and protected role within the Spanish economy (Pérez 1997). This changed when competitive pressures forced the sector to open the market and deregulate. By 1998, the Spanish banking system had experienced a significant consolidation, with the privatization of most of the state-owned banks and mergers of six of the largest banks into two: Banco Bilbao Vizcaya Argentaria (BBVA) and Banco Santander Central Hispano (BSCH). The Competition Tribunal approved these mergers on the grounds that competition would be protected by the active presence of a number of medium-sized commercial banks and a large number of saving banks[i]. However, it is to be noted that these two largest Spanish commercial banks (BBVA and BSCH) accounted for more than half of market share in Spanish commercial banking in 2002 (28.9 and 27.19 per cent, respectively), followed some way behind by the third largest bank, Banco Español de Crédito (with a 7.5 per cent market share) (El País 2003: 419). The concentration among saving banks is not as pronounced: the two largest saving banks, La Caixa and Caja de Ahorros de Madrid, held 19.1 per cent and 14.5 per cent of the savings banks' market share in 2002 (El País 2003: 420).

The removal of barriers to entry in the banking system (partly triggered by EC requirements) led to an influx of foreign banks from the 1980s and a consequent growth in competition in the banking sector. The banking liberalization coincided with a shake-out of the fragmented domestic banking system, with foreign banks allowed to rescue those in receivership. The first mover was Barclays which acquired the failing Banco de Valladolid in 1981. The proportion of foreign banks in Spain is now above the EU average even though some market entrants subsequently withdrew (OECD 2001a; *Financial Times*, 8 October 2003). According to the *Financial Times*, 'the Spanish financial system is the most profitable in the Eurozone—in terms of return on assets and second in return on equity—but with a cost-to-income ratio of 73 per cent' (*Financial Times*, 8 October 2003: 3).

In 2002, there were forty-nine foreign banks operating in Spain with ING Bank NV having the largest percentage of the foreign banks' market share (30.4 per cent), followed by BNP Paribas and Barclays Bank PLC with 8.9 per cent and 8 per cent, respectively (El País 2003: 419). The race for market share is fierce with the two main Spanish banks undertaking aggressive marketing strategies.

The role of banks in the Spanish economy is reflected in corporate financing. Leverage ratios for Spanish manufacturing firms averaged 38.2 per cent during 1992–5 and peaked at an average of 42.6 per cent in 2000–1 (Banco de España 2002). This notable reliance on debt is explained by strong ownership ties with industrial banks as well as the underdevelopment of the Spanish stock market. Leverage ratios are higher for large firms (250 employees or more) than for small firms. However, the dependence on banks decreased in the 1990s. The proportion of bank debt as a percentage of total debt fell from over 35 per cent in 1991 to just below 22 per cent in 2000, as shown in Table 8.1. A comparative analysis of bank debt as a percentage of total debt over time shows that Spanish firms' reliance on bank debt is considerably higher than German firms (who also traditionally enjoyed closed ties with industrial banks). It is, however, considerably lower than in Italy where there is a large network of small regional banks providing finance to small and medium-sized firms. Finally, most of the debt in Spanish manufacturing firms tends to be short-term, a pattern which occurs among firms in other European economies, such as France and Germany (Banco de España 2002: 121). There is little empirical evidence on the consequences of high debt leverages for labour and management behaviour. The suggestion which will be considered here is that the fact that lenders (banks) tended to own

Table 8.1. *Bank debt as a percentage of total debt (various countries)*

Country	1991	1995	2000
Spain	35.6	29.7	21.9
France	20.1	14.8	14.8
Germany	22.3	19.0	14.1
Italy	38.1	33.9	32.5
Japan	37.1	40.8	37.8
Portugal	37.6	31.1	33.4
United States	20.4	19.4	21.8

Source: Banco de España (2002: 131).

shares in the firms to which they lent money meant that company managers were able to pursue long-term strategies and did not have to seek short-term efficiencies. 'Patient capital' therefore resulted in few pressures to restructure labour management in order to improve productivity, and facilitated employment security.

The presence of institutional investors (insurance companies, investment companies, pension funds, and other forms of institutional savings funds) in Spanish financial markets in the early 1990s was relatively small compared to other OECD countries. For instance, the share of institutional investors' assets was 21.9 per cent of GDP compared with 34 per cent in Germany, 61.9 per cent in France, 127.2 per cent in the United States, and 131.3 per cent in the United Kingdom (OECD 2001b: 46). By the end of the 1990s, the share of institutional investors in the Spanish financial system had multiplied by three, and had caught up with other Continental European countries. This increase in the importance of institutional investment is explained by the entrance of foreign capital, a growing concern to supplement public pensions with private provision, and the transfer of the state's public deficit to household savings.

The Spanish stock market has historically been small, underdeveloped, and geographically segmented into four locations (Madrid, Barcelona, Bilbao, and Valencia), with the Bolsa de Madrid being the largest. During the 1990s, the stock market matured in terms of market capitalization, securitization, and the modernization of administrative procedures. Privatization, the Securities Market Law reform of 1998, and new regulations on takeover bids stimulated activity on the Spanish stock market and helped to develop a small investor culture. In addition, according to the OECD's 2003 *Financial Market Trends* (2003b), the growing reliance on private savings for retirement income explains part of the increasing consolidation and integration of European stock markets over time.

Viewed comparatively, market capitalization and the number of firms traded in the Spanish stock market have grown tremendously in the last few years and, although they remain well below that of the Anglo-Saxon markets, there is certainly a trend towards Anglo-Saxon sources of finance for companies (Tables 8.2, 8.3).

The most important reform in recent years has been the consolidation in 2001 of the four different Spanish stock markets and the financial societies within these stock markets into a single holding company with responsibility for trading, clearing, and settlement—the *Bolsas y Mercados Españoles* (BME). It is expected that this consolidation will

Table 8.2. *Market capitalization in selected OECD countries (as percentage of GDP)*

Country	1988	1990	1993	1997	2001
Australia	50.4	35.1	67.5	71.0	101.5
France	25.0	25.9	35.7	48.0	89.7
Germany	18.3	21.0	23.7	39.1	58.1
Italy	16.1	13.5	13.7	29.5	48.4
Japan	131.2	95.6	68.6	51.4	54.4
The Netherlands	47.3	40.7	55.9	124.4	120.5
Norway	14.6	22.6	23.6	42.9	41.6
Portugal	14.0	12.9	14.4	36.6	42.2
Spain	25.5	21.8	23.9	51.7	80.5
Sweden	53.1	41.1	55.8	114.2	110.8
United Kingdom	92.6	85.8	119.5	150.3	155.7
United States	55.2	53.2	78.0	137.0	137.2

Source: World Bank (2003).

Table 8.3. *Number of listed domestic companies in selected OECD countries*

Country	1988	1990	1993	1997	2001
Australia	1,380	1,089	1,070	1,159	1,334
France	646	578	472	683	791
Germany	609	413	426	700	988
Italy	211	220	210	239	288
Japan	1,967	2,071	2,155	2,387	2,471
The Netherlands	232	260	245	201	180
Portugal	171	181	183	148	97
Spain	368	427	376	384	1,458
Sweden	142	258	205	245	285
United Kingdom	2,054	1,701	1,646	2,157	1,923
United States	6,680	6,599	7,246	8,851	6,355

Source: World Bank (2003).

attract more financial resources and ensure more efficient management, in addition to the benefits from economies of scale. Two other markets within the Spanish stock market are a special market for Latin American companies (*Latibex*) created in 1999 and a new market (*Nuevo Mercado*) for new economy companies created in 2000 along the lines of the *Noveau Marché* and the erstwhile *Neuer Market*. However, the Spanish new market is very small with only seventeen companies in it by 2002.

Compared with most OECD countries, venture capital investments in Spain are underdeveloped. The immaturity of venture capital investments in Spain has long-term effects on growth and is closely related to the low levels of R&D investments at firm level. In 2000, there were only eighty-five registered venture capital entities (OECD 2001*a*: 92). Risk-averse entrepreneurs, few management buyouts or industrial spin-offs, little interest in IPOs, and financial markets which are generally oriented towards large firms contribute to this underdevelopment. To counter this, since 1999, the Spanish government has made efforts to boost venture capital investments with fiscal incentives. For example, the New Financial Law of 2002 extends tax concessions to venture capital investments even after they have been partially sold in the stock market (OECD 2003*a*: 80).

Traditionally, the market for corporate control among Spanish firms was practically non-existent because of high ownership concentration of quoted firms and poor minority shareholder rights. For instance, in 1997 nearly half of Spanish quoted-firms (representing 20.6 per cent of the capitalization of the stock market) were owned by a majority shareholder. This made it impossible for investors to bring about changes in corporate control. However, takeover bids have increased, especially by value, since the mid-1990s. As shown in Table 8.4, takeover bids reached a peak in 2001. After 2001, as elsewhere, takeovers became too expensive because of declining equity prices. This is confirmed by the fact that nine out of the nineteen authorized tender offers in 2001 were made by European groups, whereas in 2002 just three of the seventeen offers were by foreign firms. The relatively low number of takeovers indicates a weak market for corporate control, particularly if we take into account that the single largest takeover bid in 2002 (that of Aceralia for Arcelor) accounted for nearly 50 per cent of the total takeover value in the period (CNMV 2003: 65).

Table 8.4. *Spanish tender offers*

Tender offers	1997	1998	1999	2000	2001	2002
Number authorized in year	14	18	13	16	19	17
Value of authorized offers[a, b]	648	4,683	711	3,059	7,685	5,589
Number filed in year	13	18	13	14	18	17
Value of filed offers[a, b]	575	4,411	601	2,606	4,468	4,318

[a] Millions of euros.
[b] Not including withdrawn offers.

Source: CNMV (2002, 2003).

In early 2003, a Takeover Law was enacted with the primary objective of protecting minority shareholders from expropriation by majority shareholders. The rationale for this legislation lies in the reactions to takeovers in the construction and real estate sector where huge premiums had been secured by majority shareholders at the expense of minority shareholders. However, the traditional interventionist role of the Spanish state has not completely disappeared. For instance, former state-owned firms such as Telefónica, Repsol and Endesa are protected from the implications of the new legislation by the presence of a 'golden share', held by the government until 2008 to protect the national strategic interest. This is a good illustration of Schmidt's (2003) argument that 'state-enhanced' activity is replacing fully fledged 'state-led' activity.

8.3.4. *Ownership structure of Spanish firms*

Ownership structure is one of the main dimensions of corporate governance. It is widely seen to be determined by other country-level corporate governance characteristics such as the development of the stock market and the nature of state intervention and regulation (La Porta *et al.* 1998). Ownership type and concentration are the two key dimensions of ownership structure. In Spain, details of owner identity and ownership share are reported in an annual census (Empresas de la Central de Balances) of all Spanish companies conducted by the Banco de España. Table 8.5 shows the distribution of ownership type in the last decade.

Table 8.5 shows that in the early 2000s the majority of Spanish firms are owned by domestic capital, that is, domestic firms, private

Table 8.5. *Ownership structure of Spanish firms 1990–2001 (percentage of ownership)*

Owner type	1990	1993	1997	2001
State[a]	33.7	33.4	33.5	24.8
Financial institutions	5.0	4.3	5.3	4.9
Domestic firms	18.8	28.8	26.8	45.1
Other domestic owners	27.6	17.6	19.6	14.4
Foreign capital	14.9	15.9	14.8	10.8
Total	100	100	100	100

[a] Including ownership by public administrative authorities and by the state-owned holding company SEPI.

Source: Banco de España (2002).

individuals, and the state. Three main characteristics of the current ownership structure of Spanish companies are to be noted. First, state ownership continues to be predominant, despite the massive privatization programme initiated since 1996. Although state ownership has fallen since the early 1990s, the state continues to have majority ownership in a still-significant proportion of large Spanish firms. Second, there has been a steady increase in the proportion of ownership held by domestic firms, suggesting a further strengthening of business groups or holdings by former state-owned firms and industrial banks. Third, the percentage of foreign capital ownership (in the mid teens throughout the 1990s) is starting to decrease.

Firms quoted on the Spanish stock market show a somewhat different ownership structure, mainly due to the increasing consolidation of the Spanish stock market during the 1990s. As is shown in Table 8.6, in 1996 the primary shareholders were foreign institutional investors (28 per cent), closely followed by individuals and family groups (24 per cent).

The high percentage of foreign ownership is mainly due to the openness of the economy after 1986. A comparison with other OECD countries highlights a relatively high percentage of bank ownership. Domestic institutional investors own a relatively low proportion of domestic listed firms. Ownership trends over time are shown in Table 8.7.

Four recent developments stand out. First, the proportion of equity (by value) held by the state has virtually disappeared. It has fallen from 16.64 per cent in 1992 to 0.21 per cent in 2000. Second, there has been a corresponding dramatic increase in ownership by non-financial firms, including by privatized ones such as the Spanish flagship

Table 8.6. *Ownership of listed companies in 1996: various countries (percentage of ownership)*

Investor type	Spain	Germany	France	US	UK
Institutional investors (domestic)	7	20	20	41	67
Banks	14	10	10	6	1
Institutional investors (foreign)	28	9	25	5	9
State	11	4	3	0	1
Individuals	24	15	23	49	21
Non-financial firms	7	42	19	0	1
Other	10	0	0	0	0
Total	100	100	100	100	100

Source: Eguidazu (1999: 250–251); OECD (1998).

Table 8.7. *Significant shareholdings in listed Spanish firms (percentages of firm ownership)*

Owner type	1992	1996	2000
Banks	15.56	14.06	7.29
Insurance firms	3.37	2.20	2.29
Institutional investors (domestic)	1.65	5.02	4.77
State	16.64	10.87	0.21
Non-financial firms	7.72	6.90	20.26
Individuals	24.44	23.59	30.52
Foreign	30.61	37.36	34.67
Total	100	100	100

Source: World Federation of Exchanges (2002); CIA (2002).

telecommunications company (Telefónica). Third, there has been an increase in the proportion of total equity held by private households, from 24 to 31 per cent. This is a higher level of individual ownership than in other European economies (25, 16, 15.6, 13.1, and 7.5 per cent in Milan, London, Frankfurt, Stockholm, and Paris, respectively). Fourth, the proportion of equity held by foreign capital has been more or less stable over the last 10 years at around 30–35 per cent. These four trends are characteristic of liberal market economies and hence might translate into demands for higher shareholder value and accountability from managers and chief executives. However, the shifts in ownership type over the last ten years have not been accompanied by ownership dispersion. High ownership concentration of Spanish listed firms persists, with 49 per cent of quoted firms in 1997 having a single majority owner (Cuervo-Cazurra 1999).

In sum, we can observe changing patterns towards a new hybrid system of corporate governance. In this system, the state has retreated from its earlier direct and highly interventionist role and instead has attempted to enhance actions taken by other actors. Spanish firms are attempting to catch up with those in more developed countries by incorporating new institutions promoted by legislation and by developing dormant ones such as the stock market. However, other characteristics of Latin corporate governance systems, such as ownership concentration and the leading role of banks, appear to persist.

8.4. The System of Employment Relations

The main heritage of Francoist industrial relations was a paternalistic orientation of management and the state towards employees. This was reflected organizationally in a single 'vertical' union, a state-controlled syndicalist organization uniting employers and employees in a single body (Unión Sindical Obreara). During the Franco era democratic unions were declared illegal, strikes and collective bargaining were outlawed (until 1958), and the Ministry of Labour governed industrial relations by regulations (*ordenanzas labourales*) (Preston 1976; Maravall 1978; Linz 1981; Fishman 1990; Bermeo 1994). During the political transition period (1975–8), unions functioned as moderate and constructive social agents. Following the signing of the Pactos de la Moncloa in 1977, unions became partners in a large number of social pacts. Thus, labour tried to be accommodating through political compromise and concertation. There are conflicting interpretations in the academic literature on the effectiveness of the unions' strategy. For instance, Miguélez and Prieto (1991) claim that industrial relations in Spain were the poor relations of the political transition in that insufficient changes were demanded by unions of political leaders; whereas Hamann argues that 'the lack of an institutional legacy of democratic unions and the relatively high degree of institutional fluidity, left unions much leeway to adjust quickly to a rapidly changing political environment' (1998: 427). The economic restructuring of the 1980s provided another window of opportunity for deregulation and decentralization of both bargaining and the production process.

The demographic transformations during the democratic period (post-1975) led to changes in labour market structure. As in other industrializing countries, the principal demographic shift was a significant decrease in employment in the agricultural sector and an increase in the service sector. In addition, after the Franco regime, Spanish public administration was extensively reformed, with the creation of autonomous regions (*autonomías*), new ministries, and an expansion of welfare provision. As a result, the share of public administration employment as a proportion of total employment grew by more than 50 per cent between 1976 and 1994. As shown in Table 8.8, employment in the public sector has continued to grow, despite the privatization of state-owned firms.

The main transformations in the Spanish employment system are mostly explained by the rigidity of the labour market. A particularly important feature has been the expensive and lengthy dismissal procedure instituted during the Franco regime and still persisting today. This inhibits job creation and helps to explain high levels of unemployment since the 1980s. As Table 8.9 shows, unemployment rose from 16 per cent at the beginning of the 1990s to 23 per cent in 1995.

Table 8.8. *Employment by sector 1980–2000*
(thousands)

Type	1980	1990	2000
Self-employed	2,065	2,496	1,867
Employed	7,918	9,240	12,285
Public sector	1,510	2,106	2,443
Private sector	5,608	7,167	9,842

Source: Instituto Nacional de Estadística (2003).

Table 8.9. *Spanish employment activity and unemployment rates (percentages)*

Year	Activity rate (%)	Unemployment rate (%)		
		Total	Male	Female
1980	48.7	11.5	11.0	12.9
1990	49.4	16.3	12.0	24.2
1995	49.0	22.9	18.1	30.5
2000	51.3	13.9	9.6	20.5
2001	52.9	10.9	7.5	15.2

Notes: The unemployed are defined as those who are without work and who are actively looking for employment (as defined by registration with the INEM).

Source: Instituto Nacional de Estadística (2003).

In the mid-1990s unemployment was nearly double the European Community average. At 11 per cent in late 2002 it continued to be one of the highest in the OECD.

Moreover, with the emergence of foreign pressures for greater flexibility from the 1980s, the Spanish employment system evolved towards an extreme labour market dualism with numerical flexibility being the key divide between labour market segments. This duality is critical because it influences the entire system of management–labour relations. The Spanish labour market is divided into a primary stable sector composed of 'insider' workers with permanent contracts, rising wages, and social benefits (about two-thirds of the labour force), and a secondary unstable segment composed mainly of workers with temporary contracts and precarious job conditions (mostly young employees and women). According to Fernández Macías (2003: 207), the extreme division of the labour market is to be seen in the context of (1) a strong labour movement which can afford some protection to insiders and (2) the strong impact of international economic crisis and an extremely high level of unemployment.

The rigid labour market has persisted since the Franco era, mainly due to the power of the labour movement. By the late 1980s, this pattern of labour market regulation could no longer be maintained and a parallel 'secondary' labour market emerged. In fact, the structure may be more complicated than this. Pérez-Díaz and Rodriguez (1995) describe the Spanish labour market as a four-tier system, composed of a protected core, temporary workers, workers in the underground economy, and unemployed workers dependent on public subsidies. They argue that the four segments are related as follows:

> The relative rigidity of the rules concerning job stability and wages in the primary labour market are to a significant extent responsible for the scope and characteristics of the other three arenas: low competencies and low wages for temporary and underground workers, and subsidies and benefits for ex-employees and the unemployed. (1995: 190)

The approach to this labour market structure has been that state policy has focused on supporting the secondary tiers by generous benefits rather than promoting employability by training and active labour market policies. As a result, there has been a lack of connection between skills and job stability and between compensation and productivity. Furthermore, rigid forms of work organization have persisted and overall there has been little innovation in work practices. In conclusion, there is a contradiction between those pressures from the corporate governance system for reforms to labour management within the firm and those emanating from government labour market policy and favouring stability.

The remainder of this section discusses several key elements of Spanish labour–management relations and their role within the corporate governance equation. In particular, it examines (1) traditional industrial relations issues, such as collective bargaining agreements; (2) work relations issues, such as skill formation; (3) employment relations issues, such as the spread of several Human Resource Management (HRM) practices; and (4) the influence of foreign subsidiaries on Spanish work practices.

8.4.1. *Industrial relations: collective bargaining and employee voice*

Spain has a well-developed and relatively centralized system of collective bargaining. Three key characteristics of Spanish collective bargaining should be noted.

First, as in Germany, collective bargaining agreements are subject to the statutory *erga omnes* principle whereby all workers benefit from agreements within their scope (national, industry, or firm) regardless of their union affiliation. As a consequence, collective bargaining de facto covers about 80 per cent of the workforce (Hamann and Martínez Lucio 2003: 66). Second, the majority of the workforce are covered by sectoral agreements reached at provincial level (Miguélez and Rebollo 1999: 333–4). Only 11 per cent of firms (mainly large firms and state-owned firms) have enterprise agreements. Sectoral bargaining is the most important level of bargaining for establishing minimum working conditions in the workplace and for pay determination. This is also vital for workers in small and medium firms with no company-level agreement or employee representation. Third, the main representative body of workers is the work council (*comité de empresa*). This can be constituted in workplaces with fifty or more employees irrespective of trade union membership. As pointed out by Bayo-Moriones and Huerta-Arribas (2002: 710), 'although union density is very low, unions usually enjoy a high degree of influence since work councils exist in a great majority of Spanish companies'. Since all employees are entitled to vote in work council elections, union candidacies ensure that union involvement can be found in around 80 per cent of firms (Martínez Lucio 1998: 436). García-Serrano and Malo (2002) demonstrate the importance of work councils and show that establishments with firm/plant-level agreements, usually highly associated with the strong presence of organized labour in work councils, have a stronger influence on low worker mobility than establishments with higher-level agreements.

In this way, wage bargaining in Spain mainly takes the form of collective bargaining at the provincial sectoral level agreements, which might be categorized as intermediate levels of centralization in wage bargaining (Royo 2000). This differs from other Latin countries such as France where collective bargaining is increasingly taking place at the firm level, thereby enabling and supporting radical innovation in product markets (Hancké 2002). It has been argued that the Spanish sectoral collective bargaining results in a 'poverty' of bargaining (Martínez Lucio 1998), because of a narrow bargaining agenda (wages), ineffective coordination between the levels of bargaining, and fragmentation of industrial sectors into a multiplicity of sub-sectors. The sectoral level of wage bargaining has also been criticized for being insufficiently flexible 'to allow for wage differentials to reflect firm-level productivity differentials' (OECD 2001a: 64). Moreover, the most recent OECD report on Spain (2003) claims that labour costs are becoming a major obstacle to productivity growth and there is therefore a need to reform the wage bargaining system.

The rise in unemployment in Spain led to shifts in union bargaining agendas from a focus on work organization towards demands for employment security. It is also argued that unemployment, coupled with sectoral shifts in employment, have brought about a decline in trade union membership (a fall of about 15 percentage points in the 1990s). This decline of unionization is also a result of two opposing trends: the precarious labour market and the increased use of HRM practices to promote participation in the workplace. However, scholars of Spanish industrial relations agree that the decrease in union membership does not tell the full story of union representation or power because of the so-called 'dual system of worker representation', as regulated by legislation and entitling all workers to be covered by collective bargaining agreements. As in France, union participation in collective bargaining agreements is decided by representation in elections to workers' committee elections. Yet, unlike France, Spanish law defines a 'representative' trade union as one which has at least 10 per cent of the employee delegates and work council members within the area covered by the agreement. This institutional arrangement consolidates the position of the two major union confederations (Unión General de Trabajadores (UGT) and Comisiones Obreras (CC.OO.)) as the dominant bargaining agents and in effect establishes a national 'contest' between them to obtain the maximum votes. As Martínez Lucio (1998: 436) points out, union influence depends on electoral success as much as on membership figures.

The employers' association (Confederación Española de Organizaciones Empresariales (CEOE)) has existed as a social partner since the transition times. However, from the late 1980s, the growing recession and the increasingly conflictual state of industrial relations led employers' organizations to become increasingly antagonistic. As part of this, they developed their own political agenda, of which key items were calls for greater labour market flexibility, firm-level collective bargaining, and a reduction in employers' social security contributions. Employer associations saw no further mileage in containing union and government demands through concertation and support of potential expansionist economic policies. Instead they focused on corporate restructuring, flexibility, and international competitiveness (López Novo 1991; Martínez Lucio 1995, 1998).

Finally, a key feature of Spanish industrial relations is the high level of industrial conflict. Spain has the highest strike rate among EU countries as a result of 'the limited strategic options available to Spanish trade unions and Spanish employers' ambivalence toward industrial relations institutions' (Rigby and Marco Aledo 2001). The most significant labour mobilizations recently were jointly led by the two union confederations (UGT and CC.OO.): these were one-day 'general strikes' in 1988 and in 2002 to oppose government decree—laws aimed at reforming employment relations by reinforcing the dual labour market.

8.4.2. *Numerical flexibility, temporal contracts, and skill formation*

This section argues that increasing labour market duality and fragmentation leaves little motivation for investment in firm-specific human capital. Employees in the temporary labour market do not need advanced skills, while those in the core labour market have little incentive to undertake professional retraining because of job protection.

The labour market helps to define the nature of employment expectations and practices, training and development, mobility patterns, and internal versus external careers. Labour market structures 'are closely connected to types of national education and training systems, skill definitions and control institutions, union structures and policies, and the legal framework governing labour relations, as well as the diffuse norms concerning authority, loyalty, and identity' (Whitley 1999: 26). Stakeholder capitalism views competitive advantage as arising from the engagement of social partners and other stakeholders in the firm's strategies and practices. By contrast, shareholder capitalism assumes a flexible labour market where employees are hired and fired at will (Hall and Soskice 2001b). According to the latter model, continental European labour markets are seen as 'sclerotic' and 'fossilized', especially in contrast to the flexible and dynamic labour markets characteristic of the United States. Esping-Andersen and Regini (2000a), however, see this view as too simplistic. They argue instead that labour market 'flexibility' in Europe is complicated and cannot be reduced to a simple dichotomy between flexibility and rigidity. This is applied here to the Spanish experience.

Traditionally, Spain had a highly regulated labour market particularly in terms of contracting issues such as hiring and firing. In the 1980s, many employers called for greater flexibility and deregulation, and this resulted in several reforms (Toharia and Malo 2000). The most notable is the 1984 labour reform, known as 'flexibility at the margin'. This allows the creation of flexible contracts, while leaving existing contracts untouched, and it marked the beginning of the dual labour market. Hence, since the early 1980s, fifteen different types of atypical employment contracts have been introduced (Martínez Lucio 1998: 450), with forms of temporary employment being the most widespread. Although the rationale behind the introduction of temporary contracts was to encourage the creation of permanent posts, in practice transfers from temporary to permanent contracts are rare.

In 1994, measures to promote non-precarious employment were introduced by a decree which sought (unsuccessfully) to limit the use of traditional temporary contracts (the so-called *contratos basura* or trash contracts) by creating yet another kind of temporary contract (apprenticeships) and to increase incentives for part-time work. Neither of these two initiatives were successful. Three years later, in 1997, under government pressure, employers and unions signed a national agreement 'clarifying the grounds for dismissal and in effect making it easier for companies at risk of losses to declare redundancies on economic grounds' (Martínez Lucio 1998: 452). Finally, in March 2001, taking advantage of the conservative parliamentary majority, the government enacted another labour reform by decree without the support of either employers or trade unions. This reform was aimed at creating more and better employment contracts by promoting indefinite contracts and encouraging female participation in the labour market.

In sum, Spain relied on numerical flexibility as its key policy for job creation and job maintenance, by making temporary contracting the main policy instrument to persuade employers to hire workers. The 'regulation by de-regulation' of the labour market is leading to high levels of job insecurity and lack of commitment by both employers and employees. A study by Amuedo-Dorantes (2000) shows that temporary employment is non-transitional and involuntary. Esping-Andersen and Regini (2000*b*) note that, as in Germany and France, the 'controlled experiment' of labour market deregulation is accompanied by other, sometimes contradictory, measures of re-regulation. Their explanation is that de-regulation seeks to insert a degree of flexibility in some segments of the labour market, but on the whole not in a way that questions the basic framework and rules of regulation.

Table 8.10 shows that Spain has the highest percentage of temporary employees in the EU. In 2000, despite governmental efforts to

Table 8.10. *Temporary work in Western Europe 1983–94 (percentage of the workforce in temporary employment)*[a]

Country	1983	1987	1989	1991	1994
France	3.3	7.1	8.5	10.2	11.0
Germany	9.7	11.6	11.0	9.5	10.3
Italy	6.6	5.4	6.3	5.4	7.3
The Netherlands	5.8	9.4	8.5	7.7	10.9
Portugal	14.4	16.9	18.7	16.5	9.4
Spain	15.6	15.6	26.6	32.3	33.7
Sweden	12.0	–	–	–	13.5
United Kingdom	5.5	6.3	5.4	5.3	6.5

[a] National definitions of temporary employment are used. These vary from country to country. See OECD Employment Outlook (various years) for details.

Source: Waddington and Hoffman (2000: 39).

minimize this kind of contract, temporary contracts accounted for 31.6 per cent of all contracts, almost double the EU average (17 per cent) (*El País*, 8 March 2001). Conversely, part-time employment is much lower than the European average (Waddington and Hoffmann 2000: 38). This is mainly explained by the lower level of female participation in the labour market in Spain.

The use of flexible labour contracts by many firms means that, as Blyton and Martinez Lucio point out, labour is not seen as 'a resource to be qualitatively developed in order to provide the economy with a competitive edge' (1995: 278). One of the main problems with labour market segmentation is that it fosters the growth of unskilled work (Pérez-Díaz and Rodriguez 1995), which in turn may encourage employment growth in less productive sectors. New personnel management and work organization designs are scarce and only permanent workers tend to benefit from them. However, smaller employers have also been looking to HRM practices 'as a way of pre-empting strong and independent labour representation' (Martínez Lucio 1999: 447).

Spanish firms invest little in R&D and in information technology. Investments are less than one per cent of GDP in R&D compared with an EU average of 1.9 per cent. Only 1.9 per cent of GDP is invested in information technology compared with an EU average of 3.2 per cent (*El País*, 15 June 2003). The fact that for several decades Spain's main competitive advantage was low labour costs helps to explain these discrepancies. There were few incentives to develop the necessary institutions to create highly skilled employees. Proof of this is the low prestige of vocational training compared with countries such as

Germany. More recently, efforts to solve the rigidity of the labour market focused on passive labour market policies (subsidies to the unemployed and to support new permanent contracts) rather than active policies, such as the provision of training for unemployed workers (OECD 2003*a*: 59).

Another institutional constraint in the vocational training area has been the inefficiency of state interventionism. Besides the formal vocational education system for young employees, vocational training was subsidized through the state and conducted under the auspices of INEM (National Employment Institute). It is remarkable that until 1993, well into the economic crises, INEM was the mediator between employees and employer, and thus controlled the entire hiring market. All new hiring contracts had to be administrated by INEM, otherwise they were considered illegal. Rodríguez-Piñero Royo (2001) shows how INEM's activities were disconnected from firms' labour requirements and also its vocational training programmes were eroded during the 1980s and 1990s.

In Spain, training infrastructure, as well as a culture of training, are underdeveloped compared with other European countries (Martín Artiles 1999). There is no statutory requirement on employers to provide training and the few existing training schemes tend to be rigid and bureaucratic (Fina 1991). In particular, there is very little on-the-job training. Firm-level training is subsidized by public funds, although their efficacy has been questioned and continues to be the subject of reform. Investment in training is highly selective, and much of it is directed exclusively to top management teams and permanent workers.

8.4.3. *The development of HRM practices*

Work organization in Spanish firms has also traditionally been rigid as a result of state policy. The Ordenanzas Labourales in the Franco years and then the Workers' Statute of 1980 (in place until the early 1990s) severely restricted managerial capacities to innovate in work organization (Pérez-Díaz and Rodriguez 1995). The introduction of functional flexibility and HRM practices has been slow and limited, due in part to the legal and administrative constraints for change (Ferner and Quintanilla 2002). The role of personnel management consisted mainly in applying the extensive regulations. Hence, HRM was perceived as technical, bureaucratic, and legalistic.

In the post-Franco years, the main goal of personnel management was to reduce labour conflict and manage the wide range of contractual agreements, rather than to develop human capital. The personnel function was generally underdeveloped and perceived as an administrative function as opposed to a strategic management function. During the years of high unemployment, personnel managers' activities were concentrated on the management of redundancies within the context of a rigid labour market.

Thus, the introduction of HRM practices and more flexible working practices in Spanish firms has lagged behind other European countries (García Echevarría and Val Nuñez 1996). However, the personnel function in Spanish firms has undergone a steady process of modernization triggered by the increasing flexibility in the labour market, EU social policy, the growth in competition, and the emergence of new organizational principles. In recent years, the use of team briefings, team working, quality circles, and profit-sharing schemes has burgeoned, as managements have attempted to promote greater levels of commitment among workers to the enterprise. Flórez-Saborido, González-Rendón, and Alcaide-Castro (1995) also refer to the importance of foreign consulting firms and large multinationals in implanting certain HR practices such as job rotations and appraisal feedback. Gradually, the activities of HR managers are shifting from the management of redundancy towards the introduction of new systems of labour management which contribute to labour market flexibility, vocational training, and flexible compensation.

The development of flexible compensation is an interesting case in point. Until recently, the rigidity of the labour market and the low level of competition for managerial staff led to low management turnover. Geographical and organizational mobility was low. Managerial careers tended to develop within a given firm and promotions were given on the basis of seniority—hence the lack of incentive to leave the firm. Moreover, wages were seldom linked to performance. In the 1990s, increasing competition among Spanish firms and the emergence of pressures from emergent shareholder value capitalism, required greater accountability of managers and more emphasis on short-term measures of performance. These led to the introduction of new compensation strategies, some in the form of fringe benefits and some tied to stock market performance such as bonuses and stock options for senior management (Ortín and Salas Fumás 1997). In total, 80 per cent of Spanish blue chip firms (Ibex35) now offer stock options programmes to their top managers (*El País*, 15 June 2003).

The initial introduction of fringe benefits to complement pay was also motivated by fiscal advantages for the firm and the employee (Flórez-Saborido, González-Rendón and Alcaide-Castro 1995). A recent report by Mercer Human Resource Consulting (2002) indicates that the fringe benefits most used are the following (in order of use): company car, loans, pension plans, and life and accident insurance. Despite all the publicity about stock options, the most widely-used form of performance-related pay is bonuses. According to Watson Wyatt (2002), contingent pay among top managers is distributed as follows: 83 per cent of managers are offered bonuses, 37 per cent stock options, 20 per cent preferential shares, and 13 per cent profit sharing. Since the equity market in Spain is still narrow and underdeveloped, the symbolic effect of stock options is perhaps more important than their practical benefits.

There are other ways in which contingent pay in the Spanish governance system does not fully compare with the situation in the Anglo-Saxon countries. For instance, as elsewhere in Europe, senior management compensation packages are not fully disclosed. Disclosure is limited to total remuneration of the top management team, with the constituent elements not being individually itemized. In addition, unlike most Anglo-Saxon companies, where compensation committees of outside directors are established to design remuneration schemes, in Spain these committees are embryonic and shadowy institutions. It is rarely clear who is on them, or indeed whether they exist at all. Finally, Romero and Valle Cabrera's (2001) survey of 99 Spanish manufacturing firms, with more than 500 employees in the mid-1990s, found that Spanish compensation practices follow different models than those in American companies. They argue that 'Spanish companies do not design true strategies of compensation; instead compensation practices may exist that are common to all companies irrespective of the strategy followed, of the sector to which they belong, or their size' (Romero and Valle Cabrera 2001: 234). They conclude that contingent pay in Spain might simply be a search for legitimacy as a result of pressures exerted by institutional shareholders.

With the exception of managers, contingent compensation linked to firm productivity or employee skills is uncommon. There are very few employee share ownership plans, except those in the form of small cooperative arrangements and the well-known Mondragón cooperatives (Whyte 1999).

8.4.4. *Foreign direct investment and multinational corporations in Spain*

Another important factor influencing change in work organization and the introduction of HRM practices is the presence of foreign capital in the form of subsidiaries. Since the early 1960s, foreign direct investment was driven by Spain's main competitive advantage, viz. cheap labour. This meant that investment flowed to high-volume and to medium/low-skill operations such as car assembly (Blyton and Martínez Lucio 1995: 276), and was partly motivated by a concern to gain access to the European market. Spanish unions did not actively oppose these investments as they did not want to jeopardize the multinationals' job creation and technology transfer activities, although they were suspicious of the multinationals' motives for investing in a protected market with a dictatorial government. In effect, union views shifted to embrace multinationals as partners and as employers who could be 'more sensible, progressive, and democratic than the average entrepreneur' (Guillén 2000: 437).

There seems to be a tension between the need for innovation in Spanish work organization and the search for cheap labour. Some case studies consider whether the entry of foreign multinational subsidiaries in Spain had any spillover in the diffusion of HRM practices in Spanish work organization. Most studies, particularly within the automobile industry, seem to agree that the development of innovative work organization practices has been patchy, and such practices are intertwined with traditional and paternalistic work practices. Pérez-Díaz and Rodríguez state that '(foreign) automakers have been committed to introducing a variety of changes in work organization which most Spanish observers label as "Toyotism"' (1995: 181). In a similar vein, Charron shows how production organization in one of the oldest foreign automobile firms in Spain (FASA Renault) takes a post-Fordist form: 'its production was diversified with low volumes for each model, produced on relatively flexible assembly lines, using skilled labour which enjoyed significant job security' (1998: 254). Despite some significant transplant practices, there is also the case of Volkswagen's SEAT plant in Martorell which introduced labour-intensive methods such as three shift working rather than highly automated production methods (Smith 1998). Pérez-Díaz and Rodriguez also note that 'there is little evidence that innovations such as quality circles, just-in-time procedures, and group work have become wide-spread' (1995: 181).

As Martínez Lucio has noted, although multinational firms have been in the forefront of importing HRM practices such as quality circles and multi-skilling to enhance worker involvement, subsidiaries' plans are not always high value-added operations and their management structures are often subservient to the dictats of international headquarters (1998: 448). In conclusion, multinational subsidiaries' labour and management relations can be viewed as a hybrid between the parent firm's resources and strategies, company-level systems, and the problems and opportunities specific to the Spanish institutional context.

8.5. Conclusion

The Spanish case shows that change does not have to be radical or involve a transformation of the entire corporate governance system to have major effects on a national economy and significant implications for labour management. Instead, institutions and practices can change over time and be transplanted in a process of hybridization (Boyer *et al.* 1998; Aguilera and Jackson 2003). Spain has moved from a 'state-led' to a 'state-enhanced' corporate governance and labour relations system which is increasingly mixed in form.

In terms of corporate governance, Spain was traditionally characterized by high state ownership, strong state intervention, and an important role for banks. From these origins, the country has followed its own particular path to a new governance model shaped by its own traditions. It has moved towards a hybrid system, adopting practices from different countries, but in particular from the Anglo-Saxon model. As a result, there exists a tension between the new role of the state as a strong regulator, the uncommitted role of foreign capital, and the weak participation of labour within the firm alongside its stronger power in shaping sectoral employment systems. As has been shown, the current Spanish corporate governance scene is characterized by a new role for the state as a regulator, newly privatized firms in the hands of core investors (many of them foreign), a higher free float of capital on the stock market, but, still, a small equity market, a very weak market for corporate control, and the somewhat piecemeal introduction of Anglo-Saxon practices, such as increased transparency, accountability, and potentially more efficient boards. Anglo-Saxon-style codes of corporate governance practice and stock options for managers have also appeared.

In the Franco era, the labour market was characterized by extensive state regulation, welfare protection, and paternalistic management, especially in large firms. Since then, of course, trade unions have operated as in other market economies and collective bargaining has developed. These remain significant at the national and sectoral level and play a real part in regulating and constraining employment conditions. Decentralization of collective bargaining has not gone as far in Spain as in France and Italy, but there has been some tendency to use new HRM-type practices to reduce union presence at the workplace. These include team briefings, quality circles, and profit-sharing schemes.

Spain has a strong dual labour market economy, with a core of more secure and well-paid jobs, in larger firms, multinational companies, and state-owned organizations, but with a large peripheral labour force with temporary employment contracts and poor terms and conditions. Recent further changes, in part reflecting growing corporate governance pressures, include a greater ability to lay off workers, some more flexible forms of working, and a small increase in contingent pay. In terms of skill formation, job training for more flexible working remains limited. In part as a result, firms, including the growing number of foreign multinationals, have tended to opt for labour-intensive production methods and functional flexibility is limited.

Thus, as in the other Latin countries, major tensions exist. They exist between, on the one hand, a more marketized financial system, less state ownership and control, and corporate governance arrangements which are evolving in a somewhat Anglo-Saxon direction, and, on the other hand, labour management which is also becoming more flexible but which is still constrained by legal and institutional factors.

9

Corporate Governance and Industrial Relations in Italy

SANDRO TRENTO

9.1. Introduction

Over the last decade, a large literature has developed on models of capitalism, typically focusing on two ideal types: the market-based system (Anglo-Saxon) and relationship-based system (Germany, Japan). In market-based systems, equity markets are well developed, institutional investors such as pension funds play an important role, and corporate governance operates indirectly through the courts and market for corporate control. Some argue that this leads to short-term profit maximization as the primary goal of the firm. In relationship-based capitalism, long-term bank debt is the main source of financing for firms, large firms are typically closely held, equity markets are less developed, and there is little takeover activity. Banks are directly involved in *ex ante* monitoring of management via long-term relationships with firms. The two models of capitalism differ also in terms of labour relations. Where the market for corporate control is active, for instance, there is greater pressure to contain labour costs and deny long-term 'claims' by workers against the firm. Market-based systems tend to be less supportive of firm-specific training regimes because workers have limited incentives to invest in firm-specific skills. It is also said that countries with this system rely more than relationship-based systems on the external labour market and offer fewer opportunities for long-term job tenure.

In this chapter, we will argue that the Italian variety of capitalism cannot be viewed as either market-based or relationship-based. Instead, Italy has specific 'institutional complementarities', which arise from path-dependent patterns of historical evolution. The main

The opinions expressed in the present chapter are those of the author and do not represent those of the Bank of Italy.

grounds for rejecting the market or relationship characterization of the governance and labour relations systems are as follows.

The equity market in Italy is less developed than in market-based countries and institutional investment is still at an embryonic stage. Similarly, the market for corporate control is at an early stage of development. Financing of investment is heavily based on bank credit but, nevertheless, relationships between banks and firms have not taken the long-term character said to characterize relationship-based systems. Thus, banks do not hold significant direct ownership stakes in industrial corporations and are not very active as monitors. Family control plays a central role in Italian capitalism, both in the large firm sector (FIAT, Parmalat, Mediaset, Luxottica, and Benetton are all family controlled) and in the small firm sector. Firms are usually closely held by families or small coalitions of owners. Related to this, pyramidal ownership, along with cross-shareholding, is a widespread means of control.

A similar conclusion holds for labour relations. The Italian system differs substantially from those prevailing in market-based capitalism, though there has been a strong drive towards a more flexible labour market over the last 10 years. Even though the role of national bargaining in wage determination, employment relations, and to a lesser extent work relations is diminishing, it still plays a very important role especially at the industrial sector level. On the other hand, in contrast to relationship-based countries such as Germany, there is almost no tradition of a participation in bodies like the German *Aufsichtsrat* nor of cooperative working at firm level. In spite of the turning point of 1992–3, when a major new approach to industrial relations was agreed between government, employers, and unions, the extent of coordination of the Italian labour system is relatively low across the economy. In the last decade, there has been a strong drive toward greater flexibility in job tenures and forms of employment.

9.2. Italian Capitalism

The combination of corporate governance institutions and rules found in any given country depends on path-dependent patterns of industrialization and historical development. As a corollary to this, it is unlikely that any given country will fit either the market or relationship model. Italian industrial organization and corporate governance is characterized by the combination of several important features which taken together do not match either model. A major difference between Italy and other industrial nations is that financial institutions have very little involvement in monitoring companies via share equity or debt capital. Most banks have neither accumulated equity stakes in companies nor developed close long-term relationships based on lending. Institutional investment is also relatively undeveloped in Italy. Associated with this the Italian stock market is small, even by Southern European standards. Ownership of large firms is highly concentrated with family ownership being especially important. A notable feature of Italian corporate ownership has been the pyramidal form whereby a small number of owners in effect control a large number of companies. In this system, the interests of minority shareholders have been weakly protected and this has further contributed to the limited development of Italian equity markets.

The following pages will offer a brief historical analysis of the evolution of the Italian model of capitalism, before describing the current institutional variety in more depth.

9.2.1. *The evolution of the Italian model*

As Barca and Trento (1997) have shown, Italy is a typical latecomer, industrializing only at the end of the nineteenth century. The industrialization process was protracted and it was not until the post-Second World War period that the Italian economy had truly solid foundations. Italy traditionally suffered from a shortage of capital, scarcity of raw materials, and the lack of a large market (due in part to geography and in part to the historical division into small, independent states). When there is 'insufficient previous long-term accumulation of wealth in *appropriate* hands which at a propitious moment can be made available to industrial entrepreneurs' (Gerschenkron 1962: 116), the informal capital market of the early industrializers no longer suffices. During the first phase of industrialization (from the mid-1890s onwards), an important role was played by the universal banks, some founded with German capital (e.g. Banca Commerciale Italiana and Credito Italiano) (Confalonieri 1974). These financial institutions operated through a *mix* of credit relations and equity subscription. Initially, they functioned as a means to overcome deficiencies in the primitive accumulation of capital. Later, they became the channel by which diffuse, fragmented savings could be funnelled into equity, given that direct equity holdings by savers were inhibited by the underdeveloped stock market.

Equally, a corollary to the prevalence of debt capital was the failure of the stock market to take off to any significant extent. With an inadequate stock market and stable, non-competitive relations between banks and industry, the foundations were laid in the early years of the twentieth century for an intensive concentration of control and the formation of corporate pyramidal groups.

The stock market crash of 1929–31 hit the Italian financial system at a time of pronounced industrial and financial concentration. The intermingling of credit and industrial capital, the underdevelopment of the stock market, and above all the creation of corporate groups based on cross-shareholding, made the crisis particularly acute. These features both fostered the domino effect of the crash and hindered adjustment. The crisis struck the large industrial-banking groups, and the organization into pyramidal groups amplified the repercussions of the plunge in share prices. The leading banks found it impossible to turn their equity holdings and claims in the crisis-torn industrial groups into cash. This paved the way for the state to assume a central function within Italian capitalism.

The government refinanced the troubled banks by buying out their industrial holdings and transferring them to a new state-owned agency created especially for this purpose in 1933: the Institute for Industrial Reconstruction (Istituto per la Ricostruzione Industriale (IRI)). This took over the entire equity capital of the mixed banks, and thus acquired more than 20 per cent of all the existent equity capital of limited companies. For instance, IRI owned 100 per cent of Italy's defence-related mining and steel industries, 90 per cent of its shipbuilding, and 30 per cent of electricity generation. In addition, it controlled the telephone system in Central and Northern Italy and possessed extensive real estate holdings (see Castronovo 1995). Thus, unlike other countries, the Italian system of public enterprise was the by-product of a corporate salvage operation rather than the result of a clearly articulated policy of nationalization.

The creation of IRI was accompanied by the Banking Law of 1936. This prohibited banks from holding equity in industrial companies. It also created institutional specialization of their credit business. Provision of short-term credit was assigned to ordinary banks while medium and long-term credit became the remit of special credit institutions. As a result, the German-style universal or mixed bank disappeared from the scene. But the Italian solution was not intended to relaunch the stock market as a means for developing broader ownership and more diffuse control of industry. The dominant logic continued to see the banks as the linchpin of industrial finance. This contrasts with the approach taken in the United States at the same time, where financial rehabilitation and the separation between banking and industry were founded upon the recovery of the stock market, the formation of the Securities and Exchange Commission, the regulation of mutual funds, and deposit protection legislation.

For the Italian economy, the crisis of the 1930s was a key structural divide, with major changes in the model of corporate governance occuring and the consolidation of the first stage of Italian capitalism. With the direct, massive intervention of the state, Italy moved from an ownership pattern based on corporate groups and universal banks (similar in some ways to the German model) to one centred on pyramidal groups albeit subdivided into public and private entities. Thus, a characteristic feature of the Anglo-Saxon model of corporate control developed, namely the separation of banking and industry. As a result, the bank as controller, mandated to oversee the rehabilitation and restructuring of firms in crisis, disappeared. The consequent vacuum was in part filled by the state holding company (IRI), which was repeatedly required to take over companies in financial distress.

The end of Second World War and the creation of the republic consolidated the institutional structure of Italian capitalism. The return to democracy, the emergence of a new governing class (formed largely in opposition to fascism), and the potential offered by closer European integration and free trade permitted the full unfolding of the development potential inherent in the model of corporate governance installed between 1933 and 1936. In the first 10–15 years after the end of the war, features of the governance framework stimulated rapid economic and industrial development. State control gave a new generation of managers, untainted by involvement with the previous fascist regime, the chance to acquire control of large, emerging enterprises. A sense of mission linked to the post-war reconstruction climate helped make up for the monitoring weaknesses of the corporate governance model, while many of the relevant strategic choices were clear-cut (providing the country with an adequate and stable supply of energy, building a highway system, modernizing the steel industry to meet the needs of the engineering sector, etc.). At the same time, low wages (emanating from an excess supply of labour) allowed rapid growth in both large and small family-controlled firms to be fuelled by abnormally high levels of self-financing.

Although there was some debate in the immediate post-war years about privatizing IRI, the general consensus was that public enterprise had a key role to play in the reconstruction process (Bottiglieri 1984). By this time, IRI controlled over 200 companies (with over 135,000 employees). In 1948, IRI was granted greater independence from the government, while in 1953 the National Hydrocarbon Agency (Ente Nazionale Idrocarburi (ENI)) was created to act as a public holding company for the oil, petrochemical, and later the chemical sector. In the 10–15 years after the war, state-owned enterprises coexisted with a set of large private enterprises still under family and coalition control. In practice, private and public companies counterbalanced each other in terms of strategic power, prompting a degree of competition in several sectors such as engineering, oil, and chemical. A central role was played in the post-war system by the investment bank, Mediobanca. This was created in 1946 to overcome the prohibition of commercial banks offering medium and long-term finance to industry and it was itself owned by three banks in turn owned by IRI—Banca Commerciale, Credito Italiano, and Banco di Roma.

From the early 1960s, the system began a process of major transformation. The objectives of IRI and ENI were extended from reconstruction and modernization to contesting monopoly, promoting new industrial relations, sustaining employment, and fostering the economic development of the South (Barca and Trento 1997). The government nationalized the electric power industry with the formation of a directly state-run agency, the National Electricity Corporation or ENEL (Ente Nazionale Energia Elettrica).

The eventual crisis that struck the model of public ownership involved both unstable strategic objectives and the failure of political oversight. A deceleration of economic growth, the persistent backwardness of the South, and the problems caused by abrupt changes in relative prices (in both wages and raw materials) tilted the guidelines for state-owned companies from long-term objectives to more volatile, short-term ones, such as sustaining employment and rescuing ailing private firms. The complicated hierarchical structure induced by the creation of a Ministry for Public Shareholdings (Ministero delle Partecipazioni Statali) resulted in a vague definition of the official statutory 'mission' of the public groups at their creation and in their subsequent activities. As the performance of many of these companies deteriorated, it was hard to distinguish the costs of the social objectives imposed by government from those of simple mismanagement. Pressures to perform were weakened by the soft budget constraints provided by state ownership and the provision of government funds.

A failure of the market for political control added to these problems. From 1945 to 1993, the government was controlled by a series of alliances among an unchanging group of parties. Given the low risk of losing office, parties in the ruling coalition had little incentive actively to monitor the management of state-owned firms. Nor did the opposition always perform its function as a watchdog over public enterprise. Indeed, there was often collusion between government and opposition in this respect. For instance, most of the policy measures affecting public enterprises in this period, including subsidies, were approved unanimously in parliament (Maraffi 1990).

The resulting crisis for state-owned corporations had repercussions on the private sector; in particular, it upset the equilibrium of the over-all system of corporate governance in the large enterprise. Relations between public and private enterprise, which had been competitive in the 1950s became collusive insofar as the government moved to rescue failing private companies. Thus, the government's role as 'controller of last resort' grew in importance from the 1960s such that the payroll of state-owned groups rose from around 200,000 employees in the mid-1960s to 600,000 in the 1980s.

9.2.2. *The current features of Italian capitalism*

Since the 1970s, Italian capitalism has been characterized by a pro-nounced dualism between a small business sector, composed of small and medium-sized industrial firms (1–250 employees), and a large-firm industrial and service sector. Firms with less than ten employees (95 per cent of firms) employ 47 per cent of total industrial workers. Compared to other countries, Italy has a disproportionately large small-firm sector. Indeed, the share of Italian manufacturing employment accounted for by firms with more than 500 employees halved between the early 1960s and the mid-1990s (from 31.5 to 15.1 per cent of manufacturing employment). This decline is much greater than in the United States, the United Kingdom, France, and Germany. While the share of employment accounted for by firms with fewer than 100 employees rose everywhere, the increase was sharpest in Italy (from 48.8 to 68.6 per cent). In Italy, the further fractionalization of an already fragmented productive structure has been accompained by a diffusion of self-employment. As Table 9.1 shows, 27 per cent of total non-agricultural workers in Italy are self-employed, compared with 7 per cent in the United States, around 10 per cent in France and Germany, and 12 per cent in the United Kingdom.

Table 9.1. *Incidence of self-employment in OECD countries 1998*

Country	Share of self-employment in total non-agricultural employment	Per capita GDP
Australia	12.4	21,949
Austria	8.8	23,077
Belgium	16.0	23,242
Canada	15.9	23,761
Germany	9.9	22,049
Denmark	7.9	25,514
Finland	9.9	20,488
France	9.8	21,293
Greece	32.1	13,912
Ireland	14.1	20,634
Iceland	14.9	24,836
Italy	26.6	21,265
Japan	13.8	24,574
Korea	31.3	14,477
Luxembourg	7.8	33,119
Mexico	31.5	7,697
The Netherlands	10.1	22,142
New Zealand	16.9	17,846
Norway	4.3	26,771
Portugal	20.1	14,562
Spain	19.7	15,990
Sweden	9.6	20,439
Turkey	28.7	6,463
United Kingdom	12.0	20,483
United States	7.1	29,326

Source: OECD, Eurostat.

Many of the small firms produce complex, high quality, but traditional products, employ a large share of relatively skilled labour, and operate with flexible systems of organization and production. Frequently, they are also linked in groups by various forms of coordination, especially when they form part of industrial districts (Piore and Sabel 1984; Barca and Magnani 1989). The fact that small businesses predominate in all sectors suggests that institutional features specific to the Italian economy are at work (Torrini 2002).

The major difference in corporate governance between Italy and other industrial countries is the lack of financial institutions exercising monitoring via share or debt capital. Banks in Italy hold virtually no stake in non-financial companies. This was the result, as shown earlier, of the separation between banking and industry introduced in the 1930s. No other financial institutions have taken over the role of banks in the ownership structure of Italian companies, partly due to the absence of pension funds as a consequence of the country's broad pay-as-you-go public pension system. Banks also have been reluctant to participate in governance on the basis of their extensive role as creditors. Both macro-studies (Ciocca 1982, 1991) and micro-evidence (Capra *et al.* 1994) show that Italian banks have played a crucial role in financing economic growth by assessing the creditworthiness of borrowing firms. However, with a broad use of collateral, multiple bank lending, high turnover in bank–customer relations, and the pre-dominance of overdraft credits, this *ex ante* monitoring has not gen-erally been followed by adequate *ex post* monitoring. Banks have generally preferred an arm's length relationship with their customers rather than relational finance and they typically only intervene when companies are in distress. In the small business sector, banks play a role in bringing about transfers of control when a company is in financial distress, but do not actively monitor entrepreneurs' long-term strategies. Nor do they appear particularly active in soliciting or backing the adjustment of companies' ownership structures. Italy's bankruptcy law plays an important role in explaining this behaviour. No satisfactory provisions exist to allow active entrepreneurs an interim period of monitored control, while creditors are permitted to liquidate companies with small regard being taken for the efficient reallocation of the assets of the distressed company.

However, this picture of bank behaviour has some notable exceptions. A few small and medium-sized local banks operating in the small business sector and one large bank operating in the large firm sector (Mediobanca) have taken a more active role in gov-ernance (De Cecco and Ferri 1994). Mediobanca has complemented the mix of family, coalition, and group control of large private firms. The initial lack of competition (self-perpetuating because of its reputation and the slackness of state-owned banks) created a strong incentive for Mediobanca to invest in monitoring, but it has also made it slow to intervene when firms show signs of distress. In many cases, Mediobanca became involved in crisis resolution only at a very late stage. It has also biased the bank's function towards preserving and consolidating the implicit rules which hold together the prevail-ing structures of ownership and control, rather than broadening those structures. Typically, Mediobanca has encouraged other members of the elite of family capitalism to 'help' the family in trouble, without disrupting the fundamental balance of power within the family firm to be rescued. As a result, changes in control have rarely resulted from economic distress (Barca and Trento 1997).

When commercial banks are absent from the area of corporate finance, these services are generally provided by other institutions such as investment banks, fund managers, and accountancy houses. However, none of these has ever been particularly active in the Italian economy. The exit device (such as a well-developed market for corporate control) has also been missing. The failure of financial and non-financial institutions to act as advisers or intermediaries and the high concentration of ownership, as well as the lack of rules concerning public offers, have prevented this development.

Company law, securities law, and investment regulation do not provide a framework for institutional investors to play much of a role in corporate governance. Minority shareholders' interests are not strongly legally supported and accounting and company information available to shareholders is also inadequate. Moreover, little or no independent monitoring has been exercised by corporate bodies. Finally, the board of directors in Italian companies is generally fully identified with the controlling shareholders; the board of auditors, whose members are chosen by the majority shareholders, also lacks adequate enforcement power.

In the absence of financial institutions, fiduciary duties, and the market for corporate control, the state has come to play a central role in corporate governance, both as an owner and as a prime mover in the allocation of resources to the private sector. Until the privatization programme of the 1990s, the state directly controlled a majority stake in about 50 per cent of medium-sized and large companies. It held about one-sixth of the entire non-agricultural sector, as against about one-eighth in France (pre-privatization), less than one-tenth in Germany, and one-sixteenth in the United Kingdom (post-privatization). In practice, it has held about 80 per cent of the commercial banking system's deposits and an even larger stake of long-term lending banks.

As well as acting as an owner, the Italian state has constantly made up for failures in the governance environment of private companies by providing them with a steady flow of resources. Thus, it has transferred substantial funds to entrepreneurs to overcome situations of financial distress, has bought out mismanaged companies, has provided subsidies to realize delayed restructuring, and has granted subsidized credit.

State ownership is potentially a very powerful device in corporate governance since it can ensure full separation between ownership and control. However, for this model to work efficiently, the political authorities must neither interfere excessively in management by frequently shifting their goals nor collude with managers (Laffont and Tirole 1993). In order to avoid such collusion, the public must have the opportunity to punish the political authorities. In other words, in this type of system the market for corporate control is replaced by the political market. We will consider later what became of these conditions in Italy.

Together with state ownership, Italian corporate governance has relied on implicit rules elaborated in the pyramidal groups. Pyramidal group control occurs when a set of companies (ranging from two to several hundred) are controlled by the same entrepreneur via a chain of proprietary and control relations.[1] Several objectives may determine the adoption of the pyramidal rather than a divisional organizational form. These include concerns to entrench the power of owners at the apex, to limit liability, to provide incentives for unit managers, and to reap fiscal benefits and state subsidies for small firms. Here, we focus on the use of pyramidal groups intended to allow greater separation between ownership and control. By spreading out the voting rights of minority shareholders over a large number of firms and concentrating those of the entrepreneur in the company at the top of the pyramid, this model allows the latter to obtain control over the greatest possible amount of other people's capital with the smallest possible amount of his own capital (Hilferding 1910). This way of achieving separation puts the interests of minority shareholders in all the subsidiaries of the group at particular risk. These interests might in fact systematically diverge from those of the entrepreneur, whose interests are linked to the performance of the group as a whole. Monitoring devices, specifically designed for pyramidal groups, are then called in (such as the presence of the same directors on the boards of several companies belonging to the pyramid).

In Italy, this model of control has been widely diffused throughout the economy. Major firms such as FIAT, Pirelli, Mediaset, and ENI are typical examples of pyramidal groups. Almost all large industrial companies are part of a group. As Figure 9.1 shows, between 60 and 95 per cent of companies with more than 100 employees are part of a pyramid.

Using data on the ownership structure of companies which directly or indirectly own or are owned by about 250 listed companies, a map

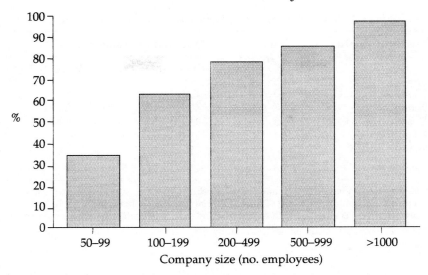

Figure 9.1. *Diffusion of pyramidal groups in Italian industry by size of company (1993)[a] (weighted percentages)*

[a] Stratified random sample of industrial firms with more than 50 employees.
Source: Barca, Bianco *et al.* (1994).

of about 180 pyramidal groups, comprising 6,500 companies has been drawn (Barca *et al.* 1994*a*, *b*). By tracing the ultimate ownership of 'listed groups' it is possible to evaluate the degree of separation between ownership and control in general, and for each type of controlling head in particular. In a pyramidal group, company A (the head company) has a controlling stake in company B, which in turn has a controlling stake in company C, and so on. There seems to be no doubt that the degree of separation of ownership and control achieved via pyramidal groups in Italy has been kept low by the fact that this organizational form is not recognized in current company law. No specific legal provision exists to safeguard the interests of minority shareholders in subsidiaries. There is not even an explicit obligation to disclose the boundaries of these groups in order to allow banks or other agents fully to evaluate the risks of dealing with them. Although regulations require that all loans to a group are added together to calculate banks' risk exposure, this is difficult to undertake due to uncertainty about the extent of pyramidal groupings.

Once the composition of pyramidal groups is identified, it is possible to assess the modes of control in them, at least for medium-sized

Table 9.2. *Models of control of medium-sized and large Italian companies*[a]

Models of control[b]	Numbers of groups	Proportion of companies	
		Unweighted (%)	Weighted[c] (%)
Absolute control	45	20.0	8.0
Family control	47	40.7	22.1
Coalition control	53	18.8	13.4
State ownership	13	15.2	53.5
Foreign control	20	5.3	3.0
Total	178	100	100

[a] Companies belonging to pyramidal groups with at least one listed parent company.
[b] The form of control at the top of the group. See the text for definitions.
[c] Each company is weighted with a composite index of its net value and of its employment.

Notes: The number of companies in the study is 4,552.

Source: Barca *et al.* (1994*b*).

and large firms. For this purpose, 'family control' is taken to be any ownership structure in which the non-controlling owners belong to the same family as the entrepreneur, while 'coalition control' is defined as a structure in which there is evidence of the entrepreneur and the non-controlling owners being linked through shared understandings and contracts. These coalitions may operate as a formal syndicate or informally via implicit agreements. Cooperatives are included in this category, since community members or workers entrust some of their peers with the task of managing their resources, drawing on the bonds established by common goals or through the political or social action of the founders.

By attributing the mode of control of the company at the top of a pyramidal group to all companies in the group, we can obtain a good estimate of the extent of these various forms of control.

Thus, 40.7 per cent are run through family control and 18.8 per cent through coalition control. Attributing to each of these top companies the size of the whole group, the first model turns out to run 22.1 per cent of total capital, the second around 13.4 per cent (see Table 9.2). In this analysis the state controls around 50 per cent, but it should be borne in mind that this pre-dates much of the privatization programme in the 1990s.

9.2.3. *An evaluation of Italian corporate governance*

The effects of any given mix of corporate governance devices can be evaluated according to two criteria. The first concerns its contribution to static efficiency. In other words, how far does corporate govern-ance and the allocation of control maximize innovation and human capital investments? The second concerns the impact of the corporate governance system on dynamic efficiency. In other words, what is its impact on the incentives for people to improve their skills, given their endowment of talents? Allowance must be made for the fact that investments in human capital not only make people more productive in performing a specific task, given their skills, but also increase these skills. Any allocation of control, then, feeds back into the allocation of skills among individuals and might have negative dynamic effects on the development of these skills (Pagano 1991*a*, *b*; Barca 1994, 1995). A system in which access to corporate control is 'reserved' to a relatively limited pool of individuals (such as the affiliates of controlling families) may cause problems for dynamic efficiency in the long run.

To assess the static efficiency of Italian corporate governance, reference can be made to three specific stages in companies' life cycles when corporate governance is especially important: the initial cre-ation and growth phase, generational changes, and crisis situations. As regards the first phase, state ownership mobilized finance for rapid economic development by making resources available to entrepreneurs. Family and coalition control allow accumulated savings to be chan-neled to investment, bearing in mind that formal intermediary institutions, such as the stock exchange, investment banks, and institutional investors, are underdeveloped. But these devices are inadequate to govern the growth of both small and large companies when there are shortages of capital, which should be rectified by long-term debt or by private risk capital. The preponderance of short-term debt and the wide use of collateral are particularly unsuitable for financing fast growth, especially when firms do not have much of a record. Similarly, both family and coalition control tend to prevent the raising of new 'outside' risk capital. For an entrepreneur to attract funds to finance his projects, requisites that most people do not possess may be demanded, such as family ties or political and social links with well-off members of society. Growth tends to be limited by the capital of incumbent families and coalitions. Several facts seem to corroborate this evaluation: the limited diffusion and high concentra-tion of ownership, the small size of the stock exchange, and the lack of medium-sized firms (Barca and Trento 1997).

Generational changes occur when an entrepreneur retires or dies. Competition for control of the company then arises between the entrepreneur's offspring (who are likely to have had a chance to acquire some of the entrepreneur's tacit knowledge), managers and workers of the company (who have also had a chance to acquire tacit knowledge), and competitors, suppliers, and customers (who also have some informational advantage). In a situation of family control, the entrepreneur's offspring enjoy an obvious advantage over all others due to their inheritance rights. However, inheritance law does not allow the legator freely to dispose of his or her wealth to the advantage of a specified heir and this tends to create family feuds for the control of companies.

Finally, during crises all three models—family, coalition, and state control—function to reduce the risk that signals of poor performance might lead to changes in the distribution of control. This is one of the main advantages of the Italian governance environment. On the other hand, due to the lack of continuous monitoring, these models may increase the risk of the opposite error: that a misallocation of control, though signalled by bad performance, does not lead quickly enough to a transfer of control. This is perhaps the main drawback of the Italian system, where insufficient incentives are provided for the various stakeholders to search for an alternative allocation of control in crisis and where the Italian state operates with a very soft budget constraint.

While an a priori judgement of the static efficiency of Italian corporate governance is therefore ambivalent, there seems to be no doubt about the negative dynamic efficiency of the system. Several factors played a role in impeding turnover within the entrepreneurial establishment: the financial obstacles to entrepreneurs, particularly new entrants, who lack the 'right connections'; the stickiness of the model of family control; and the strong collusion between the top managers of state-owned companies and top politicians, who have helped each other to stay in power. People's opportunities to use their abilities in order to develop new skills have very likely been reduced. This has undoubtedly had an adverse effect on business enterprises and the political economy.

It is probably the case that persistent dynamic inefficiencies and the related inequality of opportunity for upward social mobility explain much of the emerging consensus at the beginning of the 1990s for a reform of the corporate governance system centred on a reduced role of state ownership. But the consensus for reform must also be attributed to the perception that, on the grounds of static efficiency, the disadvantages by then largely outweighed any advantages of the system.

9.3. **Labour Relations in Italian Industry**

Historically, the Italian system of labour relations has been considered as unusual among the industrial countries. It is true it shared with France one important characteristic—the influence of a strong Communist-dominated trade union confederation. However, after 1968, the analogies ceased. The achievement of an unprecedented de facto controlling power in large firms went hand in hand with a significant direct role in politics, which to some extent displaced the activities of political parties. Several significant reforms in the area of pensions, employment protection, and health were realized in the 1970s because of strong pressure from the trade unions.

Since the beginning of the 1990s, major developments in labour relations have been the attempt to codetermine incomes policy and the desire to create of an institutional framework which is accepted by the social partners. These developments result from several important changes in the Italian economy, such as changes in terms of the increased exposure to more intense international competition, the decline in manual employment, the development of temporary and part-time employment (especially in private services), and the move of production processes away from Fordism. The common European currency has recently added to the pressures for change.

In order to assess the main features of recent changes and links with corporate governance, it is necessary to outline the main features of the labour relations system in the recent past. Since 1948, labour has been represented at national level by three trade union confederations organized on political lines. The largest and most influential—Confederazione Generale Italiana del Lavoro (CGIL)—was led by Communists and Socialists, and controlled mainly by the former. Confederazione Italiana Sindacati dei Lavoratori (CISL) reflected the social doctrine of the Catholic church, and the Unione Italiana del Lavoro (UIL) was led by right-wing Social Democrats. Each confederation has under its umbrella various national occupational trade unions.

Up to the 1960s, the political character of Italian trade unionism inhibited its development within the firm. In contrast to Germany and the United Kingdom, the existence of a strong Communist Party stifled the emergence of representational structures because of the fear that workers and unions would be incorporated into management, thereby undermining the 'unity of the working class'. More than anywhere else in Western Europe, this 'horizontal' feature of the trade union structure inhibited the development of representational structures and employee 'voice' within the firm. Italian trade unions were more interested in attempting to organize workers broadly rather than engaging in bargaining or codetermination within the firm. Once the Left had achieved electoral success, capitalist firms were expected to be transformed into socialist enterprises.

The confederations played a central role in contractual negotiations for each occupational category at sectoral level. The activity of CGIL at firm level was aimed at defensive monitoring of the terms and conditions agreed in the national sectoral contracts. At the time, the balance of power was very much in favour of Confindustria, the national employers' organization. Unions were weak and their activities were skewed towards political activity to such an extent that local union representatives undertook little activity to improve working conditions or secure wage increases via collective bargaining. Moreover, the existence of a large 'reserve army of labour' in agriculture further encouraged wage moderation.

From the mid-1950s, CISL, drawing upon a long-standing Catholic social tradition and 'human relations' philosophies, tried to build a model of union activity based on the link between productivity and wages at firm level, within the framework of a national incomes policy. This approach was widely discussed at the beginning of the 1960s, when the economic boom greatly strengthened the bargaining power of the trade unions and stimulated the emergence of centre-left governments formed from an alliance between the ruling Christian Democratic Party and the Socialists. In these years, a serious attempt was made to reform the Italian system of labour relations. The main proposal, put forward by the Socialists, focused on the development of trade union involvement in the formulation of an income policy aligned with macro-economic objectives. However, in the end, the CGIL refused to go along with this initiative. The views of its Communist main component, the (related) incapacity of the reformers to beat the conservative opponents within the government, and the hostility of Confindustria meant that this attempt to reform the system came to nothing.

The so-called 'hot autumn' of 1969 brought about major changes. For the first time since 1948, the three trade unions agreed upon a common strategy and acted on a united basis. In spite of the strong resistance of firms which had benefited from very low levels of real wages by international standards, the unions were able to achieve wage increases which exceeded the growth of productivity. They also achieved considerable control of the production process within many medium-sized and large firms. A new representational structure known as the *consiglio dei delegati* (council of delegates) was created at firm level and directly elected by workers.

The years immediately following 1969 show the Italian tendency to exploit any advantage, however temporary, in the balance of power. In the wake of the shock to the system posed by 1968, no serious attempt was made to develop an institutional framework which could represent the various interests within the firm. Events in the 1970s exhibit the lack of a cooperative culture in the Italian system at the firm level and in the formulation of macroeconomic policies. In particular, in 1970, following a long wave of union unrest, a Labour Rights Law (*Statuto dei Lavoratori*) was enacted. This introduced trade union rights such as the right for union activities within the firm and strict provisions against individual lay-offs. However, no provision was made for any sort of codetermination: union rights were strictly separated from any kind of shared governance of the firm. In 1975 the union movement was still strong enough to impose a system of wage indexation (*scala mobile*) which played a crucial role in the price–wage spiral of the second half of the 1970s. Buoyed up by this, at the same time, the goals of the trade unions widened to include reforms of the welfare system, health care, pensions, and training.

The wage shock induced by the legislation, coupled with the 1973 oil shock and the subsequent automatic wage indexation, contributed to massive inflationary pressures. The attempt by CGIL leaders at the end of the 1970s to modify the tenet of the 'wage as independent variable' was to some extent successful partly because the Communist Party was a member of coalition supporting the government. However, this met widespread resistance by local unions at firm level. The intense restructuring of production processes arising from the renewal of fixed capital in medium-sized and large firms paved the way for the historic defeat of the trade unions at FIAT in 1980 and the subsequent drastic reduction in the size of the labour force.

These violent upswings in the labour relations balance of power were of much less concern to the small firms belonging to industrial districts. These firms had developed a model of organization ('flexible specialization') which was largely autonomous of developments in larger firms. One of the success factors in this model has been a participative culture within the firm and in the local social and political context. The areas where these districts are more widespread tend to be those where the reformist political tradition is more pronounced, such as the Emilia-Romagna, Tuscany, and Marche regions. These firms might be viewed as an informal 'share economy', where workers partcipate in and benefit from the firm's growth and profits. Put differently, in these districts, there exists a complex set of rules concerning the behaviour of the players, implying mutual responsibilities and burdens supported by rewards and sanctions.

The industrial district has been a key ingredient of the competitive success of Italian manufacturing industry. This model, however, is linked to specific local factors (in particular, social capital) and cannot easily be reproduced elsewhere. Moreover, in recent years, technological innovations and related changes in organization structures seem to favour large enterprises because of the increasing globalization of product markets. Small firms usually trade in traditional sectors which typically are more exposed to price competition from goods produced in low wage countries. Hence, their employment and labour relations systems are subject to increased pressure.

9.4. The 1990s: A Decade of Change

The 1990s were a decade of significant change for Italy and major aspects of the post-war political system came to an end. Both financial and labour markets have undergone a process of major reform. The following sections outline the main aspects of change and the interaction between the different elements.

9.4.1. *Financial markets*

In the last decade, there have been extensive changes in laws and regulations. New laws have been passed affecting banking and financial sectors, a large programme of privatization has been implemented, an Antitrust Authority has been created, measures have been taken to enhance competition, and many sectors have been liberalised (gas, electricity, telecommunication, and retailing). The origins of these reforms lie in the shortcomings of Italian economic performance in the previous twenty years. During the 1970s and 1980s, static and dynamic inefficiencies increasingly hampered both large private and state-owned companies. The former went through a 'stop-go' process, in which adjustments would be effected abruptly after a long period of inactivity and delay (Barca and Magnani 1989). As a result, many state-owned companies came to a virtual standstill. Both public and private sector companies presented their shareholders and the general public with dramatic examples of abuses of control. Throughout the two decades, the small firm sector grew and partly compensated for these swings and for dynamic inefficiencies. But much of this came at the cost of massive tax evasion—the family model of control inextricably linked corporate and private interests.

By the beginning of the 1990s, increasing pressure stemming from these failures, together with EU-generated constraints on state funding, the liberalization of capital mobility, and an upheaval in the political market, led the authorities to introduce reforms.[2] The 1990s saw a thorough overhaul of the role of public intervention in the Italian economy, with direct state involvement in the management of economic activites curtailed and revisions to the rules governing the conduct of private enterprises increased. In particular, privatization of state-owned enterprises gradually gathered support in political and public circles. Some privatizations were a reaction in part to EU pressures regarding state subsidies and the related need to adjust the finances of several major state-owned groups. In 1992, following the EU currency crisis and the devaluation of the lira, the government finally introduced a radical privatization plan. The reasoning behind the strategy was twofold: on the one hand, there was a growing need to curb the rise of public debt; on the other, there was the desire to improve the competitiveness of the Italian industrial system by bringing more small investors into the financial market.

The privatization programme, which began in 1993, is one of the largest ever realized in any country. As Table 9.3 shows, it generated total gross proceeds of more than 171 trillion lire (€88,570 million) between 1993 and 2001, nearly 8 per cent of the average GDP for those years.

In the last 3 years, the proceeds of privatization were on average 1.8 per cent of GDP. By way of comparison, average annual privatization receipts in the United Kingdom were 1.2 per cent between 1985 and 1995. This process led to a steep rise in market capitalization of the Italian stock market: by 2000 it had risen to over €700 billion and to 65 per cent of GDP. Furthermore, the expansion of share ownership arising from public offerings of shares in privatized firms led to a reduction in ownership concentration of Italian firms. In many cases (e.g. Banca Commerciale, Credito Italiano, ENI, ENEL, Telecom Italia) privatization took place by public offerings, thereby giving small investors the opportunity to participate. Indirectly, also, privatization enhanced the market for corporate control in Italy. In 1998,

Table 9.3. *The main privatizations in Italy*

Corporation (group)	Method of sale	Percentage sold	Gross proceeds in billions of lire (millions of euros)
1993			
Italgel (IRI)	Private agreement	62.12	431
Cirio-Bertolli-DeRica (IRI)	Private agreement	62.12	311
Credito Italiano (IRI)	Public offering	58.09	1,801
SIV (EFIM)	Auction	100.00	210
Total for year			2,753
1994			
IMI—1st *tranche*	Public offering	32.89	2,150
COMIT (IRI)	Public offering	54.35	2,891
Nuovo Pignone (ENI)	Auction	69.33	699
INA—1st *tranche*	Public offering	47.25	4,530
Acciai Speciali Terni (IRI)	Private agreement	100.00	624
SME—1st *tranche* (*IRI*)	Private agreement	32.00	723
Other companies (*ENI*)			1,087
Total for year			12,704
1995			
Italtel (IRI)	Auction	40.00	1,000
Ilva Laminati Piani (IRI)	Private agreement	100.00	1,929
Enichem Augusta (ENI)	Auction	70.00	300
Other companies (*ENI*)			336
IMI—2nd *tranche*	Private agreement	19.03	1,200
SME—2nd *tranche* (*IRI*)	Accept takeover bid	14.91	341
INA—2nd *tranche*	Private agreement	18.37	1,687
ENI—1st *tranche*	Public offering	15.00	6,299
ISE (IRI)	Auction	73.96	370
Total for year			13,462
1996			
Dalmine (IRI)	Auction	84.08	302
Italimpianti (IRI)	Auction	100.00	42
Nuova Tirrena	Auction	91.14	548
SME—3rd *tranche* (*IRI*)	Accept takeover bid	15.21	121
INA—3rd *tranche*	Conv. bond issue	31.08	3,260
MAC (IRI)	Auction	50.00	223
IMI—3rd *tranche*	Public offering	6.94	501
Montefibre (ENI)	Public offering	65.00	183
ENI—2nd *tranche*	Public offering	15.82	8,872
Total for year			14,051
1997			
ENI—3rd *tranche*	Public offering	17.60	13,230
Aeroporti di Roma (IRI)	Public offering	45.00	541
Telecom Italia	Core investors + public offering	39.54	22,883

Table 9.3. (*Continued*)

Corporation (group)	Method of sale	Percentage sold	Gross proceeds in billions of lire (millions of euros)
SEAT editoria	Core investors + public offering	61.27	1,653
Banca di Roma (IRI)	Public offering + bond issue	36.50	1,900
Total for year			40,207
1998			
SAIPEM (ENI)	Public offering	18.75	1,140
ENI—*4th tranche*	Public offering	14.83	12,995
BNL	Public offering	67.85	6,707
Total for year			20,842
1999			
ENEL	Public offering	35.50	34,828
Autostrade (IRI)	Auction + public offering	57.00	8,105
Total for year			42,933
2000			
Autostrade (IRI)	Private agreement	30.00	4,911
Finmeccanica (IRI)	Public offering	43.70	5,505
Aeroporti di Roma (IRI)	Private agreement	51.20	1,328
Banco di Napoli	Public offering	16.16	494
Total for year			12,238 (6,320)
2001			
ENI—*5th tranche*	Accelerate book building	5.00	5,268 (2,721)
SNAM—Rete gas	Public offering	40.24	4,260 (2,200)
Total for year			9,528 (4,921)
2002			
TELECOM Italia	Accelerate book building	4.20	2,777 (1,434)
Total proceeds 1993–2002			171,495 (88,570)

Sources: Company accounts (various years); Ministry of the Treasury, *Relazione sulle privatizzazioni* (various years).

the successful leveraged takeover of Telecom Italia (the former state-owned monopoly, privatized in 1997), one of the largest hostile takeovers ever made in Europe, generated major changes in the hitherto lethargic Italian market for corporate contol.

The salient event of the decade in the area of regulatory reform of the markets was the 1990 Antitrust Law which created a new Competition Authority. In addition, a new Banking Law was passed in 1993 eliminating the prohibition on banks from purchasing shares in non-financial corporations and ending the regional specialization of banks. As a result, banks are now potentially more able to play a more active role in both corporate finance and corporate governance (Ciocca 2000).

The creation of a stock market relying on broad-based shareholding and on a market for corporate control required modification of the civil code to safeguard the rights of minority shareholders and to guarantee greater transparency in corporate management. It also required more effective oversight of the stock market by the regulatory authorities. To achieve these, a new law was passed in 1998 (Legislative Decree 58 of February 1998) on financial markets, securities arrangements, and corporate governance. In particular, new rules for corporate governance based on international standards were introduced. These new rules include the following. New takeover rules oblige an intending purchaser to bid for all of a company's ordinary shares once it has purchased more than 30 per cent of the company's capital (the mandatory bid rule). Other significant innovations are the creation of an auction system for competing bids and the possibility for a shareholders' meeting to authorize defensive tactics against hostile bids. In the area of corporate disclosure, the scope of reporting requirements has been broadened to cover unlisted companies which have issued widely held financial instruments. With the aim of making the ownership of listed companies transparent, the new law confirms the requirement to notify the Stock Market Authority of equity interests which exceed 2 per cent. The new law also enhanced the transparency of shareholder agreements and limited their maximum duration to 3 years.[3]

Shareholders with at least 1 per cent of a company's equity may engage qualified intermediaries (banks, securities firms, and asset management companies) to solicit proxies from other shareholders for use in the general meeting. Proxy votes thus collected are cast by the delegated shareholder or, at the latter's behest, by the intermediary which has been involved in the process. The role of a listed company's board of auditors in exercising control on the running of the company has been strengthened by rationalizing the division of accounting-related tasks between the board and the external auditors. Thus, the rights of minority shareholders have been given greater protection.

The other essential condition for the creation of a new corporate governance system is the emergence of activist financial institutions. Here, there have been some changes, though to date they are inadequate. The opportunity to develop universal banking has been reinforced, with banks being allowed (subject to restrictions) to acquire equity interests in non-financial companies. For the corporate culture of the banks to change, however, the legal framework is inadequate. Banks need to have a strong incentive to undertake a new role, and arguably this requires further measures such as their privatization.

9.4.2. *Labour relations*

From the early 1990s, there have also been major changes in labour relations. Thus, for example, for the first time, a credible incomes policy was agreed by the social partners. The wage increases in national labour contracts became linked to the target inflation rate set by the government 2 years ahead. They also take into account the difference between the actual and the target rates of inflation in the two preceding years, adjusted to eliminate the effects of changes in the terms of trade due, for example, to a devaluation. Such *ex post* adjustment has sometimes been the cause of fierce disputes between the parties (e.g. in the renewal of the metalworking contract in 1997).

Company-level contracts allow flexible wage increases according to the performance of the company. They are hierarchically subordinate to national contracts, which can set floors or ceilings for pay increases at the firm level and provide for their suspension in given periods. At least since 1997, all the main national contracts provide for performance-related payments. In particular, they are not to be subsequently transformed into a fixed component of earnings, as was often the case in the past. The 1992–3 agreements set a 4-year length for company-level contracts and provided for their expiry to be staggered according to respective national contracts. However, in practice, their duration has been significantly shorter, especially where they introduce performance-linked bonuses which require annual or more frequent renegotiation and monitoring.

Company-level contracts are common in the manufacturing sector and are rapidly spreading also among small and medium-sized firms. According to the annual Bank of Italy survey of manufacturing firms with fifty employees or more, the number of these contracts reached a peak in 1995–6. At the end of 1996, around 1.7 million employees, or three-quarters of these firms' employees, received a bonus linked to company performance. For one-third of these employees the bonus was also downwardly flexible. However, overall, the degree of flexibility is more limited. On average, only about 3 per cent of total earnings is related to company performance and less than 1 per cent is downwardly flexible. Firm bonuses are fairly homogeneous across workers within the same firm, so that they tend to reduce internal wage dispersion, while widening differentials between firms.

The bargaining system established by the 1992–3 agreements was effective in containing wage and inflationary pressures, especially following the depreciation of the lira. However, several weaknesses must be mentioned. First, 2-year national agreements introduce nominal wage rigidity into the system. While this worked in favour of wage moderation up to 1995, it may exacerbate the conflict when workers try to recoup *ex post* the decline in real wages, as happened with contracts renewed in 1997. Second, a source of rigidity may stem from pay scales which are relatively flat, partly as an inheritance of the earlier wage indexation mechanism and partly because of the common practice of granting all employees similar nominal increases regardless of position. This constraint may be especially severe for sectors with a need to restructure (e.g. banking, transport, and telecommunications) and for businesses in the South which are unable to compensate the lower productivity through significant geographical wage differentials. Third, national contracts often cover macro-sectors which are too broad and heterogeneous to provide unambiguous reference points for costs and productivity. For example, the metalworking sector includes electronics and precision machinery along with the production of basic steel products.

This system is now coming under pressure. Disaffection of firms is growing, because it is perceived that wages have not become as flexible with respect to productivity as competition requires. Meanwhile, trade unions are having to cope with the widespread liberalization of the labour market, the globalization of productive processes, and the shortening of the temporal horizon of investors. Key issues concern the form that employee voice should take, and what further system changes are needed to meet competitive pressures. These issues are more acute in a country such as Italy, where the market-based model has weaker historical roots. One answer, advanced in particular by the Catholic trade union CISL, points to the combination of a marked flexibility of the wage bargaining system with a 'share economy', that is, participation in firm's profit and capital. Another answer, put forward by the left-wing union CGIL, looks instead at the need to ensure sufficient contractual power for workers in all firms through national bargaining, allowing for a greater flexibility in the hiring of labour, but avoiding the direct involvement of labour in the management of the enterprises.

Since the mid-1990s, employment has increased by about 1 million workers. Almost 80 per cent of this increase has taken the form of temporary and part-time work. The increased flexibility of external labour markets and the growing diversity of contractual arrangements reflects a felt-need on the part of management to calibrate output and demand at the level of the firm. This, in turn, has posed problems for trade unions and has weakened their position as representative agencies. Such changes have occurred in particular in sectors which are open to competition and which were always less well organized and lower paid, such as textiles, footwear, and clothing. The big question now is the extent to which these changes are also likely to take place in better organized and more protected sectors, such as metalworking and the state-owned organizations.

Further steps toward flexibility have been made recently with the so-called 'Pact for Italy' signed in July 2002 by the government, employers, and trade unions (except CGIL). This agreement contained several measures regarding the structure of taxation, the labour market, and intervention in the South. The government agreed to implement the EU Directive on working time, the reform of regulations governing public and private employment agencies, training contracts, part-time work, labour-only subcontracting, and various types of atypical work contract. The Pact proposed only one derogation from Article 18 (individual lay-offs) of Labour Rights Law (*Statuto dei Lavoratori*–1970): for a 3-year period, newly hired workers at firms with fewer than sixteen employees in the 12 months prior to the enactment of the law will not be covered by the regulations governing lay-offs even if the hirings raise the number of employees above the threshold.

9.5. Conclusions

In Italy, over the last decade or so, there have been important changes in financial markets, corporate governance, and labour relations. Banks, a number of which were traditionally state-owned and tended to be small by international standards, have been privatized and have grown in size. In addition, new banking laws have enabled them to take a more active role in both equity investment and in corporate governance. At the same time, changes in financial regulations have increased the protections accorded to minority investors. There have also been massive privatizations which have further moved Italy away from its traditional model of financing. However, to date these changes have been limited in their effects on ownership concentration. Nor have they created an active market for corporate control. The size of the equity market still remains relatively small. Though also under pressure, pyramidal ownership structures, often based on family ownership, still remain significant and give top owners and firms protection from market forces.

Simultaneously, there have also been major developments in labour markets and industrial relations. Governments have attempted to create new forms of incomes policies at the national level and also to revise employment regulations and welfare state protections. At the same time, under growing pressures from product and financial markets, there has been an increase in labour market flexibility, as shown by employer attempts to do more within the firm to increase flexibility in employment, hours, and wages. There is now greater use of atypical forms of working and of variable pay. In the manufacturing sector, production systems have moved away from Fordism towards more flexible production arrangements. Over the longer term, the reduced power of trade unions at workplace level has allowed these developments, but more in some sectors and firms than others. No new role has been created for labour in corporate governance; within the firm, for the most part, the influence of labour is reactive. Outside the firm, national and sectoral bargaining continue to be important, though their role is diminishing and more adjustments are being made at company and plant level.

The Italian trajectory of reform and change has been pragmatic and negotiated, in a context where neither governments, firms, nor labour have been able to take a strong lead. Given this, there may be no wholesale move in the direction of either relational–insider or market–outsider types of arrangements. However, within this context, firms and, to some extent, unions have moved slowly to expand the menu of possible institutional solutions. Italian capitalism never fitted easily into a particular type, and today this is still the case. Nevertheless, financial and product market pressures, allied with concerns about macroeconomic performance, suggest that further major change is required. This may well come on the corporate governance side with more outside monitoring of companies and greater protection of minority owners. On the labour side, it may come with more flexible working and a further decentralization of bargaining.

NOTES

1. For a distinction between different kinds of groups see Daems (1980) and Brioschi, Buzzacchi, and Colombo (1990).
2. A series of electoral reforms resulted in a British-style, first-past-the-post electoral system. At the same time judicial inquiries into political corruption overturned the political equilibrium which had prevailed for the entire post-war period, with pressures on the two leading government parties, the Christian Democrats and the Socialists. This transition is still under way, with intensive debate over the new constitutional rules that should be adopted.
3. If the parties have not fixed an expiry date for the agreement, they may withdraw at any time after giving notice.

10

Corporate Governance, Labour, and Employment Relations in Japan: The Future of the Stakeholder Model?

TAKASHI ARAKI

10.1. Introduction: From an Employee-Centred Stakeholder to a Shareholder Model?

In Anglo-Saxon countries, corporate governance debates have focused on the relationship between shareholders and managers and have paid little attention to the role of employees in governance (Blair and Roe 1999: 1). Indeed, such debates presuppose that a corporation is the shareholders' property and the purpose of the corporation is to maximize the interest of shareholders. Corporate governance is therefore about how to control managers in the interests of shareholders. Formally, Japanese company law adopts the same presupposition and provides the shareholders' general meeting with the power to appoint the directors. In contrast to Germany, for example, Japanese law does not give employees or their representatives any formal status as a constituent of the corporation (Okushima 1991: 75).

However, in practice, in Japan it has long been held that employees are the most important stakeholders. According to Egashira (1994): 'There has been a consensus among legal commentators that, irrespective of the principles and theories embedded in corporate law, in practice larger companies are administered by prioritizing the interests of employees, both white and blue collar workers' (Egashira 1994: 3). Itami refers to the notion of 'employee-sovereign corporation' or 'employee-centred corporation' and justifies such governance on the grounds that the contribution and risk exposure of core employees are greater than those of shareholders and that employees make a major long-term investment via the seniority-based wage and retirement allowance system (Itami 1987*b*, 2000). Until the major slowdown of the Japanese economy from the early 1990s, this perspective seemed to fit the perceptions of both Japanese managers and employees.

Scholars have identified several key features that distinguish the Japanese system of governance and the role of employees in these. Fukao (1999: 177) identifies the following: the 'main bank' system in which the corporation has long-term relationships with one or a small number of banks through cross-shareholdings; the 'keiretsu' system in which companies form groups with long-term trading relationships (sometimes with cross-shareholding); and the 'lifetime employment' system guaranteeing stable employment and seniority-based wages. Inagami (2001) defines an ideal-typical Japanese corporation as follows: an insider-based monitoring model, whose purpose is to prioritize its continuing existence and development as an enterprise community; management by directors who have been promoted through an internal job hierarchy, and who simultaneously serve as employed executive officers; and an ownership system comprising cross-shareholdings and 'silent', stable shareholders, coupled with indirect financing through the main-bank system. In combination, these features underpin long-standing relationships of mutual trust between the firm, its employees, and other stakeholders.

The significance of employees' status in corporate governance is also stressed by foreign scholars. Dore emphasizes four dominant features of Japanese capitalism. One, on a continuum of 'employee-favouring' through to 'shareholder-favouring', firms lean heavily towards the former. Two, firms engage in relational trading as opposed to impersonal spot-market trading. Three, firms stress the importance of cooperation rather than competition with their competitors. Four, government has important roles in producing public goods and serving as an umpire in clashes of private interests in matters that Anglo-Saxon countries would leave to the market (Dore 2000a: 51). For his part, Milhaupt (2001: 2085) also identifies a number of central features of the governance environment in Japan: the 'main bank' system and its role in corporate governance; the absence of an external market for corporate control; the structure and role of Japanese company boards; and the lifetime employment system. He also points out that the legal supports for many aspects of the system are limited.

Thus, viewed from the perspective of three parties to corporate governance (shareholders, management, and employees), the traditional corporate governance in Japan can be summarized as follows.

One, shareholders have been less concerned with dividends than with the long-term relationships in which the firm is engaged. Thus, they have not actively intervened in corporate governance. Two, directors are mostly promoted from within the firm with a significant number having a dual function of director and employee (*Jyugyoin kenmu torishimariyaku* or 'directors-with-employee functions'). In this way, management and employees have come to share common perspectives and interests. Three, long-term employment practices and cooperative industrial relations have been created through a combination of company policy interacting with cooperative collective bargaining and voluntary joint consultation. Together, these have created Japan's employee-centred stakeholder model.

From a legal perspective, the distinctive characteristic of Japan's stakeholder model is its reliance on non-legal practices or norms (Araki 2000*a*: 259, 2000*b*: 87; Dore 2000*a*: 182, 215, 2000*b*; Milhaupt 2001: 2083). Furthermore, Japanese law does not give employees or their representatives any formal status as a constituent of the corporation (Okushima 1991: 75). This contrasts with Germany where the stakeholder model is sanctioned by legislation. One corollary of this, however, is that environmental changes may potentially modify Japan's traditional corporate governance more easily than where the stakeholder model is supported by legislation.

This possibility takes on a high degree of salience given the recent changes in the Japanese economy. Over the last 10 years, Japan has witnessed a prolonged economic slump, bankruptcies of large banks and financial institutions, and scandals involving various forms of corporate misconduct. As a result, Japan's corporate governance system, especially the absence of an external market for corporate control, has faced severe criticism (by bodies such as the Corporate Governance Forum of Japan). There have certainly been changes recently in Japanese corporate governance and its environment. Cross-shareholdings are dissolving and stable corporate shareholdings are being reduced. Major banks are selling the shares of their trading customers, especially in the light of 2001 regulations which limit banks' shareholdings to the amount of their own core capital. As we will see below, major corporate law reforms facilitating corporate restructuring have occurred since the late 1990s, and changes in 2002 introduced American-style boards of directors with outside directors. At the same time, the media highlights the alleged collapse of lifetime employment practices, the demise of wages and benefits based on seniority, and the reduction in employee voice as union density continues to decline. This raises the fundamental question as to whether Japan's traditional employee-centred stakeholder model is being transformed into a shareholder-centred model, with important consequences for employment and industrial relations.

This chapter examines traditional features and recent changes in share ownership.[1] It then reviews traditional aspects of corporate management and recent legislative changes. Next, the chapter considers the Japanese employment system and cooperative management–labour relations. Again, it looks at recent changes and at legal developments designed to cope with such changes. Finally, the chapter concludes with an evaluation of the current situation and of future prospects.

10.2. Share Ownership in Japan

Distinctive features of corporate governance in Japan in the latter half of the twentieth century were stable, long-term shareholders and extensive ownership by business corporations, often in the form of cross-shareholding. Table 10.1 shows the distribution of share ownership by key investor groups as compared with the United States and Germany.

In the years immediately after the Second World War, the so-called *zaibatsu* or pre-war financial combines had been dissolved, holding companies forbidden under Anti-Monopoly Law, and shareholding by corporations largely prohibited. Initially, the proportion of equity held by individual shareholders was as high as 69 per cent (in 1949) and share turnover was high. However, corporate shareholdings by financial institutions (especially banks and securities companies) and by business corporations increased steadily and by the mid-1960s

Table 10.1. *Ownership of equity in the United States, Germany, and Japan*

Investor type	US	Germany	Japan
Individuals	30–35	4	20
Institutional owners (e.g. banks)	2	27	40
Institutional agents (e.g. pension funds)	55–60	3	6
Corporations	2–7	41	30
Government	Negligible	6	Negligible
Foreign investors	6	19	4

Notes: Percentages of equity held by each shareholder type.
Source: Porter (1992: 42).

Table 10.2. *Proportion of equity (by volume) held by shareholder types 1950–2002*

Year	Financial institutions	Business corporations	Individuals	Foreigners
1950	12.6	11.0	61.3	—
1960	30.6	17.8	46.3	1.3
1970	32.3	23.1	39.9	3.2
1980	38.8	25.0	29.2	4.0
1990	45.2	25.2	23.1	4.2
1995	41.4	23.8	23.6	9.4
2000	37.0	22.3	26.3	13.2
2001	36.2	23.2	25.9	13.7
2002	34.1	24.8	23.4	16.5

Source: National Conference of Stock Exchanges (2002).

surpassed shareholding by individuals. In 1990, the combined shareholding of banks, financial institutions, and business corporations had reached 70 per cent and the proportion of individual shareholding stood at 23 per cent of total equity by value. Table 10.2 shows the evolution of share ownership by investor types over time in Japan.

It became common for large business partners to own each other's stock. When such cross-shareholding existed among banks from which other companies obtained long-term credit, these banks came to be known as 'main banks' for those companies (Yamakawa 1999: 5). According to the Top Management Survey conducted by RIALS (Inagami 2000), a massive 98 per cent of companies considered they had 'stable' shareholders.[2] The percentage of shares held by stable shareholders is 54 per cent. In total, 39 per cent of surveyed companies have cross-shareholdings with stable shareholders.

Several factors explain this structure of shareholding. Though the *zaibatsu* were dissolved by the Occupation Authorities in 1945, personal networks among the *zaibatsu* families led to a regrouping of the *zaibatsu*-related companies. The relaxation of Anti-Monopoly regulations facilitated such trends. Japan's accession to the OECD in 1964—entailing liberalization of capital markets to foreign investment—further induced Japanese companies to develop a pattern of cross-shareholding to defend themselves against foreign acquisition (Ito 1993: 154).

These stable shareholders are not motivated by short-term profit. Their purpose is to promote growth and to provide protection against hostile takeovers. In the case of cross-shareholding between banks and business corporations, the main concern of banks is to secure their loans and also to grow their own business. Therefore, the stable, long-term prosperity of the business corporation is much more important than short-term profit. As a consequence of this, shareholders of large Japanese companies tend to act as 'silent shareholders' (*mono iwanu kabunushi*) and do not readily become involved in company affairs (Charkham 1994: 81; Yamakawa 1999: 5). This has allowed Japanese companies to pursue long-term strategies. Until the collapse of the so-called 'bubble economy' in the early 1990s, these features of the Japanese system were well regarded.

10.2.1. *Recent changes in share ownership*

Cross-shareholdings and long-term shareholdings, especially those between banks and customer corporations, have declined substantially in recent years. Cross-shareholding refers to the mutual shareholding relationship when a company, some of whose shares are held by another company, owns shares in that other company.[3] It includes shareholdings registered in the name of trust banks operating as benefit trusts and shareholdings held through holding companies. Long-term shareholdings are a broader category, defined by Kuroki as cross-shareholdings, non-cross-held shares owned by domestic banks (excluding trust banks) and domestic insurance firms, and shares held by listed affiliate companies (Kuroki 2002: 5). As Table 10.3 shows, the cross-shareholding ratio in the overall market fell from

Table 10.3. *Percentage of total equity held as cross-shareholdings and long-term shareholdings*

Year	Cross-shareholding[a] by value	Cross-shareholding by volume	Long-term shareholding[b] by value	Long-term shareholding by volume
1987	18.4	14.5	45.8	42.5
1992	17.8	14.8	45.7	42.8
1997	15.1	13.1	40.5	37.7
2001	9.1	8.9	30.2	30.5

[a] Cross-shareholding is defined as a mutual shareholding relationship where a company, whose shares are owned by another company, owns the shares of that other company. It includes indirect mutual shareholding where a company X's shares are held by a company Y, a sister company of a holding company Z, and the company X owns shares in company Z.
[b] Long-term shareholding includes cross-shareholding as defined above, shareholding by financial institutions (banks, domestic life, and non-life insurers), financial institutions' shares held by business corporations, and sister company's shares held by its parent or holding company.

Source: Kuroki (2002).

18 per cent in 1987 to 9 per cent in 2001 on a value-basis. The stable, long-term shareholding ratio including cross-shareholding in the overall market declined from 46 per cent in 1987 to 30 per cent in 2001 on a value-basis. Although the stable, long-term shareholding ratio in business corporations declined modestly from 12 per cent in 1996 to 11 per cent in 2001, that in financial institutions fell drastically from 30 per cent in 1996 to 19 per cent in 2001 and that in banks from 15 per cent in 1996 to 9 per cent in 2001 on a value-basis (Kuroki 2002).

Such drastic declines in cross-shareholdings and stable shareholding have occurred under the following circumstances. The introduction of the market-to-market method of calculating the value of holding shares at market prices from 2001 and the continuous decline of stock prices induced many companies to sell unprofitable stocks. Furthermore, the 2001 Law Restricting Banks' Shareholding calls for banks to reduce shareholdings so as not to exceed the amount of their own capital. This legislation forced banks to sell their shares in customer companies and triggered a reciprocal sale of banks' stocks by their customers.

However, a survey conducted by the Ministry of Finance shows that more than 80 per cent of companies still maintain cross-shareholding even though there has been a decline recently (see Table 10.4). Moreover, 70 per cent of surveyed companies believed that cross-shareholdings have a merit in creating stable and long-term trading relations.

Furthermore, although cross-shareholdings with banks and other financial institutions are dissolving, those among business corporations have not changed as much. For the future, according to a survey conducted by the Japan Productivity Centre for Socio-Economic Development (JPC-SED) (2003), company directors are equally divided on the advantages and disadvantages of maintaining cross-shareholdings. It is therefore premature to state that cross-shareholdings

Table 10.4. *The extent of cross-shareholdings in 1999 and 2002*
(percentages of companies with cross-shareholding)

Year	Company size categories by capital (billion yen)					
	Under 1	1–3	3–10	10–30	30 plus	All
1999 (875 companies)	89.5	87.6	85.7	92.0	90.0	88.4
2002 (1,216 companies)	77.4	82.2	83.2	86.8	84.6	83.2
Change 1999–2002	−12.1	−5.4	−2.5	−5.2	−5.9	−5.2

Source: Ministry of Finance, Policy Research Institute (2003: tables 3–4).

Table 10.5. *The proportion of equity (by value) held by shareholder types 1970–2002*

Year	Financial institutions	Business corporations	Individuals	Foreigners
1970	31.8	23.9	37.7	4.9
1975	35.5	27.0	32.1	3.6
1980	36.2	26.2	27.9	5.8
1985	39.8	28.8	22.3	7.0
1990	43.0	30.1	20.4	4.7
1995	41.1	27.2	19.5	10.5
2000	39.1	21.8	19.4	18.8
2001	39.4	21.8	19.7	18.3
2002	39.1	21.5	20.6	17.7

Source: National Conference of Stock Exchanges (2002).

are uniformly dissolving and that recent trends will necessarily continue.

Another important development in the structure of share ownership in the 1990s was a rapid increase in the importance of foreign shareholders. The proportion of shares (by value) held by foreign owners rose from 4.7 per cent in 1990 to 18.8 per cent in 2000 (see Table 10.5). Although this percentage fell slightly to 17.7 per cent in 2002, their presence in the Japanese stock market is now significant. Unlike traditional Japanese shareholders, foreign investors are likely to require more shareholder value-oriented corporate governance. Since their investments tend to be concentrated in larger, leading companies, their interests and views on investment goals may have a disproportionate effect on corporate governance (Ministry of Finance 2003).

At the same time, there have been legal changes which have strengthened the position of shareholders vis-à-vis managers. To facilitate shareholders' representative lawsuits and to promote more active monitoring by shareholders, the 1993 Commercial Code fixed the costs of lawsuits by shareholders at a nominal amount. Until then, the cost of a lawsuit by shareholders against managers could be prohibitively high. However, faced with the increase in the number of lawsuits and under pressure from business, the government later limited directors' financial liability. Thus, the 2001 Commercial Code makes it possible for the shareholders' meeting to limit the directors' liability to between 2 and 6 years' remuneration. However, this does not gainsay the fact that in total there has been an increase in external control through shareholders' representative lawsuits.

10.3. **Corporate Management and Monitoring Arrangements**

Influenced initially by German and subsequently by American law, the legal underpinnings of the Japanese corporate management and monitoring system developed some unique features (Oda 1999: 216). The Commercial Code of 1899 introduced a dual monitoring structure of managing directors and company auditors modelled on German law. In 1950, under American influence, Japanese company law introduced boards of directors to supervise corporate management. However, since the older auditor role was never abolished, Japan has had a system where corporate management has been monitored by both a board of directors and auditors. This is referred to as the 'dual monitoring system'.

In addition, as discussed below, the 2002 revision of the Commercial Code introduced a further, American-style governance model, based on three committees composed mainly of outside directors. The new model is called a 'company with the three committees' (*iinkai-tou secchi gaisha*) as opposed to the traditional governance

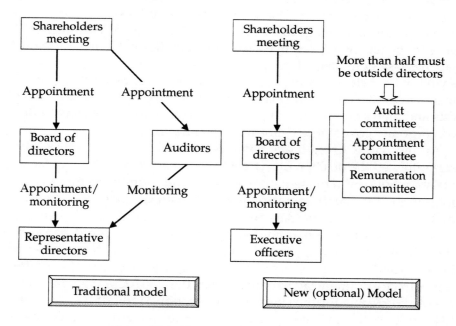

Figure 10.1. *Two competing governance models*

model called a 'company with auditors' (*kansa-yaku sonchi gaisha*). Its adoption, however, is optional. As a result, Japan now has two different governance models, in potential competition with one another (Kansaku 2000: 169; Egashira 2002: 412; Kanda 2003: 153). The two systems are illustrated in Figure 10.1.

10.3.1. *The traditional governance model (the dual monitoring system)*

10.3.1.1. *The board of directors*
From a comparative perspective, the first major feature of the Japanese board of directors is its large size: boards with more than twenty members have been common in Japan (Kawahama 1997: 38). This large size has been cited as a major cause of board dysfunction in terms of decision-making and monitoring.[4] In the late 1990s, there was a tendency to reduce the number of directors and to increase the number of executive officers. Nonetheless, by the late 1990s, the average number of directors was 17.5 which is still much larger than in the United States where the average number is 12 (Charkham 1994: 188; Inagami 2000: 337).

A further feature of the Japanese board is that there is no sharp difference between board members and employees in terms of background, remuneration, and function. The Top Management Survey shows that 76 per cent of board members are promoted from within, not hired from outside (Inagami 2000: 324). Moreover, most of the remainder are from parent or affiliated companies. Thus, there are usually no 'outsider' directors in the company. In part, this internal promotion practice stems from measures to democratize Japan's economy after the Second World War: older directors were purged and a younger set of managers was promoted from within (Okazaki 1993: 103, 114, 125). With the spread of long-term career employment, the promotion of incumbent employees to board membership became commonplace. Thus, board membership is a final stage of promotion for managerial employees who have performed well over the course of their career. The need to accommodate these employees in part explains the large size of the typical Japanese board.

With regard to remuneration, the gap between board members and other employees is much smaller than that in the United States or the United Kingdom. The average annual remuneration of board members amounts to just nine times that of new graduate entrants

(Inagami 2000). There is continuity of the remuneration profile between a department head who is a managerial employee and a low level director. As a result, the remuneration gap between senior employees and board members is quite narrow.

Junior directors usually have a double function as both board members and managers of their respective departments. According to the Top Management Survey, half of all board members fit into this category of directors.[5] According to another survey, three-quarters of the annual salary of these so-called 'directors-with-employee-functions' rewards their employee function while one-equarter is for their directorial activities (Romu Gyosei Kenkyu-jo 1999: 2). The main role of these junior directors is to represent their department (including conveying the voice of ordinary employees) rather than to develop corporate strategy.

This feature of the board of directors has facilitated cooperative labour relations and arguably has also enhanced the efficiency of corporate administration. However, the 'insider' nature of the traditional board system has been less effective in preventing misconduct by management and in making directors and top managers accountable to shareholders. In practice, the president and senior directors nominate those below them, with the result that these other directors are beholden to them. As a result, the board of directors tend to be subject to the leadership of the president and senior directors rather than vice versa.

10.3.1.2. *The role of auditors*

The role of the auditor was initially to audit the finances of the company and this remains the case in smaller firms. In larger firms the role is both to oversee finances and to scrutinise the administration of the company. Their scrutiny is understood to be confined to ensuring legal compliance. It does not extend to evaluating the appropriateness of corporate administration.[6]

Though this dual structure of management originally stems from German law, there are significant differences between the German supervisory board (*Aufsichtsrat*) and the Japanese board of auditors. One, whereas the German supervisory board has the power to appoint and discharge board members as well as to audit finance and monitor business administration, Japanese auditors are restricted to the latter. Two, whereas a German supervisory board in companies with more than 500 employees consists of representatives of both shareholders and employees, the Japanese auditor system does not allow for worker-participation. The appointment of Japanese auditors has been de facto determined by the directors, who have a right to propose a list of nominees to a general shareholder meeting. It has been common for auditors to be selected from board members or senior managers (Kubori 1994: 41).

Since it is difficult to expect the board of directors to supervise their own business administration, efforts to reform the Japanese monitoring system have concentrated on measures to strengthen the power of auditors and ensure their independence. In 1974, the supervisory power of auditors was expanded to cover corporate administration as well as finance. In 1981, it became compulsory to have three or more auditors, at least one of whom in larger companies has to be full time. In 1993, the term of office for auditors was expanded from 2 to 3 years so as to strengthen their independence. The 2001 revisions of the Commercial Code further strengthened the auditors' power and independence by further extending the term of office to 4 years and by requiring that in larger companies at least half of the auditors must be outsiders. The board of auditors in larger companies has been given a right to veto proposals to nominate auditors at the shareholder meeting and a right to submit its own proposals (Egashira 2002: 390; Kanda 2003: 139).

In spite of these amendments to strengthen the power and independence of auditors, the auditor system still falls short of expectations (Keizai Doyukai 1996: 7; Yoshihara 2001: 185). In this context, in 1998, the Corporate Governance Forum of Japan (1998: 43) proposed a radical reform plan: to allow companies to abolish the auditor system by adopting an American-style 'board of directors' system utilizing outside directors. This reform was located in a broader critique of the Japanese system. In its *Corporate Governance Principles* the Forum states:

Global competition may be interpreted as a survival race between two corporate systems for higher corporate efficiency: one system predominantly promoting value for shareholders—so called 'shareholder value'; and the other pursuing multiple values including those of employees ... What should be done in Japan is to promote the idea that shareholders are owners of corporation and the purpose of corporation is to pursue their interest. (Corporate Governance Forum of Japan 1998: 8–10)

The proposal resulted in a new corporate governance model in the 2002 corporate law revision. This is outlined below.

10.3.2. *Introduction of a new governance model with outside directors and with three committees*

The draft of the 2002 corporate law revision referred to the defects of the existing Japanese board of directors system. Monitors are primarily insiders and the number of directors is too large to function effectively. Moreover, 'directors-with-employee-functions' are in reality subject to senior directors. To cope with these problems, it was felt necessary to institute the following: to separate the monitoring mechanism from corporate administration in order to strengthen the former; to delegate more power to executive officers (*shikko-yaku*) in order to enhance business operations; and to establish three committees (audit, appointments, and remuneration) with outside directors so as to enhance the independence of the monitoring function from the board of directors.

Thus, a new governance model called a 'company with the three committees' (*iinkai-to secchi kaisha*) was introduced. To adopt this model, it is necessary to establish committees for audit, appointments, and remuneration. Each committee must have more than three directors, the majority of whom must be outside or non-executive directors. Where this new governance model is adopted, boards of auditors are to be abolished and replaced by the audit committee. Such companies must have one or more executive officer(s) (*shikko-yaku*). The directors and board of directors are to concentrate on monitoring while corporate administration is entrusted to the executive officers (see Figure 10.1). However, it should be noted that this model is optional. Therefore, companies can maintain the traditional dual monitoring system.

The above reform is one of the most fundamental changes in postwar corporate law. Unlike the traditional governance model with internally promoted directors, this model consists of outside directors representing the interests of shareholders. If widely adopted, the new governance model might have a significant impact on the labour and employment relations. So far, however, the number of companies that have adopted the new governance model is limited. According to the *Nikkei* (15 June 2003), only thirty-five listed companies have adopted the new governance model although they include such leading corporations as Sony, Toshiba, Mitsubishi, and Hitachi. Many Japanese managers prefer the old system on the grounds that it makes for clearer leadership and greater flexibility in the running of the company (Ministry of Finance, Policy Research Institute 2003: table 3-24).

The scarcity of suitable candidates for outside directors has further hindered the adoption of the new governance model. As a result, the majority of listed corporations have maintained the traditional governance model.

10.4. Employment

Employment security and worker flexibility have had a high priority in the Japanese enterprise. It has been supported by aspects of the corporate governance system referred to above and that employees are an integral part of Japanese corporate governance. However, in the last 10 years, circumstances surrounding employment relations have changed substantially. Since the economic slowdown from the early 1990s, unemployment has increased to unprecedented levels for Japan, reaching nearly 6 per cent by 2002. The traditional lifetime employment system is said to be collapsing. Reflecting pressures for corporate restructuring, judge-made law has started to relax the legal regulations concerning economic dismissal. This section reviews the traditional employment system and its recent changes.

10.4.1. *Long-term employment practices*

Japan's long-term or lifetime employment incorporating job security was created and sustained by various social institutions: legal rules concerning dismissals, state policy to maintain employment, and social norms respecting employment. Even after the two oil crises of the 1970s, Japan boasted of its low unemployment and managed to maintain employment security for core workers.

10.4.1.1. *Law restricting dismissals without just cause*
From a comparative perspective, Japanese law on job tenure and dismissals has several features. Until the 2003 revision of the Labour Standards Law, employment security was provided by case law rather than statute. Japanese courts established a case law rule called the 'abuse of the right to dismiss' which regards a dismissal without just cause as an abuse of the right to dismiss and thus null and void. This doctrine arose in the context of post-war socio-economic conditions which made protection of employment security imperative. In the extremely difficult circumstances following the Second World

War, dismissal meant extreme privation for workers. Even when recovery was well underway and the practice of long-term employment had started to become established, dismissal was viewed as detrimental to a worker's seniority (a decisive factor in the Japanese personnel management and wage system) because seniority accrued in previous employment could not usually be carried over to new employment. Given strong internal labour markets in Japan, dismissal has traditionally had more serious consequences for workers than in countries where external labour markets are more developed.

In such circumstances, Japanese courts developed the doctrine that workers should be protected through restrictions on the employer's right to dismiss at will. Relying on the general clause of the Civil Code that prohibits abuse of rights, Japanese courts handed down a series of decisions holding that an objectively unreasonable or socially unacceptable dismissal was an abuse of the right to dismiss, and thus null and void. The doctrine of abuse of the right to dismiss was finally endorsed by the Supreme Court in 1975. Under subsequent case law, an employer is required to demonstrate the existence of just cause. Courts interpret just cause very strictly and tend to deny the validity of dismissal unless there has been serious misconduct by the worker.

In addition, Japanese case law sets stringent restrictions on economic dismissals. In effect, the courts adopted the emerging practice of large companies and their unions as the basis for general rules concerning economic dismissals. These practices had come to involve extensive consultation to avoid employment-adjustment dismissal except as a very last resort. What resulted was case law which dictates that any adjustment dismissal should be rejected as an abuse of the right to dismiss unless it meets four requirements.

First, there must be a real and demonstrable business-based need to resort to reduction of personnel. Second, the employer must take every possible measure to avoid adjustment dismissals including the following: reductions in overtime, reductions in recruitment, voluntary retirement, non-renewal of fixed-term and part-time contracts, and implementation of transfers (*haiten*) or 'farming out' (*shukko*) of redundant workers. In other words, dismissals must be the action of last resort. The 'last resort' requirement is particularly stringent. Since Japanese employers have many alternatives for cost reduction and maintaining redundant workers, it is difficult for them to readily satisfy this requirement. Third, the selection of workers to be dismissed must be made on an objective and reasonable basis. Fourth, management is required to explain the need, timing, scale, and method of dismissal to the union or other worker body (if no union exists) and consult with them in good faith concerning the dismissals.

The remedies against unjust dismissals are highly protective. In many countries, unjust dismissals results in the payment of damages or redundancy payments. By contrast, in Japan, the abuse of the right to dismiss doctrine obliges the employer to pay wages during the period of dismissal and to reinstate the dismissed employee. As a result, if a dismissal is held to be abusive, the employer cannot dissolve the employment relationship no matter how much the employer might wish to pay the employee. These are, therefore, real disincentives for Japanese employers to resort to arbitrary dismissals.

10.4.1.2. *Internal flexibility to secure long-term employment*
To compensate for restrictions on external numerical flexibility, the Japanese employment system has promoted internal or functional flexibility. In other words, through flexible deployment of workers, Japanese companies have accommodated changing socio-economic circumstances while maintaining employment security (Araki 2002: 48). There are a number of ways in which this takes place.

First, flexible modification of working conditions is rendered possible in that the employment contract does not specify the conditions of employment, particularly the place and type of work. In drafting work rules, employers reserve the right to deploy workers based on business necessity, including the right to order transfers which entail changes in the place and/or type of work. Therefore, the employer can unilaterally order such changes without obtaining the worker's consent. However, modifications in the place and/or type of work may be reviewed for their validity by the courts where such changes cause workers significant personal inconvenience.

Second, the Supreme Court ruled that a 'reasonable modification' of work rules has a binding effect on all workers, including those who opposed the modification. In drawing up or modifying work rules, the employer is required to ask the opinion of the union or of a person representing a majority of the workers (in the absence of a union). However, an agreement is not required. Thus, the employer can unilaterally establish and modify work rules, provided they are reasonable. Moreover, the Supreme Court has repeatedly ruled that such modified work rules are binding on all employees in the establishment.

The underlying notion is, therefore, that workers are expected to accept and be subject to reasonable changes in working conditions in return for employment security. This is the legal basis of the internal or qualitative flexibility of the Japanese employment relationship.

10.4.1.3. *Governmental policy to maintain employment*

Government employment policy has contributed to employment security. Initially after the Second World War, policy focused on unemployment benefit programmes and job-creation measures to absorb unemployment through public works. From the mid-1960s, however, economic growth and the spread of long-term employment shifted government policy to providing various subsidies to enable employers suffering from economic difficulties to retain their workers rather than resorting to dismissals. In particular, the Employment Adjustment Allowance programme for firms that were compelled to shut down operations temporarily was extensively used, thereby contributing to the maintenance of employment security. Thus, the main focus of policy became to maintain employment and prevent unemployment rather than to absorb prior existing unemployment. This is reflected in Japan's vocational training policy which focuses less on providing vocational training to unemployed workers than on supporting companies in their on-the-job and off-the-job training, thereby enabling the employers to retain their workers (Araki 1994: 385; Takanashi 1997: 5, 1999: 7; Ohtake 2000: 5).

However, in response to the prolonged recession over the last decade, Japan's employment policy is shifting its emphasis from avoiding dismissals and maintaining employment to promoting the smooth reallocation or transfer of redundant workers. Government is increasing expenditure to encourage labour mobility to cope with increasing unemployment while maintaining the traditional policy of employment security.[7] In sum, the current state of employment policy can be viewed as a diversification of measures to mirror growing workforce diversity and to partially adjust employment policy away from too great a reliance on maintaining employment of regular workers (Araki 1999: 5).

10.4.1.4. *Norms concerning employment security*

Apart from the law and government policy, the notion that dismissals should only be condoned as a last resort is widely and deeply rooted in Japanese society. In truth, case law and government employment policy have resulted in an outgrowth of voluntary practices incorporating employment security. In practice, it should be noted that the number of dismissal cases in Japan is extremely small compared to other countries.[8]

In 1993, in response to the recession triggered by the collapse of the bubble economy, some Japanese employers cancelled their agreed promises of employment to new graduate recruits. These unilateral cancellations attracted considerable public attention and received wide media coverage because they violated social norms. The Ministry of Labour publicized the names of the companies that had cancelled their agreements to stigmatize them. These events reflected the social norm that employment relationships should not be unilaterally broken by the employer and furthermore that this principle even applies to situations where the formal employment relationship has not actually begun.

Corporate governance arrangements have arguably also played a part in promoting norms and practices favourable to employment security. Patient shareholders, the absence of a market for corporate control, and relatively weak pressures from financial markets until recently have allowed firms to maintain jobs. In addition, directors are as responsive to employee needs as much as they are to shareholder value.

10.4.2. *Changing employment security*

Employment is becoming unstable, and atypical or non-regular employment is increasing. Between 1990 and 2002, non-regular employees rose from 20.2 per cent of the Japanese work force to 29.8 per cent. To cope with increased mobility, the government has introduced a series of measures to activate the external labour market (Araki 1999).

Regulations on fixed-term contracts in Japan have been progressively relaxed. Unlike many European countries where objective grounds are required to conclude fixed-term contracts, no such grounds are required in Japan either to reach or renew such contracts. The sole legal restriction on fixed-term contracts has been that the agreed term of the contract may not exceed one year. However, the 2003 revision of the Labour Standards Law further relaxed the upper limit to 3 years. In addition, temporary work agencies have been progressively legalized. After several moderate revisions in the 1990s, the 1999 revisions of the law lifted the general prohibition on 'worker dispatching'. The 2003 revisions extended legalized worker dispatching to production sites that had continued to be prohibited under the 1999 revision.

Recently, there has been an important legal development concerning economic dismissals. As mentioned above, the validity of economic

dismissals had traditionally depended on whether all four requirements were met or not. If one of four requirements was not satisfied,
the dismissal was regarded as an abuse of the right to dismiss.
A recent decision by the important Tokyo District court has rejected this
interpretation, arguing that there are no good grounds for insisting
that all four requirements must be satisfied for economic dismissals
to take place.[9] According to the decision, courts should determine
whether a dismissal is abusive. The so-called 'four requirements' are
merely 'four factors' to analyse abusiveness. Therefore, an economic
dismissal can be legal and valid even if one of the four 'factors' is not
met by taking all other factors surrounding the dismissals into consideration. Nevertheless, despite the changes, it is arguable that the
restrictions are still more stringent than in European countries and
certainly more so than in the United States.[10]

The 2000 Labour Contract Succession Law. In the context of corporate
restructuring and growing labour mobility, several counter-measures
have been adopted to protect employees' interests. This can be shown
with reference to recent changes to facilitate corporate sell-offs and
transfers. To facilitate corporate restructuring and reorganization, the
so-called 'corporate division scheme' was introduced by an amend-
ment of the Commercial Code in 2000. Prior to this, corporation division was carried out through transfer of the business or undertakings.
In order to transfer a business, the company (transferor) had to obtain
individual consent from all creditors and from workers who were to
be transferred to the other company (transferee). This procedure was
thought to be cumbersome and to have hindered restructuring and
reorganization. The 2000 revision of the Commercial Code introduced
a simplified procedure. When a plan to sell part of a company is
approved by the shareholders meeting by special resolution, the division becomes legally binding on all parties concerned without the
need to obtain their individual consent (though dissenting creditors
can express objection and seek liquidation). However, it was feared
that this could be easily abused to downsize workforces and that
employment security would be severely damaged. To protect
employees' interests in the event of a corporate division, the Labour
Contract Succession Law (LCSL) was introduced in 2000. Under this
law, employment relationships are automatically transferred to the
newly established corporation as a principle. However, a worker who
is only partially connected to the spun-off unit can object to moving.
Workers not involved in the unit can only be transferred with their

consent. Also workers can object to exclusion from a transfer if the work in the transferee organization is their usual work (Yamakawa 2001; Araki 2002: 142, 2003: 27).

In terms of effects, when an employment contract is passed to the transferee corporation, the effect of succession is automatic and as comprehensive as in the case of a merger. Therefore, all rights and duties in the employment contract or terms and conditions of employment are transferred to the transferee without modifications. However, adjustments in the terms and conditions of employment are not prohibited before or after the corporation division. Given the necessity to establish uniform working conditions and adjust them to changing corporate circumstances, it is possible for the transferor or transferee to vary working conditions through reasonable modification of work rules as well as through agreement with individual workers or with labour unions (Yamakawa 2001: 10).

In the case of collective agreements, the fear is that workers lose the protection provided by the collective bargaining agreement in the previous company. Though terms and conditions of employment provided by a collective agreement are to be transferred as they are, they can be changed unfavourably (to workers) by individual consent as long as there is no normative effect of the collective agreement. Therefore, the LCSL provides that when an employment contract between union members and the transferor is passed to the transferee, it shall be deemed that a collective bargaining agreement with the same contents is concluded between the transferee and the union to which those workers belong.

The LCSL is a Japanese version of the acquired rights legislation implementing the EC Directive on Transfer of Undertakings. However, an important difference is that application of the LCSL is confined to dismemberment of companies whereas the EC Directive covers transfers of undertakings as well as division of corporations and mergers. Under Japanese law including the LCSL, automatic and mandatory transfer of an employment contract is not required in the event of transfer of undertakings.

Finally, there have been several other attempts to change the legal regulation of employment. Battles have been fought between the government seeking to promote economic recovery, employers wanting more liberalization, and unions and their supporters wanting to defend and extend labour protection. For instance, the unions and their supporters have tried unsuccessfully to reverse the 'four factors' rule in the case of economic dismissals. They have won some victories against employer proposals which would have given employers a freer hand at law to dismiss employees. One example was a requirement in the Labour Standards Law 2003 that strengthens employers' obligation to provide written reasons for dismissal. The unions also successfully opposed the introduction of monetary solutions to dismissal disputes.

10.5. Industrial Relations, Employee Participation, and Corporate Governance

For many years, a prominent feature of Japan's industrial relations has been stable and cooperative relations between labour and management. This is not the result of some deep cultural predisposition on the part of Japanese managers and workers. Indeed, it should be remembered that, from the end of the Second World War up to the 1960s, Japan experienced turbulent management–labour confrontations (Hiwatari 1999: 276; Koshiro 2000). Japan's current stable industrial relations should be understood as the result of the following three factors: (1) enterprise unionism, (2) widespread joint management–labour consultation practices, and (3) internal promotion of management.

10.5.1. *Enterprise unionism*

Enterprise unionism is a hallmark of Japanese industrial relations (Sugeno and Suwa 1996). Currently around 20 per cent of the Japanese labour force are union members: 96 per cent of unions in Japan are enterprise-based unions and 91 per cent of all unionized workers belong to enterprise unions. Enterprise unionism is a system under which unions are established within an individual enterprise, collectively bargain with a single employer, and conclude collective agreements at the enterprise level. An enterprise union organizes workers in the same company irrespective of their jobs. As a result, both blue and white-collar workers are organized in the same union. Enterprise unions normally confine their membership to regular workers, though there are no legal obstacles to prevent them from organizing part-time or temporary workers. Within an industry, enterprise unions often join an industrial federation of unions, though collective bargaining at that level is very rare. In their turn, industrial federations are affiliated to national confederations.

There are several reasons for the dominance of this pattern of union organization. Prior to the Second World War, Japan had little experience with industry-wide unionism. The mobilization of workers into units at the enterprise level during the war may have had some influence in its emergence. After the war, when employers had defeated radical left-wing unions but could no longer suppress union activities altogether, workers resorted to enterprise-level workplace organization and this was recognized by management.

Enterprise unionism has continued to predominate because it has served well as a key component of Japanese employment relations. Under the long-term employment system, dismissals are avoided at all cost. In exchange, workers accept the flexible adjustment of working conditions and are prepared to be transferred within a company and receive in-house education and on-the-job training. Promotion and wages are decided mainly by that individual's length of service and performance. In this context, industry-level bargaining makes little sense. Enterprise unions and enterprise-level collective bargaining have been the main mechanism for reconciling worker demands and employer expectations in the context of strong internal labour markets. In further defence of the system, it might be argued that, when unions have their basis in a particular company, they tend to be more pragmatic than ideological and more conscious of their own company's productivity and competitiveness.

10.5.1.1. *Wages and enterprise unionism*
However, enterprise unionism also arguably has defects. These include weaker bargaining power, the lack of a universal impact across an industry, and the lack of political influence on national labour policy (Sugeno and Suwa 1996).

To compensate for weakness in bargaining power and the lack of industry or nation-wide influence, union leaders in the 1950s devised a unique wage determination system called '*Shunto*' (Spring Wage Offensive) (Takanashi 2002). In this system, industrial federations of enterprise unions and national confederations set a target every spring for wage increases and seek to coordinate negotiations and strikes across enterprises and industries. Strong enterprise unions in a prosperous industry are selected as a pattern-setter to start negotiations and to establish the market price for that year. Other unions then follow suit. The market price established in *Shunto* has also been reflected in the public sector where strikes are prohibited and also in regional minimum wages which are fixed under the Minimum Wages Law.

In this manner, the *Shunto* strategy has compensated for the limitations of enterprise unionism in terms of bargaining power and establishing social standards across companies.

Where union influence is confined to particular enterprises, as in enterprise unionism, it is difficult to deal with national issues. To fill this gap, enterprise unions have also operated through industry federations and national confederations. In 1989, four former national confederations merged to form the Japanese Trade Union Confederation (*Rengo*). This has eight million members and covers two-thirds of all union members in Japan. Through *Rengo* and its predecessors, unions have been involved in national level corporatist-style consultation. A tripartite council called the Industry and Labour Round Table Conference (*Sangyo Rodo Konwa-Kai*) has operated since 1970. In this forum, representatives of labour, management, and the public interest (the government and academic experts) meet periodically to discuss and exchange opinions on industrial and labour policy. In addition, from time to time, the government creates other tripartite bodies to advise on labour and social policies. These have become important in determining the content of labour policies and labour legislation. It is an established practice that the content of drafts proposed to the Diet by the government is deliberated and developed in these bodies.

At the industry level, major companies and federation of labour unions in the same industry voluntarily establish management–labour councils. They exchange information and opinions on the state of the industry, working conditions, and future strategies for the growth of the industry and the enhancement of workers' welfare.

In these ways, Japanese labour has obtained a say in economic and social policy at industry and national level even though *Rengo* and its predecessors have never resorted to direct actions to promote labour legislation. Thus, it should not be forgotten that Japanese industrial relations, though based on enterprise unionism, are supplemented by corporatist-type mechanisms (Shinoda 1994).

10.5.2. *Joint management–labour consultation*

At plant and company level, joint management–labour consultation is an established practice in Japanese industrial relations and this complements collective bargaining over wages and basic conditions. Currently, 42 per cent of all establishments have such consultation bodies, and, in unionized establishments, the figure is higher at

85 per cent. In Japan, management–labour consultation is voluntary and operates without any legal supports.

The origins of this system are to be found in the period of conflict after the Second World War. By the mid-1950s, leaders on both sides of industry had become increasingly unhappy with the tendency towards adversarial relations and had begun to look for new, more pragmatic and cooperative relations. In 1955, the Japan Productivity Centre was established by business circles under the auspices of the Ministry of International Trade and Industry (MITI) and the American authorities in order to promote joint consultation and productivity improvements. Left-wing union confederations, especially *Sohyo*, were sceptical and regarded the movement as a new type of rationalization or exploitation. However, the confederation of moderate unions *(Sodomei)*, agreed to participate on condition that consultation should not be used to bypass unions and that their opinions should be fully respected. Thus, three basic principles were agreed. One, management–labour consultation should be promoted in order to increase productivity. Two, productivity increases should enhance employment security, with any problems of surplus labour being resolved by transfers and the like rather than by lay-offs. Three, the fruits of increased productivity should be distributed fairly between the firm, employees, and customers, in accordance with the conditions in the national economy.

On this basis (and after the defeat of the leftist union movement during the major dispute at the *Miike* coal mine in 1960), pragmatic and cooperative labour relations gradually became established in Japanese industrial relations. Labour and management voluntarily established consultation arrangements and developed extensive communication channels. Employers provided information to employees and their unions, and unions cooperated with management in increasing productivity. However, it should be remembered that joint consultation has been supported by the sanction of a union's right to bargain.

10.5.3. *Internal promotion of management*

Internal promotion of management has also contributed to Japan's cooperative industrial relations and employee-centred corporate governance. In most larger companies, union shop agreements oblige all employees to join the union. This means that senior managers and directors were members of the enterprise union when they were rank-and-file white-collar workers. Furthermore, according to the Top Management Survey, 28 per cent of top management had previously been leaders of an enterprise union (Inagami 2000: 339). In a sense, management–labour relations are relations between present union members and former union members (sometimes between current union leaders and former union leaders). This fosters a consciousness that both labour and management belong to the same community, facilitates the pursuit of common interests, and leads Japanese management to adopt a consultative approach.

In addition, in firms with the traditional governance model, nearly half of board members are 'directors-with-employee-functions'. It can be argued that this gives employees a further channel to voice their opinions to corporate management. However, in firms adopting the new governance model with the three committee structure, the majority of committee members must be outside directors. The adoption of the new governance model will significantly affect the internal promotion system and the acceptance of 'directors-with-employee-functions' practice. However, as mentioned earlier, few companies have adopted this model so far.

10.5.4. *Recent developments in industrial relations*

In industrial relations, there have been no major legislative changes in recent years. However, recent changes in the industrial relations environment have started to raise questions about the traditional system of worker representation.

10.5.4.1. *Legislative developments promoting corporate restructuring*

From the late 1990s, the government has taken a number of measures to promote corporate restructuring and market-oriented management in the hope of dealing with the prolonged economic slump. In 1997, it legalized holding company arrangements which had been prohibited by the anti-monopoly legislation of early post-war period. In the same year, changes were made to both the stock exchange and employee transfer systems, thereby further facilitating the formation of holding companies. Around this time, the law on stock options was also liberalized. As discussed above, the corporate division scheme was introduced in 2000 to promote corporate reorganization and under the 2002 law the adoption of US-type corporate governance became possible.

These legislative changes are aimed at promoting corporate reorganization and have implications for industrial relations. There is the possibility, and the beginnings of a trend, for companies to be divided into several units, with each unit becoming an independent firm. The headquarters of the original company becomes a holding company governing the newly created subsidiaries. This raises a number of issues for unions. The most important is whether the union can bargain with the holding company. Another concerns the role it will play in the different parts of the holding company. According to the traditional interpretation, the holding company has no obligation to bargain with the union organizing workers in the subsidiary company when there is no evidence that the new holding company intervenes in and decides the actual working conditions of the subsidiary. However, since the holding company decides whether the subsidiary exists or not, unions and their supporters contend that holding companies have a duty to bargain.

10.5.4.2. *Declining union density and emergence of a new representation system*

Union density has declined continuously since 1975 and fell to 19.6 per cent in 2003. In addition, the growing diversity of the workforce has started to challenge the representative legitimacy of enterprise unionism. Traditionally enterprise unions organized only regular employees; non-regular employees such as part-time and fixed-term contract workers remained unorganized. However, 30 per cent of all employees are now non-regular employees. In addition, in the 1990s, middle management employees were often the main losers in corporate restructuring. But, since employees promoted to middle management are supposed to leave unions, they have little protection by unions and under law. Together, these factors prompt a reconsideration of the traditional arrangements for employee voice. They might provide support for a case to introduce a system of employee representation similar to continental European works councils whereby all employees in an establishment would be represented irrespective of union membership.

Indeed, there are some very early signs that this could happen. The 1998 revised Labour Standards Law introduced a new representation system called the 'management–labour committee' (*Roshi Iinkai*). Half of the members of these committees must be appointed by the labour union representing a majority of workers at the workplace concerned or by persons representing a majority of the workers where no such union exists. This management–labour committee must be established when the employer wants to introduce a white-collar exemption from overtime regulation. (Araki 2002: 94). The management–labour committee is the first permanent organ with parity membership that represents all the employees in the establishment. Therefore, this committee can be regarded as an embryonic form of works council in Japan, although the jurisdiction of this committee is currently confined to working hour regulations, and its establishment is not compulsory. To date, few such committees have been created. However, further changes to the law in 2003 have simplified the procedure for introducing the white-collar exemption and this may stimulate the establishment of more committees of this type.

10.6. Conclusions: Future of Japan's Stakeholder Model

As outlined in the introduction, the Japanese employee-centred stakeholder model relies heavily on a number of customary practices, such as long-term cross-share ownership, internal promotion of management and the existence of 'directors-with-employee-functions', long-term (lifetime) employment, and voluntary joint management–labour consultation.

The chapter has reviewed how these practices contributed to and sustained the traditional stakeholder model in Japan. It then considered recent changes which might affect the traditional governance model. These include the following: there are important changes in share ownership, with the dissolution of cross-shareholdings and the rise of foreign ownership. With a shift from indirect finance via banks to direct finance, the importance of banks in Japanese corporate governance has been reduced. There have been changes in corporate law giving large companies an option to adopt a US-type corporate governance system utilizing outside directors. The revision of corporate law in the 1990s has facilitated shareholders' representative lawsuits and may stimulate 'shareholder value conscious' corporate governance. In this context, the concept of shareholder value has emerged.

The employment system is also changing. In the last decade, Japan has experienced the highest unemployment rate in the post-war period. Labour mobility has increased and the state's labour market policy has shifted toward the promotion of the external labour market. Stable regular employment has gradually shrunk and currently non-regular and contingent workers account for 30 per cent of all workers. Courts have started to relax economic dismissal restrictions. In industrial relations, the decline in union density and the growing diversification of the workforce raise a question mark over the traditional collective labour relations system.

Compared to the legally based stakeholder model in Germany, Japan's system might be described as a 'practice-dependent' stakeholder model. As such, this is more vulnerable to changes. Although it is undoubtedly difficult to transform a system made up of interdependent institutions (Aoki and Okuno 1996: 1), in an era of disequilibrium, when several institutions change simultaneously, such change may occur. Therefore, the question is whether these changes will fundamentally transform the current stakeholder model into the shareholder value maximizing model.

Given the existence of counter-pressures working against shareholder value-oriented governance, the most likely outcome is that the current stakeholder model will survive for the time being. Recent developments can best be viewed as the realignment of the priorities of various stakeholders within the framework of the stakeholder model. A number of counter-pressures and tendencies may be cited.

First, although cross-shareholdings are dissolving, more than 80 per cent of companies still maintain cross-shareholdings and recognize the merit of forming stable and long-term trading relations. Moreover, the proportion of equity held by foreign investors has levelled out (or even declined) after rising in the 1990s. Though it is now easier to mount shareholders' representative lawsuits against management, the 2001 Commercial Code revisions enable the shareholder meeting or the board of directors to limit the amount of directors' liability. Although the 2002 corporate law revisions introduced a US-style governance model, the vast majority of Japanese corporations maintain the traditional model.

As for employment security, the enactment of the Labour Contract Succession Law in 2000 was a typical countermeasure to protect employees' interests in the increasing number of corporate reorganizations. The 2003 revisions of the Labour Standards Law, incorporating the case law rule on abusive dismissals, have a symbolic significance confirming the social norm of employment security in Japanese society. Though union density is declining, new forms of worker representation are emerging and joint consultation remains a key part of the Japanese system. These developments serve to sustain the stakeholder model centred on employees' interests or at least put a brake on a radical transformation into a shareholder value model.

Second, survey evidence suggests that the stakeholder model is still widely supported in Japan despite some moves towards a shareholder value model. According to one survey, directors believe that any increase in profits should be distributed evenly between shareholders, employees, and the firm's business needs, rather than going predominantly to shareholders. Similarly, only a quarter of directors believe shareholders should have any special place in management decision-making (JPC-SED 2003). Another survey by the Ministry of Finance Policy Research Institute (2003) found that while banks and trading companies have become less important and customers and shareholders regarded as more important between 1999 and 2002, employees are still regarded as an equal stakeholder. Indeed, there is evidence that their perceived importance is rising. As for the external control of corporate governance, it is also notable that customers and product markets are seen as more important than shareholders or the stock market. Another survey (Japan Institute of Labour 2002) examined the factors affecting restructuring and downsizing decisions. Prominent factors are not changes in corporate governance (14 per cent) but intensified competition in the domestic market (85 per cent) and 'limited demand due to market maturity' (74 per cent).

In terms of industrial relations, the JPC-SED 2003 survey showed that a majority of directors think labour–management consultation does not hinder the management decision-making. Moreover, 59 per cent of directors and 66 per cent of HRM directors believe that unions should be involved in management decision-making in the future. This reflects the deep-rooted consciousness in Japan that employees are the important constituents of corporations.

Given this evidence of attitudinal stability, coupled with the various counter-trends and counter-measures to protect employees' interests, it appears that Japan's stakeholder model will not be drastically modified in the near future. Financial market pressures will have a growing effect, but so will product market pressures. Japanese firms hope they can cope with these through their internal flexibility. Current changes in shareholder structure and management organization require some reconsideration of the priority of various stakeholders' interests. Shareholders' interests cannot be ignored and employment security is no longer an absolutely supreme value in corporate governance. However, such reconsideration seems to be occurring within the framework of the traditional stakeholder model.

NOTES

1. Some parts of the analysis of the traditional model are based on Araki (2000*b*).
2. The survey of the top management and corporate governance (here-inafter 'Top Management Survey') was conducted in February 1999 by a study group headed by Inagami, for the Research Institute for Advancement of Living Standards (RIALS), a think tank of Rengo (The Japanese Trade Union Confederation). The study group distributed questionnaires to the top management of all the 1,307 companies listed in the first section of the Tokyo Stock Exchange and received responses from 731 companies. The resultant analysis was published in Inagami (2000).
3. Cross-shareholding includes indirect relationships where a company X's shares are held by a company Y, a sister company of holding company Z, and the company X owns a share of company Z.
4. Dore (2000*a*: 87–8, 2000*b*: 163–4) points out that critics of traditional governance disregard various positive functions of Japanese boards of directors, such as information sharing and commitment reinforcing.
5. According to Nitta (2000: 87), the average number of board members is 17.5 and average number of directors-with-employee-functions is 8.3.
6. While the debate continues over whether auditors' scrutiny covers the issue of efficiency and the appropriateness of corporate administration the majority opinion is that auditors' scrutiny is confined to checking on legality and it is the board of directors which supervises the issue of efficiency and the appropriateness of corporate administration (Maeda 2000: 238; Yoshihara 2001: 192).
7. However, subsidies for declining industries are being reduced since such payments are criticized for delaying structural changes and hindering labour reallocation.
8. Although rapidly increasing, the number of labour-related cases newly filed in Japanese local courts (first instance) in 2001 was only 3,029 (2,119 ordinary civil cases; 749 provisional disposition cases; and 161 administrative cases).
9. The National Westminster Bank case (3rd Provisional Disposition), 782 Rodo Hanrei 23 (Tokyo District Court, 21 January 2000).
10. German law requires detailed procedures for economic dismissals, including drawing up a 'social plan'. However, if employers follow the procedures, it seems easier to get rid of redundant employees in Germany than in Japan. In the United States, the classic employment-at-will doctrine is eroding and is being modified by case law. Stringent anti-discrimination laws also restrain American employers from arbitrarily dismissing employees. However, compared to Europe and Japan, American employers still enjoy more freedom to dismiss employees and restriction on economic dismissals hardly exists (Summers 1995: 1036).

11

Towards a Comparative Perspective on Corporate Governance and Labour Management: Enterprise Coalitions and National Trajectories

GREGORY JACKSON

11.1. Two Families of Nations?

The study of corporate governance has become ever more pressing for students of labour management. This book has illustrated important linkages which cut across boundaries of finance, management, industrial relations, and politics and law. This development challenges traditional theories of the firm and suggests areas for new interdisciplinary work. The book has approached the subject largely through the method of country case studies which feature rich institutional description and to a lesser extent evidence from firms within a particular country. In looking across these case studies, what conclusions can be drawn from a comparative perspective? Rather than trying to summarize the main findings for each country, this chapter will return to an explicitly comparative perspective to draw out tentative conclusions and to raise issues for further study.

The Introduction to the volume started by sketching out two types of country patterns—market/outsider and relational/insider regimes. Very similar typologies are widely used in other comparative research. These typologies reflect strong correlations in aggregate country-level data between national capital market development (e.g. shareholder rights, market capitalisation, ownership dispersion, merger and acquisition (M&A) activity), labour market regulation (e.g. employment protection law), and coordination of industrial relations (e.g. coordination of wage bargaining and employment turnover) across OECD countries (Hall and Gingerich 2001; Höpner 2003b; Waldenberger 2003).

Table 11.1 shows a set of such correlations for twenty-two OECD countries in the mid-1990s. Ownership dispersion is associated with shorter employee tenures. In addition, high market capitalization, private pension funds, and M&A were all associated with shorter tenures or higher rates of corporate downsizing. Conversely, less marketized capital coincides with more stable employment. One caveat is that highly concentrated ownership is not correlated with stable employment, suggesting stronger affinity on the market end of

Table 11.1. *Correlation of corporate governance and labour management in OECD countries in the mid-1990s*

	Employee board	Unionization	Employment protection law	Long-term employment	Downsizing rate
Corporate governance indicators					
Dispersion[a]	−0.18	−0.03	−0.60*	−0.69*	0.33
Concentration[b]	0.04	0.05	0.51*	0.35	−0.33
Family owner[c]	−0.21	0.03	0.35	0.09	−0.09
Investor rights[d]	−0.21	−0.13	−0.54*	−0.52*	0.13
Accounting rules[e]	0.14	0.30	−0.58*	−0.38	0.39
Private pensions[f]	−0.23	−0.08	−0.63*	−0.47*	0.10
Market cap.[g]	−0.34	−0.20	−0.48*	−0.33	0.48*
M&A[h]	−0.16	0.24	−0.53*	−0.56*	0.46*
Bank restrictions[i]	−0.30	−0.18	−0.07	0.06	0.08
State banks[j]	0.29	0.06	0.52	0.32	−0.11
Labour indicators					
Employee board[k]	1	—	—	—	—
Unionization[l]	0.56*	1	—	—	—
Employment protection legislation	0.20	−0.06	1	—	—
Long-term employment[m]	0.16	−0.03	0.71*	1	—
Downsizing rate[n]	−0.20	0.00	−0.34	−0.40	1

* Indicates significance at the 0.05 level.
[a] Dispersion: percentage of listed firms with less than 25% of their shares 'closely held'.
[b] Concentration: the average percentage of shares held by the top 3 shareholders.
[c] Family ownership: percentage of top firms with a family owner holding a block of 10% or more.
[d] Investor protection: index of anti-director rights.
[e] Accounting: strictness of accounting standards.
[f] Private pensions: assets of pension funds as percentage of GDP.
[g] Market cap: stock market capitalization as percentage of GDP.
[h] M&A: value of mergers and acquisitions as percentage of GDP, average 1990–5.
[i] Bank restrictions: index of restrictions on banks holding corporate equities.
[j] State banks: assets of state-owned banks as percentage of GDP.
[k] Employee board: index of representation on corporate board.
[l] Unionization: union membership as percentage of the labour force.
[m] Long-term employment: average tenure of male employees in years.
[n] Downsizing rate: percentage of firms making a cut of 10% of more in total employment, average 1991–2001.

Sources: La Porta, Lopez-de-Silanes, and Schleifer (1999); Barth, Caprio, and Levin (2000); OECD (1997); www.fibv.com, SDC Platinum Worldwide Merger, Thomson/Worldscope Data and various national sources.

the spectrum. Caution is required in interpreting these relationships because the outcomes are also correlated with patterns of legal regulation. Dispersion and M&A are strongly associated with legal protections for shareholders and employee tenure is associated with employment protection law. Yet, few countries appear to have strong legal rights for both shareholders and employees. Thus, it is difficult to differentiate between direct linkages between corporate governance and labour management or indirect relationships due to the (perhaps unintentional) interaction of regulatory choices.

Relatively few studies have explored these linkages by comparing firms across countries. A small number of studies use company data in the context of one country. For Japanese firms, several studies confirm significant relationships between foreign investors and downsizing (Ahmadjian and Robinson 2001) or main banks and employment stability (Abe 2002). Table 11.2 shows correlations across a pooled sample of listed firms in the same twenty-two OECD countries. Generally, the expected associations exist between ownership patterns and share price volatility or price–book ratios (on the one hand) and rates of downsizing and average wages (on the other hand). Beyond that, concentrated ownership is also associated with strategic management outcomes such as less divestment of fixed assets and lower profitability. Notably, the strength of association is very low compared to the country data.

Nor are the relationships identical across countries. The United States, the United Kingdom, and several countries with strong employment protection (such as France, Spain, Sweden, and the Netherlands) show no significant correlation between ownership and downsizing. In Japan and Italy, concentration has the expected association with fewer employment cuts. Japanese corporate networks may concentrate ownership, but also tend to reinforce managerial control—capitalism without capitalists—and thereby support commitments to stakeholders within the firm. In Germany, the pattern appears quite complex. Dispersed firms are more likely to make big cuts in employment, but highly concentrated firms are also likely to make more small cuts in employment, not less. Perhaps German blockholders, such as family owners, provide a counterweight to employee interests, whereas dispersed manager-controlled firms remain more subject to employee influence?

Despite this complexity, most comparative research still relies on a dichotomous contrast between market-oriented systems such as the United States and the United Kingdom (on the one hand) and countries

Table 11.2. Correlation of corporate governance and labour outcomes: firm-level measures for 1992–2001

	Employment growth[b]	10% employment cut[d]	5% employment cut[d]	Average wage[c]	Δ Wage[a]	Δ Labour as % of value-added[e]
Dispersed ownership[f]	0	0.04*	0.03*	0	0	0
% Closely-held shares[g]	0.01	−0.03*	−0.02*	0.02*	0	0
Δ Closely-held shares[h]	−0.02*	0	0.01*	0	0	0
Price volatility[i]	0.01	0.12*	0.10*	−0.07*	−0.01	−0.03
Price–book ratio[j]	0	−0.01	−0.02*	−0.01	−0.01	0
Dividend yield[k]	0	0	0.01*	−0.01	0	0
Δ Dividend as % VA[l]	0	0.04*	0.03*	0.01	0	0
Sale of stock options[m]	−0.01	0	0	0.10*	0	0
Disposal of fixed assets[n]	−0.01	0.05*	0.05*	0.05*	−0.01	0

* Indicates significance at the 0.05 level.

a Δ in average wage: percentage change in average wage.

b Employment growth: annual percentage change in total employees.

c Average wage: total salary and benefit expense divided by the number of employees.

d Employment cut: equals 1 if negative change in percentage employees was greater than 10% or 5% in a given year.

e Δ Labour as percentage of value-added: percentage change in the share of value-added of total labour costs as a percentage of firm value-added.

f Dispersed ownership: equals 1 if less than 25% of total shares are not closely held.

g Closely held shares: percentage of shares held by insiders or other stable owners based on various national definitions.

h Δ Closely held shares: percentage change in percentage of shares held by insiders or stable owners

i Price volatility: index of share price volatility.

j Price–book ratio: ratio of total market capitalization to the book value of total assets.

k Dividend yield: dividends per share as a percentage of average share price.

l Δ Dividend as percentage of value-added: percentage change in share of dividends as a percentage of total firm value-added.

m Sale of stock options: total value of stock options exercised in U.S. Dollars.

n Disposal of fixed assets: total value of fixed assets sold as a percentage of total assets.

Notes: Own calculations from Thomson/Worldscope Database. This data set covers all listed firms with over 2,000 employees in 22 OECD countries. Number of observations in the table = 33,094 firm-years.

Source: Thomson/Worldscope.

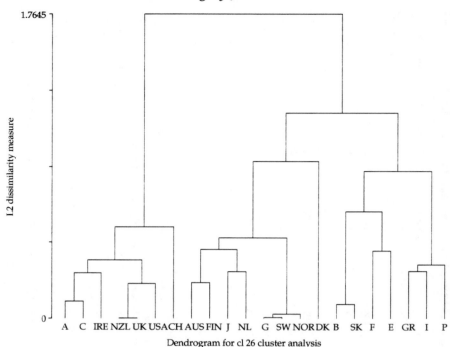

Figure 11.1. *Country clusters based on industrial relations*

Notes: The clusters are based on average linkages between employee representation, employment protection, and downsizing.

List of countries: A: Australia; C: Canada; IRE: Ireland; NZL: New Zealand; UK: United Kingdom; USA: United States of America; CH: Switzerland; AUS: Austria; FIN: Finland; J: Japan; NL: Netherlands; G: Germany; SW: Sweden; NOR: Norway; DK: Denmark; B: Belgium; SK: South Korea; F: France; E: Spain; GR: Greece; I: Italy; P: Portugal.

where markets play a lesser role such as Germany and Japan (on the other hand). As noted in the Introduction, many countries do not fit too well within this broad typology. Figure 11.1 shows a cluster analysis of countries based on three labour variables—employee representation, employment protection, and downsizing—resulting in at least three major groups. The group of Anglo-Saxon countries is the most homogeneous with very marketized employment on all three measures. This group is distinct from all the other clusters which have more stable employment. However, among countries with stable employment, a further division exists based on the degree of institutionalized voice within the firm. Then, within each of these groups, we can find countries with greater or lesser legal employment protection. When adding several governance variables such as ownership

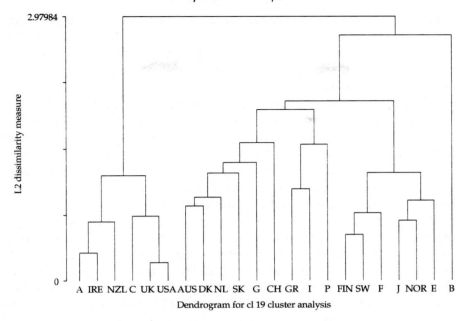

Figure 11.2. *Country clusters based on finance, governance, and industrial relations measures*

Notes: The clusters are based on average linkages between ownership dispersion, investor protection, pension assets, downsizing, and employment protection.

List of countries: A: Australia; C: Canada; IRE: Ireland; NZL: New Zealand;
UK: United Kingdom; USA: United States of America; CH: Switzerland; AUS: Austria;
FIN: Finland; J: Japan; NL: Netherlands; G: Germany; SW: Sweden; NOR: Norway;
DK: Denmark; B: Belgium; SK: South Korea; F: France; E: Spain; GR: Greece; I: Italy; P: Portugal.

patterns and investor protection to the cluster analysis, the market/ insider group is largely reproduced again (see Figure 11.2). However, the relational/insider group falls into a large and confusing number of clusters.[1]

In fact, the relational/insider group subsumes a great deal of diversity. Little consensus exists on how to label this group, as is evident in comparative typologies such as insider, relationship-oriented, stakeholder, or coordinated economies. Concentrated ownership encompasses family firms, diverse forms of corporate networks, and various forms of relationship banking. Cooperative industrial relations involve diverse forms of unionism and labour–management consultation. Employment security may result from legal employment protections as in continental Europe or be based on more informal norms and firm-specific investments such as in Japan. The state also plays very different roles in regulating both capital and labour depending on particular regulatory styles and state capacities. In contrast to the apparent homogeneity of market/outsider systems, the linkages between different social forms of non-market organization are much less well understood.

It is important to take this diversity seriously in order to study the linkages between corporate governance and labour management. Many relational/insider regimes incorporate significant market elements. Countries such as Japan, the Netherlands, or Sweden have strong investor protection law or high stock market capitalization, but continue to have cooperative industrial relations and high employment security. By contrast, few countries with predominantly market govern- ance regimes have relational employment institutions. The absence of capital market pressure, at least very strong pressure, may thus be a necessary condition for relational employment. But not all elements of market systems are equally linked to all elements of relational systems. One reason is that not all 'relationship-oriented' institutions are alike. The social forms of those institutions matter, although their effects may display certain functional equivalence.[2] For example, the impact of cap- ital market pressures on employment security may depend upon whether such security is based on strict legal regulation, is a by- product of strong firm-specific investments in training, or is due to insti- tutional opportunities for employees to exercise 'voice' rather than 'exit'.

Markets also come in various shapes and colours. When considering the US or UK cases historically, the pressures emanating from capital markets vary greatly over time. The heyday of 'managerial capitalism' which arose through a high separation of ownership and control was also a strong period for 'welfare capitalism' for labour in the United States. Then the wave of hostile takeovers in the United States and the United Kingdom in the 1980s led to a scaling back of large conglomer- ates through de-diversification and also with a new harsher deal for employees. Whereas the dispersed ownership of the post-war Golden Age left much autonomy for management, dispersed ownership evolved into a market for corporate control threatening that autonomy. An interesting contrast to this is Japan, which also underwent a brief period of high ownership dispersion in the early post-war years. Japanese managers responded with initiatives to build up dense net- works of stable shareholding centred around banks which historically suppressed markets for corporate control. Such freedom from capital market pressures is often seen as being an important prerequisite in the emergence of the employee-oriented Japanese firm.

Further progress in understanding these relationships depends on the ability to disaggregate various elements within these broad types and assess their interrelationships in a more systematic way. By looking at the specific configurations of institutions, linkages can be understood as conjunctural causation. The impact of one institutional variable is treated in conjunction with a wider set of institutions. Economic theory considers such interaction effects in terms of institutional complementarities, where the returns to one institution increase in the presence of another institution or set of institutions (Aoki 2001). But more work is needed to develop and refine such approaches to integrate multiple dimensions of economic activity, as well as to compare a wide and sociologically informed range of institutional forms.

A more configurational approach has also become relevant to understand the issue of potential 'hybrid' configurations or cases which mix elements of market and relational regimes. Major changes are presently underway in the organization of capital markets and corporate governance around the world. As the various country chapters have shown, since the mid-1990s, almost all OECD countries have been engaged in efforts to re-evaluate and reform their corporate governance arrangements. For its part, the European Union (EU) has placed great pressure on member countries to liberalize their financial markets. Stock markets have grown in importance, and reforms have been introduced to strengthen investor protection and accounting standards. The past influence of Japanese main banks and German universal banks in corporate finance and governance of large firms has declined (Jackson 2003). Cross-border mergers and acquisitions have also been rising. In sum, liberalization has made relational/insider regimes not just considerably more market-oriented, but in some ways also less 'national' through their adaptation to international regulatory standards and other Anglo-Saxon practices.

How have such changes in the area of corporate governance impacted labour management thus far? Also what role has labour played in shaping efforts to reform governance practices? If the absence of capital markets is a necessary condition for relational patterns of employment and industrial relations, then these changes may result in the convergence of relational employment on a market model. For the most part, the chapters in this volume suggest that the patterns of change are more complex. While the diversity across countries appears to be narrowing, the force of such change falls short of achieving convergence in the foreseeable future. Firms are increasingly being forced to cope with new capital market pressures, but do so by piecemeal adaptation of their existing inherited employment relations and industrial relations.

These issues bring us back to the major questions which motivated this book. How tight are the linkages between corporate governance and labour management? What scope for managerial discretion exists in mediating between the interests of investors and labour? How do the specific institutional forms of ownership and control, as well as industrial relations, shape the nature of such linkages? What role has corporate governance played in the historical evolution of labour management in shaping diverse patterns of the present day? And, in turn, how does labour impact on corporate governance?

In the rest of this chapter, Section 11.2 will briefly review different economic theories helpful for understanding the linkages between corporate governance and labour management, but will argue that these represent multiple dimensions of economic activity which need to be examined in an integrative fashion. Section 11.3 outlines a more sociological approach to governance arrangements as coalitions between capital, labour, and management within the firm. This view stresses how the interests and rights of different groups of investors, managers, and employees may overlap. Section 11.4 moves back to macro-level country patterns by introducing a configurational approach to examining institutional linkages. Some evidence is examined to assess whether corporate patterns act as necessary or sufficient conditions for different labour outcomes. Section 11.5 extends this discussion by discussing historical trajectories and patterns of change in different national cases. Such patterns have both similarities, and important differences, across cases. Finally, Section 11.6 concludes with thoughts about the future diversity of labour management in the light of corporate governance trends.

11.2. Linkages in Economic Theory

Given two domains such as 'corporate governance' (CG) and 'labour management' (LM), their linkages may be studied in several general models:

(a) CG → LM
(b) CG ← LM
(c) CG ← → LM
(d) CG ↘
          Firm Strategy
      LM ↗

Thus, corporate governance may be seen as independent variables facilitating or constraining patterns of labour—or vice versa. Or both factors can be seen as independent variables whose interaction effects are important for some third institution or performance outcome. Even more complex models may consider additional institutional domains, such as welfare state institutions which may impact on financial markets via the pension system (Jackson and Vitols 2001) or through facilitating employment adjustment by 'externalising' costs on the welfare state (see Chapter 4, this volume).

These domains each contain a number of different institutions which may be linked in different ways. Thus, more accurately, we can actually disaggregate such relationships as

CG ←—→ LM

according to various types such as

market vs. relational ←—→ market vs. relational

or even a series of single dimensions:

(ownership, banks, M&As, etc.) ←—→ (participation, employment security, etc.)

Understanding the relationship between corporate governance and labour management poses the challenge of integrating such multiple linkages. Here, economic theory offers several models of the linkages between corporate governance (ownership and finance) and labour management.

First, transaction cost models suggests that commitment by investors to specific firms supports stable long-term employment, investment in worker training, and cooperative industrial relations (Hall and Soskice 2001b). These institutional complementarities are closely linked to dynamic (X-) efficiency in lower-volume, higher-quality product markets which require high skills (Streeck 1992a, 1997b). This view fits both models (a) and (d) above in terms of credible commitments by management to labour directly or to particular firm strategies.

Second, agency theory argues that employee strength increases the agency costs to diffuse shareholders (Jensen and Meckling 1979) and therefore reinforces the advantages of direct control coming from relational finance, which are needed to counterbalance the strength of labour. For example, Roe (1999: 194) argues that, in countries like Germany, 'diffuse owners may be unable to create a blockholding balance of power that stockholders would prefer as a counterweight to the employee block'.[3] This model stipulates a direct causal impact of labour management on corporate governance, as shown above in model (b).

Third, the economics of information and cooperation offer a further perspective which stresses potential positive-sum aspects between corporate governance and labour management. For example, information and disclosure may enhance the prospect of voice for both investors and employees, thereby increasing the accountability of management (Hirschman 1972; Aoki 1988).

This list is not intended as an exhaustive survey and other authors could be cited within each school. The point is to illustrate that each model stresses different causal arrows and different types of linkages. However, rather than see these as competing models, each model may represent different dimensions. These multiple dimensions of economic exchange (Z_1, Z_2, Z_n) have potential trade-offs or opposing effects. Strong labour participation may increase agency costs but lower transaction costs. Takeovers may lower agency costs for minority shareholders, but increase transaction costs for employees. Or some elements of market regimes, such as strict accounting rules, may be neutral or beneficial for some elements of relational regimes such as employee participation. Making inferences about the overall complementarity between two institutions (let alone two institutional domains) would require a complex integrative model to sum up all the possible dimensions.[4] This makes empirical applications complex.

In addition, we cannot tell a priori which dimension will drive overall performance. Different dimensions may be more relevant to economic performance under a given set of exogenous conditions. For example, the relative costs of 'over-investment' by overly secure managers or vested employee influence versus 'under-investment' due to short-termism by investors may depend on the life cycle of firms, sectors, and economies. Moreover, efficiency is always relative to the context of particular strategies. Institutions may have different comparative advantages for different sorts of strategies, as discussed in the literature on varieties of capitalism (Hall and Soskice 2001*a*) or national business systems (Whitley 1999). Yet, corporate strategies are not a simple matter of choosing the best 'fit' to market conditions. Rather, strategy is also a result of negotiation between different stakeholder groups and coalitions formed among different subgroups among investors, management, and employees. This raises the issue of power among major corporate stakeholders in the firm.

11.3. Enterprise Coalitions

Even where economic models remain ambiguous, stakeholders must cope with such ambiguity and potential trade-offs. The interests of investors and employees may be opposed in a negative-sum fashion, as stressed by agency theory. But, positive-sum outcomes are also possible, such as when improved labour cooperation benefits shareholders through productive efficiency or when corporate disclosure sought by investors improves transparency for organized labour. The potential degree of overlap depends on the institutionalized identities and interests of each group. Thus, different patterns of coalitions may arise between different subgroups of investors, management, and employees.

The notion of corporate governance as coalition has important roots in economics (Aoki 1994), but also in more sociological and political models of the firm (Cyert and March 1963). This section draws specifically upon a sociological framework for studying corporate governance in terms of coalitions between capital, management, and labour (Aguilera and Jackson 2003). It begins by reviewing how the institutionalized identities and interests of each group vary and then proceeds to discuss three patterns of coalitions between them.

Investors may have different degrees of commitment or liquidity with regard to their stakes in particular firms. Commitment may arise from ownership concentration, but also other stable shareholding arrangements related to cross-shareholding or relational contracting. Liquidity is associated with dispersion, but may also depend on the size of investor or other rules such as indexing used by institutional investors. Investors also differ in the extent to which they pursue purely financial interests or other strategic interests related to control rights. For example, inter-corporate cross-shareholdings in Japan have been motivated by various strategic interests related to mutual assurance of managerial autonomy, but also by the coordination of relational contracting across networks of allied firms. The preferences of these owners may be quite different than family owners, who are more willing to intervene in company affairs, let alone institutional investors such as pension funds. These dimensions have parallels among employees. Employees may be bound to the firm by the relative weight of firm-specific versus portable human capital. In turn, this factor is strongly influenced by external institutions such as national systems of education and training. Another dimension relates to the orientation of organized labour toward external control versus internal participation in corporate decision-making. Here, different traditions of union organization have vastly different ideas about corporate governance.

Less attention has been paid to the independent role of management and different group identities of managers based on their career patterns and cultural context. A most obvious dimension is the forms of managerial compensation, particularly the extent to which managers are given strong financial incentives aligned to the stock market. But other dimensions are also relevant. Managers may specialize in different forms of expertise, such as engineering or finance. Their careers may be more dependent on lateral moves across firms or internal promotions through orderly quasi-bureaucratic career tracks. Decision-making within the board itself may require greater degrees of consensus building, delegation, or hierarchy depending on the composition and structure of the board. For example, US boards tend to have strong centralized power held by the chief executive, but potentially balanced by independent outside directors. German and Japanese boards are more consensual in terms of their internal composition, but differ in the degree to which outsiders are involved.

These various dimensions point to different lines of conflicts and different types of coalitions forming across these three groups of stakeholders.

Class coalitions may arise when the interests of capital and management oppose the interests of labour, particularly regarding distributional issues. Where capital and management pursue financial interests such as in the United States, conflict is likely to arise around trade-offs between wages and profits, capital re-investments and dividends, or levels of employment and shareholder returns. Management may use employee ownership or contingent pay as a means to align employee interests with capital and to minimize governance conflicts. In Japan, class conflict is lessened because cross-shareholding and the main banking relationships tend to be complementary with lifetime employment (Aoki 1994). Here, the strategic interests and long-term commitment of capital support managerial alignment with employees and facilitate investments in firm-specific skills and stable employment. Management may also play different roles in mediating class conflict. For instance, whereas the dominance of functional orientations among German managers helps balance financial interests, US managers are mostly aligned with shareholders' financial interests due to the prevalence of external careers and contingent pay incentives.

Insider–outsider coalitions may arise when the interests of labour and management (insiders) oppose the interests of capital (outsiders). Insiders may favour internal diversification ('empire building'), block efforts at restructuring, or erect takeover defences, all to the potential disadvantage of external capital. Insider–outsider conflicts are often evident in Japan due to highly committed management, the strong internal participation of core employees, and the fixed commitment of capital to specific firms. Insiders' interests conflict with minority shareholders' interests in greater liquidity and financial returns, as well as the interests of certain employees, for example, mobile professionals and non-core employees. In the US context of portable employee skills and liquid capital, such conflicts may be less severe. The introduction of more autonomous independent directors over the last decades has helped insiders further to align management with outside interests, and favour more severe methods of corporate reorganization.

Finally, *accountability coalitions* concern the common interests of capital and labour *vis-à-vis* management. Shareholders and employees may form coalitions to remove poorly performing management or to demand higher corporate transparency. Here, managerial accountability to different stakeholders is not a zero-sum relationship. In Germany, strong labour participation in the supervisory board complements committed blockholders in actively monitoring management. But, where the interests of capital and labour diverge too sharply, such coalitions may break down and give management increasing autonomy to pursue its own agenda and thereby damage accountability.

Different strategic issues cut across these lines in different ways. Conflicts between capital and labour often play out in struggles over corporate strategy—such as favouring growth or profits, target rates of return, paying dividends or reinvesting capital, the definition of core competence and so on. Here, different institutional configurations may favour different coalitions which stress the latent positive-sum or negative-sum aspects of such changes. The next section turns to the diversity of such arrangements.

11.4. Beyond Correlation: Studying Diversity as Institutional Configurations

Evaluating the impact of institutions faces some particular methodological challenges. Strongly institutionalized patterns of organization may vary relatively little within a single national context. Thus, only a few Japanese firms do not have cross-shareholding, few US firms do not use stock options, and all firms in a given country may be subject to the same employment protection law. Institutional traits may also co-vary strongly with other variables. For example, the strength of codetermination among German firms depends, according to law, on the size of firms. Strong isomorphism often leads to an absence of an appropriate control group when using firm-level data.

Let us consider one example. Table 11.3 shows that the rate of corporate downsizing displays significant differences across countries, as well as between firms with dispersed and concentrated ownership. This appears broadly consistent with the notion of market finance being associated with market-oriented labour management. However, Table 11.4 reports the results of a logit model predicting the likelihood of firms making a 10 per cent cut in employment between 1992 and 2001 across twenty-two OECD countries. After controlling

Table 11.3. *Rates of corporate downsizing for selected countries 1991–2001*

Country	10% cut 2001	10% cut 1991	Average annual rate 1999–2001	Cumulative likelihood for each firm
Australia	0.099	0.057	0.093	0.301
Canada	0.094	0.212	0.096	0.312
France	0.083	0.079	0.069**	0.306
Germany	0.093	0.099	0.101	0.402
Italy	0.147	0.088	0.096	0.413
Japan	0.059	0.020	0.041**	0.213
Korea	0.140	0.104	0.153**	0.548
The Netherlands	0.070	0.077	0.065*	0.351
Spain	0.015	0.122	0.077	0.292
Sweden	0.154	0.276	0.095	0.384
Switzerland	0.131	0.096	0.091	0.426
UK	0.179	0.164	0.129**	0.473
US	0.206	0.092	0.106**	0.445
Dispersed	—	—	0.105**	—
Concentrated	—	—	0.082**	—

* *T*-test for the difference of means with the overall sample is significant at 0.05.
** Significant at 0.01.

Notes: Sample covers listed corporations with over 2,000 employees. Downsizing is counted as a negative shift in total employment of 10% over a one year period. Cumulative likelihood is calculated as the probability of each firm within the sample undergoing one or more employment cuts within the time period. $N = 33,094$ firm-years.

Source: Own calculations from Thomson/Worldscope.

Table 11.4. *Logit model of the likelihood of a 10% cut in employment, selected countries in 2001*

	Odds ratio	Standard error	z	Significance
Assets (ln)	0.9174195	0.0368193	−2.15	0.032
ROA ($t-1$)	0.9895516	0.0023990	−4.33	0.000
Sales Growth	0.9391732	0.0036168	−16.30	0.000
Dispersed	1.000280	0.1923223	0.00	0.999
Closely-held	0.9968440	0.0039829	−0.79	0.429
France	0.5290478	0.1611784	−2.09	0.037
Germany	0.5609505	0.1637352	−1.98	0.048
The Netherlands	0.4319714	0.2151003	−1.69	0.092
Japan	0.3223691	0.0620804	−5.88	0.000
UK	1.018149	0.1782022	0.10	0.918
Spain	0.1444043	0.1476633	−1.89	0.058
Italy	1.219077	0.4264672	0.57	0.571

Diagnostics: n = 3414; LR chi^2 = 546.15; Chi^2 significance = 0.000; Log-likelihood = −1181.966; Pseudo R^2 = 0.1877.

Notes: The base model includes data from firms in twenty-two countries. This table reports seven selected country dummies using the United States as a baseline. Controls for general industrial classification are not reported.

Source: Company data taken from Thomson/Worldscope Database. The sample includes all listed firms with over 2,000 employees in each country.

for firm performance and industrial sector, country differences persist but the impact of ownership dispersion was no longer significant.[5] While this result is only a tentative illustration, it suggests that broad institutional effects at the national level may be much larger than the effects of ownership on employment at the firm level. Put another way, the effects appear to be contingent on the overall institutional setting in a country. So, while corporate governance may constrain patterns of labour management, significant scope for variation within and between distinct institutional settings remains.

When dealing with aggregate cross-national evidence, work on corporate governance faces a situation common in other areas of comparative research—namely, a small number of cases and a large number of potential explanatory variables which are highly correlated with one another (Lijphart 1971; Ragin and Zaret 1983; Tilly 1984). The cases also display limited diversity. For example, few or no countries have very strong legal protection for both investors and employees. Given these problems, traditional statistical methods cannot be applied or may be highly misleading. Statistical methods also have difficulty dealing with issues of institutional complementarity, because linear models make assumptions about how variables combine by looking at marginal effects while holding other factors constant based on their average value.

A common research strategy in this situation is to undertake individual country case studies or paired cases, as witnessed in this book. Case studies do well in examining the complexity and rich causal textures in a given case, but only permit limited generalization. In an effort to bridge the gap between the findings of the country cases and the country-level correlations, this section presents a brief analysis of the cross-national data from Table 11.1 using the methods of qualitative comparative analysis and the logic of fuzzy sets.[6]

Fuzzy-set methods are tools for making inferences about necessary and sufficient conditions for an outcome (Ragin 2000). Variables are scored between 0 and 1 according to the degree of membership in the conceptual category. A score of 1 represents a case which is 'fully in' the category and 0 represents a case which is 'fully out', whereas 0.5 represents the transition point where a case is 'neither in, nor out'. Necessary and sufficient conditions are evaluated using the membership scores of an outcome across cases. When a necessary condition is present, membership in the cause will be greater than or equal to membership in the outcome. Here, the outcome is a subset of the cause (e.g. all countries with ownership dispersion are rich). When a sufficient condition is present, membership in the cause will be less than or equal to membership in the outcome (e.g. all countries with developed private pension systems have ownership dispersion). This chapter adopts a benchmark proportion to determine whether a factor can be considered probabilistically necessary or probabilistically sufficient based on the proportion of cases.

Five sets of outcomes are examined: employee representation at board level, unionization, employment protection law, centralization of collective bargaining, and downsizing. Tables 11.5 and 11.6 report the results of the fuzzy-set tests for necessary and sufficient conditions of each variable individually. The coefficients show the proportion of cases which meet these conditions. None of the corporate governance variables were necessary conditions for any of the labour management outcomes. Likewise, none of the governance variables were individually sufficient to produce any of the labour management outcomes. However, some combinations of governance variables or conjunction of governance and labour management variables proved sufficient to produce labour outcomes.[7]

Table 11.5. *Results of fuzzy-set test: necessary conditions*

Measure	Cause >= employee represention	Cause >= unionization	Cause >= employment protection	Cause >= downsizing	Cause >= collective bargaining centralization
Ownership dispersion	0.25	0.41	0.53	0.50	0.33
—owner	0.50	0.59	0.79	0.50	0.44
Investor protection	0.42	0.55	0.53	0.56	0.28
—investor	0.58	0.59	0.68	0.61	0.50
Accounting rules	0.58	0.64	0.58	0.67	0.44
—accounting	0.25	0.36	0.37	0.33	0.11
Private pensions	0.33	0.36	0.37	0.50	0.33
—pension	0.75	0.64	0.84 (0.46)	0.67	0.50
Market capitalization	0.42	0.41	0.37	0.44	0.28
—market cap.	0.42	0.45	0.79	0.50	0.61
M&A	0.42	0.45	0.42	0.67	0.28
—m&a	0.67	0.55	0.74	0.61	0.50

Note: The level of significance for all proportions >0.80 is listed in parentheses. An adjustment factor of 0.17 was used in determining membership in each set.

Table 11.6. *Results of fuzzy-set test: sufficient conditions*

Measure	Cause <= employee representation	Cause <= unionization	Cause <= employment protection	Cause <= downsizing
Ownership dispersion	0.55	0.68	0.68	0.64
—owner	0.50	0.50	0.68	0.55
Investor protection	0.41	0.64	0.59	0.50
—investor	0.41	0.55	0.50	0.50
Accounting rules	0.45	0.50	0.55	0.55
—accounting	0.55	0.68	0.82	0.64
Private pensions	0.45	0.82	0.64	0.68
—pension	0.41	0.45	0.41	0.45
Market capitalization	0.41	0.59	0.55	0.54
—market cap.	0.41	0.55	0.50	0.45
M&A	0.50	0.68	0.59	0.68
—m&a	0.41	0.64	0.45	0.50

Note: All proportions greater than 0.80 (using an adjustment factor of 0.17) and 0.65 were tested for significance, $P <= 0.05$.

(a) *Employee representation at board level.* Corporate governance variables alone did not prove sufficient. However, strong centralized unions plus strong investor rights and accounting, but low dispersion and market value, were sufficient for board-level codetermination. This pattern fits closely to Norway and Finland, but also fits relatively well to the other Scandinavian countries. This configuration is consistent with a linkage to union power in the national arena and a lack of capital market development. The lack of capital market development might be interpreted in two ways—as a response to employee strength (as predicted by agency theory) or in political terms such that the absence of widespread popular involvement in the stock market limited opposition for employee rights in the board. More puzzling is the positive association with investor rights and good accounting.

(b) *Unionization.* One configuration of corporate governance variables proved sufficient for strong unions, namely an absence of dispersion, investor rights, and private pension fund development. Germany, Italy, Belgium, and Austria have high membership in this category. But the Scandinavian countries fit less well to this pattern, and it underestimates the level of unionization in the United Kingdom, Ireland, and Australia.

(c) *Employment protection law.* The tests for this outcome are slightly ambiguous. Several combinations were consistent with the test of sufficiency, but did not achieve a good fit for countries with high positive outcomes of employment protection. The absence of very strong capital market development is a necessary condition—measured by the joint presence of high values on market capitalization, mergers, and pension funds. This suggests that the high correlation found in other analyses with market finance is probably driven by the outlying cases of the United States and the United Kingdom. It is perhaps noteworthy that weak legal rights for shareholders are neither necessary nor sufficient for strong employment protection. For example, Japan and Norway have moderately high investor protection and employment protection law, but an absence of high dispersion and M&A.

(d) *Centralization of collective bargaining.* Here, one pattern of governance variables proved sufficient and had a very high degree of fit, namely countries with high ownership concentration but weak investor protection and low merger activity. Belgium, Germany, Austria, and Greece have the highest scores in this set. These conditions are consistent, but fit less well, with Sweden and Norway. This combination supports the notion that high coordination or cooperation among business facilitates multi-employer bargaining, as discussed in the Introduction.

(e) *Downsizing.* The fifth outcome of downsizing is particularly relevant, since capital market pressures are often related to the propensity of firms to cut their labour force. No necessary or sufficient relationships were detected between ownership, investor protection, accounting, private pension fund development, market capitalization, or M&A (on the one hand) and the rate of downsizing (on the other hand). Looking at ownership and downsizing, for example, countries such as Japan, Greece, Portugal, Austria, and Norway appear relationship-oriented on both ends, and contrast with the United Kingdom and the United States at the opposite extreme. But a large number of countries fall in the middle. Some countries with moderate dispersion do not have particularly high downsizing rates—specifically, Ireland and Australia, but also to a lesser extent France, Denmark, and the Netherlands. The Netherlands appears to be an interesting case with highly 'marketized' capital but not too marketized labour.

Nor did industrial relations institutions alone offer a consistent explanation of downsizing. Neither board representation, unionization or employment protection law appears to be necessary or sufficient for low rates of corporate downsizing. Countries with board representation such as Germany, Austria, Sweden, and Finland are not countries with particularly low downsizing rates. Countries with low unionization rates such as France and Spain also have low downsizing rates, but Finland and Sweden again represent cases of strong unions but frequent downsizing. Employment protection law seems to have the strongest relationship, but falls short of being a necessary condition for low downsizing. Here, Japan and Denmark prove to be exceptions in having employment security 'in excess' of the legal mandates. Conversely, Spain and Italy have strong employment protection but this proves insufficient to produce very low downsizing rates. However, downsizing is associated with particular combinations of governance and labour variables. Dispersed ownership and private pension funds may lead to high downsizing when combined with weak unions. Pension funds and high M&A are also sufficient for downsizing when combined with weak unions.

Two further labour outcomes were examined by combining the various measures related to relational employment in two ways—a logical OR which takes the highest membership in any of the other five sets and a logical AND taking the lowest value in any of the five sets. The first indicator shows membership in the set of countries with any type of strong employee rights, thus allowing us to consider possible functional equivalence between different institutional forms. Here, all countries with the absence of some combination of investor protection, market capitalization, and M&A had some form of employee strength. The second indicator looks at membership in the set of countries which are relational across all of the measures, thus conforming to an ideal-typical relational employment regime. Here, the corporate governance scores were neither necessary nor sufficient for strong relational employment institutions.

A composite indicator for strong market-oriented corporate governance regimes was also computed by taking membership among countries with high scores on market capitalization, mergers and pension funds. The absence of market-oriented capital is a necessary condition for relational employment; however, relational capital is not a sufficient condition. Conversely, the presence of market-oriented capital is not necessary for market employment, but is sufficient for it. What about the reverse impact of labour on corporate governance? Again the absence of relational employment is necessary for strong capital market development, but not sufficient to explain it. Thus, we can expect a very high correlation between these measures despite the fact the employment variables alone are insufficient to explain capital market outcomes.

In sum, the linkages between corporate governance and labour management seem strongest at the extreme ends of the spectrum. Strongly market-oriented corporate governance may preclude strongly relational regimes of employment, and vice versa. But corporate governance factors alone are not sufficient to explain employment patterns. Nor is relational employment sufficient to explain weak capital market development or patterns of ownership across countries. This finding usefully qualifies the broad conclusions about the impact of employee power on ownership and finance drawn from cross-national correlations, such those by Roe (2003) or Pagano and Volpin (1999). The findings also have several other interesting implications. First, legal rights for investors may be relatively neutral towards systems of relational employment, compared to the degree of market activity and presence of institutional investors. In particular, employee participation is quite compatible with strong investor protections. Second, ownership dispersion itself is only related to labour outcomes in the context of other capital market or employment variables. Meanwhile, ownership concentration is only related to centralized collective bargaining. Third, the degree of capital market activity by pension funds or through M&A seem to be particularly important elements for labour.

11.5. National Trajectories

The discussion above confirms the linkages between corporate governance and labour management, particularly the potential incompatibility between market-oriented capital and relational employment. But it also suggests that the linkages may be rather loose, given intermediate levels of capital market activity, or the effects may be highly contingent on industrial relations institutions. Given the shift among OECD countries to stronger shareholder rights and more capital market orientation, what can be concluded about the impact of such liberalization on labour management across countries?

A starting point is to remember that the shift toward more market-oriented corporate governance has different starting points and takes on different forms in different countries. In France, de-concentration is largely a process of privatization and untangling of dense state–industry networks. In Germany, universal banks are central players which are reducing their large stakes and playing a less active role in governance in the boardroom. In Japan, the ties between firms and their main banks have also weakened, but this process has been driven by the post-'bubble' asset deflation, the non-performing loan issue, and changes in accounting which now put banks at greater risk by reporting the current market values of long-term holdings. This situation has sparked rapid unwinding of cross-shareholdings since the late 1990s.

Such processes may also have different end points. Ownership dispersion itself may lead to increased managerial autonomy as relational monitors no longer provide effective external control, or firms may be subjected to intense market pressures through the market for corporate control. In Europe, this process may still depend very much on the political developments in the EU regarding takeover regulation. However, privatization in France looks to be quite thorough, and has subjected a large number of firms to pressures from foreign investors. Likewise, the shift of German bank strategy has left firms increasingly vulnerable to hostile takeover bids. Yet, Germany maintains a large sector of family firms which are largely unaffected by recent developments. Meanwhile, Japanese firms have sought to restructure stable shareholdings rather than eliminate them and risk exposure to hostile bids. The pressure from foreign investors remains limited to a small group of top companies, while the decline of the main bank may have reinforced managerial autonomy. This analysis could be extended by looking at how these different pressures are magnified or diminished through the specific national patterns of corporate law.

Looking across the eight countries studied in this volume, the shifts in corporate governance are parallel to a number of common trends in labour management. First, elements of variable or performance-related pay are becoming more widespread—linked either directly to firm or business unit performance measures, or less directly through target setting at individual or small group level. Employee share ownership has been an important change to align employee interests with those of shareholders. Second, employment has become less stable. Firms have come under pressure to maximize shareholder returns by reducing excess employment or to divest from less profitable or non-core businesses. Third, employee participation has been challenged to adapt to new decision-making structures within large firms and to manage increased organizational restructuring, via the growth of direct participation and joint consultative arrangements. Fourth, pressures for the decentralization of collective bargaining are increasing, and more decisions are being taken at workplace level, either jointly with labour or unilaterally by management. But despite these common trends, variation can also be seen in labour outcomes.

In Germany, elements of performance pay have largely come 'on-top' of existing pay schemes, rather than replacing them. They have been implemented in a manner consistent with centralized industry-level collective bargaining, thus representing only a controlled decentralization of the German system. German patterns of employment adjustment have largely been reinforced, if not intensified. The welfare state, strong legal position of the works council and industrial unionism work together to externalize employment adjustment from large German firms. On the one hand, this also reinforces the cooperative character of firm-level employee participation, as works councils are increasingly called upon to 'co-manage' decisions over corporate restructuring and to make employees an increasingly valuable asset for the corporation. But, on the other hand, the character of codetermination as an encompassing and solidaristic political and legal institution is changing dramatically. Participation has become an increasingly 'contractual' affair, as decision-making structures are adapted to new organization boundaries and hierarchies. Works councils often lack access to centralized management decisions of parent companies. In addition, greater divisions between core 'insider' employees and peripheral 'outside' employees are straining the internal articulation of employee interests. On issues such as core competence and spin-offs, the interests of works councils may be divided between weaker versus stronger business units, rather than on class lines, with the result that a new type of insider–outsider conflict is emerging.

In Japan, similar pressures are playing out in quite different ways from Germany. Japanese enterprise unions lack legal rights for participation as in Germany. Participation is not vested in particular business units, but depends upon unions maintaining total membership and solidarity across business units as a source of strength *vis-à-vis* management. As shown in the case of NTT, Japanese unions have a strong incentive to defend the boundary of the firm or corporate group in order to internalize employment adjustment processes across various business units (Sako and Jackson 2004). However, the lack of integration into multi-employer agreements may mean that enterprise-based unions may also be more willing to accept pay cuts or wage freezes in order to assure job security. Japanese unions do not face the German problem where performance pay threatens equal pay for equal work across firms bound together under centralized collective agreements. However, performance measures may be very difficult to adapt to a context of seniority-based pay scales and stable internal career patterns. Here, pressures are to differentiate internally between different 'specialist' systems of employment stressing performance and job-related pay in contrast to traditional company careers.

Both Germany and Japan contrast to cases where labour plays a weaker role in the firm. Whereas Germany, Japan, and to a lesser extent the Netherlands represent cases of adapting and modifying a strong role of labour in the corporation, the changes in France, Spain, and Italy seem to reinforce the weakness of labour. (See the respective country chapters in this volume.) To be sure, these countries have some degree of centralized collective bargaining and strong legal employment protection. But such constraints outside the firm are increasingly placed in tension with developments inside the firm. French firms have engaged in very rapid de-diversification and have done so unilaterally with little voice from organized labour. Similarly, Spanish firms continue to face strong external constraints on employment adjustment through strict legal regulations, but have made intensified use of labour market dualism in the form of temporary employment outside these institutions. Italy seems also to be pressured by tendencies toward dualism and decentralization of collective bargaining.

11.6. Conclusion

The linkages between corporate governance and labour management will remain an exciting subject of study in coming years. National differences still matter and the common trends observed in this book do not seem to indicate convergence on a single model. At least, not yet. What agenda emerges for new comparative studies of national diversity?

In the future, international comparisons may be less categorical. Differences in the areas of finance, ownership patterns, corporate law, accounting rules, boardroom practices, or executive compensation are narrowing. The question is no longer dispersion versus concentration, banks versus markets, good versus weak shareholder rights, independent directors or zero independence, or the presence or absence of stock options. These differences have become much more ones of degree, rather than kind. In some sense, it is helpful to remember that they always were differences of degree, as this conclusion has tried to suggest. Nor will differences in kind disappear completely. But the diversity of the future may be harder to measure by traditional indicators. For example, what differences exist between stock options schemes in Germany and the United States? Or who are outside directors in Japan versus the United Kingdom? Here, our interest will not just be the presence or absence of a practice, but on how such practices are implemented in different contexts.

Along with corporate governance, the diversity of labour management and industrial relations in large firms will also narrow, but not disappear. Employment security and employee participation will remain in those countries which already have them, but this type of security and rights may cover an ever shrinking core. The prospects of diversity depend very much on whether countries with strong employee 'voice' and participation find a way to use that strength to promote greater corporate accountability alongside investors. In practice, there seems nothing antithetical in extending strong legal rights to both shareholders and employees. A form of labour management which is complementary to capital markets is not simply one which responds quickly to the forces of the market, but one which can constrain the excesses and short-term failures of such markets.

It remains to be seen whether organized labour can play a role in promoting an 'enlightened' version of shareholder value that can stress the positive-sum aspects of corporate governance. The prospects for such a model will have a very real and substantial impact of the welfare of employees in corporations around the world.

NOTES

1. The quality of such typologies depends on identifying the empirically relevant dimensions which vary across contexts. Other variables might be added, such as whether unions are organized around industry, occupation/craft, or enterprise lines, resulting in a different clustering of industrial relations systems.
2. On the concept of functional equivalence, see Merton (1949).
3. German codetermination is sometimes argued to promote poor managerial accountability by dividing the supervisory board into factional benches, diluting the board's overall powers and promoting collusion between management and employees (Pistor 1999).
4. See Aoki (2001) on the concept of complementarity. This concept is widely used within discussion of corporate governance to specify the increased returns to an institution in particular combination with another institution.
5. After controlling for various performance variables but no country variables, the odds of downsizing increase by a factor of 1.27 for dispersed firms relative to concentrated firms.
6. This analysis draws on data from another project with Ruth Aguilera on determinants of corporate ownership. Further details on the dataset, coding of membership scores, and the method of analysis can be found in Jackson and Aguilera (2004).
7. Unless otherwise noted, the test for sufficiency required a proportion of positive cases to exceed 80% and achieve a significance of 0.05. An adjustment of 0.17 (generally equivalent to one degree of membership) was allowed to control for measurement error.

Bibliography

Abe, M. (2002). 'Corporate governance structure and employment adjustment in Japan: an empirical analysis using corporate finance data'. *Industrial Relations*, 41: 683–702.

Abowd, J. and Bognanno, M. (1995). 'International Differences in Executive and Managerial Compensation', in R. Freeman and L. Katz. (eds.), *Differences and Changes in Wage Structures*. Chicago: Chicago University Press.

Adams, M. (1999). 'Cross Holdings in Germany'. *Journal of Institutional and Theoretical Economics*, 155: 80–109.

Addison, J., Schnabel, C., and Wagner, J. (1998). 'Betriebsräte in der Deutschen Industrie—Verbreitung, Bestimmungsgründe und Effekte', in K. Gerlach, O. Hübler, Olaf and W. Meyer (eds.), *Ökonomische Analysen Betrieblicher Strukuren und Prozesse*, Frankfurt/M: Campus.

—— ——, and ——. (1999). Verbreitung, Bestimmungsgründe und Auswirkungen von Betriebsräten: Empirische Befunde aus dem Hannoveraner Firmenpanel, in B. Frick, N. Kluge, and W. Streeck (eds.), *Die wirtschaftlichen Folgen der Mitbestimmung*, Frankfurt/M: Campus.

—— ——, and —— (2001). 'Works Councils in Germany: Their Effects on Establishment Performance'. *Oxford Economic Papers*, 53: 659–94.

Addison, J., Siebert, W., Wagner, J., and Xiandong, W. (2000). 'Worker Participation and Firm Performance: Evidence from Germany and Britain'. *British Journal of Industrial Relations*, 38: 7–48.

Agarwal, R. and Elston, J. (2001). 'Bank-Firm Relationships, Financing and Firm Performance in Germany'. *Economics Letters*, 72: 225–32.

Aguilera, R. (1998). 'Directorship Interlocks in Comparative Perspective: The Case of Spain'. *European Sociological Review*, 14: 319–42.

—— (1999). 'Elites, Corporations and the Wealth of Nations: How Do Historical Institutional Settings Shape Inter-Corporate Relations in Italian and Spanish Capitalism?' Harvard University, Ph.D. dissertation.

—— and Cuervo-Cazurra, A. (2004). 'Codes of Good Governance Worldwide. What is the Trigger?'. *Organization Studies*, 25: 415–44.

—— and Jackson, G. (2003). 'The Cross-National Diversity of Corporate Governance: Dimensions and Determinants'. *Academy of Management Review*, 28: 447–65.

Ahmadjian, C. L. and Robinson, P. (2001). 'Safety in numbers: Downsizing and the Deinstitutionalization of Permanent Employment in Japan'. *Administrative Science Quarterly*, 46: 622–54.

Alchian, A. (1984). 'Specificity, Specialization, and Coalitions'. *Journal of Institutional and Theoretical Economics*, 140: 34–49.

Alexander, D. and Nobes, C. (2001). *Financial Accounting, an International Introduction'*. London: Prentice Hall.

Allen, F. and Gale, D. (2000). *Comparing Financial Systems*. Cambridge, MA: MIT Press.

Amable, B. and Hancké, B. (2001). 'Innovation and Industrial Renewal in France in Comparative Perspective'. *Industry and Innovation*, 8: 113–34.

Amuedo-Dorantes, C. (2000). 'Work Transitions Into and Out of Involuntary Temporary Employment in a Segmented Market: Evidence from Spain'. *Industrial and Labor Relations Review*, 53: 309–25.

Aoki, M. (1986). *The Co-operative Game Theory of the Firm*. Oxford: Clarendon Press.

—— (1988). *Information, Incentives, and Bargaining in the Japanese Economy*. Cambridge: Cambridge University Press.

—— (1994). 'The Japanese Firm as a System of Attributes: A Survey and Research Agenda'. In M. Aoki, and R. Dore (eds.), *The Japanese Firm: the Sources of Competitive Strength*. Oxford: Oxford University Press.

—— and Dinc, S. (1997). 'Relational Financing as an Institution and its Viability under Competition.' Stanford: Stanford University Center for Economic Policy Research, Stanford University, Paper No. 488.

—— (2001). *Toward a Comparative Institutional Analysis*. Cambridge, MA: MIT Press.

—— and Okuno, M. (1996). *Keizai Shisutemu No Hikaku Seido Bunseki (Comparative Institutional Economic Analysis)*. Tokyo: Tokyo University Press.

—— and Serdar, D. (1997). 'Relational Financing as an Institution and its Viability under Competition'. Stanford, CA: Stanford University, Center for Economic Policy Research, CEPR Publication No. 488.

Araki, T. (1994). 'Promotion and Regulation of Job Creation Opportunities', in *International Society of Labour Law and Social Security, Promotion and Regulation of Job Creation Opportunities* (Proceedings of XIV World Congress of Labour Law and Social Security).

—— (1995). 'Modification of Working Conditions Through Dismissals?' *Japan Labour Bulletin*, 5: 34–8.

—— (1998). 'Accommodating Terms and Conditions of Employment to Changing Circumstances: A Comparative Analysis of Quantitative and Qualitative Flexibility in the US, Germany, and Japan', in C. Engels and M. Weiss (eds.), *Labour Law and Industrial Relations at the Turn of the Century*. Deventer: Kluwer.

—— (1999). '1999 Revisions of Employment Security Law and Worker Dispatching Law: Drastic Reforms of Japanese Labour Market Regulations'. *Japan Labour Bulletin*, 5: 38–9.

—— (2000a). 'Nichi-Bei-Doku no Koporeto Gabanansu to Koyo Roshi Kankei (Corporate Governance and Employment and Labour Relations in Japan, US and Germany)' in T. Inagami (ed.), *Gendai Nihon No Koporeto*

Gabanansu (*Corporate Governance In Contemporary Japan*). Tokyo: Toyo Keizai.

—— (2000*b*). 'A Comparative Analysis: Corporate Governance and Labour and Employment Relations in Japan'. *Comparative Labour Law and Policy Journal*, 22: 67–96.

—— (2002). *Labour and Employment Law in Japan*. Tokyo: Japan Institute of Labour.

—— (2003). 'Corporate Restructuring and Employment Protection: Japan's New Experiment', in R. Blanpain and M. Weiss (eds.). *Changing Industrial Relations and Modernisation of Labour Law—Liber Amicorum in Honour of Professor Marco Biagi*. Deventer: Kluwer.

Armour, J., Deakin, S., and Konzelmann, S. (2003). 'Shareholder Primacy and the Trajectory of UK Corporate Governance'. *British Journal of Industrial Relations*, 41: 531–56.

Augar, P. (2001). *The Death of Gentlemanly Capitalism*. London: Penguin.

Backes-Geller, U. (1996). *Betriebliche Bildungs und Wettbewerbsstratgien im Deutsch-Britischen Vergleich*. Munich: Hampp.

—— Frick, B. and Sadowski, D. (1997). 'Codetermination and Personnel Policies of German Firms: The Influence of Works Councils on Turnover and Further Training'. *International Journal of Human Resource Management*, 8: 328–47.

Bacon, N. and Berry, B. (2003). 'Shareholders, Stakeholders and HRM: The Impact of Financial Orientation on the Standing, Style of Operation and Policies of HRM', paper presented to 18th Workshop on Strategic Human Resource Management, EIASM, Brussels, April.

Bagley, C. and Page, K. (1999). 'The Devil Made Me Do It: Replacing Corporate Directors' Veil of Secrecy with the Mantle of Stewardship'. *San Diego Law Review*, 36: 897.

Banco de España. (2002). *Central de Balances. Resultados Anuales de las Empresas No Financieras 2002*. Madrid: Banco de España.

Barca, F. (1994). *Imprese in cerca di padrone. Proprietà e controllo nel capitalismo italiano*. Bari: Laterza.

—— (1995). 'Alternative Models of Control: Efficiency, Accessibility and Market Failures', in J. Roemer (ed.), *Property Rights, Welfare and Incentives*. Aldershot: Macmillan.

—— and Magnani, M. (1989). *L'industria fra capitale e lavoro*. Bologna: Il Mulino.

—— and Trento, S. (1997). 'State Ownership and the Evolution of Italian and Japanese Corporate Governance Models: the Roles of Institutional Shocks'. *Economic Systems*, 23: 35–60.

——, Bianco, M., Cannari, L., Cesari, R., Gola, C., Manitta, G., Salvo, G., and Assetti, L. (1994*a*). *Proprietary e Mercato delle Imprese Proprieta, Modelli di Controlle e Riallocazione nelle Imprese Industriah Italiano*, Vol. 1. Bologna: Il Mulino.

——, Bianchi, M., Brioschi, F., Buzzacchi, L., Casavola, P., Filippa L., and Pagnini, M. (1994*b*). *Assetti Proprietari e Mercato dellelimprese. Gruppo, Proprietà e Controllo nelle Imprese Italiane Medio-grandi*, Vol. 2. Bologna: Il Mulino.

Barker, R. (1998). 'The Market for Information—Evidence from Finance Directors, Analysts and Fund Managers'. *Accounting and Business Research*, 29: 3–20.

Barney, J. (1991). 'Firm Resources and Sustained Competitive Advantage'. *Journal of Management*, 17: 99–120.

Barth, J. R., Caprio, G., and Levin, R. (2000). 'Banking Systems Around the Globe: A New Database', World Bank, Economics Working Paper, No. 2325.

Bassi, L., Lev, B., Low, J., McMurrer, D., and Siesfeld, G. A. (2000). 'Measuring Corporate Investments in Human Capital', in M. Blair and T. Kochan (eds.), *The New Relationship*, Washington, DC: Brookings Institution.

Bauer, M. and Bertin-Mourot, B. (1997). Administrateurs et Dirigeants du CAC 40, Paris: Boyden.

Baums, T. (1996). 'Corporate Governance Systems in Europe—Differences and Tendencies of Convergence', Osnabrück: University of Osnabrück, Working Paper No. 8/96.

—— and Frick, B. (1998). 'Co-determination in Germany: The Impact of Court Decisions on the Market Value of Firms', *Economic Analysis*, 1: 143–161.

—— and —— (1999). 'The Market Value of the Codetermined Firm', in M. Blair and M. Roe (eds.), Employees and Corporate Governance, Washington, DC: Brookings Institution.

Bayo-Moriones, A. and Huerta-Arribas, E. (2002). 'The Adoption of Production Incentives in Spain'. *British Journal of Industrial Relations*, 40: 709–724.

Bebchuk, L., Fried, J., and Walker, D. (2002). 'Managerial Power and Rent Extraction the Design of Executive Compensation'. *University of Chicago Law Review*, 69: 751–846.

Becht, M. and Boehmer, E. (1997). 'Transparency of Ownership and Control in Germany' in *The Separation of Ownership and Control: A Survey of Seven European Countries (Preliminary Report to the European Commission)*. Brussels: European Corporate Governance Network.

—— (1999). 'European Corporate Governance: Trading Off Liquidity Against Control'. *European Economic Review*, 43: 1071–1089.

—— and Roel, A. (1999). 'Blockholdings in Europe: an International Comparison'. *European Economic Review*, 43: 1049–1056.

Beckmann, T. and Forbes, W. (2003). 'An examination of takeovers, job loss and the wage decline within UK industry', paper presented to 18th Workshop on Strategic Human Resource Management, EIASM, Brussels, April.

Bellmann, L. and Frick, B. (1999). 'Umfang, Bestimmungsgründe und wirtschaftliche Folgen betrieblicher Zusatz- und Sozialleistungen', in B. Frick, R. Neubäumer, and W. Sesselmeier (eds.), *Die Anreizwirkungen betrieblicher Zusatzleistungen*. München:.

—— and Kohaut, S. (1995). 'Betriebliche Determinanten der Lohnhoehe und der Uebertarifliche Bezahlung. Eine empirische Analyse auf der Basis des IAB-Betriebspanels', *Mitteilungen aus der Arbeitsmarkt und Berufsforschung*, 1: 62–75.

—— and —— (1995a). 'Effektiv- und Tariflöhne in der Bundesrepublik Deutschland: eine empirische Analyse auf der Basis des IAB-Betriebspanels', in K. Gerlach and R. Schettkat (eds.), *Determinanten der Lohnbildung*. Berlin:.

—— and —— (1995b). 'Betriebliche Determinanten der Lohnhöhe und der übertariflichen Bezahlung'. *Mitteilungen aus der Arbeitsmarkt- und Berufsforschung*, 28: 62–75.

—— and —— (1997). Pay Differentials Between Public and Private Sector Employees: An Empirical Analysis based on the German Establishment Panel, in J. Kühl, M. Lahner, and J. Wagner (eds.), Die Nachfrageseite des Arbeitsmarktes. Ergebnisse aus Analysen mit Deutschen Firmenpaneldaten. Nürnberg: Institut für Arbeitsmarkt und Berufsforschung.

—— and —— (1999). 'Betriebliche Lohnbestimmung in ost- und westdeutschen Betrieben. Eine Analyse mit den Daten des IAB-Betriebspanels', in L. Bellmann et al. (eds.), *Zur Entwicklung von Lohn und Beschäftigung auf der Basis von Betriebs- und Unternehmensdaten*. Nürnberg: Institut für Arbeitsmarkt und Berufsforschung.

——, ——, and Schnabel, C. (1998). 'Ausmaß und Entwicklung der übertariflichen Entlohnung'. *IW-Trends*, 2: 1–10.

—— ——, and —— (1999). 'Flächentarifverträge im Zeichen von Abwanderung und Widerspruch: Geltungsbereich, Einflussfaktoren und Öffnungstendenzen', in L. Bellmann and V. Steiner (eds.), *Panelanalysen zu Lohnstruktur, Qualifikation und Beschäftigungsdynamik*. Nürnberg: Institut für Arbeitsmarkt und Berufsforschung.

—— and Möller, J. (1995). 'Institutional Influences and Inter-Industry Wage Differentials', in F. Buttler, F. Wolfgang, R. Schettkat, and D. Soskice (eds.), *Institutional Frameworks and Labour Market Performance. Comparative Views on the U.S. and German Economies*. New York: Routledge.

Benders, J., Huijgen, F., Pekruhl, U., and O'Kelly, K. (2000). *Useful but Unused. The Fate of Group Work in Europe*, Dublin: European Foundation for the Improvement of Working and Living Conditions.

Benelli, G., Loderer, C., and Lysm, T. (1987). 'Labor Participation in Corporate Policy-Making Decisions: West Germany's Experience with Co-determination'. *Journal of Business*, 60: 663–75.

Béret, P. (1992). 'Salaires et Marchés Internes: Quelques évolutions Récentes en France'. *Economie Appliquée*, 45: 5–22.

Berger, P. and Ofek, E. (1995). 'Diversification's Effect on Firm Value'. *Journal of Financial Economics*, 37: 39–65.

Berle, A. and Means, G. (1932). *The Modern Corporation and Private Property*. New York: Macmillan.

Bermeo, N. (1994). 'Sacrifice, Sequence, and Strength in Successful Dual Transitions: Lessons from Spain'. *Journal of Politics*, 56: 601–27.

Bertrand, M. and Mullainathan, S. (1998). 'Is There Discretion in Wage Setting? A Test Using Takeover Legislation'. Boston: National Bureau of Economic Research, no. 6807.

Beyer, J. (1996). 'Governance Structures: Unternehmensverflechtungen und Unternehmenserfolg in Deutschland'. *Zeitschrift für Betriebswirtschaft, Ergänzungsheft*, 3: 79–101.

—— (1998). *Managerherrschaft in Deutschland? 'Corporate Governance' unter Verflechtungsbedingungen*. Opladen: Westdeutsche Verlag.

—— (2003). 'Deutschland AG a.D.: Deutsche Bank, Allianz und das Verflechtungszentrum des deutschen Kapitalismus', in W. Streeck and M. Höpner (eds.), *Alle Macht dem Markt? Fallstudien zur Abwicklung der Deutschland AG*. Frankfurt: Campus.

—— and Hassel, A. (2002). 'The Effects of Convergence: Internationalisation and the Changing Distribution of Net Value Added in Large German Firms', *Economy and Society*, 31: 309–32.

—— and —— (2002). 'The Effects of Convergence: Internationalization and the Changing Distribution of Net Value Added in Large German Firms'. *Economy and Society*, 31: 309–32.

Bhagat, S., Shleifer, A., and Vishny, R. (1990). 'The Hostile Takeover Boom in the 1980s: The Return to Corporate Specialization'. *Brookings Papers on Economic Activity: Microeconomics*, 1–72.

Biggart, N. (1991). 'Explaining Asian Economic Organization. Toward a Weberian Institutional Perspective'. *Theory and Society*, 20: 199–232.

Black, B. and Coffee, J. (1994). 'Hail Britannia: institutional investor behavior under limited regulation'. *Michigan Law Review*, 92: 1997–2087.

Blair, M. (1995). *Ownership and Control: Rethinking Corporate Governance for the Twenty-first Century*. Washington, DC: Brookings Institution.

—— (1999). 'Team Production in Business Organizations: An Introduction'. *The Journal of Corporation Law*, 24: 743–50.

—— and Kochan, T. (2000). *The New Relationship: Human Capital in the American Corporation*. Washington, DC: Brookings Institution.

—— and Kruse, D. (1999). 'Worker Capitalists? Giving Employees an Ownership Stake'. *Brookings Review*, 17: 23–6.

—— and Blasi, J. R. (2000). 'Employee Ownership: An Unstable Form or a Stabilizing Force?', in M. Blair and T. Kochan (eds.), *The New Relationship: Human Capital in the American Corporation*. Washington, DC: Brookings Institution.

Blair, M. and Roe, M. (1999). *Employees and Corporate Governance.* Washington, DC: Brookings Institution.

—— and Stout, L. (1999). 'A Team Production Theory of Corporate Law'. *Virginia Law Review*, 85: 247–328.

Blasi, J. and Kruse, D. (1991). *The New Owners.* New York: Harper Business.

—— and Bernstein, A. (2002). *In the Company of Owners.* New York: Perseus.

Blyton, P. and Martinez Lucio, M. (1995). 'Industrial relations and the management of flexibility: factors shaping developments in Spain and the United Kingdom'. *The International Journal of Human Resource Management*, 6: 271–91.

Boehmer, E. (1998). 'Ownership Structure and Firm Performance in Germany: Institutional Background and Empirical Evidence', Berlin, Humboldt University, Working Paper (www.wiwi.hu-berlin.de/~boehmer).

—— (1999). 'Corporate Governance in Germany: Institutional Background and Empirical Results', Berlin, Humboldt University, Working Paper (www.wiwi.hu-berlin.de/~boehmer).

Bolton, P. and von Thadden, E. (1998a). 'Blocks, Liquidity, and Control'. *Journal of Finance*, 53: 1–25.

—— and —— (1998b). 'Liquidity and Control: A Dynamic Theory of Corporate Ownership Structure'. *Journal of Institutional and Theoretical Economics*, 154: 177–215.

Boockmann, B. and Hagen, T. (2001). 'The Use of Flexible Working Contracts in West Germany: Evidence from an Establishment Panel', Mannheim, ZEW Discussion Paper.

Borio, C. (1990). 'Leverage and Financing of Non-financial Companies: An International Perspective'. Basle: Bank for International Settlements, Economic Paper 27.

Bottiglieri, B. (1984). 'Linee interpretative del dibattito sulle partecipazioni statali nel secondo dopoguerra'. *Economia Pubblica*, 5: 239–44.

Boyer, R. (1990). *The Regulation School.* New York: Columbia University Press.

—— (2003). 'The Embedded Innovation Systems of Germany and Japan: Distinctive Features and Futures', in K. Yamamura and W. Streeck (eds.), *The End of Diversity? Prospects of German and Japanese Capitalism.* Ithaca, NY: Cornell University Press.

—— Charron, E., Jurgens, U., and Tolliday, S. (1998). *Between Imitation and Innovation.* Oxford: Oxford University Press.

Brioschi, F., Buzzacchi, L., and Colombo, M. (1990). *Gruppi di imprese e mercato finanziario.* Roma: La Nuova Italia Scientifica.

Bronars, S. and Deere, D. (1991). 'The threat of unionization, the use of debt and the preservation of shareholder wealth'. *Quarterly Journal of Economics*, 106: 231–54.

Bundesbank, Deutsche (2000). 'Ergebnisse der gesamtwirtschaftlichen Finanzierungsrechnung für Deutschland 1991 bis 1999'. *Statististische Sonderveröffentlichung 4*.

Burkart, M., Gromb, D., and Panunzi, F. (1997). 'Large Shareholders, Monitoring, and the Value of the Firm'. *Quarterly Journal of Economics*, 112: 693–728.

Cable, J. (1985). 'Capital Market Information and Industrial Performance: The Role of West German Banks'. *Economic Journal*, 95: 118–132.

Cadbury Report (1992). *Report of the Committee on the Financial Aspects of Corporate Governance*. London: Gee Publishing.

Calmfors, L. and Driffill, J. (1988). 'Bargaining Structure, Corporatism and Macroeconomic Performance'. *Economic Policy*, 6: 14–61.

Campa, J. and Guillén, M. (1996). 'Spain: A Boom From Economic Integration', in J. Dunning and R. Narula (eds.), *Foreign Direct Investment and Governments*. New York: Routledge.

Capdevielle (1981). *France De Gauche Vote á Droite*. Paris: Presses de la Fondation Nationale des Sciences Politiques.

Capra, L., D'Amico, N., Ferri, G., and Pesaresi, N. (1994). *Assetti Proprietari e Mercato delle Imprese. Gli Intermediari della Riallocazione Proprietaria in Italia*, Vol 3. Bologna: Il Mulino.

Cappelli, P. (1999). *The New Deal at Work*. Boston: Harvard Business School Press.

—— Bassie, L., Katz, H., Knoke, D., Osterman, P., and Useem., M. (1997). *Change at Work*. New York: Oxford University Press.

Carr, C. and Tomkins, C. (1998). 'Context, culture and the role of the finance function in strategic decisions. A comparative analysis of Britain, Germany, the USA, and Japan'. *Management Accounting Research*, 9: 213–239.

Carstensen, V., Gerlach, K., and Hübler, O. (1995*a*). 'Erfolgsbeteiligung von Arbeitnehmern: Motive, Ausgestaltung und empirische Befunde' in K. Semlinger and B. Frick (eds.), *Betriebliche Modernisierung in personeller Erneuerung*, Berlin: Sigma.

—— —— and —— (1995*b*). 'Profit Sharing in German Firms: Institutional Framework, Participation, Microeconomic Effects and Comparisons with the US', in F. Buttler, F. Wolfgang, R. Schettkat, and D. Soskice (eds.), *Institutions and Labor Market Performance: Comparative Views on the US and German Economies*, London: Routledge.

Casper, S. and Hancké, B. (1999). 'Global Quality Norms within National Production Regimes : ISO 9000 Norm Implementation in the French and German Car Industries'. *Organization Studies*, 20: 961–85.

Castronovo, V. (1995). *Storia Economica d'Italia. Dall'Ottocento ai Giorni Nostri*. Torino: Einaudi.

Central Statistical Office (2002). *Share Ownership: A Report on Ownership of Shares as at 31st December 2001*. London: Central Statistical Office.

318   *Bibliography*

Chamberlain, N. (1948). *The Union Challenge to Management Control*. New York: Harper.
Chandler, A. (1962). *Strategy and Structure: Chapters in the History of the American Industrial Enterprise*. Cambridge, MA: MIT Press.
—— (1977). *The Visible Hand: the Managerial Revolution in American Business*. Cambridge, MA: Harvard University Press.
—— (1990). *Scale and Scope: The Dynamics of Industrial Capitalism*. Cambridge, MA: Harvard University Press.
Chang, R. (2001). *Downsizing Announcements and Stock Market Reaction in the United Kingdom*. University of Nottingham: MA Dissertation.
Charkham, J. (1994). *Keeping Good Company: A Study of Corporate Governance in Five Countries*. Oxford: Oxford University Press.
Charron, E. (1998). 'FASA Renault: Innovation in Productive Flexibility and Job Security', in R. Boyer, J. Charron, and S. Tolliday. *Between Imitation and Innovation*. Oxford: Oxford University Press.
Child, J. (1972). 'Organizational Structure, Environment, and Performance: the Role of 'Strategic Choice'. *Sociology*, 6: 1–22.
Chirinko, R. and Elston, J. (1996). 'Finance, Control, and Profitability: An Evaluation of German Bank Influence', Baltimore: The John Hopkins University, American Institute for Contemporary German Studies, Working Paper No. 28.
Chorin, J. (1990). 'L'Adaptation de la Représentation du Personnel de Droit Commun aux Entreprises Publiques a Statut: les Exemples d'EDF-GDF et de la SNCF'. *Droit Social*, 12: 886–95.
CIA (Central Intelligence Agency) (2002). *The World Factbook 2002*. www.cia.giv/cia/publications/factbook/index.html.
Ciocca, P. (1982). *Interesse e profitto*. Bologna: Il Mulino.
—— (1991). *Banca, Finanza, Mercato: bilancio di un decennio e nuove prospettive*. Torino: Einaudi.
—— (2000). *La Nuova Finanza in Italia. Una Difficile Metamorfosi (1980–2000)*. Torino: Boringhieri.
Cioffi, J. (2000). 'Governing globalization? The state, law, and structural change in corporate governance'. *Journal of Law and Society*, 27: 572–600.
Clark, G. (2000). *Pension Fund Capitalism*. Oxford: Oxford University Press.
Clarke, T. and Bostock, R. (1997). 'Governance in Germany: The Foundations of Corporate Structure?', in K. Keasey, S. Thompson, and M. Wright (ed.), *Corporate Governance: Economic and Financial Issues*. Oxford: Oxford University Press.
CNMV (Comisión Nacional del Mercado de Valores) (2002). *Memoria de la CNMV. Informe Anual sobre sus Actividades 2001*. Madrid: CNMV.
—— (2003). *Memoria de la CNMV. Informe Anual sobre sus Actividades 2002*. Madrid: CNMV.
Coffee, J. (1988). 'Shareholders versus Managers: the Strain in the Corporate Web', in J. Coffee, Jr., L. Lowenstein, and S. Rose-Ackerman (eds.), *Knights,*

Raiders and Targets: The Impact of the Hostile Takeover. New York: Oxford University Press.

—— (1999). 'The future as history: The prospects for global convergence in corporate governance and its implications'. *Northwestern University Law Review*, 93: 641–707.

Coff, R. W. (1991). 'Corporate Acquisitions of Human-asset Intensive Firms: Let the Buyer Beware', Los Angeles: UCLA Anderson School of Management, unpublished PhD thesis.

Cole, R. (1999). *Managing Quality Fads: How American Business Learned to Play the Quality Game*. New York: Oxford University Press.

Comment, R. and Jarrell, G. (1995). 'Corporate focus and stock returns'. *Journal of Financial Economics*, 37: 67–87.

Commissie Corporate Governance (Commissie Peters) (1997). *Aanbevelingen inzake Corporate Governance in Nederland*. Amsterdam: AEX beurs.

Commissie Corporate Governance (Commissie Tabaksblad) (2003). The Dutch code of corporate governance. Principles of good corporate governance and best practice provisions, www.commissiecorporategovernance, July 2003.

Confalonieri, A. (1974). *Banca e Industria in Italia, 1894–1906, 3 volumes*. Milano: Banca Commerciale Italiana.

Conference Board (2002). *Commission on Public Trust and Private Enterprise*. New York: The Conference Board.

Conte, M. and Svejnar, J. (1990). 'Employee Ownership Plans', in A. Blinder (ed.), *Paying for Productivity*. Washington, DC: Brookings Institution.

Conyon, M. and Schwalbach, J. (2000). 'Executive compensation: evidence from the UK and Germany'. *Long Range Planning*, 33: 504–26.

—— Peck, S., Reed, L., and Sadler, G. (2000*a*). 'The structure of executive compensation contracts: UK evidence'. *Long Range Planning*, 33: 478–503.

—— Sourafel, G., Thompson, S., and Wright, P. (2000*b*). *The Impact of Mergers and Acquisitions on Company Employment in the United Kingdom*. Nottingham: Nottingham University Centre for Research on Globalization and Labour Markets, Research Paper 2000/5.

Cools, K. and van Praag, M. (2000). 'Topsalarissen en Aandelenopties' *Economisch Statistische Berichten*, 85: 69–73.

Corbett, J. and Jenkinson, T. (1996). The Financing of Industry, 1970–1989: An International Comparison'. *Journal of the Japanese and International Economies*, 10: 71–96.

Core, J., Guay, W., and Larcker, D. (2003). 'Executive Equity Compensation and Incentives: A Survey'. *Federal Reserve Bank of New York Economic Policy Review*, 9: 27–51.

Corporate Governance Forum of Japan (1998). *Corporate Governance Principles*. Tokyo: Corporate Governance Forum of Japan.

Courtois, G. (1995). 'Education et Formation: Grandes Tendances', in S. Cordellier and E. Poisson (eds.), *L' Etat de la France*. Paris: La Découverte.

Coy, P. (2002). 'High Turnover, High Risk', *Business Week 50* (Spring 2002), 24. David and Brierley 1985.

Crozier, M. (1964). *Le Phénomene Bureaucratique*, Paris: Le Seuil.

Cubbin, J. and Leech, D. (1983). 'The Effect of Shareholding Dispersion on the Degree of Control in British Companies: Theory and Measurement', *Economic Journal*, 93: 351–369.

Cully, M., Woodland, S., O'Reilly, A., and Dix, G. (1999). *Britain at Work: as Depicted by the 1998 Workplace Employee Relations Survey*. London: Routledge.

Cuervo-Cazurra, A. (1999). 'Grandes Accionistas y Beneficios Privados: El Caso de Bancos Como Accionistas de Empresas no Financieras'. *Investigaciones Europeas de Dirección y Economía de la Empresa*, 5: 21–44.

Culpepper, P. (2001). 'Employers, Public Policy, and the Politics of Decentralized Cooperation', in P. Hall and D. Soskice (eds.), *Varieties of Capitalism: The Institutional Foundations of Comparative Advantage*. Oxford: Oxford University Press.

Cyert, R. and March, James G. (1963). *A Behavioral Theory of the Firm*. Englewood Cliffs, NJ: Prentice Hall.

Daems, H. (1980). 'The Rise of the Modern Industrial Entreprise: a New Perspective', in A. Chandler and H. Daems (eds.), *Managerial Hierarchies. Comparative Perspectives and the Rise of Modern Industrial Enterprise*. Cambridge, MA: Harvard University Press.

Deakin, S. and Slinger, G. (1997). 'Hostile takeovers, corporate law, and the theory of the firm'. *Journal of Law and Society*, 24: 124–151.

—— Hobbs, R., Konzelmann, S., and Wilkinson, F. (2002). 'Partnership, Ownership and Control: The Impact of Corporate Governance on Employment Relations'. *Employee Relations*, 24: 335–352.

De Cecco, M. and Ferri, G. (1994). 'Origini e natura speciale dell'attività di banca d'affari in Italia'. *Temi di Discussione, n. 242*. Roma: Banca d'Italia.

De Jong, A. (2001). 'The Netherlands', in K. Gugler (eds.), *Corporate Governance and Economic Performance*, Oxford: Oxford University Press.

De Jong, D., De Jong, A., Mertens, G., and Wasley, C. (2001*a*). 'Corporate governance in Nederland: de invloed van de Commissie Peters', *Maandblad voor Accountancy en Bedrijfseconomie*, 74: 150–161.

—— —— —— and —— (2001*b*). 'Corporate Governance in Nederland: Governance en Financiële Prestaties'. *Maandblad voor Accountancy en Bedrijfseconomie*, 74: 103–116.

De Jong, H. (1995). 'European Capitalism: Between Freedom and Social Justice'. *Review of Industrial Organization*, Vol. 10: 399–419.

—— (1996). 'European Capitalism Between Freedom and Social Justice', in J. McCahery, W. Bratton, S. Picciotti, and C. Scott (eds.), *International Regulatory Competition and Coordination: Perspectives on Economic Regulation in Europe and the United States*. Oxford: Clarendon Press.

Deeg, R. (2001). 'Institutional Change and the Uses and Limits of Path Dependency: The Case of German Finance'. Cologne: Max Planck Institute, MPIfG Discussion Paper 01/6.

Delsen, L. (2000). *Exit podermodel? Sociaal-Economische Ontwikkelingen in Nederland*, Assen: Van Gorcum.

—— (2002). *Exit Polder Model? Socio-Economic Changes in the Netherlands*, Westport: Preager Publishers.

—— and De Jong, E. (eds.) (1998). *The German and Dutch Economies. Who follows whom?* Heidelberg: Physica Verlag.

Demsetz, H. (1983). 'The Structure of Ownership and the Theory of the Firm'. *Journal of Law and Economics*, 26: 375–90.

Desseigne, G. (1995). *L'Evolution du Comité d'Entreprise*. Paris: Presses Universitaires de France.

Deutsche Bundesbank (2000). *Wertpapierdepots, Statistische Sonderveröffentlichung*, Frankfurt/M: Deutsche Bundesbank.

Dickens, R., Gregg, P., and Wadsworth (2001). 'The State of Working Britain', London: Centre for Economic Performance, London School of Economics.

Dietl, H. (1998). *Capital Markets and Corporate Governance in Japan, Germany, and the United States*. London and New York: Routledge.

Dilger, A. (2002). *Ökonomik betrieblicher Mitbestimmung: Die wirtschaftlichen Folgen von Betriebsräten*, München: Hampp.

—— and Frick, B. (2000). 'Kapitalmarktreaktionen auf Veränderungen und Veröffentlichungen der Stimmrechtsverteilung'. *Zeitschrift Führung + Organisation*, 69: 18–24.

——, ——, and Speckbacher, G. (1999). 'Mitbestimmung als zentrale Frage der Corporate Governance', in B. Frick, N. Kluge, and W. Streeck (eds.), *Die wirtschaftlichen Folgen der Mitbestimmung*, Frankfurt/M: Campus.

DiPrete, T. and McManus, P. (1995). 'Institutions, Technical Change, and Diverging Life Chances: Earnings Mobility in the U.S. and Germany'. *American Journal of Sociology*.

Donaldson, G. (1994). *Corporate Restructuring: Managing the Change Process from Within*. Boston: Harvard Business School Press.

Donnelly, S., Gamble, A., Jackson, G., and Parkinson, J. (2001). *The Public Interest and the Company in Britain and Germany*. London: Anglo-German Society for the Study of Industrial Society.

Dore, R. (2000a). *Stock Market Capitalism: Welfare Capitalism*. Oxford: Oxford University Press.

—— (2000b). 'Comment: Papers on Employees and Corporate Governance'. *Comparative Labour Law and Policy Journal*, 22: 159–60.

—— (2000c). *National Capitalisms in a Globalized World*. Oxford: Oxford University Press.

Düll, H. and Ellguth, P. (1999). 'Atypische Beschäftigung: Arbeit ohne betriebliche Interessenvertretung?'. *WSI-Mitteilungen*, 52: 165–76.

Duval, G. (1996). 'Les Habits Neufs du Taylorisme'. *Alternatives Economiques*, 137: 30–9.

Easterbrook, F. and Fischel, D. (1991). *The Economic Structure of Corporate Law*. Boston, MA: Harvard University Press.

Edwards, J. (1999). 'Corporate Governance in Germany: The Influence of Banks and Large Equity-Holders', München: CES, Working Paper No. 180.

—— and Fischer, K. (1994). *Banks, Finance and Investment in Germany*. Cambridge: Cambridge University Press.

—— and Nibler, M. (2000). 'Corporate Governance in Germany: The Role of Banks and Ownership Concentration'. *Economic Policy*, 31: 237–260.

—— and Weichenrieder, A. (1999). 'Ownership Concentration and Share Valuation: Evidence from Germany', München: CESifo, Working Paper No. 193.

Egashira, K. (1994). 'Koporeto Gabanansu wo Ronzuru Igi (The Significance of Corporate Governance)', 1364 *Shoji Homu* 2.

—— (2002). *Laws of Stock Corporations and Limited Liability Companies*. Tokyo: Yuhikaku.

Eguidazu, S. (1999). *Creación de Valor y Gobierno de la Empresa*. Barcelona: Gestión 2000.

Eironline (2001). 'Corus announces large-scale redundancies', www.eiro. eurofound.ie.

El País (2003). *Anuario El País 2003*. Madrid: Ediciones El País.

Elston, J. A. and Albach, H. (1995). 'Bank Affiliations and Firm Capital Investment in Germany', *Ifo-Studien*, 41: 3–16.

—— and Horst, A. (1995). 'Bank Affiliations and Firm Capital Investment in Germany'. *Ifo-Studien*, 41: 3–16.

Emmons, W. and Schmid, F. (1998). 'Universal Banking, Control Rights, and Corporate Finance in Germany'. *Review of the Federal Reserve Bank of St. Louis*, 80: 19–42.

Erickson, C. and Jacoby, S. (2003). 'The Effect of Employer Networks on Workplace Innovation and Training'. *Industrial and Labor Relations Review*, 56: 203–223.

Esping-Andersen, G. and Regini, M. (2000a). 'Introduction', in G. Esping-Andersen and M. Regini (eds.), *Why Deregulate Labor Markets?* Oxford: Oxford University Press.

—— (2000b) 'Conclusions', in G. Esping-Andersen and M. Regini (eds.), *Why Deregulate Labor Markets?* Oxford: Oxford University Press.

Estevez-Abe, M., Iversen, T., and Soskice, D. (2001). 'Social Protection and the Formation of Skills: A Reinterpretation of the Welfare State, in P. Hall and D. Soskice (eds.), *Varieties of Capitalism: the Institutional Foundations of Comparative Advantage*. Oxford: Oxford University Press.

Eyraud, F. and Tchobanian, R. (1985). 'The Auroux Laws and Company Level Industrial Relations in France'. *British Journal of Industrial Relations*, 23: 241–59.

Fabel, O. and Lehmann, E. (2001). 'The Degree of Universality in Banking: Regulatory Policy Effects versus Strategic Choices', Konstanz: University of Konstanz, mimeo.

Faccio, M. and Ameziane, L. (2001). 'Institutional shareholders and corporate governance: the case of UK pension funds', paper presented to CEPR conference, March.

Faccio, M. and Lasfer, A. (2000). 'Do Occupational Pension Funds Monitor Companies in Which They Hold Large Stakes?'. *Journal of Corporate Finance*, 6: 71–110.

Farber, H. and Hallock, K. (1999). 'Have employment reductions become good news for shareholders? The effects of job loss announcements on stock prices, 1970–97'. Princeton: Princeton University, Industrial Relations Section, Working Paper No. 417.

Fernández Macías, E. (2003). 'Job Instability and Political Attitudes toward Work: Some Lessons From the Spanish Case'. *European Journal of Industrial Relations*, 9: 205–22.

Ferner, A. (2000). 'The Underpinnings of 'Bureaucratic' Control Systems: HRM in European Multinationals'. *Journal of Management Studies*, 37: 521–540.

—— and Hyman, R. (1998). *Changing Industrial Relations in Europe*, Oxford: Blackwell.

—— and Quintanilla, J. (2002). 'Between Globalization and Capitalist Variety: Multinationals and the International Diffusion of Employment Relations'. *European Journal of Industrial Relations*, 8: 243–50.

Fina, L. (2001). *Mercado de Trabajo y Políticas de Empleo*. Madrid: CES.

Financial Markets Center (2000). *Employee Stock Options: Background Report'*. Philomont, Virginia: FMC.

Financial Times (2003). *Special Report: Spain Finance*. Tuesday, 21 October.

Fishman, R. (1990). *Working-Class Organization and the Return to Democracy in Spain*. Ithaca, NY: Cornell University Press.

FitzRoy, F. and Kornelius, K. (1993). 'Economic Effects of Codetermination'. *Scandinavian Journal of Economics*, 95: 365–75.

—— and —— (2000). 'Co-determination, Efficiency, and Productivity', Essen: University of Essen, mimeo.

Fligstein, N. (1990). *The Transformation of Corporate Control*. Cambridge, MA: Harvard University Press.

—— (2001). *The Architecture of Markets: An Economic Sociology of Twenty-First Century Societies*. Princeton: Princeton University Press.

Flórez-Saborido, I., González-Rendón, M., and Alcaide-Castro, M. (1995). 'Spain', in I. Brunstein (ed.), *Human Resource Management in Western Europe*. New York: Walter de Gruyter.

Foss, N. (ed.), (1997). *Resources, Firms, and Strategies*, Oxford. Oxford University Press.

Fox, M. (1998). 'Required Disclosure and Corporate Governance'. *Law and Contemporary Problems*, 62: 113–27.

Franks, J. and Mayer, C. (1997a). 'Corporate Ownership and Control in the U.K., Germany, and the U.S.', in D. Chew (ed.), *Studies in International Corporate Finance and Governance Systems.* New York: Oxford University Press.

—— and —— (1997b). 'Ownership, Control, and Performance of German Corporations', paper presented at the Center for Financial Studies, 19–20 November, Frankfurt/M.

—— and —— (2000). 'Governance as a source of discipline', paper prepared for the Company Law Review Committee on Corporate Governance, www.dti.gov.uk.

Freeman, R. (2000). 'Single-Peaked vs. Diversified Capitalism: The Relation Between Economic Institutions and Outcomes', Boston: National Bureau of Economic Research, Working Paper no. 7556.

—— and Lazear, E. (1995). 'An Economic Analysis of Works Councils', in J. Rogers and W. Streeck (eds.), *Works Councils: Consulation, Representation, and Cooperation in Industrial Relations,* Chicago: University of Chicago Press.

—— and Medoff, J. (1984). *What Do Unions Do?* New York: Basic Books.

—— and Rogers, J. (1999). *What Workers Want.* New York: ILR Press.

Frick, B. (1992). *Interne Arbeitsmärkte und betriebliche Schwerbehindertenbe-schäftigung: Theoretische Analysen und empirische Befunde,* Frankfurt/M: Campus.

—— (1994). 'Betriebsverfassung und betriebliche Schwerbehindertenbe-schäftigung'. *Arbeit,* 3: 331–45.

—— (1996). 'Co-determination and Personnel Turnover: The German Experience'. *Labour,* 10: 407–30.

—— (1997a). *Mitbestimmung und Personalfluktuation: Zur Wirtschaftlichkeit der bundesdeutschen Betriebsverfassung im internationalen Vergleich,* München.

—— (1997b). 'Die Funktionsfähigkeit der bundesdeutschen Betriebsverfassung: Quantitative und qualitative Evidenz im Überblick'. *Industrielle Beziehungen,* 4: 172–95.

—— (1999). 'Corporate Governance and Corporate Takeovers: A German Perspective', in L. Funk (ed.), *The Economics and the Politics of the Third Way.* Münster: Lit-Verlag.

—— (2000). 'Die Anreizwirkungen betrieblicher Zusatzleistungen: Möglichkeiten und Grenzen', in W. Schmähl (ed.), *Soziale Sicherung zwischen Markt und Staat,* Berlin: Duncker and Humblot.

—— (2002). 'High Performance Work Practices und betriebliche Mitbestimmung: komplementär oder substitutiv? Empirische Evidenz für den deutschen Maschinenbau'. *Industrielle Beziehungen,* 9: 79–102.

—— and Möller, I. (2002). 'Works Councils, Profit Sharing and Firm Performance: Empirical Evidence from (East and West) Germany', Witten/Herdecke: University of Witten/Herdecke, mimeo.

—— and Sadowski, D. (1995). 'Works Councils, Unions, and Firm Performance', in F. Buttler, F. Wolfgang, R. Schettkat, and D. Soskice (eds.),

Institutional Frameworks and Labour Market Performance. London: Routledge.

—— Speckbacher, G., and Wentges, P. (1999). 'Arbeitnehmermitbestimmung und moderne Theorie der Unternehmung'. *Zeitschrift für Betriebswirtschaft*, 69: 745–63.

Froud, J., Haslam, C., Johal, S., and Williams, K. (2000*a*). 'Restructuring for Shareholder Value and its Implications for Labour'. *Cambridge Journal of Economics*, 24: 771–97.

—— —— Sukhdev, J. L., and Williams, K. (2000*b*). 'Shareholder Value and Financialization: Consultancy Promises, Management Moves'. *Economy and Society*, 29: 80–110.

Fukao, M. (1999). 'Nihon no kinyu sisutemu fuan to koporeto gabananse kozo no jakuten (Insecure Financial System and Weakness of Corporate Governance in Japan)', in M. Aoki *et al.* (eds.), *Shijo no Yakuwari, Kokka no Yakuwari* (*The Role of the Market, the Role of the State*). Tokyo: Toyo Keizai.

Furubotn, E. (1985). 'Codetermination, Productivity Gains, and the Economics of the Firm'. *Oxford Economic Papers*, 37: 22–39.

—— (1988). 'Codetermination and the Modern Theory of the Firm: A Property Rights Analysis'. *Journal of Business*, 61: 165–81.

Galbraith, J. (1969). *The New Industrial State*. London: Penguin.

Gámir, L. (1999). *Las Privatizaciones en España*. Madrid: Ediciones Pirámide.

García Echevarría, S. and Val Nuñez, M. (1996). *Los Recursos Humanos en la Empresa Española*. Madrid: Díaz de Santos.

García-Serrano, C. and Malo, M. (2002). 'Worker Turnover, Job Turnover and Collective Bargaing in Spain'. *British Journal of Industrial Relations*, 40: 69–85.

Gaved, M. (1998). *Institutional Investors and Corporate Governance*. London: Foundation for Business Responsibility.

Gedaljovic, E. and Shapiro, D. (1998). 'Management and Ownership Effects: Evidence from Five Countries'. *Strategic Management Journal*, 19: 533–53.

Gelauff, G. and den Broeder, C. (1996). 'Governance of stakeholder relationships: The German and Dutch experience'. *Research Memorandum No. 127*, The Hague: CPB Netherlands Bureau for Economic Policy Analysis.

Gerlach, K., Lehmann, K., and Meyer, W. (1998). 'Entwicklung der Tarifbindung im Verarbeitenden Gewerbe Niedersachsens', in K. Gerlach, O. Hübler, and W. Meyer (eds.), *Ökonomische Analysen betrieblicher Strukturen und Entwicklungen*, Frankfurt/M: Campus.

Gerlach, K. and Jirhahn, U. (2001). 'Employer Provided Further Training: Evidence from German Establishment Data', *Schmollers Jahrbuch*, 121: 139–64.

Gerschenkron, A. (1962). *Economic Backwardness in Historical Perspective*. Cambridge, MA: Belknap Press.

Ghilarducci, T., Hawley, J., and Williams, A. (1997). 'Labor's Paradoxical Interests and the Evolution of Corporate Governance'. *Journal of Law & Society*, 24: 26–43.

Gilson, R. and Kraakman, R. (1991). 'Reinventing the Outside Director: an Agenda for Institutional Investors'. *Stanford Law Review*, 43: 863–906.

Gittleman, M., Horrigan, M., and Joyce, M. (1998). 'Flexible Workplace Practices: Evidence from a Nationally Representative Survey'. *Industrial and Labor Relations Review*, 52: 99–115.

Godard, J. (2002). 'Institutional Environments, Employer Practices, and States in Liberal Market Economies'. *Industrial Relations*, 41: 249–85.

Goergen, M. (1998). *Corporate Governance and Financial Performance*. Cheltenham: Edward Elgar.

Golding, T. (2001). *The City: Inside the Great Expectation Machine*. London: Financial Times/Prentice Hall.

Gompers, P. and Metrick, A. (2001). 'Institutional Investors and Equity Prices'. *Quarterly Journal of Economics*, Volume 116: 229–59.

Goodijk, R. (2001). 'Corporate Governance and Workers' Participation in the Netherlands', in R. Markey *et al.* (eds.), *Models of Employee Participation in a Changing Global Environment: Diversity and Interaction*. Aldershot: Ashgate.

Goold, M. and Campbell, A. (2002). *Designing Effective Organizations: How to Create Structured Networks*. San Francisco: Jossey-Bass.

Gordon, D. (1996). *Fat and Mean: The Corporate Squeeze of Working Americans and the Myth of Managerial Downsizing*. New York: Martin Kessler Books.

Gorton, G. and Schmid, F. (2000*a*). 'Universal Banking and the Performance of German Firms'. *Journal of Financial Economics*, 58: 29–80.

—— and —— (2000*b*). 'Class Struggle Inside the Firm: A Study of German Codetermination', Philadelphia: University of Pennsylvania, mimeo.

Gospel, H. (1992). *Markets, Firms, and the Management of Labour in Modern Britain*. Cambridge: Cambridge University Press.

—— and Pendleton, A. (2003). 'Finance, Corporate Governance, and the Management of Labour: A Conceptual and Comparative Analysis'. *British Journal of Industrial Relations*, 41: 557–82.

Goyer, M. (1998). 'Privatization and corporate governance in France', paper presented at the annual meeting of the American Political Science Association, Boston.

—— (2001). 'Corporate governance and the innovation system in France'. *Industry and Innovation*, 8: 135–58.

—— (2002). 'The Transformation of Corporate Governance in France and Germany: the Role of Workplace Institutions'. Max Planck Institute Working Paper #02/10, Cologne: Max Planck Institute.

—— (2003). 'Corporate Governance and the Focus on Core Competencies in France and Germany', in C. Milhaupt (ed.), *Global Markets, Domestic Institutions: Corporate Law and Governance in a new era of Cross-Border Deals*. New York: Columbia University Press.

—— 'The transformation of corporate governance in France', in P. Culpepper, P. Hall, and B. Palier (eds.), *The Changing Balance Between the Economy, Society, and the State*, forthcoming.

Green, F. (1999). 'Training the Workers', in P. Gregg and J. Wadsworth (eds.), *The State of Working Britain*. Manchester: Manchester University Press.

Greenbury Report (1995). *Directors' Remuneration*. London: Gee.

Grieger, J. (2001). 'Shareholder Value und Mitbestimmung in Deutschland— Theoretische Perspektiven und normative Implikationen'. *Zeitschrift für Personalforschung*, 15: 62–96.

Grinyer, J., Russell, A., and Collison, D. (1998). 'Evidence of Managerial Short-Termism in the UK'. *British Journal of Management*, 9: 13–22.

Groot, W. and Maassen van den Brink, H. (1998). 'Bedrijfsopleidingen: wie neemt er aan deel en wat levert het op?' *Maandschrift Economie*, 62: 28–40.

Groves, M. (1998). 'In Tight Job Market, Software Firm Develops Programs to Keep Employees', *Los Angeles Times* (June 14, 1998), D-5.

Gugler, K. (eds.) (2001). *Corporate Governance and Economic Performance*, Oxford: Oxford University Press.

Guillemard, A. (1991). 'France: Massive Exit through Unemployment Compensation', in M. Kohli, M. Rein, A. Guillemard, and H. van Gunsteren (eds.), *Time for Retirement. Comparative Studies of Early Exit from the Labor Force*. Cambridge and New York: Cambridge University Press.

Guillén, F. (2000). 'Organized Labor's Images of Multinational Enterprise: Divergent Foreign Investment Ideologies in Argentina, South Korea, and Spain'. *Industrial and Labor Relations Review*, 53: 419–42.

Gurdon, M. and Anoop, R. (1990). 'Codetermination and Enterprise Performance: Empirical Evidence from West Germany'. *Journal of Economics and Business*, 42: 289–302.

Hall, B. and Murphy, K. (2002). 'Stock Options for Undiversified Executives'. *Journal of Accounting and Economics*, 33: 3–42.

Hall, P. A. and Gingerich, D. W. (2001). 'Varieties of Capitalism and Institutional Complementarities in the Macroeconomy: An Empirical Analysis', mimeo.

Hall, P. A. and Soskice, D. (2001a). *Varieties of Capitalism. The Institutional Foundations of Comparative Advantage*. Oxford: Oxford University Press.

—— and —— (2001b). 'An Introduction to Varieties of Capitalism' in P. Hall and D. Soskice (eds.), *Varieties of Capitalism: The Institutional Foundations of Comparative Advantage*. Oxford: Oxford University Press.

Hamel, G. and Prahalad, C. (1994). *Competing for the Future*. Boston: Harvard Business School Press.

Hamann, K. (1998). 'Spanish Unions: Institutional Legacy and Responsiveness to Economic and Industrial Change'. *Industrial and Labor Relations Review*, 51: 424–44.

Hamann, K. and Martínez Lucio, M. (2003). 'Strategies of Union Revitalization in Spain: Negotiating Change and Fragmentation'. *European Journal of Industrial Relations*, 9: 61–78.

Hancké, B. (2000). 'European Work Councils and Industrial Restructuring in the European Motor Industry'. *European Journal of Industrial Relations*, 6: 35–59.

—— (2001). 'Revisiting the French Model: Coordination and Industrial Restructuring in the 1980s', in P. Hall and D. Soskice (eds.), *Varieties of Capitalism*, New York: Oxford University Press.

—— (2002). *Large Firms and Institutional Change: Industrial Renewal and Economic Restructuring in France*. Oxford: Oxford University Press.

Hanka, G. (1998). 'Debt and the terms of employment'. *Journal of Financial Economics*, 48: 245–82.

Hansmann, H. and Kraakman, R. (2000). 'The End of History for Corporate Law', Newhaven, CT: Yale University, Law and Economics Working Paper 235.

Harris, H. (1982). *The Right to Manage: Industrial Relations Policies of American Business in the 1940s*. Madison: University of Wisconsin Press.

Hart, O. (1995). 'Corporate Governance: Some Theory and Implications'. *Economic Journal*, 105: 678–89.

Harzing, A. and van Ruysseveldt, J. (1995). *International Human Resource Management. An Integrated Approach*, London: Sage.

Haveman, G. (2003). 'Wie gaat er eigenlijk over de Arbeid? 'Van sociaal beleid naar Human Resource Management', in A. Nagelkerke, W. de Nijs, *Sturen in het laagland. Over continuiteit en verandering van de Nederlandse arbeidsverhoudingen*, Delft: Eburon.

Hazama, H. (1997). *The History of Labour Management in Japan*. London, Macmillan.

Helias, S. (1997). *Le Retour de l'Actionnaire: Pratiques du Corporate Governance en France, aux Etats-Unis, et en Grande-Bretagne*. Paris: Gualino Editeur.

Hempel Report (1998). *Report of the Committee on Corporate Governance*. London: Gee.

Hendry, C., Wodward, S., Harvey-Cooke, J., and Gaved, M. (1997). *Investors views of People Management*, London: Institute of Personnel and Development.

Hernando, I. and Martínez Pagés, J. (2001). 'Is There a Bank Lending Channel of Monetary Policy in Spain?' Madrid: Servicio de Estudios. Banco de España, Working Paper 0117.

Heywood, J., Hübler, O., and Uwe, J. (1998). 'Variable Payment Schemes and Industrial Relations: Evidence from Germany'. *Kyklos*, 51: 237–57.

Hilferding, R. (1910). *Das Finanzkapital*. Frankfurt am Main: Europäische Verlagsansstalt, reprinted, 1968.

Hilbert, J., Südmersen, H., and Weber, H. (1990). *Berufsbildungspolitik. Geschichte, Organisation, Neuordnung*. Opladen: Leske and Budrich.

Hill, C. (1988). 'Internal Capital Market Controls and Financial Performance in Multidivisional Companies'. *Journal of Industrial Economics*, 37: 67–83.

Hirschman, A. (1972). *Exit, Voice, and Loyalty: Responses to Decline in Firms, Organizations, and States*. Cambridge, MA: Harvard University Press.

HM Treasury (2001). *Institutional Investment in the UK: A Review*. London: HM Treasury.

Hiwatari, N. (1999). 'Employment Practices and Enterprise Unionism in Japan', in M. Blair and M. Roe (eds.), *Employees and Corporate Governance*. Washington, DC: Brookings Institution.

Hoffmann, S. (1963). 'Paradoxes of the French Political Community', in S. Hoffmann, C. Kindleberger, L.Wylie, J. Pitts, J. Duroselle, and F. Goguel (eds.), *In Search of France*. Cambridge, MA: Harvard University Press.

Höland, A. (1985). *Das Verhalten von Betriebsräten bei Kündigungen*, Frankfurt/M: Campus.

Holland, J. (1995). *The Corporate Governance Role of Financial Institutions in their Investee Companies*, London: Chartered Association of Certified Accountants, Research Report 46.

—— (1998). 'Influence and Intervention by Financial Institutions in their Investee Companies'. *Corporate Governance*, 6: 249–64.

Hoogendoorn, J. (1999). 'Strategisch human resource management in Nederland en Europa'. *Tijdschrift voor HRM*, 3: 27–46.

Höpner, M. (2000). 'Unternehmensverflechtung im Zwielicht. Hans Eichels Plan zur Auflösung der Deutschland AG'. *WSI-Mitteilungen*, 53: 655–663.

Höpner, M. (2001). 'Corporate Governance in Transition: Ten Empirical Findings on Shareholder Value and Industrial Relations in Germany'. Cologne: Max Planck Institute, MPIfG Discussion Paper 01/5.

—— (2003a). 'What Connects Industrial Relations with Corporate Governance? A Review on Complementarity'. CEPREMAP, September 2003.

—— (2003b). *Wer beherrscht die Unternehmen? Shareholder Value, Managerherrschaft und Mitbestimmung in großen deutschen Unternehmen*. Frankfurt am Main: Campus Verlag.

—— and Jackson, G. (2001). 'An Emerging Market for Corporate Control? The Case of Mannesmann and German Corporate Governance'. Cologne: Max Planck Institute, MPIfG Discussion Paper 01/4.

—— and Krempel, L. (2003). 'The Politics of the German Company Network', Cologne: Max-Planck Institut für Gesellschasftsforschung, Working Paper 2003–9.

Howell, C. (1992). *Regulating Labor*. Princeton: Princeton University Press.

Hübler, O. and Uwe, J. (1998). 'Zeit-, Leistungs- und Gruppenentlohnung— Empirische Untersuchungen mit Betriebsdaten zur Entlohnungsart', in K. Gerlach, O. Hübler, and W. Meyer (eds.), *Ökonomische Analysen betrieblicher Strukturen und Entwicklungen*. Frankfurt/M: Campus.

Hübler, O. and Meyer, W. (2000). 'Industrial Relations and the Wage Differentials between Skilled and Unskilled Blue-Collar Workers within Establishments: An Empirical Analysis with Data of Manufacturing Firms', Bonn: Institut Zukunft der Arbeit, Discussion Paper No. 176.

Hutton, W. (1996). *The State We're In*. London: Vintage.

Ide, M. (1998). *Japanese Corporate Finance and International Competition: Japanese Capitalism versus American Capitalism*. London: Macmillan.

Inagami, T. (2000), *Gendai Nihon No Koporeto Gabanansu* (*Corporate Governance In Contemporary Japan*). Tokyo: RENGO Research Institute.

—— (2001). 'From Industrial Relations to Investor Relations? Persistence and Change in Japanese Corporate Governance, Employment Practices, and Industrial Relations', *Social Science Japan Journal*, 4: 225–41.

Instituto Nacional de Estadistica (2003) *Encuesta de Población Activa* (*EPA*), www.ine.es.

International Labour Office (2001). *The Employment Impact of Mergers and Acquisitions in the Banking and Financial Services Sector*. Report for discussion at the Tripartite Meeting on the Employment Impact of Mergers and Acquisitions in the Banking and Financial Services Sector. Geneva: International Labour Office.

Itami, H. (1987a). *Mobilizing Invisible Assets*. Cambridge, MA: Harvard University Press.

—— (1987b). *Jinpon Shugi Kigyo* (*Employee-Centred Corporation*). Tokyo: Chikuma Shobo.

—— (1993). 'Kabushiki Gaisha to Jyugyoin Shuken', in H. Itami *et al.* (eds.), 1 *Nihon No Kigyo Shisutemu: Kigyo To Ha Nanika* (*Corporation System In Japan: What is the Corporation?*) Yuhikaku: Tokyo.

—— (2000). *Nihon-Gata Koporeto Gabanansu* (*Japanese-Style Corporate Governance*) Tokyo: Nihon Keizai Shinbun Sha.

Ito, K. (1993). 'Kabushiki Mochiai (Cross-shareholding)', in H. Itami *et al.* (eds.), 1 *Nihon No Kigyo Shisutemu: Kigyo To Ha Nanika* (*Corporation System In Japan: What is the Corporation?*) 154 (Yuhikaku).

Jackson, G. (1996). 'Labour Market Structure in Comparative Perspective: Germany, Japan and the United States', in Institute for Western Europe, Columbia University (eds.), *Europe and the World: External Relations and Internal Dynamics*. New York: Columbia University.

—— (2000). 'Comparative Corporate Governance: Sociological Perspectives', in J. Parkinson, A. Gamble, and G. Kelly (eds.), *The Political Economy of the Company*. Oxford: Hart Publishing.

—— (2001). 'The Origins of Nonliberal Corporate Governance in Germany and Japan', in W. Streeck and K. Yamamura (eds.) (pp. 121–70) *The Origins of Nonliberal Capitalism: Germany and Japan Compared*, Ithaca, NY: Cornell University Press.

—— (2003). 'Corporate Governance in Germany and Japan Liberalization Pressures and Responses,' in Yamamura, K. and Streek, W. (eds.), *The End of Diversity? Prospects for German and Japanese Capitalism*. Ithaca, NY: Cornell University Press.

—— and Aguilera, R. (2004). 'Some Determinants of Cross-National Diversity in Corporate Ownership: A Fuzzy Sets Approach', Tokyo: RIETI, Discussion Paper.

—— and Sako, M. (2004). 'Enterprise Boundaries and Employee Representation: NTT and Deutsche Telekom Compared'. Tokyo: RIETI, Discussion Paper.

—— and Vitols, S. (2001). 'Between Financial Commitment, Market Liquidity and Corporate Governance: Occupational Pensions in Britain, Germany, Japan and the USA', in B. Ebbinghaus and P. Manow (eds.), *Comparing Welfare Capitalism: Social Policy and Political Economy in Europe, Japan and the USA*. London: Routledge.

Jacobs, M. (1991). *Short-Term America: The Causes and Cures of Our Business Myopia*. Boston: Harvard Business School Press.

Jacoby, S. (1985). *Employing Bureaucracy: Managers, Unions and the Transformation of Work in American Industry 1900–1945*. New York: Columbia University Press.

—— (1995). 'Current Prospects for Employee Representation in the US: Old Wine in New Bottles?' *Journal of Labor Research*, 16: 387, 391–397.

—— (1997). *Modern Manors: Welfare Capitalism since the New Deal*. Princeton: Princeton University Press.

—— (1999). 'Are Career Jobs Headed for Extinction?' *California Management Review*, Fall 1999, 42(1): 123–45.

—— (2000). 'Corporate Governance in Comparative Perspective: Prospects for Convergence'. *Comparative Labor Law and Policy Journal*, 22: 5–32.

—— (2001). 'Employee Representation and Corporate Governance: A Missing Link'. *University of Pennsylvania Journal of Labor and Employment Law*. 3/3: 449–89.

—— (2002). 'For More Honesty with Stock Options'. *Christian Science Monitor*, July 29.

—— and Saguchi, K. (2002). 'The Role of the Senior HR Executive in Japan and the United States'. Working paper, The Anderson School, UCLA.

Januszewski, S., Köke, F., and Winter, J. (1999). 'Product Market Competition, Corporate Governance and Firm Performance: An Empirical Analysis for Germany', Mannheim: ZEW, Discussion Paper No. 99–63.

Japan Productivity Council for Socio Economic Development (2003). Shakai-Keizai Seisan-sei Honbu (JPC-SED), Roshi Kankei Tokubetsu Iinkai (Management-Labour Relations Committee), *21 Seiki: Kigyo Keiei no Henka to Roshi Kankei: Wagakuni ni okeru Koporeto Gabanansu no Henyo wo Fumaete* (*Changes in Corporate Management and Management-Labour Relations in the 21st Century: Responding to Transformations in Corporate Governance in Japan*) (JPC-SED).

Japan Institute of Labour (2002). www.jil.go.jp/press/koyo/020617_03.html

Jensen, M. and Meckling, W. (1976). 'Theory of the Firm: Managerial Behavior, Agency Costs and Ownership Structure'. *Journal of Financial Economics*, 3: 305–360.

—— and —— (1979). 'Rights and Production Functions: An Application to Labor-Managed Firms and Codetermination'. *Journal of Business*, 52: 469–506.

Jimeno, J. (1997). 'La Negociació Col.lectiva: Aspectes Institucionals I les seves Consequencies Economiques, *Revista Economica de Catalunya'*. 72–7.

Jirjahn, U. (1998). *Effizienzwirkungen von Erfolgsbeteiligung und Partizipation: Eine Mikroökonomische Analyse*, Frankfurt/M: Campus.

—— and Klodt, T. (1998). 'Betriebliche Determinanten der Lohnhöhe', in K. Gerlach, O. Hübler, and W. Meyer (eds.), *Ökonomische Analysen betrieblicher Strukturen und Entwicklungen*, Frankfurt/M: Campus.

—— and —— (1999). 'Lohnhöhe, industrielle Beziehungen und Produktmärkte', in L. Bellmann *et al.* (eds.), *Zur Entwicklung von Lohn und Beschäftigung auf der Basis von Betriebs- und Unternehmensdaten*, Nürnberg: Institut für Arbeitsmarkt und Berufsforschung.

Johnston, J. (2002). 'Tenure, Promotion and Executive Remuneration'. *Applied Economics*, 34: 993–997.

Jürgens, U., Naumann, K., and Rupp, J. (2000). 'Shareholder Value in an Adverse Environment: The German Case'. *Economy and Society*, 29: 54–79.

—— Rupp, J., and Vitols, K. (2000). 'Corporate Governance und Shareholder Value in Deutschland: Nach dem Fall von Mannesmann'. Berlin: Wissenschaftszentrum Berlin für Sozialforschung.

Kabir, R., Cantrijn, D., and Jeunink, A. (1997). 'Takeover Defenses, Ownership Structure and Stock Returns in the Netherlands: an Empirical Analysis'. *Strategic Management Journal*, 18: 97–109.

Kanda, H. (1992). 'Future of Corporate Law', *Shihon Shijo*, 23: 87.

—— (2003). *Corporate Law*, Tokyo: Kobundo.

Kansaku, H. (2000), 'Koporeto Gabanansu-ron to Kaisha-ho (Debate on Corporate Governance and Corporate Law)', in T. Inagami *Gendai Nihon No Koporeto Gabanansu (Corporate Governance in Contemporary Japan)*. Tokyo: RENGO Research Institute.

Kaplan, S. (1989). 'The Effect of Management Buyouts on Operating Performance and Value'. *Journal of Financial Economics*, 24: 217–54.

—— (1994). 'Top Executives, Turnover, and Firm Performance in Germany'. *Journal of Law, Economics and Organization*, 10: 142–59.

Katz, H. and Darbishire, O. (1997). *Converging Divergencies: World-wide Changes in Employment Relations*. Ithaca, NY: Cornell University Press.

—— and —— (1999). *Converging Divergencies: Worldwide Changes in Employment Systems*, Ithaca, NY: Cornell University Press.

Kaufman, B. (1999). 'Does the NLRA Constrain Employee Involvement and Participation Programs in Nonunion Companies? A Reassessment'. *Yale Law and Policy Review*, 17/2: 729–812.

Kawahama, N. (1997). 'Torishimariyaku-kai no Kantoku Kino (Supervisory Function of a Board of Directors)', in S. Morimoto *et al.* (ed.), *Kigyo no Kenzen-Sei Kakuho to Torishimariyaku no Sekinin (Maintaining Sound Corporate Management and Directors' Responsibility).* Tokyo: Yuhikaku.

Keizai Doyukai 1996: Keizaidoyukai, 12 *Kigyo Hakusho (White Paper On Corporation)* Tokyo: Keizai Doyukai.

Khurana, R. (2002). *Searching for a Corporate Savior: The Irrational Quest for Charismatic CEOs.* Princeton: Princeton University Press.

Kitschelt, H., Lange, P., Marks, G., and Stephens. J. (1999). 'Convergence and Divergence in Advanced Industrial Economies', in H. Kitschelt, P. Lange, G. Marks, and Stephens. J. (eds.), *Continuity and Change in Contemporary Capitalism.* Cambridge: Cambridge University Press.

Kleinknecht, A., Oostendorp, R., and Pradhan, M. (1997). 'Patronen en economische effecten van flexibiliteit in de Nederlandse arbeidsver-houdingen', *Wetenschappelijke Raad voor het Regeringsbeleid.* Den Haag: SDU.

Kochan, T. (2002). 'Addressing the Crisis in Confidence in Corporations', *Academy of Management Online,* www.aom.pace.edu.

—— Katz, H., and McKersie, R. B. (1986). *The Transformation of American Industrial Relations.* New York: Basic Books.

Kohaut, S. and Bellmann, L. (1997). 'Betriebliche Determinanten der Tarifbindung: Eine empirische Analyse auf der Basis des IAB-Betriebspanels 1995'. *Industrielle Beziehungen,* 4: 317–34.

Koike, K. (1988). *Understanding Industrial Relations in Modern Japan.* London: Macmillan.

Kommission Mitbestimmung (1998). *Mitbestimmung und neue Unternehmenskulturen—Bilanz und Perspektiven.* Gütersloh: Bertelsmann Stiftung.

Kono, T. (1984). *Strategy and Structure of Japanese Enterprises.* Armonk: M. E. Sharpe.

Koshiro, K. (2000). *A Fifty Years History of Industry and Labour in Postwar Japan,* Tokyo: Japan Institute of Labour.

Kotthoff, H. (1998). 'Mitbestimmung in Zeiten interessenpolitischer Rückschritte. Be-triebsräte zwischen Beteiligungsofferten und 'gnadenlosem Kostensenkungsdiktat'. *Industrielle Beziehungen,* 5: 76–100.

Kroll, D. (2000). 'Der Borsengang ist eine Chance', *Die Mitbestimmung,* 46(5), 26–9.

Kubori, H. (1994). 'Nihon no Kaisha Soshiki no Jittai to Kororeto Gabanansu (The Reality of Japanese Corporation and Corporate Governance)', *Jurisuto,* 41.

Kurdelbusch, A. (2002). 'The Rise of Variable Pay in Germany: Evidence and Explanations'. *European Journal of Industrial Relations,* 8: 325–50.

Kuroki, F. (2002). *Cross-Shareholdings Decline (FY2001 Survey),* Tokyo: NLI Research Institute.

Lafferty, K. (1996). 'Economic Short-termism: the Debate, the Unresolved Issues, and the Implications for Management'. *Academy of Management Review*, 21: 825.

Laffont, J. and Tirole, J. (1993). *A Theory of Incentives in Procurement and Regulation*. Cambridge, MA: MIT Press.

—— (1989). *Management and Labour in Europe: the Industrial Enterprise in Germany, Britain, and France*, Brookfield, VT: Edgar Elgar.

Lane, C. (1995). *Industry and Society in Europe: Stability and Change in Britain, Germany, and France*. Cheltenham: Edward Elgar.

—— (2003). 'Changes in Corporate Governance in German Corporations: Convergence to the Anglo-American Model?', *Competition and Change*, 7, 2–3: 79–100.

La Porta, R., Lopez-de-Silanes, F., and Schleifer, A. (1999) 'Corporate Ownership Around the World'. *Journal of Finance*, 54: 471–517.

—— —— —— and Vishny, R. W. (1997). 'Legal Determinants of External Finance'. *Journal of Finance*, 52: 1131–50.

—— —— —— and —— (1998). 'Law and Finance'. *Journal of Political Economy*, 106: 1113–1155.

—— —— and —— (2000). 'Investor Protection and Corporate Governance'. *Journal of Financial Economics*. 58: 3–27.

Lazear, E. (2000). 'Performance Pay and Productivity'. *American Economic Review*, 90: 1346–1361.

Lazonick, W. and O'Sullivan, M. (1997a). 'Big Business and Skill Formation in the Wealthiest Nations: the Organization Revolution in the Twentieth Century', in A. Chandler, A. F. Amatori, and T. Hikino (eds.). *Big Business and the Wealth of Nations*. Cambridge: Cambridge University Press.

—— and —— (1997b). 'Finance and Industrial Development: Japan and Germany'. *Financial History Review*, 4: 113–34.

—— and —— (2000). 'Maximizing Shareholder Value: A new Ideology for Corporate Governance'. *Economy and Society*, 29: 13–35.

—— and Prencipe, A. (2002). 'Corporate Governance, Innovation, and Competitive Performance in the Commercial Turbofan Industry: The Case of Rolls-Royce'. Mimeo, Fontainebleau: Insead.

Lehmann, E. and Weigand, J. (2000). 'Does the Governed Corporation Perform Better? Governance Structures and Corporate Performance in Germany'. *European Finance Review*, 4: 157–95.

—— and Neuberger, D. (2001). 'Do Lending Relationships Matter? Evidence from Bank Survey Data'. Journal of Economic Behavior and Organization, 339–60.

Lepsius, M. (1990). *Interessen, Ideen und Institutionen*. Opladen: Westdeutsche Verlag.

Levine, D. (1989). 'Just-Cause Employment Policies when Unemployment is a Worker Discipline Device'. *American Economic Review*, 79: 902–5.

—— (1991). 'Just-Cause Employment Policies in the Presence of Worker Adverse Selection'. *Journal of Labor Economics*, 9: 294–305.

—— (1992). 'Public Policy Implications of Imperfections in the Market for Worker Participation'. *Economic and Industrial Democracy*, 13: 183–206.

—— (1993). 'Demand Variability and Work Organization', in S. Bowles, H. Gintis, and B. Gustafsson (eds.), *Markets and Democracy: Participation, Accountability and Efficiency*, Cambridge: Cambridge University Press.

—— (1995). *Reinventing the Workplace: How Business and Employees Can Both Win*. Washington, DC: Brookings Institution.

—— and Laura Tyson, D' Andrea (1990). 'Participation, Productivity and the Firm's Environment', in A. Blinder (ed.), *Paying for Productivity: A Look at the Evidence*, Washington, DC: Brookings Institution.

Liebeskind, J., Opler, T., and Hatfield, D. (1996). 'Corporate Restructuring and the Consolidation of US Industry'. *Journal of Industrial Economics*, 44: 53–68.

Lijphart, A. (1971). 'Comparative Politics and the Comparative Method'. *American Political Science Review*, 65: 682–93.

Lindner-Lehmann, M. (2001). *Regulierung und Kontrolle von Banken. Prinzipal-Agenten-Konflikte bei der Kreditvergabe*, Wiesbaden: Gabler.

—— and Neuberger, D. (1995). Bankeneinfluß auf Industrieunternehmen: Kritik an der Studie von Perlitz und Seger. *Die Bank*, 11: 690–2.

Linhart, D. (1991). *La Modernisation des Entreprises*, Paris: La Découverte.

Linz, J. (1981). 'A Century of Politics and Interests in Spain', in S. Berger (ed.), *Organizing Interests in Western Europe: Pluralism, Corporatism, and the Transformation of Politics*. Cambridge: Cambridge University Press.

Long, W. and Ravenscraft, D. (1993). 'Decade of Debt: Lessons from LBOS in the 1980s', in M. Blair (ed.), *The Deal Decade*. Washington, DC: Brookings Institution.

Looise, J. and Drucker, M. (2000). 'De ondernemingsraad in tijden van overgang'. *Tijdschrift voor HRM*, 4: 115–40.

López Novo, P. (1991). 'Empresarios y Relaciones Laborales: Una Perspectiva histórica', in F. Miguélez and C. Prieto (eds.), *Las Relaciones Laborales en España*. Madrid: Siglo Veintiuno.

Lütz, S. (2002). 'From Managed to Market Capitalism? German Finance in Transition'. *German Politics*, 9: 149–71.

Macher, J., Mowery, D., and Hodges, D. (1998). 'Reversal of Fortune? The Recovery of the US Semiconductor Industry'. *California Management Review*, 41: 107–36.

Machin, S. (1999). 'Wage Inequality in the 1970s, 1980s and 1990s', in P. Gregg, and J. Wadsworth (eds.), *The State of Working Britain*. Manchester: Manchester University Press.

Madrick, J. (2002). 'Welch's Juice,' *New York Review of Books* (February 14, 2002), 16–18.

Maeda, H. (2000). *Kaisha Ho Nyumon (Primer On Corporate Law)*, Tokyo: Yuhikaku.

Mancini, C. and Visser, W. (1995). *Continuing Vocational Training and SME's*. Zoetermeer: EIM.

Manne, H. (1965). 'Mergers and the Market for Corporate Control'. *Journal of Political Economy*, 3: 110–20.

Maraffi, M. (1990). *Politica ed Economia in Italia. La Vicenda dell'impresa Pubblica dagli anni Trenta agli Anni Cinquanta*. Bologna: il Mulino.

Maravall, J. (1978). *Dictadura y Disentimiento Político*. Madrid: Alfaguara.

Markides, C. (1995). *Diversification, Refocusing, and Economic Performanc*. Cambridge, MA: MIT Press.

Marsden, D. (1999). *A Theory of Employment Systems: Micro-foundations of Societal Diversity*. New York: Oxford University Press.

Martínez Lucio, M. (1995). 'Interpreting Change: Debates in Spanish Industrial Relations'. *European Journal of Industrial Relations*, 1: 369–83.

—— (1992). 'Spain: Constructing Institutions and Actors in the Context of Change', in A. Ferner and R. Hyman (eds.), *Industrial Relations in the New Europe*. Oxford: Blackwell.

—— (1998). 'Spain: Regulating Employment and Social Fragmentation', in A. Ferner and R. Hyman (eds.), *Changing Industrial Relations in Europe*. Oxford: Blackwell.

Martín Artiles, A. (1999). 'Organización del Trabajo y Nuevas Formas de Gestión Laboral', in F. Miguélez and C. Prieto (eds.), *Las Relaciones Laborales en España*. Madrid: Siglo Veintiuno.

Maug, E. (1998). 'Large Shareholders as Monitors: Is There a Trade-Off Between Liquidity and Control?' *Journal of Finance*, 53: 65–98.

Maurice, M., Sellier, F., and Silvestre, J. (1986). *The Social Foundations of Industrial Power: A Comparison of France and Germany*. Cambridge, MA: MIT Press.

Mayer, C. (1990). 'Financial Systems, Corporate Finance, and Economic Development', in Hubbard, R. (ed.), *Asymmetric Information, Corporate Finance and Investment*. Chicago: University of Chicago Press.

—— and Alexander, I. (1990). 'Banks and Securities Markets: Corporate Financing in Germany and the United Kingdom'. *Journal of the Japanese and International Economies*, 4: 450–75.

—— (1997). 'Corporate Governance, Competition, and Performance'. *Journal of Law and Society*, 24: 152–176.

—— (2000). 'Institutions in the New Europe: The Transformation of Corporate Organization'. Presented at conference on 'What do we know about institutions in the New Europe? First Saint-Gobain Foundation for Economics Conference, Paris, November.

Mayer, M. and Whittington, R. (1999). 'Strategy, Structure and 'Systemness': National Institutions and Corporate Change in France, Germany and the UK, 1950–1993'. *Organization Studies*, 20: 933–59.

McConnell, J. and Servaes, H. (1995). 'Equity Ownership and the Two Faces of Debt'. *Journal of Financial Economics*, 39: 163–84.

McNamee, M. (2002). 'Pitt's Accounting Fix Leaves a Lot Broke', *Business Week* (February 4, 2002).

McNulty, S. (2002). 'Unions Urge Groups to Act on Enron Directors', *Financial Times* (Jan. 26, 2002).

Meihuizen, H. (2000). 'Productivity Effects of Employee Stock Ownership and Employee Stock Options Plans in Firms Listed on the Amsterdam Stock Exchanges: an empirical analysis'. Paper for the International Association for the Economics of Participation, Trento, 6–8 July 2000.

Mercer Human Resource Consulting (2002). *Estudio de Compensación Total (TRS)*. Madrid, memo.

Merton, R. K. (1949). *Social Theory and Social Structure*. Glencoe, IL: Free Press.

Meyer, W. (1995a). 'Tarifbindung—Ein Hemmnis auf dem Weg zu niedrigeren Lohnkosten?' in: U. Schasse and J. Wagner (eds.), *Erfolgreich Produzieren in Niedersachsen*. Hannover: Niedersächsisches Institut für Wirtschaftforschung.

—— (1995b). 'Analyse der Bestimmungsfaktoren der 'übertariflichen' Entlohnung auf der Basis von Firmendaten', in K. Gerlach and R. Schettkat (eds.), *Determinanten der Lohnbildung*. Berlin: Sigma.

—— and Swieter (1997). 'Übertarifliche Bezahlung im Verarbeitenden Gewerbe'. *WSI-Mitteilungen*, 2: 119–25.

Midler, C. and Charue, F. (1993). 'A French-style Socio-technical Learning Process: the Robotization of Automobile Body Shops', in B. Kogut (ed.), *Country Competitiveness. Technology and the Organization of Work*. New York: Oxford University Press.

Miguélez, F. and Prieto, C. (1991). *Las Relaciones Laborales en España*. Madrid: Siglo Veintiuno.

—— and Rebollo, O. (1999). Negociación Colectiva en los Noventa, in F. Miguélez, and C. Prieto (eds.), *Las Relaciones Laborales en España*. Madrid: Siglo Veintiuno.

Milhaupt, C. (2001). 'Creative Norm Destruction: The Evolution of Non-legal Rules in Japanese Corporate Governance', 149 *University of Pennsylvania Law Review*, 149: 2083–2119.

Millward, N., Bryson, A., and Forth, J. (2000). *All Change at Work? British Employment Relations 1980–1998*. London: Routledge.

Ministry of Finance, Policy Research Institute (2003). *Shinten suru Koporeto Gabanansu Kaikaku to Nihon Kigyo no Saisei (Developing Corporate Governance and Regeneration of Japanese Corporations)*. Tokyo: Ministry of Finance.

Ministry of Labour (1999). *Survey of Communication between Labour and Management*. Tokyo: Ministry of Labour.

Mitbestimmung, Kommission (1998). *Mitbestimmung und neue Unternehmenskulturen Bilanz und Perspektiven*. Gütersloh: Verlag Bertelsmann Stiftung.

Mitchell, L. (1992). 'A Theoretical and Practical Framework for Enforcing Corporate Constituency Statutes'. *Texas Law Review*, 70: 579.

Mitchell, M. and Mulherin, H. (1996). 'The Impact of Industry Shocks on Takeover and Restructuring Activity'. *Journal of Financial Economics*, 41: 193–229.

338   Bibliography

Möbus, M. and Verdier, E. (eds.) (1997). *Les Diplomes Professionnels en Allemagne et en France: Conception et Jeux d'Acteurs*. Paris: L'Harmattan.

Moerland, P. (1995). 'Alternative Disciplinary Mechanisms in Different Corporate Systems'. *Journal of Economic Behaviour and Organization*, 26: 17–34.

Mol, R., Meihuizen, H., and Poutsma, E. (1997). 'Winstdeling, aandelen en opties voor werknemers'. *Economische Statische Berichten*, 13: 613–15.

Morin, F. (1995). 'Le Coeur Financier Francais', *Marches et Techniques Financieres*, number 72.

—— (1996). 'Privatisation et Devolution des Pouvoirs: le Modele Francais du Gouvernement d'Entreprise'. *Revue Economique*, 6: 1253–68.

—— (2000). 'A Transformation in the French model of Shareholding and Management'. *Economy and Society*, 29: 36–53.

Morin, F. (2002). 'Evolution et Structure de l' Actionnariat en France'. *Revue Francaise de Gestion*, 141: 155–81.

Morville, P. (1985). *Les Nouvelles Politiques Sociales du Patronat*. Paris: La Découverte.

Murphy, K. (1999). 'Executive Compensation', in O. Ashenfelter, and D. Card (eds.) *Handbook of Labor Economics*. Amsterdam: North Holland.

Myers, S. (1984). 'The Capital Structure Puzzle'. *Journal of Finance*, 39: 575–92.

Nagel, B., Tiess, B., Rüb, S., and Beschorner, A. (1996). *Information und Mitbestimmung im internationalen Konzern*. Baden-Baden: Nomos.

Nagelkerke, A., de Nijs, W. F. (Red.) (2003). *Sturen in het laagland. Over continuïteit en verandering van de Nederlandse arbeidsverhoudingen*, Delft: Eburon.

National Conference of Stock Exchanges (2002) *The 2002 Share Ownership Survey*. Tokyo: National Conference of Stock Exchanges.

Neuberger, D. (1997). 'Anteilsbesitz von Banken: Wohlfahrtsverlust oder Wohlfahrtsgewinn?' *Ifo-Studien*, 43: 15–34.

—— and Neumann, M. (1991). 'Banking and Antitrust: Limiting Industrial Ownership by Banks?' *Journal of Institutional and Theoretical Economics*, 147: 188–99.

New Bridge Street Consultants. (2002). *Paying for Performance: Executive Long-Term Incentives in FTSE350 Companies*. London: New Bridge Street Consultants.

Nitta, M. (2000). 'Nihon Kigyo no Koporeto Gabanansu: Genjo to Tenbo (Japanese Corporation and Corporate Governance: present state and future)', in T. Inagami (ed.) *Gendai Nihon No Koporeto Gabanansu (Corporate Governance in Contemporary Japan)*. Tokyo: RENGO Research Institute.

O'Connor, M. (1991). 'Restructuring the Corporation's Nexus of Contracts: Recognizing a Fiduciary Duty to Protect Displaced Workers'. *North Carolina Law Review*, 69: 1189.

—— (1993). 'The Human Capital Era: Reconceptualizing Corporate Law to Facilitate Labor-Management Cooperation'. *Cornell Law* Review, 78: 901–65.

—— (1998). 'Rethinking Corporate Financial Disclosure of Human Resource Values for the Knowledge-based Economy'. *University of Pennsylvania Journal of Labor and Employment Law*, 527.

—— (2000). 'Labor's Role in the American Corporate Governance Structure'. *Comparative Labor Law and Policy Journal*, 22: 97–134.

Oda, H. (1999). *Japanese Law*. Oxford: Oxford University Press.

Odean, T. (1999). 'Do Investors Trade Too Much?' *American Economic Review*, 89: 1279–98.

OECD (1993). 'Enterprise Tenure, Labour Tunrover, and Skill Training.' *Employment Outlook*. Paris: OECD.

—— (1997a). *Economic Survey: France*. Paris: Organization for Economic Cooperation and Development.

—— (1997b) 'Employment Protection and Labour Market Performance.' *Employment Outlook*. Paris: OECD.

—— (1998a). *Financial Market Trends*, No. 69. Paris: OECD.

—— (1998b). 'Training of Adult workers in OECD Countries: Measurement and Analysis'. *Employment Outlook*. Paris: OECD.

—— (1999). *Principles of Corporate Governance (draft)*. Paris: OECD, Directorate for Financial, Fiscal and Enterprise Affairs

—— (2000). *Financial Market Trends*, No. 78. Paris: OECD.

—— (2001a). *OECD Economic Surveys: Spain. 2000–2001*. Paris: OECD.

—— (2001b). *Financial Market Trends*, No. 80. Paris: OECD.

—— (2002). *Financial Market Trends*, No. 82. Paris: OECD.

—— (2003a). *OECD Economic Surveys: Spain, 2003*. Paris: OECD.

—— (2003b). *Financial Market Trends*, No. 84. Paris: OECD.

Office of National Statistics (2002). *Share Ownership: A Report on the Ownership of Shares at 31st December 2001*. London: HMSO.

Ohtake, F. (2000). 'Special Employment Measures in Japan'. *Japan Labour Bulletin 39*.

Okazaki, T. (1993). 'Senji Keikaku Keizai to Kigyo (Wartime Planned Economy and Corporation)', in K. Kenkyujo (ed.), *4 Gendai Nihon Shakai: Rekishiteki Zentei*. Tokyo: Tokyo University Press.

Okushima, T. (1991). 'Employees' Participation in Corporate Administration'. *Hogaku Kyoshitsu*, 132: 74.

Ortín, A. and Salas Fumás, V. (1997). 'The Compensation of Spanish Executives: A Test of a Managerial Talent Allocation Model'. *International Journal of Industrial Organization*, 15: 511–32.

Ortiz, L. (1998). 'Union Response to Teamwork: the Case of Opel Spain'. *Industrial Relations Journal*, 29: 42–57.

—— (1999). 'Unions' Responses to Teamwork: Differences at National and Workplace Levels'. *European Journal of Industrial Relations*, 5: 49–69.

—— (2002). 'The Resilience of Company-Level System of Industrial Relations: Union Responses to Teamwork in Renault's Spanish Subsidiary'. *European Journal of Industrial Relations*, 8: 277–99.

Orts, E. (1992). 'Beyond Shareholders: Interpreting Corporate Constituency Statutes'. *George Washington Law Review*, 61: 14–35.

Osterman, P. (1999). *Securing Prosperity*. Princeton: Princeton University Press.

O'Sullivan, M. (2000a). 'The Innovative Enterprise and Corporate Governance'. *Cambridge Journal of Economics*, 24: 393–416.

—— (2000b). *Contests for Corporate Control: Corporate Governance and Economic Performance in the United States and Germany*. New York: Oxford University Press.

Owen, G. (1999). *From Empire to Europe*. London: Harper Collins.

Pagano, M. and Volpin, P. (1999). 'The Political Economy of Corporate Governance', Salerno: Universita Degli Studi di Salerno, CSEF Working Paper No. 75.

Pagano, U. (1991a). 'Property Rights, Asset Specificity, and The Division of Labour under Alternative Capitalist Relations'. *Cambridge Journal of Economics*, 15: 315–42.

—— (1991b). 'Property Rights Equilibria and Institutional Stability'. *Economic Notes*, 20: 189–228.

Parkinson, J. (1993). *Corporate Power and Responsibility: Issues in the Theory of Company Law*. Oxford: Clarendon Press.

Parrat, F. (1999). *Le Gouvernement d' Entreprise*. Paris: Editions Maxima.

Pendleton, A. (1997). 'Characteristics of Workplaces with Financial Participation'. *Industrial Relations Journal*, 28: 103–19.

—— Poutsma, E., van Ommeren, J., and Brewster, C. (2001). *Employee Share Ownership and Profit Sharing in the European Union*, Luxembourg: Office for Official Publications of the European Union.

—— Wilson, N., and Wright, M. (1998). 'The Perception and Effects of Share Ownership: Empirical Evidence from Employee Buy-outs'. *British Journal of Industrial Relations*, 36: 99–124.

—— Blasi, J., Kruse, D., Poutsma, E., and Sesil, J. (2002). *Theoretical Study on Stock Options in Small and Medium Enterprises*. Report to the Enterprise Directorate General, Commission of the European Communities.

Pérez-Díaz, V. and Rodriguez, J. (1995). 'Inertial Choices: An Overview of Spanish Human Resources, Practices and Policies', in R. Locke, T. Kochan, and Michael Piore (eds.), *Employment Relations in a Changing World Economy*. Cambridge, MA: MIT Press.

Pérez, S. (1997). *Banking on Privilege: The Politics of Spanish Financial Reform*. Ithaca and London: Cornell University Press.

Perlitz, M. and Seger, F. (1994). 'The Role of Universal Banks in German Corporate Governance'. *Business and the Contemporary World*, 4: 49–67.

Perotti, E. and Spier, K. (1993). 'Capital Structure as a Bargaining Tool: the Role of Leverage in Contract Negotiation'. *American Economic Review*, 83: 1131–41.

Perry, C., Kramer, A., and Schneider, T. (1982). *Operating during Strikes: Company Experience, NLRB Policies, and Governmental Regulations*.

Philadelphia: Industrial Research Unit, Wharton School, University of Pennsylvania.

Peters Report (1997). *Corporate Governance in Nederland*. De Veerig Aanbevelingen.

Pfeffer, J. (1998). *The Human Equation: Building Profits by Putting People. First*. Boston: Harvard Business School Press.

Piore, M. and Sabel, C. (1984). *The Second Industrial Divide*. New York: Basic Books.

Pistor, K. (1999). 'Codetermination: A Socio-Political Model with Governance Externalities', in M. Blair and M. Roe (eds.), *Employees and Corporate Governance*. Washington, DC: Brookings Institution.

Plender, J. (1998). 'Ownership and Pensions'. *Political Quarterly*, 69: 394–403.

Poensgen, O. (1982). 'Der Weg in den Vorstand. Die Characteristiken der Vorstandsmitglieder der Aktiengesellschaften des Verarbeitendedn Gewerbes.' *Die Betriebswirtschaft*, 42: 3–25.

Porter, M. (1980). *Competitive Strategy: Techniques for Analyzing Industries*. New York: Free Press.

—— (1990). *The Competitive Advantage of Nations*. New York: Free Press.

—— (1992). *Capital Choices: Changing the Way America Invests in Industry*, Boston: Harvard Business School and Council on Competitiveness.

—— (1997). 'Capital Choices: Changing the Way America Invests in Industry', in D. Chew (ed.), *Studies in International Corporate Finance and Governance Systems*, New York: Oxford University Press.

Pound, J. (1993). 'The Rise of the Political Model of Corporate Governance and Corporate Control'. *New York University Law Review*, 68: 1003–71.

—— (1995). 'The Promise of the Governed Corporation'. *Harvard Business Review*, March–April, 89–98.

Poutsma, E. and van den Tillaart, H. (1996). '*Financiële Werknemersparticipatie in Nederland: tijd voor beleid!*'. Den Haag: Nederlands Participatie Instituut.

—— and Nagelkerke, A. (2003). 'De Ontwikkeling en Betekenis van Financiele Participatierelingen' in P. Duffhues and R. Kabir (eds.) *Personeelsopties en Andere Vormen van Variabele Beloningen in Nederland*. Tilburg: Center for Applied Research.

Preston, P. (1976). *España en Crisis*. Madrid: Fondo de Cultura Económica.

Prigge, S. (1998). 'A Survey of German Corporate Governance', in K. Hopt, H. Kanda, M. Roe, E. Wymeersch, and S. Prigge (eds.), *Comparative Corporate Governance—the State of the Art and Emerging Research*. Oxford: Oxford University Press.

Proshare (1999). *Employee Share Schemes—Do They Create Employee Shareholders?* London: Proshare.

Prowse, S. (1995). 'Corporate Governance in an International Perspective: a Survey of Corporate Control Mechanisms among Large Firms in the U.S., U.K., Japan and Germany'. *Financial Markets, Institutions and Instruments*, 4: 1–63.

Purcell, J. (1995). 'Corporate Strategy and Its Link with Human Resource Management Strategy' in J. Storey, (ed)., *Human Resource Management: A Critical Text* (1995). London: Routledge.

Putzhammer, H. and Köstler, R. (2000). 'Eckpunkte für ein Ubernahmegesetz', Die Mitbestimmung 46: 22–3.

Pye, A. (2001). 'Corporate Boards, Investors and Their Relationships: Accounts of Accountability and Corporate Governing in Action'. *Corporate Governance*, 9: 186–95.

Ragin, C. (2000). *Fuzzy-Set Social Science*. Chicago, IL: University of Chicago Press.

—— and Zaret, D. (1983). 'Theory and Method in Comparative Research: Two Strategies', *Social Forces*, 61: 731–54.

Rehder, B. (2003a). *Betriebliche Bündnisse für Arbeit in Deutschland. Mitbestimmung und Flächentarif im Wandel*. Frankfurt am Main/New York: Campus.

—— (2003b). 'Corporate Governance im Mehrebenensystem. Konfliktkonstellationen im Investitionswettbewerb deutscher Großunternehmen', in M. Höpner, W. Streeck (eds.), *Alle Macht dem Markt? Fallstudien zur Abwicklung der Deutschland AG*. Frankfurt: Campus.

Reichheld, F. (1996). *The Loyalty Effect: the Hidden Force Behind Growth, Profits, and Lasting Value*. Boston: Harvard Business School Press.

Rhodes, M. and Van Apeldoorn, B. (1997). 'Capitalism versus Capitalism in Western Europe', in M. Rhodes, P. Heywood, and V. Wright (eds.), *Developments in Western European Politics*. London: St. Martin's Press.

Rigby, M. and Marco Aledo, M. (2001). 'The Worst Record in Europe?: A Comparative Analysis of Industrial Conflict in Spain'. *European Journal of Industrial Relations*, 7: 287–305.

Rodríguez-Piñero Royo, M. (2001). 'Temporary Work and Employment Agencies in Spain'. *Comparative Labor Law and Policy Journal*, 23: 129–71.

Roe, M. J. (1993). 'Takeover Politics', in M. Blair (ed.), *The Deal Decade*. Washington, DC: Brookings Institution.

—— (1994). *Strong Managers, Weak Owners: The Political Roots of American Corporate Finance*, Princeton, NJ: Princeton University Press.

—— (1999). 'German Codetermination and Securities Markets', in M. Blair and M. Roe (eds.), *Employees and Corporate Governance*. Washington, DC: Brookings Institution.

—— (2000). 'Political Foundations for Separating Ownership from Corporate Control'. *Stanford Law Review*, 53: 539–606.

—— (2003). *Political Determinants of Corporate Governance*. Oxford: Oxford University Press.

Romero, M. and Vallé Cabrera, R. (2001). 'Strategy and Managers' Compensation: The Spanish Case'. *International Journal of Human Resource Management*, 12: 218–42.

Romu Gyosei Kenkyu-jo. (1999). 'Saishin Yakuin Hoshu-shoyo, Irokin no Jittai (The Current State of Executives' Remuneration, Bonus, and Severance Pay)', *Rosei Jiho*, 2: 3395.

Rosanvallon, P. (1988). *La Question Syndicale*. Paris: Editions du Seuil.

Ross, G. (1982). 'The Perils of Politics', in P. Lange, G. Ross, and M. Vannicelli (eds.), *Unions, Change and Crisis: French and Italian Union Strategies, and the Political Economy*, London: Allen and Unwin.

Roy, W. (1997). *Socializing Capital: The Rise of the Large Industrial Corporation in America*. Princeton: Princeton University Press.

Royo, S. (2000). *From Social Democracy to Neoliberalism. The Consequences of Party Hegemony in Spain, 1982–1996*. New York: St. Martin's Press.

Ryan, P. (1996). 'Factor Shares and Inequality in the UK'. *Oxford Review of Economic Policy*, 12: 106–26.

Sabel, H. (1996). 'Governance Structures in Deutschland: Mißerfolge, Leitungsstrukturen und Führungsverhalten. Zeitschrift für Betriebswirtschaft'. *Ergänzungsheft*, 3: 103–23.

Sako, M. and Sato, S. (eds.) (1997). *Japanese Labour and Management in Transition*. London: Routledge.

Sadowski, D., Backes-Gellner, U., and Frick, B. (1995). 'Betriebsräte in Deutschland: Gespaltene 'Rationalitäten?' *Jahrbuch für Neue Politische Ökonomie*, 14: 157–82.

—— and Frick, B. (1990). 'Betriebsräte und Gesetzesvollzug: Eine ökonomische Analyse am Beispiel des Schwerbehindertengesetzes'. *Zeitschrift für Personalforschung*, 4: 165–78.

—— and —— (1992). *Die Beschäftigung Schwerbehinderter: Betriebswirtschaftliche Analysen und politische Empfehlungen*. Idstein: Schulz–Kirchner.

—— Junkes, J., and Lindenthal, S. (2001). 'Labour Co-Determination and Corporate Governance in Germany: The Economic Impact of Marginal and Symbolic Rights', in J. Schwalbach (ed.), *Corporate Governance. Essays in Honor of Horst Albach*. Berlin: Springer.

Salais, R. (1988). 'Les Stratégies de Modernisation de 1983 a 1986'. *Economie & Statistique*, 213: 51–74.

—— (1992). 'Modernisation des Entreprises et Fonds National de l'Emploi: une Analyse en Termes de Mondes de Production'. *Travail et Emploi*, 51: 49–69.

Scheibe-Lange, I. and Prangenberg, A. (1997). 'Mehr Mitbestimmung via US-Borsen-aufsicht?' *Die Mitbestimmung*, 43: 45–9.

Schettkat, R. (1992). *The Labour Market Dynamics of Economic Restructuring. The United States and Germany in Transition*. New York: Praeger.

Schmid, F. and Seger, F. (1998). 'Arbeitnehmermitbestimmung, Allokation von Entscheidungsrechten und Shareholder Value'. *Zeitschrift für Betriebswirtschaft*, 68: 453–73.

Schmidt, R. (1997). 'Corporate Governance: The Role of Other Constituents', paper presented at the conference on Workable Corporate Governance: Cross-Border Perspectives, 17–19 March 1997, Paris.

Schmidt, V. (1996). *From State to the Market? The Transformation of French Business Under Mitterrand*. New York: Cambridge University Press.

Schmidt, V. (2003). 'French Capitalism Transformed, yet still a Third Variety of Capitalism'. *Economy and Society*, 32: 526–54.

Schnabel, C. and Wagner, J. (1996). 'Ausmaß und Bestimmungsgründe der Mitgliedschaft in Arbeitgeberverbänden: Eine empirische Untersuchung mit Firmendaten'. *Industrielle Beziehungen*, 3: 293–306.

—— and —— (1999). 'Betriebliche Altersversorgung: Verbreitung, Bestimmungsgründe und Auswirkungen auf die Personalfluktuation', in B. Frick, R. Neubäumer, and W. Sesselmeier (eds.), *Die Anreizwirkungen betrieblicher Zusatzleistungen*. München: Hampp.

Schwab, S., and Thomas, R. (1998). 'Realigning Corporate Governance: Shareholder Activism by Labor Unions'. *Michigan Law Review*, 96: 1043–1045.

Scott, J. (1997). *Corporate Business and Capitalist Classes*, Oxford: Oxford University Press.

Scott, M. and Rothman, H. (1994). *Companies with a Conscience: Portraits of Twelve Firms that Make A Difference*. Secaucus: Carol Pub. Group.

Sengenberger, W. (1987). *Struktur und Funktionsweise von Arbeitsmärkten: Die Bundesrepublik Deutschland im internationalen Vergleich*. Frankfurt am Main: Campus Verlag.

Sharpe, S. (1994). 'Financial Market Imperfections, Firm Leverage, and the Cyclicality of Employment'. *American Economic Review*, 84: 1060–1074.

Shinoda, T. (1994). 'Ima Mata Corporatism no Jidai Nanoka? (The Era of Corporatism?)', in T. Inagami *et al.* (eds.), *Neo-Corporatism no Kokusai Hikaku* (International Comparison of Neo-Corporatism). Tokyo: Japan Institute of Labour.

Shleifer, A. and Summers, L. (1988). 'Breach of Trust in Hostile Takeovers', in A. Auerbach (ed.), *Corporate Takeovers: Causes and Consequences*, Chicago: University of Chicago Press.

—— and —— (1986). 'Large Shareholders and Corporate Control'. *Journal of Political Economy*, 94, 461–88.

—— and Vishny, R. (1990). 'Equilibrium Short Horizons of Investors and Firms'. *American Economic Review*, 80: 148–53.

Shleifer, A. and Vishny, R. (1996). A Survey of Corporate Governance, Boston: National Bureau of Economic Research, working paper.

—— and —— (1997). 'A Survey of Corporate Governance'. *Journal of Finance*, 52: 737–83.

Shiller, R. (2000). *Irrational Exuberance*. Princeton: Princeton University Press.

Short, H. (1994). 'Ownership, Control, Financial Structure and the Performance of Firms'. *Journal of Economic Surveys*, 8: 203–47.

—— and Keasey, K. (1997). 'Institutional Shareholders and Corporate Governance in the United Kingdom', in K. Keasey, S. Thompson and M. Wright (eds.), *Corporate Governance: Economic, Management, and Financial Issues*. Oxford: Oxford University Press.

Signorini (1994). *Assetti Proprietari e Mercato delle Imprese. Proprietà, Modelli di Controllo e Riallocazione nelle Imprese Industriali Italiane, v. I.* Bologna: Il Mulino.

Slomp, H. (2001). 'The Netherlands in the 1990's: Towards 'Flexible Corporatism' in the Polder Model', in S. Berger and H. Compston (eds.), *Policy Concertation and Social Partnership in Western Europe*, Oxford: Berghahn.

—— (2004). 'The Netherlands: Resilience in Structure, Revolution in Substance' in H. Katz (ed.) *The New Structure of Labor Relations: Tripartism and Decentralization*. Ithaca NY: Cornell University Press.

Smith, A. (1990). 'Corporate Ownership Structure and Performance'. *Journal of Financial Economics*, 27: 143–64.

Smith, W. (1998). *The Left's Dirty Job. The Politics of Industrial Restructuring in France and Spain*. Pittsburgh: University of Pittsburgh Press.

Sorge, A. (1991). 'Strategic Fit and the Societal Effect: Interpreting Cross-National Comparisons of Technology, Organization and Human Resources'. *Organization Studies*, 12: 161–90.

Sorkin, A. R. 'Back to School, But This One is for Top Corporate Officials,' *New York Times* (September 3, 2002).

Soskice, D. (1997). 'German Technology Policy, Innovation, and National Institutional Frameworks'. *Industry and Innovation*, 4: 75–96.

—— (1999). 'Divergent Production Regimes: Coordinated and Uncoordinated Market Economies in the 1980s and 1990s', in H. Kitschelt, P. Lange, G. Marks and J. Stephens (eds.), *Continuity and Change in Contemporary Capitalism*. Cambridge: Cambridge University Press.

Stabile, S. (1998). 'Pension Plan Investments in Employer Securities: More Is Not Always Better'. *Yale Journal on Regulation*, 15: 61–116.

Stark, D. (2001). Ambiguous Assets for Uncertain Environments: Heterarchy in Postsocialist Firms', in P. DiMaggio (ed.), *The Twenty-First-Century Firm. Changing Economic Organization in International Perspective*. Princeton, NJ: Princeton University Press.

Steele, M. (1999). *The Challenges of Leadership*. Cranfield: Cranfield School of Management.

Steiger, M. (2000). *Institutionelle Investoren im Spannungsfeld zwischen Aktienmarktliquidität und Corporate Governance*. Baden-Baden: Nomos.

Steen, T. and Pedersen. T. (2000). 'Ownership Structure and Economic Performance in the Largest European Companies'. *Strategic Management Journal*, 21: 689–705.

Stiglitz, J. (1985). 'Credit Markets and the Control of Capital'. *Journal of Money, Credit and Banking*, 17: 133–52.

Streeck, W. (1991). 'On the Institutional Conditions of Diversified Quality Production', in E. Matzner and W. Streeck (eds.), *Beyond Keynesianism: the Socio-Economics of Production and Full Employment*. Brookfield, VT: Edward Elgar.

—— (1992a). 'Productive Constraints: On the Institutional Conditions of Diversified Quality Production', in W. Streeck (ed.), *Social Instititions and Economic Performance*. London: Sage.

Streeck, W. (1992*b*). *Social Institutions and Economic Performance: Studies of Industrial Relations in Advanced Capitalist economies*. London: Newbury Park.

—— (1996). *Mitbestimmung: Offene Fragen*. Gütersloh: Verlag Bertelsmann Stiftung.

—— (1997*a*). Beneficial Constraints: On the Economic Limits of Rational Voluntarism, in J. Rogers Hollingsworth and R. Boyer (eds.), *Contemporary Capitalism: The Embeddedness of Institutions*. Cambridge, UK: Cambridge University Press.

—— (1997*b*). 'German Capitalism: Does it Exist? Can it Survive?', in C. Crouch and W. Streeck (eds.), *Political Economy of Modern Capitalism. Mapping Covergence and Diversity*. London: Sage.

—— (2001). 'The Transformation of Corporate Organization in Europe: An Overview'. Cologne: Max Planck Institute, MPIfG Working Paper, 01/8.

—— and Höpner, M. (eds.) (2003). *Alle Macht dem Markt? Fallstudien zur Abwicklung der Deutschland AG*. Frankfurt: Campus Verlag.

Sugeno, K. (2002). *Japanese Employment and Labour Law*, Durham: Carolina Academic Press.

—— and Suwa, Y. (1996). 'The Three Faces of Enterprise Unions: The Status of Unions in Contemporary Japan', Japan International Labour Law Forum Paper No. 6.

Sunstein, C. (1996). 'Social Norms and Social Roles'. *Columbia Law Review*, 96: 903–68.

Sutton, F.X., Harris, S.E., Kaysen, C. and Tobin, J. (1956). *The American Business Creed*, New York: Shocken Books.

Swenson, P. (2002). *Capitalists Against Markets: The Making of Labor Markets and Welfare States in the United States and Sweden*. New York: Oxford University Press.

Takanashi, A. (1997). *Employment Insurance Law*. Tokyo: Japan Institute of Labour.

—— (1999). *Japanese Employment Practice*. Tokyo: Japan Institute of Labour.

—— (2002). *Shunto Wage Offensive*. Tokyo: The Japan Institute of Labour.

Teece, D. (1998). 'Capturing Value from Knowledge Assets: The New Economy, Markets for Know-How, and Intangible Assets'. *California Management Review*, 40: 55–79.

Teece, D. (2000). *Managing Intellectual Property*. Oxford: Oxford University Press.

Thelen, K. (1991). *Union of Parts*. Ithaca, NY: Cornell University Press.

Thomson, S. and Pedersen, T. (2000). 'Ownership structure and economic performance in the largest European Companies'. *Strategic Management Journal*, 21: 689–705.

Thonet, P. and Poensgen, O. (1989). 'Managerial Control and Economic Performance in West Germany'. *Journal of Industrial Economics*, 28: 23–37.

Tilly, C. (1984). *Big Structures, Large Processes, Huge Comparisons*. New York: Sage.

Tirole, J. (2001). 'Corporate Governance'. *Econometrica*, 69: 1–35.

Tobin, J. (1956). *The American Business Creed*. Cambridge, MA: Harvard University Press.

Toharia, L. and Malo, M. (2000). 'The Spanish Experiment: Pros and Cons of Flexibility at the Margin', in G. Esping-Andersen and M. Regini (eds.), *Why Deregulate Labor Markets?* Oxford: Oxford University Press.

Torrini, R. (2002). 'Cross-country Differences in Self-employment Rates: The Role of Institutional Variables'. *Temi di Discussione, n. 459*. Roma: Banca d'Italia.

Towers Perrin (2003). *Executive Compensation Study*, annual publication, Philadelphia: Towers Perrin.

Tros, F. (2001). 'Arbeidsverhoudingen: decentralisatie, deconcentratie en empowerment'. *Tijdschrift voor Arbeidsvraagstukken*, 17: 304–18.

Trumbull, Gunnar (2002). 'Policy Activism in a Globalized Economy: France's 35 hour Working Week'. *French Politics, Culture and Society*, 20: 1–20.

Ulman, L. (1974). 'Connective and Competitive Bargaining'. *Scottish Journal of Political Economy*, 21: 77–109.

UNESCO. (1999). *UNESCO Statistical Yearbook*. Paris: UNESCO.

Useem, M. (1996). *Investor Capitalism: How Money Managers Are Changing the Face of Corporate America*. New York: Basic Books.

Van den Tillaart, H. (1999). *Macht, Onmacht en Deskundigheid van Ondernemingsraden*, Ubbergen: Tandem Felix.

Van der Goot, L. and Roosenboom, J. (2001). 'Corporate governance en de Waardering van Beursgenoteerde Ondernemingen'. *Maandblad voor Accountancy en Bedrijfseconomie*, 74: 91–102.

Van der Hoeven, B. (1995). 'Beschermingsconstructies Nederlandse beursfondsen: een burcht met vele verdedigingswallen', *F&O Monitor*, 1/2: 23–31.

Van het Kaar, R. (1995). *Ondernemingsraad en Vertrouwenscommissaris; Structuurregeling en Medezeggenschap*, Den Haag: SDU.

—— and Looise, J. (1999). *De volwassen OR*. Alphen aan de Rijn: Samsom.

Van Kampen, M. and van de Kraats, B. (1995). 'Grootaandeelhouderschap en Aandelenrendement'. *Economisch Statistische Berichten*, 7: 534–57.

Van Kersbergen, K. and van Waarden, F. (2001). '*Shifts in Governance: Problems of Legitimacy and Accountability*', paper for Social Science Research Council of the Netherlands Organisation for Scientific Research, The Hague: NOW.

Van Witteloostuijn, A. (1999). *De Anorexiastrategie: over de Gevolgen van Saneren*, Amsterdam: de Arbeiderspers.

Veersma, U. (1995). 'Multinational corporations and industrial relations: policy and practice', in A. Harzing and J. van Ruysseveldt (eds.), *International Human Resource Management. An Integrated Approach*, London: Sage.

Verboon, F. (2001). 'Prestatiebeloning: wat willen werknemers?'. *Tijdschrift voor HRM*, 2: 59–78.

Verdier, E. (1997). 'L'Action Publique en Matiere de Formation Professionnelle et les Grandes Enterprises: entre Normes et Décentralisation', paper presented at the workshop on *Mutations industrielles et dynamiques territoriales*. Maison des Sciences de L'Homme, Nantes, 28–29 March.

Viénot Report, (1999). *Le Conseil d'Administration des Sociétés Cotées*, Paris: CNPF.

Vinke, R. and Larsen, S. (2001). *Jaarboek Personeelsmanagement 2002*. Deventer: Kluwer.

Visser, J. and Hemerijck, (1997). *A Dutch Miracle: Job Growth, Welfare Reform and Corporatism in the Netherlands*. Amsterdam: Amsterdam University Press.

Vitols, S. (2002). 'Shareholder Value, Management Culture and Production Regimes in the Transformation of the German Chemical-Pharmaceutical Industry'. *Competition and Change*, 6: 309–25.

—— Casper, D., Soskice, D., and Woolcock, S. (1997). *Corporate Governance in Large British and German Companies*. London: Anglo-German Foundation for the Study of Industrial Society.

Voogd, R. (1989). *Statutaire beschermingsmiddelen bij beursvennootschappen*, Academisch proefschrift, Deventer: Kluwer.

Wada, K. (1995). 'The Emergence of the "Flow Production" Method in Japan', in H. Shiomi and K. Wada (eds.), *Fordism Transformed*. Oxford: Oxford University Press.

Waddington, J. and Hoffmann, R. (eds.) (2000). *Trade Unions in Europe. Facing Challenges and Searching for Solutions*. Brussels: ETUI.

Waldenberger, F. (2003). 'The Link Between Finance and Employment', in H. Nutzinger (ed.), *Regulierung, Wettbewerb und Marktwirtschaft*. Vandenhoech & Ruprecht.

Watson Wyatt (2002). *Top Management Compensation. Western Europe, Israel & USA*, www.watsonwyatt.com.

Weber, H. (1990). *Le Parti des Patrons*, Paris: Le Seuil.

Weigand, J. (1999). *Corporate Governance, Profitability, and Capital Structure*, Nürnberg: University of Nürnberg, post-doctorial thesis (Habilitationsschrift).

Weiler, P. (1990). *Governing the Workplace: The Future of Labor and Employment Law*. Cambridge, MA: Harvard University Press.

Weimer, J. and Pape, J. (1999). 'A Taxonomy of Systems of Corporate Governance'. *Corporate Governance*, 17: 152–66.

Wenger, E. and Kaserer, C. (1998). 'The German System of Corporate Governance—A Model that Should not be Imitated', in S. Black and M. Moersch (eds.), *Competition and Convergence in Financial Markets*. Amsterdam: North-Holland.

Westney, E. (1987). *Imitation and Innovation*. Cambridge, MA: Harvard University Press.

Whadwani, S. and Wall, M. (1990). 'The Effects of Profit Sharing on Employment, Wages, Stock Returns, and Productivity: Evidence from UK Micro-data'. *Economic Journal*, 100: 1–17.

Whitley, R. (1999). *Divergent Capitalisms: The Social Structuring and Change of Business Systems*. Oxford: Oxford University Press.

Whittington, R. and Mayer, M. (2000). *The European Corporation: Strategy, Structure, and Social Science*. New York: Oxford University Press.

Whyte, W. (1999). 'The Mondragón Cooperatives in 1976 and 1998'. *Industrial and Labor Relations Review*, 52: 478–81.

Williams, K. (2000). 'From Shareholder Value to Present-day Capitalism'. *Economy and Society*, 29: 1–12.

Williamson, O. (1975). *Markets and Hierarchies: Analysis and Antitrust Implications*. New York: Free Press.

Windolf, P. (1994). 'Die neuen Eigentümer: Eine Analyse des Marktes für Unternehmenskontrolle'. *Zeitschrift für Soziologie*, 23: 79–92.

—— (1999). 'L'évolution du Capitalisme Moderne. La France dans une Perspective Comparative'. *Revue Francaise de Sociologie*, 40: 501–30.

—— (2002). *Corporate Networks in Europe and the United States*. Oxford: Oxford University Press.

Wood, B. (1996). 'Shareholding in practice: the role of shareholders—an investment manager's view', Trades Union Congress Seminar on What's at Stake, May.

World Bank (2003). *WDI Indicators*. Http://devdata.worldbank.org/dataonline/

World Federation of Exchanges (2002). *Annual Report*. Paris: World Federation of Exchanges.

Yamakawa, R. (1999). 'The Silence of Stockholders: Japanese Labour Law from the Viewpoint of Corporate Governance', *Japan Labour Bulletin*, 38.

—— (2001). 'Labour Law Issues Relating to Business Reorganization in Japan', *Japan Labour Bulletin*, 40.

Yoshihara, K. *et al.* (2001). 1 *Kaisha Ho (Corporate Law)*, Yuhikaku.

Zanglein, J. (1998). 'From Wall Street Walk to Wall Street Talk: The Changing Face of Corporate Governance'. *DePaul Business Law Journal*, 11: 43–122.

Ziegler, N. (1997). *Governing Ideas: Strategies for Innovation in France and Germany*, Ithaca, NY: Cornell University Press.

Zingales, L. (1998). 'Corporate Governance'. in P. Newmann (ed.), *The New Palgrave Dictionary of Economics and the Law*, Vol. 1. London: Palgrave.

Zugehör, R. (2003). 'Kapitalmarktorientierung und Mitbestimmung: Veba and Siemens', in W. Streeck and M. Hoepner (eds.), *Alle Macht dem Markt? Fallstudien zur Abwicklung der Deutschland AG*. Frankfurt: Campus Verlag.

Index